Henry James and the Problem of Audience
An International Act

Studies in Modern Literature, No. 49

A. Walton Litz, General Series Editor
Professor of English
Princeton University

Thomas C. Moser
Consulting Editor for Titles on Joseph Conrad
Professor of English
Stanford University

Daniel Mark Fogel
Consulting Editor for Titles on Henry James
Professor of English
Louisiana State University
Editor, The Henry James Review

Other Titles in This Series

No. 43	*Conrad's Heroism: A Paradise Lost*	Michael P. Jones
No. 44	*Ernest Hemingway: Journalist and Artist*	Jasper Kobler
No. 45	*The Indestructible Woman in the Works of Faulkner, Hemingway, and Steinbeck*	Mimi R. Gladstein
No. 46	*The Making of* Romance	Raymond Brebach
No. 47	*The* Nouvelle *of Henry James in Theory and Practice*	Lauren T. Cowdery
No. 48	*Women of Grace: James's Plays and the Comedy of Manners*	Susan Carlson
No. 50	*The Religious Design and the Problem of Audience: An International Act*	Larry E. Grimes
No. 51	*Hemingway and the Hispanic World*	Angel Capellan

Henry James and the Problem of Audience
An International Act

by
Anne T. Margolis
Assistant Professor of English
Williams College
Williamstown, Massachusetts

UMI RESEARCH PRESS
Ann Arbor, Michigan

Copyright © 1985, 1981
Anne Throne Margolis
All rights reserved

Produced and distributed by
UMI Research Press
an imprint of
University Microfilms International
A Xerox Information Resources Company
Ann Arbor, Michigan 48106

Library of Congress Cataloging in Publication Data

Margolis, Anne Throne.
Henry James and the problem of audience.

(Studies in modern literature ; no. 49)
Revision of thesis (Ph.D.)—Yale University, 1981.
Bibliography: p.
Includes index.
1. James, Henry, 1811-1882—Criticism and interpretation. 2. James, Henry, 1811-1882—Authorship.
3. Authors and readers—United States. 4. Authors and readers—Great Britain. 5. Theater audiences—United States. 6. Theater audiences—Great Britain. I. Title.
II. Series.

PS2127.A9M37 1985   813'.4   84-24073
ISBN 0-8357-1624-4 (alk. paper)

The man himself... we directly touch, to my consciousness, positively nowhere; we are dealing too perpetually with the artist, the monster and magician of a thousand masks, not one of which we feel him drop long enough to gratify with the breath of the interval that strained attention in us which would be yet, so quickened, ready to become deeper still.
—Henry James on William Shakespeare in his
1907 Introduction to *The Tempest*

Those prefaces [to the New York Edition] have given us all great satisfaction, as read aloud by me. We especially enjoyed you where you rounded upon yourself, and as it were took yourself to pieces, in your self-censure.... You have done a lot of good work, but nothing better than the last half of each of those prefaces; and I think the public will understand from them what I tried to note to you...: the fact, namely, that you have imagined your fiction, as a whole, and better fulfilled a conscious intention in it than any of your contemporaries.
—William Dean Howells to Henry James, 2 August 1908

For Brian and Jennifer

Contents

Acknowledgments *ix*

Introduction *xi*

1 Prolific Novelists and "Scribbling Women" *1*

2 "The Mill of the Conventional" *25*

3 "A Most Unholy Trade" *55*

4 "The Larger Latitude" *97*

5 A Second Chance *137*

6 A Substitute Performance *165*

Notes *195*

Bibliography *231*

Index *239*

Acknowledgments

My intense interest in Henry James dates back to my undergraduate years at Goucher College. There, as a student in William Hedges' survey courses on American literature, I began not only to read and admire James's novels but also to note the extraordinary devotion which he was able to elicit from one of his "initiated" readers, in this case my professor. However, my fascination with James's career began to take its present shape several years later while I was auditing a graduate seminar devoted exclusively to his work. As the course progressed I was struck by the intensity of response (both positive *and* negative) which the novelist's different styles or "phases" evoked. Impressed by the sheer quantity (as well as the remarkable quality) of James's productions and highly skeptical of the retrospective account which the master gives in his Prefaces of the circumstances surrounding their creation (as well as his own development as a writer), I turned to Leon Edel's invaluable five-volume biography of James for "the facts." It was only then that I learned about James's disastrous (and periodic) attempts to turn himself into a popular dramatist, one aspect of the master's career which is carefully avoided in the Prefaces and which Edel has, almost single-handedly, salvaged from obscurity (much to his credit and much to the benefit of subsequent scholars). James's theater years, like his letters to his literary agent, provided me with ample evidence that the problem of audience loomed very large throughout the novelist's long career. So my scholarly indebtedness begins with James's biographer. I am grateful to both Professor Edel and the Yale University Library for kindly permitting me to quote from the correspondence between James and his literary agent, James B. Pinker, now in the American Literature Collection of the Beinecke Rare Book and Manuscript Library at Yale. I would also like to thank Yale and Charles Scribner's Sons for allowing me to cite letters in the same collection written by James's nephew, Henry James Jr., and Charles Scribner to James B. Pinker.

My indebtedness extends even more deeply to my former advisor, Charles Feidelson, whose profound knowledge of nineteenth-century American literature and Henry James in particular has served as an admirable example of what James liked to refer to as "saturation" in one's subject matter. The present study has benefited immensely from Professor Feidelson's penetrating criticism and his helpful suggestions. Alan Trachtenberg, the late Sydney Ahlstrom, Larry Graver and especially Martha Banta and Dan Fogel each deserve thanks for reading and making valuable comments upon different versions of this manuscript. I would also like to express my appreciation to Nadene Lane and Eileen Sahady for typing multiple drafts and seemingly endless rounds of revisions and to the Giles Whiting Foundation for providing me with research time and financial support in 1976-77. And finally there is my debt to my husband, Brian Margolis, which is much harder to describe. If I may be permitted to borrow a metaphor from our childbirth preparation classes, he coached me through a long gestation and a difficult labor with prodigious patience and affection.

Introduction

There are certain American writers whose works have been so overmined that we can hardly imagine a critic writing yet another study of one of them and having anything really important or original left to say. Henry James scholarship epitomizes this situation. "Not another work on James!" we seem to hear readers say, or rather plead, especially when we remember that there are other groups of novelists whose works have been deliberately ignored or largely neglected, at least until recently.[1] Those nineteenth-century American writers sometimes referred to as the "scribbling women" illustrate well this second category; and we are tempted to demand that under such circumstances, any new interpretation of James must either justify or apologize for its existence. It is my belief that this study justifies itself, at least in part, precisely because I have proceeded on the assumption that these two categories of writers, the canonized and the popular, are more intricately interrelated than most modern critics have suspected (or wanted to admit). An exception to this rule is William Veeder, a scholar who has reopened the question of James's relationship both to his more popular contemporaries and to the reading public. In *Henry James—The Lessons of the Master,* Veeder states that his subject is "how conventional materials, received and gradually transformed, contribute to the meaning of James's novels." Using evidence from the texts themselves as well as from the apprentice novelist's letters and his reviews of his contemporaries, Veeder documents conclusively not only James's opinions of the "scribbling women" and the popular male authors of his day but the extent to which he is indebted to them in terms of style, plot, and characters. By focusing upon the novelist's early fiction from *Watch and Ward* (1871) through *The Portrait of a Lady* (1881), Veeder is able to demonstrate the surprising degree to which James's works resemble the productions of his more popular colleagues on both sides of the Atlantic. But this valuable study leaves its audience with the mistaken impression that by the end of this crucial decade, James had outgrown his own desire to become a truly popular writer and was prepared to defy or ignore the expectations of the reading public.[2]

Henry James's determination to achieve commercial success and his consequent dependence upon the conventional themes and devices of popular fiction did not end abruptly or even significantly diminish with the publication of his early masterpiece, *The Portrait*. His plays (most of which were written in the first half of the 1890s), his experimental post-theater fiction, and even the novels of his so-called "major phase" testify to his enduring fascination with and reliance upon the literary and theatrical conventions of his day. Indeed, the very sequence as well as the content of James's productions suggest that the curious shape which his career gradually assumed can best be understood in terms of his *continuing* interaction with and anticipation of his perceived audience. I use the theatrical term "audience" here rather than the more literary terms "reader" or "public" because I feel (and hope to show) that it comes closest to capturing both James's ultimate sense of what he was doing and the corresponding response he hoped to evoke, at least from his "initiated" readers. Thematically as well as structurally, James's fiction implies the contemporaneous Anglo-American public which he alternately tried to accommodate and resist as well as the more select audience he needed to impute or create in order to continue to develop and perform as an artist. These works can therefore be used as documents by the critic who wishes to reconstruct a composite portrait of the evolving reading public as James perceived it, a portrait which is perhaps our most direct indicator of his assessment of the possibilities and limitations of nineteenth-century Anglo-American culture.

One of the few treatments of James which does focus on the problem of audience can be found in Henry Nash Smith's recent study of popular resistance to classic American literature, *Democracy and the Novel*. Building upon Veeder's thesis regarding James's pre-*Portrait* career, Smith fruitfully examines other aspects of James's relationship with popular culture, especially as it was embodied in what he refers to as James's "middlebrow or lowbrow" novels.[3] Although Smith's general outline of the stages through which the novelist's reputation passed is accurately drawn and his analysis of the reading conventions embedded in the contemporaneous reviews is quite useful, he pays little attention to the complex role played in James's career by the emerging English-speaking avant-garde. Like so many other portraits of this prodigious artist, Smith's version of the middle and late James presents us with a master who held the taste of the "babyish" public in all but total contempt and whose primary motive for artistic compromise was an exaggerated sense of economic insecurity. Appropriately enough, Smith entitles the first of his two chapters on James "Sows' Ears and Silk Purses" (a phrase taken from "The Next Time," one of the novelist's most bitter tales of writers and artists), for he subscribes to and reinforces the widely accepted view that the master had nothing but contempt for readers and critics.[4] Falling into James's artfully baited trap, Smith ignores the possibility that there is a disjunction between James's treatment of the problem of audience in these devious (and, as Smith does point out) melodramatic tales of the literary life and other of his words and actions during the second and third phases of his career.[5] As I hope to demonstrate, there is ample evidence in James's correspondence as well as in the texts themselves to prove (or at least to strongly suggest) that the master who produced these literary tributes to a life devoted exclusively to art for art's sake found himself unwilling to cut himself off deliberately from what he perceived to be the taste of the general public.

To explain why this was, in fact, the case is no easy task, but the chapters which follow should be regarded as an effort in that direction. To begin with, James's attitude towards both his work and the reading public is extremely difficult to classify. As we shall see, he was an artist who repeatedly called for the overthrow of the most cherished conventions of Anglo-American fiction and frequently challenged (or subverted) these genteel prescriptions in his own work. Yet at the same time, he was a writer who evinced a chronic obsession with the idea of popular success on a grand scale, an obsession which cannot be written off entirely as financial need or mere jealousy of his more successful competitors. In the last two decades of his life, James penned elaborately phrased (and justifiably famous) letters to old friends and young disciples in which he urged them to remain among the discriminating few who valued literature not as a trade but as a highly demanding art. Less well known are the blunt businesslike letters which James wrote to his literary agent, James B. Pinker, during this same period, letters which dwell on matters of compensation and reveal his seemingly unconquerable expectation that (despite multiple past experiences to the contrary) big sales and popular success would ultimately reward the efforts of a lifetime of exhausting labor in the literary marketplace. (As late as January of 1910, for example, the master can be found complaining to his literary agent, James B. Pinker, about the fact that *Putnam's Magazine* had reduced their rate of payment to him. He made it clear that at the very least, he expected the same terms as the author of *The Inner Shrine,* exclaiming: "I'll be hanged if each of my installments won't be worth as much as each of his—or even [if it's a She,] Hers!")[6]

While such misplaced hopes and disappointed expectations are reminiscent of Ralph Limbert, the fictional master in "The Next Time" who is determined to make a hit but can "only" produce masterpieces, "poor Limbert's" inept efforts to woo the general public pale into insignificance when compared with those of his creator. Although James's ironic tales of the literary life have usually been viewed as his hostile portrait of (and, to a large extent, his reaction against) the rise of mass culture and its effects upon his potential audience, James's career as a whole can still be seen as a valiant attempt to resist the increasingly seductive logic which these tales embody, the logic of an incipient literary modernism. James's modernist successors were to take it for granted that popularity and literary greatness were mutually exclusive terms and fates; and no less a champion of modernism than his fellow expatriate Ezra Pound would embrace James in 1918 as a precursor and an ally in the avant-garde battle for freedom of expression against "all sorts of intangible bondage."[7] Quite symptomatically, Pound had lost his temper a year earlier when H. L. Mencken lumped James and William Dean Howells together indiscriminately in his *Book of Prefaces*. Writing to Mencken, Pound insisted that "you shouldn't treat a great man and a mutton-shank in one page as if there were no gulph [*sic*] between 'em."[8] Yet despite his periodic railings against the debased taste of the Anglo-American public, the master himself stubbornly clung to a vision of his own work as an ongoing attempt to educate and initiate his less developed readers, a project which might best be described as the "civic use of the imagination" (a phrase James introduces in his New York Edition preface to "The Lesson of the Master").[9] Thus in 1914, only two years before his death, we can find James registering perplexity and dismay over the fact that he was widely (and, in his opinion, wrongly) perceived as an avant-garde writer. Advising his literary agent against allowing a German publisher to translate his late fiction, he moaned: "My late ones are things to be read in the original, for proper appreciation—the appreciation of that very minor and 'cultivated' public to whom, alas, almost solely, my productions *appear* to address themselves." In a similar vein, less than three months later the master responded with considerable enthusiasm to the news that Nelson had proposed a reprint of an apprentice novel, *The American,* in his popular "Sevenpenny Series" and that Dent was preparing yet another cheap edition of one of the novels for his "Wayfarer's Library."[10] Clearly, James never entirely gave up the hope that he could capture the imagination and hold the attention of the public at large—if only he were granted another chance.

Unlike Pound, Eliot, and others among the rising generation of modernist writers who transformed the Anglo-American literary scene, Henry James retained a decidedly ambivalent attitude towards the avant-garde version of artistic success throughout his professional life. There is no little irony in the fact that the novelist's exaggerated reputation for difficulty (the joint creation of the master and his disciples) as well as the very expensive format of his books (especially the New York Edition) were at least contributing factors in his own failure to achieve popular success during the later stages of his career, for they created an artificial and unnecessary barrier between his admittedly complex style and the attention of the Anglo-American reading public (as the circumstances of his occasional breakthroughs into relative popularity suggest). Indeed, the novelist's nephew, Henry James Jr. (son of William James) endorsed this point of view when he implied to James B. Pinker that even the New York Edition might have sold better (if not well) had the advertising only been "skillfully managed" and the fiction been made available in separate volumes or a cheaper edition.[11] But that is getting ahead of my story.

A word about my sub-title and sources. I have taken the sub-title, "An International Act," from the text of Pound's *Little Review* essay on James (an article written to convince readers that the master ought to be "more read"), though there the phrase refers not to the master's entire career but to his last and perhaps his most dramatic public gesture, his "abandonment" of his citizenship "out of shame" (to use Pound's somewhat melodramatic words).[12] There is a deliberate irony in my use of this phrase for a study of James and the problem of audience, for the novelist's change of allegiance (along with his early expatriation) has served as one of the most convenient weapons in the hands of his detractors in Pound's and subsequent generations.[13] Yet these three words concisely evoke my sense of James as an artist who came to regard himself as a strange mixture—part writer, part actor, and part magician— precisely because he made a career of (and built his reputation by) performing a delicate balancing act on the tightrope of his audience's contrasting expectations.

Of course, exactly who made up James's Anglo-American audience and what their expectations actually were is difficult if not impossible to determine with any precision more than a century after the fact, though part of the answer is embedded in the contemporaneous reviews. But James's changing *perceptions* of the reading public are the most crucial elements in a study such as this; and these perceptions can be fleshed out by a careful analysis of his correspondence, his notebooks, and his writings in conjunction with the published reviews of his work. Because not only the quantity but the quality of direct and indirect commentary by James on the reading public varies greatly from one stage of his career to another, I have had to adopt a slightly different strategy for each of the three phases. My first two chapters (which follow the novelist's apprentice years through the triumph of *The Portrait*) draw upon comments he makes regarding the Anglo-American public in his correspondence as well as in his early reviews. In these chapters I have relied heavily upon indirect evidence from his novels and tales as well as from my research on the development of the Anglo-American book trade. (In order to convey a sense of the historical dimensions of the problem of audience, I also compare James's attitude towards the public and the literary marketplace with that of some of his most notable predecessors and contemporaries, namely Nathaniel Hawthorne, Mark Twain, William Dean Howells, and Gustave Flaubert and his circle. However, their respective attitudes must receive an admittedly superficial treatment in a study which focuses exclusively on James's career.) In chapters 3 and 4, my attention shifts to James's vacillating theatrical and literary intentions and the contrast between his relationship with "common" or conventional readers and his increasing following among the

English-speaking avant-garde. This shift entails emphasis upon James's correspondence, his notebooks, his theater essays, Richard Foley's and Roger Gard's extremely useful surveys of the English and American reviews, and Leon Edel's biographical account of the theater years.[14] My final two chapters are devoted to the unique relationship which developed among James, his characters, and his audience in the novels of the major phase and the Prefaces to the New York Edition of his work. While I continue to make use of the above-mentioned sources, my interpretation here rests primarily on the evidence of the texts themselves, although it is informed and reinforced by my reading of the correspondence between James and his literary agent—much of which remains unpublished.[15]

Although I discuss each of James's major novels and several of his minor works in some depth, my main focus is on the overall shape, texture, and meaning of his career (especially his evolving identity as "the master") rather than on the significance and achievement of individual texts. If there is some reductiveness inherent in such an approach, my hope is that this limitation is counterbalanced by the new point of view which it enables me to offer on particular works.[16] However, it should be clear by now that the present study was conceived and is being offered largely as a corrective to the tendency of modern criticism to accept with little or no reservation the extremely seductive but historically unreliable retrospective account of James's career which he presents in the Prefaces (and elsewhere).[17] The master's justifiably celebrated but quite devious self-portrait of the artist and his craft has not only done much to fix James's place in the development of modern literature but has exerted a decisive (and not entirely beneficial) influence upon the way his novels have been read by subsequent generations of writers, critics, and literary scholars (in turn influencing *their* self-image and practice). Yet only by restoring a sense of the very real contingencies and compromises which impinged upon James's actual working life can we begin to understand the complex motivation behind and significance of this "exemplary" fiction.[18] I have therefore used the historical problem of audience as a means of reconstructing and illuminating those cultural circumstances which helped to shape his career.

Finally, a note about the term "avant-garde." Beginning in chapter 3 the phrase "English-speaking avant-garde" is used to refer to English and American readers who responded appreciatively to James's "super-subtle" tales and his experimental post-theater fiction (including the novels of the major phase). This looseness of application is perhaps justified by Renato Poggioli's observation that the Anglo-American avant-garde is "less theoretical and self-conscious, more instinctive and empirical" than its Continental counterpart.[19] Following Poggioli's example, I have treated this aesthetic phenomenon primarily as a "sociological fact"; and thus I group together a rather wide variety of unconventional readers who may have had little in common except their taste for the master's late work and their distaste for more popular forms of fiction. My intention here is threefold. First—I want to establish the fact that during James's middle years, a split developed between those who "got" James (or at least wanted to act as if they did) and those who did not (or would rather not even try!).[20] Second—I argue that James recognized this split not only in the reviews (which he professed not to read but which the evidence suggests he *was* familiar with) but also in terms of the contrast between the poor sales of his books and the intense response of his admirers and disciples. And furthermore—I try to demonstrate the extent to which James's most demanding fiction can be interpreted as subtle (if not always successful) attempts to undercut and heal this split by alternately wooing and trying to educate the undeveloped imagination of his "uninitiated" readers.[21] Obviously, more work can and should be done to document and analyze the development of the Anglo-American reading public and to gauge its effect upon James's career (as well as the careers of other English-speaking writers). But, as the master himself reminds us in his essay on "Criticism":

> We must be easy with him [the critic] if the picture, even when the aim has really been to penetrate, is sometimes confused, for there are baffling and there are thankless subjects; and we make everything up to him by the peculiar purity of our esteem when the portrait is really, like the happy portraits of that other art, a text preserved by translation.[22]

1

Prolific Novelists and "Scribbling Women"

As he approached the final decade of the nineteenth century, Henry James found himself at a critical turning point in his career. His reputation as an Anglo-American novelist then rested largely if not exclusively on his authorship of the international novels and tales which he had been producing for over twenty years, the most popular of which was *Daisy Miller* (1878). Yet after having devoted nearly a quarter of a century to observing the American and European scenes and exploiting the literary possibilities of the contrasts between the types of character they produced, this international novelist was suddenly forced to confess that he had become "deadly weary of the whole 'international' state of mind—so that I *ache,* at times, with fatigue at the way it is constantly forced upon me as a sort of virtue or obligation." As he confided to his older brother William, the psychologist:

> It is always a great misfortune, I think, when one has reached a certain age, that if one is living in a country not one's own and one is anything of an ironic or critical disposition, one mistakes the inevitable reflections and criticisms that one makes, more and more as one grows older, upon life and human nature etc., for a judgment of that particular country, its nature, peculiarities, etc., to which, really, one has grown exceedingly accustomed.

Here was James at a certain age, forty-five, living in a country not (yet) his own, England, and leveling self-criticism at the very quality which had helped to build his career, his tendency to interpret differences in temperament and human nature as national traits. Now he noted:

> I can't look at the English-American world, or feel about them, any more, save as a big Anglo-Saxon total, destined to such an amount of melting together that an insistence on their differences becomes more and more idle and pedantic...[1]

True to his word, James had just begun work on a serial for the *Atlantic Monthly* in which he did manage to break away from the international theme. *The Tragic Muse* deals primarily with the English social and artistic scene and it largely fulfills his current ambition (as stated in the same letter to William) of writing "in such a way that it would be impossible to an outsider to say whether I am at a given moment an American writing about England or an Englishman writing about America...."[2] But even before this novel could appear in book form in 1890, the "'international' state of mind" was forced upon James once again as he began work upon a stage version of one of his earliest novels, *The American* (1877). James had agreed to dramatize this apprentice novel after being approached by Edward Compton, a highly successful British actor-manager. Despite his recent protestation to William that he had outgrown this phase of his career, Henry now set out to convince himself that he must "take what there *is,* and use it, without waiting in vain for the preconceived—to dig deep into the actual and get something out of *that*—this doubtless is the right way to live." This admonition appears in James's notebooks where it is promptly followed by a reminder of how little money his novels make for him, a reminder which revives his old dream of writing for the theater.[3]

James's willingness to trade on his early fame as inventor of the international novel at this advanced stage of his career dramatizes his dependence on his Anglo-American audience, for the implications of Compton's choice of material could hardly have been lost on James. Access to the London stage depended upon his readiness to ignore his mature convictions and return to what he now regarded as outdated material and undeveloped habits of mind. In this light James's subsequent venture onto the London stage begins to take on the appearance of a retreat rather than an assault, for he was also responding (at least in part) to what he perceived to be the public's displeasure with his recent development as a writer. Their displeasure was represented for James not only by the negative reviews but also by the poor sales of his recent novels, *The Bostonians* and *The Princess Casamassima,* both published in 1886.

The role played by public pressure at this juncture of James's career comes into clearer focus when we learn that on January 2, 1888, he had admitted to William Dean Howells, his American friend and frequent literary advisor:

> ...I am still staggering a good deal under the mysterious and (to me) inexplicable injury wrought—apparently—upon my situation by my last two novels, the *Bostonians* and the *Princess,* from which I have expected so much and derived so little. They have reduced the desire, and the demand, for my productions to zero—as I judge from the fact that though I have for a good while past been writing a number of good short things, I remain irremediably unpublished.

The following day James wrote to thank his good friend Edmund Gosse for reassuring him about his literary position and recommending the services of A.P. Watt, a leading London literary agent.[4] (James used Watt only temporarily: James B. Pinker became his permanent agent shortly after the premature death in 1891 of Wolcott Balestier, the young American to whom the novelist had entrusted his negotiations with Compton.) Although James's biographer, Leon Edel, his marshalled evidence that 1888 turned out to be "a successful and prosperous year" for the novelist in order to argue that this is the complaint of "an impatient rather than of an unpublished or unpopular author," the fact of the poor reception and sales of these two ambitious novels remains unchanged. Furthermore, the very fact that James felt the need to seek the advice of Howells and Gosse as well as professional assistance in his dealings with the Anglo-American literary marketplace underscores his fears regarding his present status and future prospects. And while several of his short stories did appear almost simultaneously in the *Atlantic,* the *Century, Scribner's,* and *Harper's* later that year (causing Howells to liken them to an artist's exhibition of masterpieces), James had no way of knowing that what he had despairingly referred to as his "buried prose" would surface so soon. In fact, it is quite likely that Howells had reacted to his friend's mournful request for advice by taking it upon himself to intervene with his fellow editors on James's behalf. Edel quotes statements made by Howells in his October 1888 *Harper's Magazine* column to the effect that James was unanimously sought after by editors, "now the real avenues towards the public." But Howells' effort to present James as a truly popular writer whose work received "only a feeble and conditional acceptance" from what he condescendingly refers to as the "'best' criticism" reads more like a press release than a statement of fact. (In *A Hazard of New Fortunes,* his 1890 novel about the rise of mass culture and the commercialization of American literature, Howells would demonstrate just how well versed he was in the tricks of his trade. As one of his thoroughly modern characters notes with approval, the old belief that the demand creates the supply has become obsolete: "I contend that we've got a real, substantial success to celebrate now; but even if we hadn't, the celebration would do more than anything else to create the success, if we got it properly before the public."[5])

Indeed, there is ample ground for suspecting that James continued to regard his "unpublished" state, however temporary, not as a mere accident or as a delay due to illustrators (as Edel suggests) but as a distressing symptom of the public's mounting dissatisfaction with his experiments with new subject matter. It is important to remember that *The Bostonians,* as its title suggests, deals exclusively with America, in this case with a uniquely Bostonian mixture of post-Civil War feminism and spiritualism. It was immediately followed by *The Princess Casamassima,* Henry James's one venture into the realm of the political novel, accomplished via a rather melodramatic treatment of the controversial anarchist movement. Together these two novels represented the most extreme and sustained departure James had yet dared to make from his familiar terrain of international marriages and morals. Their unpopularity suggested that the public was set on denying him the freedom to break out of the international mold which they had mutually fashioned over the years. The curious evolution of James's next published fiction, *The Reverberator* (1888), gives us reason to believe that this was the conclusion which James himself had drawn. In a November 1887 notebook entry we find the germ of the story, a reference touched off by some gossip he had heard concerning a young American woman who betrayed the hospitality of Venetian society by writing an "inconceivable letter" about her hosts for publication in the New York *World*. At this point James saw such a confrontation between "the scribbling, publishing, indiscreet, newspaperized American girl and the rigid, old-fashioned, conservative, still shockable and much shocked little society she plays tricks upon" as highly illustrative of modern life, except for one thing. It was becoming harder and harder to find people in Europe who were still shockable. Privately he was forced to admit:

> I don't in the least see them in England, where publicity is far too much, by this time, in the manners of society for my representation to have any verisimilitude here ... people write to the newspapers about every thing—it is in short also a newspaperized world, and, allowing for a rather better form, there is about as little delicacy as *là bas*.

Here it sounds as though James is preparing to launch a direct attack on the newspaperized whole which he sees Anglo-American society as fast becoming. Instead, in the course of writing the story he diplomatically sidestepped this issue and reverted to typecasting (of both himself and his characters) by churning out yet another international production.[6]

Set in Paris, this slight yet entertaining novel centers on the competition for the hand of what had by now become the obligatory "young unmarried American female," a staple of Jamesian fiction. The invasion of privacy theme is treated comically and subordinated to an equally obligatory international courtship plot by means of one George Flack, an energetic American journalist who writes for an American newspaper, the *Reverberator*. Flack would like to steal Francie Dosson, the American girl, away from her fiancé Gaston, scion of one of those exclusive Franco-American families which make repeated appearances in James's fiction and which typify an obsession with propriety. Clearly this reversion to standard Jamesian types presented advantages for everyone concerned, especially for James, who was still recovering from what he considered to be a serious blow to his career. He had apparently decided that he was in no position in 1888 to take the risk of further alienating his Anglo-American audience. An attractive American girl's international dilemma of having to choose between two ardent suitors, one thoroughly American and one thoroughly Europeanized, was what transatlantic readers had come to expect from James, and this time they would not be disappointed. His American readers could accept a mildly satirical picture of themselves, especially if it came packaged in conventional and agreeable form. James proved to be just as eager to please his English readers. By presenting the new journalism as a characteristically American phenomenon, he could flatter their prejudices while relieving their anxiety in a highly entertaining manner. "Newspaperism" as portrayed here was essentially an American problem, imported from overseas rather than indigenous to the home scene. In deference to the female segment of his audience, James further blunted the satire by making Flack, not Francie, directly responsible for the offensive newspaper item. Just how far James had retreated from his original donnée in this respect can best be measured by the fact that when Howells reviewed the novel for *Harper's New Monthly Magazine,* he was able to pronounce Francie "lovable" and present her as "a marvelous expression of the best of American girlhood."[7]

Perhaps most significantly the denouement (in which Francie, her family, and her Gallicized suitor turn their collective backs on his overly fastidious and hypocritical family) was strictly calculated to please the conventional expectations of all components of James's audience. These expectations had been enumerated and criticized by James in "The Art of Fiction," an 1884 essay which he later revised and republished in 1888 as part of a collection entitled *Partial Portraits.* His partial portrait of Anglo-American readers revealed that for many of them "the 'ending' of a novel is... like that of a good dinner, a course of dessert and ices, and the artist in fiction is regarded as a sort of meddlesome doctor who forbids agreeable aftertastes." (James's analogy of the meddlesome doctor is probably an oblique reference to one of the conventional charges levelled against his preoccupation with psychological analysis. As we shall see, both James and the French practitioners of literary realism were often accused by English-speaking critics of dissecting or experimenting upon their characters.) Although a pervasive current of irony runs throughout *The Reverberator,* subtly undercutting what on the surface appears to be a happy international ending, James's indulgence in this sort of private revenge upon his audience's expectations is intended to be strictly covert. The last paragraph of *The Reverberator* is especially revealing in this regard, for in several respects it resembles the concluding paragraph of *The Bostonians* where James not so subtly subverted the happy ending implied by Basil and Verena's future marriage. Yet as Howells' review demonstrates, James could safely assume that his sleight of hand would go largely undetected by a public which he had accused (in "The Art of Fiction") of reading novels "as an exercise in skipping."[8] Only the most discriminating and attentive of readers could be expected to notice or enjoy the delicate balancing act which James was performing in (and for) his own interest (especially when a well-intentioned and highly-placed friend like Howells tried so earnestly to distract their attention from it). However, discriminating and attentive readers were precisely what Henry James periodically feared that he lacked. Ironically, it was primarily James's sense of their symptomatic absence from American culture which had shaped his early career as both a critic and a writer, for his chronic complaints about the American reading public had led, both directly and indirectly, to his decision to leave America during his apprentice years and his subsequent development of (and ever-increasing reliance upon) the international novel.

The strong misgivings concerning the character of the American reading public which were to persist throughout James's entire career surfaced quite early in his first published criticism. Although in these anonymous reviews James presented himself as a highly cosmopolitan if fledgling critic (he had cited Arnold and Taine as his models), when he contemplated the taste of American readers the evident mixture of anxiety and antagonism in his tone revealed that he was actually speaking from the point of view of an aspiring novelist.[9] In his 1864 critical debut (a notice of Nassau Senior's *Essay on Fiction* which appeared in the *North American Review*), James inadvertently revealed the source of this anxiety and antagonism when he described the ideal audience which he would like to have addressed. "For our own part, we should like nothing better than to write stories for weary lawyers and schoolmasters," he admits. These busy men, who come home from a hard day's work and read fiction to relax, sound more like common readers than the discriminating elite which we might expect James to evoke. But their prosaic character appears almost poetic to the apprentice writer when he compares them to their daughters and sisters "who stay at home all day to practice listless sonatas and read the magazines." (One cannot help wondering whether Henry had in mind here his own sister, Alice, and her friends; though it is worth noting that these young women lead lives of prescribed rather than voluntary leisure and that they frequently suffered from the debilitating effects of such enforced uselessness.)[10] The fact that this was written for a magazine audience, albeit a very select one, adds an ironic dimension to James's condescending attitude towards American magazines and their readers.

James is equally uneasy about the character of the writer of fiction. He imagines the wife and friends of a prolific novelist asking the writer whether he ever wearies of "this constant grinding out of false persons and events." The imaginary male writer responds with the assertion that the habitually busy man is the best novel-writer as well as the best novel-reader. "It is, as you say, because I 'grind out' my men and women that I endure them. It is because I create them by the sweat of my brow that I venture to look them in the face. My *work* is my salvation." The prolific author continues in his passionate outburst: "The pains of labor regulate and consecrate my progeny. If it were as easy to write novels as to read them, then, too, my stomach might rebel against the phantom peopled atmosphere which I have given myself to breathe."[11] All this talk of phantom peopled atmosphere may remind the reader of James's foremost American predecessor, Nathaniel Hawthorne. We are almost transported back into the rarified atmosphere of one of Hawthorne's romances; perhaps "The Custom House" preface to *The Scarlet Letter* comes most readily to mind. But here we see something new. Unlike Hawthorne, who was content to portray himself (however facetiously and deviously) as a mere "idler," James is straining after a definition of the producer of fiction which will place him in the same occupational category as the audience he would like to write for, skilled professional men.

The specific content of James's uneasiness with any other definition of his role was private as well as public. Not surprisingly, there was social and financial pressure on James (as on any middle-class American male of his age) to settle upon some respectable and profitable line of work, although this pressure was qualified by the peculiar status of the James family. Henry James Sr.'s inheritance of a substantial fortune from his father, a self-made millionaire, enabled the family to avoid contact with the antebellum business world almost entirely and to concentrate almost exclusively on questions of sensibility and self-cultivation. Henry Sr. placed a unique emphasis on the pleasures and responsibilities of being rather than doing, an emphasis which took practical effect in the highly eccentric education which he provided for his children. Yet his five children (as well as his wife) conformed to middle-class American expectations in many respects. All four sons attempted, with varying degrees of success, to become self-supporting while Alice, the lone daughter, never sought and was never given this opportunity. Of the four sons, the two eldest, William and Henry Jr., were the most successful; yet it was Henry, the younger of the two, who made the earliest and most consistent effort to be self-supporting (a reversal deliberately obscured by the self-effacing stance Henry would later adopt in his autobiography). While William vacillated between painting and science and eventually turned from medicine to psychology and a post on the Harvard faculty, Henry fixed upon literature as a career at the age of twenty-one after a very brief detour, an unsuccessful attempt to study law at Harvard. The aspiring novelist's desire to achieve financial and psychological independence from his family and his determination to pay back all parental advances promised a certain kind of freedom; but it forced him (at a very early stage in his career) into yet another kind of dependence, dependence upon the expectations of the American reading public.[12]

If James's desire to write for professional men is thus a reflection of his personal need to become one, at the same time it is also a reaction against his assumptions concerning the nature of both fiction and the reading public. These assumptions become explicit in his highly critical response to *The Schoenberg-Cotta Family*. In his review of this popular novel James labelled its public "respectable in everything but its literary taste." He regarded such fiction as part of an attempt to provide "books which grown women may read aloud to children without either party being bored" and he contrasted such "Sunday reading" unfavorably with the productions of the French realist school, novels which he associated with "great brilliancy and great immorality." His sarcastic comments about magazine and novel-readers in these apprentice reviews thus represent an early version of later diatribes in which he would rail against an infantile Anglo-Saxon public that consumes and demands inferior productions and in whose name critics placed artificial restrictions on the art of the novel (thereby perpetuating the chronic lack of appreciation and discrimination in Anglo-Saxon culture). The sisters and daughters of James's first review should therefore be regarded as native American versions of this transatlantic phenomenon. Because they stay at home all day, their exposure to the world is severely limited; and therefore, unlike their fathers and brothers, their judgment is largely unformed. Their prime "feminine" occupations, playing "listless sonatas" and reading the magazines, represent the kind of second-rate knowledge and second-hand experience which stunts intellectual growth and blunts artistic discrimination. In short, these women are the prototype of what James will later refer to as "the babyish public," his own label for what other writers would eventually refer to as the stupid public.

Sarcastic references to women who read fiction were as old as the novel itself. But while eighteenth-century critics often objected to female novel-reading on the grounds that it unsuited women for their modest station in life or schooled them in vice, James turned the tables in his early reviews by insinuating that it was literature which needed protection from women readers and not vice versa.[13] It is also worth noting that James was not alone when he assumed that women not only formed a substantial segment of the American magazine public but that they had a detrimental effect on the quality of magazine fiction. In August of 1866 another observer commented in the *Nation* on the way in which the general magazines were influenced by "the preponderance of female names on the subscription lists." Frank Luther Mott, a modern historian of American magazines, presents this comment as typical and accepts it as accurate. He also claims that "this petticoat rule" is particularly noticeable in American magazines between 1865 and 1885, especially in *Appleton's Journal, Harper's,* and *Scribner's,* and that it is only slightly less evident in the *Atlantic,* the *Galaxy,* and *Lippincott's.* Although it is difficult if not impossible to determine now whether women actually made up the greater part of the magazine audience in America, there is no doubt that the reading public was *assumed* to be predominantly female.[14] Thus, when we remember that James published much of his own early fiction in the *Atlantic* and the *Galaxy,* we can perceive that his recurring slurs on female readers were in fact acts of verbal aggression against what he must have assumed to be the majority of his own potential public, at least in America. Similarly, his portrait of the hardworking male novelist who grinds out novels by the sweat of his brow is an implicit attack on the omnipresence of cheap and easy writing, a state of affairs which, interestingly enough, James also seems to blame on women.

In a review of Miss Prescott's *Azarian* James charged:

> The fine writing in which "Azarian" abounds is the cheapest writing of the day. Every magazine story bears traces of it. It is so widely adopted because to a person of clever fancy there is no kind of writing that is so easy,—so easy, we mean, considering the effect produced.

He revealingly contrasts this type of writing with the "minuteness of presentation" in Balzac's "scientifically done" work, and goes on to evoke the example of "the *paternally* governed French tongue." Like his critical mentor Matthew Arnold, James greatly admires French literature and offers it as a welcome antidote to Anglo-Saxon "vulgarity," but he gives this international contrast a curious turn of the screw by recasting it in explicitly sexual terms and projecting it as a split between "masculine" and "feminine" literature. James's sexual bias becomes fully apparent as he goes on to explain that "like the majority of female writers,—Mrs. Browning, George Sand, Gail Hamilton, Mrs. Stowe,—she [Miss Prescott] possesses in excess the fatal gift of fluency." While James does not lay the blame for this state of affairs exclusively on women writers, he seems to apply an entirely different set of standards to the male writers whom he catches in the act of perpetrating similar literary crimes. Reviewing Trollope's *Lindisfarn Chase,* for example, James attributes its faults not to any fatal gift of fluency but to "the present condition of literature, when novel-writing is at once a trade and a past-time..." He continues by observing that "[s]uch works... are plentiful because they are so easy to write; they are popular because they are so easy to read." Here he seems to be suggesting that a male Anglo-Saxon author is only as good as his public will allow him to be.[15]

Again, in a review of Miss Braddon's *Aurora Floyd* James contrasts Wilkie Collins' public, capable of reading his "works of science" which require "very much the same intellectual effort as to read Motley or Froude," with Miss Braddon's public, "which reads nothing but novels, and yet which reads neither George Eliot, George Sand, Thackeray, nor Hawthorne." The fledgling critic reminds his readers that "people who read nothing but novels are very poor critics of human nature. Their foremost desire is for something new."[16] The unspoken assumption here is that Miss Braddon's public, unlike Wilkie Collins' public, is predominantly female. At the very least these people who (allegedly) read nothing but novels are part of the same public as the daughters and sisters James had described in his first review. Both typify an audience whose experience of life as well as literature is severely limited (a point of view he was to restate forcefully in his 1880 review of Zola's *Nana*). When read collectively, then, James's early criticism implies that male writers stoop to the cheap and easy only in order to achieve popularity with the reading public, while women writers churn out the cheap and easy simply because they do not know any better. These reviews further imply that the American reading public in particular is composed largely of women (and children) who are incapable of demanding or appreciating productions which require more intellectual effort. In effect, James holds women rather than men responsible (both as writers *and* as readers) for novel-writing's low status as a trade and a pastime rather than a skilled profession.

Even George Eliot, one of James's lifelong favorites, does not completely escape his application of this literary double standard. While he praises Eliot's "union of the tenderest and most abundant sympathies with a body of knowledge so ample—so active as to be absolutely free from pedantry," James condescendingly ends his 1866 review of *Felix Holt* by concluding that Eliot wrote no masterpieces because "with a certain masculine comprehensiveness which they [Miss Austen and Miss Edgeworth] lack, she is eventually a feminine—a delightfully feminine—writer."[17] His antipathy towards women writers as a group becomes a little more understandable (if not defensible) when we learn that Eliot herself tended to share in this disparaging attitude and largely for the same reason: both feared the consequences of literary amateurism. Eliot was so appalled by some of the amateurish productions of her literary sisters that she vented her displeasure in an extremely witty and entertaining article entitled "Silly Novels by Lady Novelists" (though unlike James, she did not prescribe French realism as the antidote). Published in the *Westminster Review* in October of 1856, this piece voiced her discomfort regarding the lack of standards in writing and reviewing as well as the critics' tendency to ignore or attack the best women writers while over-praising inferior female fiction. Although she insisted that there were enough great women novelists to prove that women could equal men in fiction, she blamed the "intrusions of mere left-handed imbecility" upon the fact that no other art form is so free from rigid requirements. According to Eliot, it was this situation which "constitutes the fatal seduction of novel-writing to incompetent women."[18] She might easily have extended her censure to incompetent men as well, but she did not.

Neither did her young admirer, Henry James. Although the literary male's animosity towards women writers in Anglo-American culture had as long a tradition as his hostility towards female readers, James sounds more like his American predecessor, Nathaniel Hawthorne, than like the eighteenth-century English critics whose fears centered primarily upon the social ramifications of the rise of literary women.[19] It was the phenomenal sales of *The Lamplighter,* a sentimental novel written by fellow Salemite Maria S. Cummins, which drove Hawthorne to complain bitterly to his publisher, George Ticknor, in the mid-1850s: "America is now wholly given over to a d----d mob of scribbling women, and I should have no chance of success while the public taste is occupied with their trash—and should be ashamed of myself if I did succeed." Hawthorne had gone on to ask: "What is the mystery of these innumerable editions of the 'Lamplighter,' and other books neither better nor worse?— worse they could not be, and better *they need not be,* when they sell by the 100,000..." Obviously Hawthorne's outburst can be attributed to mere professional jealousy of his more successful female competitors, but it also suggests his mounting anxiety over what he perceived as the public's loss of taste and the serious consequences for American literature.[20]

Evidence to support this line of reasoning can be found in a subsequent letter to Ticknor. Here Hawthorne praised Fanny Fern and her novel, *Ruth Hall,* very highly, despite the fact that it was another overwhelming success which went into "innumerable editions" (it sold 50,000 copies in eight months). He noted that "the woman writes as if the Devil was in her, and that is the only condition under which a woman ever writes anything worth reading," and he elaborated by adding: "Generally women write like emasculated men, and are only to be distinguished from male authors by greater feebleness and folly..."[21] James would later give vent to similar complaints about the many novels he read which seemed to him to have been written by "eunuchs or sempstressess [*sic*]." But as this second letter suggests, the crucial element in Hawthorne's complaint was not the sex of the writers but the quality of their fiction and the scale on which their novels were selling. *Uncle Tom's Cabin* (which James would nostalgically refer to late in his career as "a wonderful 'leaping' fish"), published as a two-volume novel in 1852, sold 200,000 copies within the first year; and this figure does not include its sales in England, where it was even more popular. Books of lesser quality did almost as well: Fanny Fern's *Fern Leaves* sold 70,000 copies in one year and Cummins' *The Lamplighter* sold 40,000 in eight weeks.[22]

These books (and other works from predominantly female pens) were mid-nineteenth-century versions of what we would today call best sellers. That is, they achieved high sales very rapidly and continued to sell steadily over long periods of time. Selling as they did in such unprecedented quantities, they threatened to redefine the very meaning not only of literary success but of literature itself.[23] Although we now tend to think of the 1850s as the period in which the American Renaissance writers predominated, Fred Pattee seems closer to the contemporaneous point of view when he refers to this decade as "the feminine fifties." It is well known that with the exception of *Typee,* Herman Melville was not widely read in his own day. However, compared to Melville, Hawthorne *was* relatively popular: William Charvat states that *Moby-Dick* sold only 2,500 copies in its first five years and less than 3,000 in its first twenty, while *The Scarlet Letter* sold 10,800 and 25,200 in identical periods. This means that *Moby-Dick* was an economic failure, while *The Scarlet Letter* was a steady (if not a best) seller; and Charvat suggests that

Hawthorne's relative success was due to the fact that he was more in harmony with the taste of the reading public of his day (a public Charvat also assumes to be predominantly female).[24] Yet when we compare the sales of Hawthorne's novels with that of the so-called "scribbling women," Hawthorne can hardly be considered a popular writer, a fact which he would have been the first to admit. His realization that he had "no chance of success while the public is occupied with their trash" and his declaration that he would be ashamed of himself if he did succeed has a peculiarly modern ring. In effect, Hawthorne is acknowledging the presence and the pressure of the reading public in a literary scene from which the individual patron has departed. In doing so, he became one of the first writers to introduce the note of contempt into the history of writer-reader relations in America; and this contempt was to constitute one of the essential elements in the literary legacy which he bequeathed to his foremost American successor, Henry James.

It is also important to remember that Hawthorne had to supplement his literary income with earnings from his tenure first as a custom house inspector and then as American consul to Liverpool in order to support his family. By the 1850s, several respectable literary monthlies had been founded in America. This meant that Hawthorne could have doubled his literary income by publishing his romances (as he called them) twice, first in serial form and then in book form. But it appears that Hawthorne considered his productions to be inherently unsuitable for serialization. Charvat reports that Hawthorne was approached by several editors but turned down every request. "'In all my stories...' he wrote one editor, 'there is one idea running through them like an iron rod.' If this idea were 'dragged slowly before the reader' for weeks and months, he said, 'it would become intolerably wearisome.'" (Hawthorne went on to contrast his works with the productions of Dickens and Thackeray which, he said, had the "variety of scene and multiplicity of character" necessary for serial publication.)[25] As an apprentice writer based in America, young Henry James inherited Hawthorne's dilemma in regard to the "scribbling women" and the American reading public. Without recourse to political patronage, he had to support himself by publishing his short stories and serializing his novels in the magazines, especially the *Atlantic* and the *Galaxy*. And although most of his apprentice reviews were addressed to the more exclusive audience of the *Nation* and the *North American Review*, we can almost picture the young James bravely wading through a sea of petticoats as we read these early literary notices. Between 1864 and 1866 alone, he reviewed works written by the following women, many of them now long forgotten: Miss Braddon, Miss Prescott, Mrs. A. M. C. Seemuller, Miss Alcott, Mrs. E. R. Charles, Mrs. Gaskell, and Mrs. D. M. M. Craik. In these anonymous reviews, James might criticize women writers and ridicule the public's taste for their productions, or he might try to educate literary producers and consumers alike.

In fact, he pursued all three strategies. But because James was also a writer of fiction he would have to compete with these women if he was to gain an audience and make a comfortable income.

In this context an early story, published in the *Galaxy* magazine in August of 1875, takes on an interesting dimension. "Benvolio" is uncharacteristic of James's early fiction in two respects: it is an allegory and its narrator makes only a weak attempt to disguise what is obviously a lack of confidence in his readers' taste. James even goes so far as to address his public openly as if it were almost exclusively female. As a direct result his narrative voice, which ranges between exaggerated politeness and barely concealed contempt, clearly lacks its usual subtlety and restraint. After describing his poet-hero, Benvolio, as a man of "no regular profession," the narrator comments:

> Having said this, it were perhaps well that I should let you—you especially, madam—suppose that he exactly corresponded to your ideal of manly beauty; but I am bound to explain definitely wherein it was that he resembled a fairy prince, and I need furthermore to make a record of certain little peculiarities and anomalies in which it is probable that your brilliant conception would be deficient.[26]

This practice dates back to the mid-eighteenth century when hack writers (as well as more talented novelists such as Fielding) confided in their "dear" or "gentle" readers. But what is new here is the obvious discomfort, bordering on open contempt for both himself and his audience, which James displays when he tries to give the public what he thinks it wants.

What James thinks his public wants turns out to be a highly ornamental style, a plot centering upon courtship, and a conventional happy ending. His attempts to oblige his readers can be seen in his conspicuously artificial style, as when he tells them that Benvolio is "about to enter upon the third decade of our mortal span" or when he reveals to them that their hero is endowed not with hair but with "clustering locks." "The sweet, clear, lingering, caressing tone" of Benvolio's voice is that of a man whose habit it is "to pluck the wayside flowers, and chase the butterflies afield." James's effort to supply a darker shading to this flat and rosy character sketch amounts to the disclosure that a surprising number of "silver threads" can be found among Benvolio's "golden locks," a discovery intended to quicken the readers' attention to "something grave and discreet in his smile—something vague and ghostly, like the dim adumbration of the darker half of the lunar disk."[27]

Not surprisingly, the tale recounts Benvolio's alternating but equally intense devotion to two women, a nun-like "bluestocking" whom he calls Scholastica and a worldly temptress referred to only as the Countess. As James rather perfunctorily puts it: "Benvolio was of course in love. Who was his mistress, you ask (I flatter myself with some impatience), and was she pretty, was she kind, was he successful? Thereby hangs my tale, which I must relate in due form."[28] The lack of enthusiasm and spontaneity in such passages could hardly be more complete. James almost sounds as if part of him wants to direct his readers' attention to his disdainful dependence upon the cliché-ridden plot and flowery diction which they have come to expect. But perhaps this *is* his intention. Indeed, the conflict between James's undisguised dependence upon and contempt for these devices forms a kind of inner tale which alternately competes with and compliments the more conventional plot-line in which Benvolio is alternately dependent upon and disdainful of both Scholastica and the Countess.

Leon Edel has interpreted the Countess as Europe and Scholastica as "the very breath of New England" in order to suggest that in this tale James "faces the duality of his nature and his response to the double environment of his childhood and youth." Yet the Countess and Scholastica represent contrasting versions of life in general and the literary life in particular which need not necessarily be defined in terms of nationality. As James himself tells us, the Countess "was an epitome of the gossip, the rumours, the interests, the hopes and fears of polite society." Regardless of her title, the Countess's preference for amusement over self-cultivation makes her an ideal representative of the type of common reader for whom reading is an exercise in skipping; and it is in this character that she accuses Benvolio of having "too much imagination." We also learn that although the Countess displays Benvolio's book of poems on her table, half of the leaves remain uncut.[29]

In contrast Benvolio first discovers Scholastica as she is intently reading this very volume. Her father, a blind philosopher who refuses to be read anything published later than the sixth century, has totally shielded her from contaminating contact with the Countess's world. Furthermore, the old man's dependence upon his daughter's eyes has provided her with a unique education and transformed her into the very type of the attentive reader. She is thus an ideal audience, for unlike her opposite, the Countess (who cannot remember what Benvolio has said after three minutes), she not only attends but follows (as the narrator pointedly notes). Quite significantly, it is Benvolio's repeated exposure to the glamorous Countess which eventually results in his writing first a private theatrical and then several highly successful plays. When we learn that James made periodic attempts to achieve popular success as a playwright throughout his career, we can see that Benvolio's "tolerably inexpensive" wooing of the Countess in some degree represents and prophesies his own uneven yet protracted courtship of popular success, both on and off the stage. By a similar logic, Benvolio's admiration for and attraction to Scholastica, despite her plainness of appearance, suggests his competing devotion to less obvious forms and measures of achievement.

However, Benvolio cannot seem to commit himself, for he continues to alternate back and forth between the two women. As James observes: "It was as if the souls of two very different men had been placed together to make the voyage of life in the same boat, and had agreed for convenience' sake to take the helm in alternation."[30] The same might be said of the narrator as well, for he displays a doubleness of artistic intention which matches Benvolio's vacillating matrimonial intentions. The two in fact become one in the last paragraph of the story when the narrator mechanically ends Benvolio's career as a suitor by half-heartedly marrying him off to Scholastica. James first withholds, then provides, and finally apologizes for this hackneyed denouement, displaying an indecisiveness not unlike his hero's. In effect, then, "Benvolio" reveals and unsuccessfully attempts to exorcise James's own ambivalent attraction to the rewards and possibly even the time-worn formulas of the cheap and easy. While this may seem to be an inappropriate way to refer to the Countess, it is Scholastica who represents the expensive in the sense of the difficult and the scientifically done (even though James characteristically undercuts his own terms by suggesting that Benvolio's poetry becomes "dismally dull" after his marriage to the somewhat prosaic Scholastica).

In suggesting that neither woman alone can stimulate or sustain Benvolio's imagination, James is also indirectly acknowledging his own similar reliance upon vividly contrasting forms of experience. Benvolio's admiration for the paternally-governed Scholastica, who reads only learned works ("disquisitions on philosophy, on history, on the natural sciences"), represents the attraction which exact science and classical tradition exerted upon a powerful mind committed to a profession whose lack of formal laws and rigid requirements often resulted in the predominance of the cheap and easy. (This is the side of James which would respond so enthusiastically to Flaubert and his circle because of their "scientific" emphasis upon fictional laws and technique.) Yet James's esteem for form and order was more than matched by his passionate love of all that was vivid, unpredictable, and colorful in the spectacle of life (hence his periodic efforts to clear the field of fiction of *all* a priori rules). Over the course of his career, he would continually vacillate between these two extremes: an exaggerated respect for formal consistency which could degenerate into lifelessness and an almost child-like fascination with the drama and suspense of the presented surface of life which tended to lapse into a taste for the melodramatic. (Although James frequently deals with and attempts to disguise these conflicting tendencies by projecting them onto two or more distinct characters, such internal conflict is a recurring theme in his work. Hyacinth Robinson in *The Princess Casamassima,* Peter Sherringham and Nick Dormer in *The Tragic Muse,* and Guy Domville in the play which bears his name would all lead lives of similar vacillation.)

It was in his taste for melodrama that James came closest to resembling the reading public for which he seemed to have so little respect. As "Benvolio" progressed, the narrator's irony was increasingly directed inward towards his artist-hero rather than outward towards his readers, almost as if James were struggling to distance himself from his own worst tendencies. However, these tendencies continued to predominate in a serial he created for the *Atlantic* in 1871. *Watch and Ward,* James's first full-length fiction, opens with a highly melodramatic suicide scene and centers upon the somewhat ambiguous relationship between the suicide's orphaned daughter Nora and a young bachelor, Roger Lawrence. Lawrence adopts Nora shortly after witnessing her father's death and eventually becomes her husband—though not without protracted competition from her handsome but ne'er-do-well cousin. If James's plot sounds quite elaborate, it is no more so than the overwrought prose which pervades this apprentice work. For example, James writes of his hero's face: "Beneath its simple serenity, over which his ruddy blushes seemed to pass like clouds in a summer sky, there slumbered a fund of exquisite expression." We are also treated to a generous dose of expletives diluted by means of copious dashes and frequent excerpts from lengthy epistles. Suspense is provided by postponing the inevitable nuptuals until Roger can demonstrate his worthiness by providing Nora with an exemplary education, vanquishing his two ardent competitors, and surviving a near-fatal illness.[31]

While it is certainly conceivable that James could have intended this serial to be a parody of the sentimental novels then in vogue, for the most part he seems to be playing it straight, possibly for several reasons. Although the trite plot is largely a concession to the debased taste of the public, it begins to take on deeper significance as the story progresses, for it is freighted with emotions whose source seems to be the apprentice novelist's extremely ambivalent attitude towards his audience. James's bachelor-hero sets the plot in motion by deciding that he must become both "nurse and governess" to his adopted daughter in order to remedy her "makeshift education" and transform her into the perfect wife. Roger then realizes that if he is to educate Nora properly, he must first educate himself so that daily contact with him will constitute a "liberal education" for her. His liberal education is to consist of prolonged travel abroad during which he will keep a diary addressed to Nora. This diary will later be read aloud to his daughter and future wife, "she being implied throughout as the reader or auditor." Roger's curious double "apprenticeship to the profession of husband and father" bears a strange resemblance to his young creator's literary apprenticeship, for parenthood and marriage implicitly function in this novel as metaphors for the advancing stages of reciprocal intimacy, trust, and devotion which each of these bachelors are bent on achieving vis à vis their feminine readers. Both men share a conspicuous inability to decide whether to woo or to educate their respective audience. Like his hero, James apparently decided that self-cultivation could function as the necessary prelude to (and possibly even an initiation into) courtship, for he would soon continue his own liberal education in Europe. In spite of the self-confident pose he displayed in his anonymous early reviews, in his guise as an author James seems to have also had moments when he wondered (like Roger) whether he could ever have "that charm of infalliability, that romance of omniscience, that a woman demands of her lover" and a novel-reader demands of an author. "She has seen me scratching my head, she has seen me counting on my fingers!" laments Roger, who cannot decide whether to woo Nora by going to exotic lands and returning "in glory" or by "snubbing and scolding her" and telling her she is "deplorably plain," treating her, in short, "as Rochester treats Jane Eyre."[32]

Roger's creator seems to have similarly experimented with alternative strategies. In productions such as *Watch and Ward* and "Benvolio," James can be caught in the act of catering to the lowest common denominator of the reading public; while in his more ambitious fiction we can watch him as he attempts to develop a style that is both difficult and demanding. In such works he began to defy the literary conventions of his day by engaging in minute and subtle analysis of character and motive, partly in emulation of continental realism and partly, it may be assumed, in an effort to curb his own deep-seated tendency to lapse into melodramatic expression. The dangers of this more aggressive strategy can be gauged by the fact that when readers began to criticize James's fiction, it was the resulting remoteness and lack of warmth which they noticed and reacted against (rather than the ill-concealed sarcasm and irony which accompanied his occasional lapses into melodrama). As Richard Foley points out, reviewers frequently complained "that in his persistent desire to dissect human nature James created personages easy and interesting to dissect rather than real, true-to-life characters—a complaint which was to become conventional."[33]

Such was the case with *Roderick Hudson* (1875), James's first novel to appear in book form. This work was poorly received precisely because of its unhappy ending and "the lack of warm, human feeling in the story."[34] It is not hard to see why *Roderick Hudson* would leave most contemporaneous readers cold. Roderick's endowments as an American sculptor include the extravagant kind of speech which James's native audience had come to expect from a man of "true genius." But by telling his story from the point of view of Roderick's highly restrained patron, Rowland Mallet, James manages to undercut thoroughly both the sculptor's inflated rhetoric and, we may assume, his countrymen's equally inflated expectations. As the novel progresses it becomes increasingly clear that James is prepared to provide his readers with entertainment of a highly sophisticated variety that can only be enjoyed at the hero's expense. The purchase price of such amusement is a critical stance towards those literary conventions most cherished by the Anglo-American reading public, a price most contemporaneous readers were obviously unwilling to pay.

All of this is also true of James's next novel, *The American* (1877), but to a much lesser degree. Although the narrator's tone is quite ironic when he assures his readers in the opening pages of the novel that Christopher Newman's eye "was by no means the glowing orb of a hero of romance," in the last scene of the book James can unblushingly refer to his patriotic hero's "remarkable good nature." Over the course of the novel, Newman is transformed from a comically naive and tactless American type (who is first seen wandering in the Louvre with his Bädeker in hand and "an aesthetic headache") into a romantic hero who nobly forsakes an underhanded opportunity to avenge his wronged sweetheart. While *The American* does end unhappily, we are encouraged to see Newman's renunciatory gesture as a triumph of American integrity over European corruption. James's melodramatic imagination prevails throughout much of the book and effectively forestalls what was by then the standard complaint about his work, the charge that his stories had no heart in them. Whether or not this was an altogether intentional maneuver on James's part is difficult if not impossible to determine.[35]

It should be clear by now that James's earliest relations with the American reading public were less than smooth, despite the fact that he met with early success, enjoyed easy access to the magazines, and received the encouragement and praise of influential countrymen such as Charles Eliot Norton, editor of the *North American Review,* and William Dean Howells, then assistant editor of the *Atlantic Monthly.* The relationship between Howells and James is especially revealing in this respect, for it illustrates the extent to which James was prepared to compromise with American magazine conditions and conventions. Although he never did so enthusiastically, James was often willing to defer to Howells' better judgment as when, for example, Howells objected to passages in an 1873 story entitled "The Madonna of the Future." Leon Edel suggests that the "immoral aspects" which prompted Howells' complaint were the speeches of the "cynical artist . . . who constantly compared the human race to 'cats and monkeys.'" James's willingness to let Howells make any cuts he deemed necessary is a sign that he clearly recognized the extent to which his career depended on American magazines. The artist in James was moved to write his father: "With such a standard of propriety, it makes a bad look out ahead for imaginative writing. For what class of minds is it that such very timorous scruples are thought necessary?" But James's alter-ego, the cool professional, had the last word. He conceded that Howells had a better idea of the common public's taste and concluded that he was obliged to Howells for "performing the excision personally."[36]

Another highly illustrative confrontation between James and American magazine conventions occurred when Howells objected to the unhappy ending of *The American* while it was still appearing as a serial in the *Atlantic* during 1876 and 1877. James responded to Howells with a long letter justifying his decision not to conclude his novel with the conventional happy ending. He insisted that an international marriage between Newman and the French widow, Claire de Cintré, would not be true to the facts of life and indicated that he expected more from Howells. "I quite understand that as an editor you should go in for a 'cheerful ending'" he wrote, "but I am sorry that as a private reader you are not struck with the inevitability of the American dénouement." He further argued that the prettier ending would only have been "a rather vulgar sop to readers who don't really know the world and who don't measure the merit of a novel by its correspondence to the same. Such readers assuredly have a right to their entertainment, but I don't believe it is in me to give them, in a satisfactory way, what they require." Nevertheless, James promised that his next production for the *Atlantic* would be a "very joyous little romance" complete with a happy ending and a hero with whom all the women would fall in love.[37]

By the time James made this promise he was living in England and travelling on the Continent where he was learning to know the world at firsthand. He was forced to accept the fact that in his capacity as editor of the *Atlantic,* Howells had become not only a representative of all that was limited and provincial about the Amerrican literary scene but also a spokesman for that class of minds for which "such very timorous scruples" were thought necessary. (As Howells himself would later admit, when he became a magazine editor he entered into "a tacit agreement" with his family of subscribers whereby he would "print nothing which a father may not read to his daughter, or safely leave her to read herself.")[38] This developing transatlantic conflict between the principles of an increasingly cosmopolitan artist and the standards of a highly respected American magazine editor dramatizes James's uneasy relations with his native public. It also suggests why he had already begun to think of Europe not only as an essential ingredient in the liberal education which he sought for both himself and his American readers but as the source of an alternative public.

From the outset, James had attracted a group of readers who would follow his artistic development avidly (if not always with approval) throughout the better part of his career, a group which was composed in part by his family (especially his father, his sister Alice, and his elder brother, William), his Cambridge friends and neighbors (such as Grace Norton, Charles's sister), and his editorial acquaintances, Howells included. It was, altogether, an appreciative and impressive audience for a beginning writer to lay claim to. But it had neither the cosmopolitan quality nor the democratic quantity to satisfy James's growing ambition and guarantee him literary success. Howells seemed to sense this very early in James's career. In August of 1867 he expressed his anxieties in a letter to their mutual friend, Charles Eliot Norton. As he revealed to Norton:

> Harry James has written us [the *Atlantic*] another story, which I think admirable; but I do not feel sure of the public any longer, since the *Nation* could not see the merit of *Poor Richard*. It appeared to me that there was remarkable strength in the last scenes of that story; and I cannot doubt that James has every element of success in fiction. But I suspect that he must in a great degree create his audience.

Presumably speaking as a private reader (and an aspiring author) rather than as a magazine editor, Howells concluded: "In the meantime I despise existing readers."[39]

Howells' suspicion that James "must in a great degree create his audience" was to prove prophetic. As the success of the "scribbling women" testifies, the American novelist had available a reading public of unprecedented size, but only on the condition that she or he was willing to take the necessary steps to attract its attention and cater to its taste. In 1860, the very year in which the Civil War began and just four years before Henry James made his literary debut, the Beadle firm unveiled the dime novel, a type of fiction designed expressly to meet the needs of this ever-expanding audience. "BOOKS FOR THE MILLION! A Dollar Book for a Dime!" ran the historic ad in the New York *Tribune*. Historian John Tebell reports that despite all its disruptions, the war itself helped to facilitate rather than retard the spread of the habit of reading. He also observes that while people eager for news of the conflict turned to the newspapers as never before, fiction flourished as well:

> The creation of a mass audience that had begun before the war with the first paperback revolution was hardly more than slowed down by the struggle between North and South, since paperbacks distributed wholesale to the soldiers added considerably to the reading audience.[40]

Wilky James, Henry's younger brother, was a member of this audience. While serving as an officer in the first Black regiment, the Mass. 54th, Wilky wrote home from the front in December of 1864 to make the following request of his brother, the apprentice writer. "Tell Harry that I am waiting anxiously for his 'next.' I can find a large sale for any blood and thunder tale among the darks."[41] But Henry obviously did not fit the role in which his brother tried to cast him, that of the author of blood and thunder tales. As we have seen, his emphasis was becoming quite the reverse: he was beginning to pay such acute attention to psychological detail and analysis rather than to plot or incident (at least as these terms were then understood) that his manner would soon be compared to that of a scientist cooly performing a dissection. Soldiers, Black or white, were hardly the type of reader who could appreciate this finesse, nor were they the public James himself had in mind (as we learned from his first review).[42]

Yet in reconstructing the postbellum American literary scene as it appeared to James, it is important to note that another friend and protégé of

Howells, Mark Twain, achieved literary greatness as well as pecuniary success by writing for this very public. After the war, hopes of tapping this new mass audience lured Twain into publishing his novels by subscription. This strategy represents the primary alternative open to an American novelist who wanted to expand his public as well as his profits beyond the limitations of the regular magazine and book trade. For reasons which should already be obvious, this alternative was poorly suited to James's priorities as a professional writer; but as we shall see, the contrast between his early career and Twain's is less great than one might at first imagine. For one thing, both men launched their careers as journalists. Twain began by writing newspaper journalism and only started to write novels after Elisha Bliss's American Publishing Company, a Hartford, Connecticut, subscription firm, successfully published a collection of his newspaper articles in book form as *The Innocents Abroad* in 1869. Twain's continued preference for subscription publication of his work reveals a great deal about his attitude towards the reading public as well as his priorities. As his biographer, Justin Kaplan, admits:

> In stating his goal [making lots of money] and choosing Bliss's publishing company as the way to reach it, Clemens implicitly defined his audience and the character of the books he would write for it. The subscription book, in Bliss's terms, was the people's book, and he was soon to advertise Mark Twain as "the people's author."[43]

Subscription books were sold door to door by the firm's army of book agents. Bypassing the bookstores enabled subscription publishers like Bliss to tap a wider market while reducing financial risk, for subscription books did not go to press until a sufficient number of advance orders had been secured.[44] But Twain's books had to be priced higher than regular trade books in order to pay the subscription agents as well as the author and publisher. As a result the subscription public, which was typically rural and relatively uneducated, expected very bulky books; and Twain was thus obliged to manufacture long manuscripts. Kaplan observes that "even padded out with steel engravings, decorations of all sorts, elaborate tables of contents, a six-hundred-page book would strain the integrity and imagination of an author who had only a three-hundred-page idea to begin with." On the basis of these considerations, he concludes that subscription publishing was detrimental to Twain's development as an artist. "It forced him to go on grinding out a manuscript long after he lost interest in the subject, and it conditioned him to think of his writing as a measurable commodity like eggs and corn." (Twain himself may have held a not unsimilar opinion of his own work, for the running satire on subscription books and their readers which punctuates the chapters devoted to the Grangerford-Shepherdson feud in *Huckleberry Finn* reads at times as if it were intentionally self-reflexive.)[45]

As Kaplan pointedly notes: "Authors whose aspirations were of a different sort and who, while needing money no less than Clemens did, were willing for a while to accept its equivalent in reputation, went to publishers whose books were sold in bookstores." He cites the firm of Ticknor and Fields as one of those regular publishing houses whose reputation was so high that their imprint on an author's book was a reward in itself. When we learn that Henry James published his first books with James R. Osgood and Company of Boston, proud successor to the "late Ticknor and Fields, and Fields, Osgood and Company," we can see that he epitomizes Kaplan's description of the author whose aspirations were of a different sort.[46] James's first book, a collection of short stories entitled *A Passionate Pilgrim and Other Tales,* was published in 1875 in a first printing of 1500 copies for sale at $2 each. By contrast, Twain's subscription novels usually sold at $3.50 and reached an audience estimated by one historian at roughly 40,000. Such figures help to explain why Twain once remarked to Howells: "Anything but subscription publishing is printing for private circulation."[47] However, the characteristic overstatement of this remark should not obscure the fact that the regular book trade, though certainly less profitable than subscription publishing, was a business (like any other) which subjected Henry James to pressures not totally unlike those which Mark Twain experienced. As an author who wrote articles for American magazines and who published his longer works serially, James was not above thinking of his work as a measurable commodity, although he never thought of it as just that (obviously, neither did Twain). In an early letter, written to his young friend Thomas Sargeant Perry in 1868, James had confided: "I write very little and only tales, which I think it likely I shall continue to manufacture in a hackish manner, for that which is bread." But he went on to add: "They *cannot* of necessity be very good; but they *shall not* be very bad."[48]

Given James's misgivings about the widespread taste for the cheap and easy and his disdain for readers who "don't know the world and who don't measure the merit of a novel by its correspondence to the same," it is obvious that neither Twain's subscription public nor the regular book trade readers who made the "scribbling women" so successful were the kind of audience he craved as a novelist. Yet for financial as well as for artistic reasons, James was faced with the necessity of extending the dimensions of his literary arena beyond the confines of the regular book trade in America. Some American writers, like Howells, had attempted to relieve the financial pressures by taking editorial positions; and, indeed, James did receive repeated "overtures" from both the *Nation* and the *North American Review.* But these offers of regular literary employment were just as repeatedly turned down by James, perhaps because he realized that editorial responsibilities might threaten his artistic development and would certainly limit his geographical mobility.[49] Mobility was important to a writer who sensed that his solution lay in extending his market geographically, not westward across America (as Twain was doing) but eastward to Europe. There James might continue his "liberal education" and satisfy his ambition to achieve popularity, fame, and profits by conquering and annexing the wider English-speaking public. His invention, the international novel, was to become both the vehicle for the journey and the weapon he would perfect in the course of this campaign. Extremely ambitious and highly cosmopolitan by temperament, Henry James sought an equally cosmopolitan audience which would combine size and taste, democratic quantity and aristocratic quality.

2

"The Mill of the Conventional"

In the summer of 1875 Henry James turned to an American newspaper for the first time in his career as part of his effort to secure financing for his assault upon the European literary scene. The New York *Tribune* owed its reputation for respectability largely to its former editor, Horace Greeley, a man who had attracted contributions to its pages from such widely varying talents as Henry James Senior and Margaret Fuller in the antebellum period. Ironically enough, the *Tribune* was also the weekly which had begun urging its readers to buy dime novels back in 1860 when it reverberated with ads proclaiming "BOOKS FOR THE MILLION! A Dollar Book for a Dime!" Whether or not the apprentice novelist appreciated this irony we do not know, for if James harbored any reservations about making his entrance upon the European scene in the character of an American newspaper correspondent, he effectively concealed them when he approached John Hay (assistant to *Tribune* publisher Whitelaw Reid) and suggested that he begin a regular correspondence of a non-political nature from Paris. "There is apparently in the American public an essential appetite, and a standing demand, for information about all Parisian things," he assured Hay. He followed this up by observing:

> It is as a general thing rather flimsily and vulgarly supplied, and my notion would be to undertake to supply it in a more intelligent and cultivated fashion—to write in other words from the American (or if it doesn't seem presumptuous to say so, as far as might be from the cosmopolitan) point of view a sort of *chronique* of the events and interests of the day.

What was perhaps presumptuous about this business proposition was the fact that the *Tribune* already had a Parisian correspondent, Arsene Houssaye, as James himself noted in his letter to Hay. James disposed of this obstacle by hinting both that Houssaye's efforts might be inadequate and that his relations with the paper might be coming to an end. Quite characteristically, James was anything but modest about his own qualifications.[1]

When the *Tribune* offered to pay the aspiring journalist $20 in gold per letter, James's eagerness to accept was qualified only by what he considered to be the smallness of the sum. He seems to have been totally unaware of the fact that newspaper journalism would place quite new demands on him, from the point of view of both content and tone as well as regularity of production. Up to this point James had written exclusively for magazines whose public was inferior in size but superior in taste to that of the *Tribune*. His only previous experience with transatlantic journalism had been the travel letters which he had addressed to the readers of the stately and subdued *Nation* back in 1872, and he should have been forewarned by this experience. Both his brother William and his friend Howells had criticized these efforts, aimed at the *Nation's* small but highly cultivated public, for their tendency to over-refinement. At the time James had agreed with them both, responding from Paris that he was not afraid of not being able to "work it off with practise." But he had also insisted:

> Beyond a certain point, this would not be desirable I think—for me at least, who must give up the ambition of ever being a free-going and light-paced enough writer to please the multitude. The multitude, I am more than ever convinced, has absolutely no taste—none at least that a thinking man is bound to defer to.

James followed this dismissal of the taste of the general public with a declaration which would become a familiar refrain later in his career whenever his work received an unfavorable reception:

> To write for the few is doubtless to lose money—but I am not afraid of starving. *Au point ou nous en sommes* all writing not really leavened with thought—of some sort or other—is terribly unprofitable, and to try to work one's own material closely is the only way to form a manner on which to keep afloat—without intellectual bankruptcy at least.[2]

This letter to William reveals that as early as the fall of 1872 Henry was aware of the difficulty of trying to balance two sets of account books, one financial and one intellectual. Though he was always worrying about money, James could never forget that a writer could go bankrupt in the second sense as well as the first. Yet only three years later we find him seeking to finance his European literary debut by proposing to satisfy the appetite of the American newspaper public, a public which was surely less cultivated and cosmopolitan than the "tasteless multitude" of magazine readers to which James refers in the preceding letter. It should come as no surprise, then, to learn that James soon experienced second thoughts concerning the terms of his bargain with Reid. James's uneasiness about appearing in newsprint may have represented an oblique acknowledgment of the false position in which he had placed himself. He mailed off his first piece to Reid from Paris in November of 1875 with the request that "any heading prefixed to the letter will be as brief and simple as possible." By February he was complaining to William that the heading and editorial remarks which the *Tribune* inserted over his letters sickened him "to the soul." While the private correspondence which James addressed to his family and friends during this period are full of interesting description and abound in literary gossip, they express his difficulty in finding enough topics for his *Tribune* letters as well as his acute discomfort over their format.[3] This discomfort could only have been reinforced by James's newly established friendship with Ivan Turgenev and his introduction to Gustave Flaubert and his literary cénacle, most notably Emile Zola, the Goncourt brothers, and Alphonse Daudet. (James's early essay on Turgenev, coupled with a cordial note from his father to the expatriate Russian novelist, had served as a convenient entrée into their exclusive circle.) For years Balzac and the French literary fraternity had been James's companions via the printed page where they constituted his standard of excellence (as both a reader and a critic) by representing the "expensive" qualities of consummate aesthetic taste and discrimination (if not the virtues of high morality). Now that James had set out to transform himself into a serious professional novelist, Flaubert and his followers embodied and endorsed these same qualities at firsthand; and while James was quick to note a certain narrowness of outlook on their part, he clearly admired and hoped to emulate their "scientific" emphasis upon technique and questions of form.[4] (Although he was always to hold Turgenev in particularly high regard, James never thought of himself as a disciple of Flaubert and his school. However, as we shall see, his defense of the French realists and his open sympathy with their literary intentions as well as the leading role which he was to play in introducing their work to Anglo-American readers would eventually combine with his own deep-seated tendency towards fictional experimentation to link his reputation with theirs in the eyes of hostile as well as sympathetic critics.)

Not surprisingly, these intense fellow professionals proved to be a frequent source as well as subject of some of the most colorful anecdotes which figure in James's private correspondence of this period. In a letter to Thomas Sergeant Perry written in early 1876 (almost entirely in French), he can be found boasting of his contacts with these elite French writers: "Tu vois que je suis dans les conseils des dieux—que je suis lancé en plein Olympe." He proceeded to announce that he was fascinated by Zola's "petite *école*" with its "garçons d'un grand talent," though he condescendingly confided that he found them to be *"affreusement bornés."* Another letter to Perry dated three months later suggests that this mild condescension could turn to outright disapproval, especially in the case of Zola, perhaps in part a reaction to James's frustrating lack of success in penetrating this tightly-knit clique and altering their attitude of open indifference with regard to the work of Anglo-American authors. (The young novelist singled out their lack of interest in George Eliot for criticism, but he undoubtedly felt this neglect himself.) James made no effort to conceal his disgust from Perry when he referred to Zola's latest production as *"merde au naturel,"* a play on Zola's recent characterization of his own manner as *"merde à la vanille."* However, he preferred to strike a more amused pose when addressing Howells, whom he assured—in English—that they were all "charming talkers." James seemed to hope that his behind-the-scenes accounts of the French coterie would shock his friend, the highly respectable editor of "the austere *Atlantic*"; and he took obvious pleasure in repeating bits of dialogue between Flaubert and his followers which would in all probability have scandalized the readers of the *Tribune* (while raising its circulation). One such discussion ended with Edmond de Goncourt's announcement of his next projected subject, "a whore-house *de province.*" While James carefully confined such tidbits to the pages of his private correspondence, he precipitated another sort of crisis when he asked Reid for a fifty percent raise in July of 1876. According to Leon Edel, Reid responded with a good-natured compromise. "He explained that James's subjects were often 'too remote from popular interests' and that it was possible to overestimate the newspaper's 'literary culture.'" Reid reminded James that newspaper readers, often in a hurry, preferred brevity and variety; and he suggested that James write shorter newsier letters, but at the same price. Reid summed up the situation this way: "The difficulty has sometimes been not that it was too good, but that it was magazine rather than newspaper work."[5]

Given the prominence of Turgenev and Flaubert and his circle in both James's life and his private correspondence during this period, it may be that James felt Reid's request for newsier letters as pressure not only to cheapen his manner but to turn his relations with them into grist for his journalistic mill. This would help to explain his rather extreme and somewhat self-pitying response to Reid (a preview of the way in which he would respond to similar disappointments during his theater negotiations in the 1890s). He revealed that he had been half expecting Reid's criticism; yet his reaction to this, his first real editorial rebuff, was, in effect, to quit. Somewhat stiffly he replied: "If my letters have been 'too good' I am honestly afraid that they are the poorest I can do, especially for the money! I had better, therefore, suspend them altogether." Never one to offend an editor, James ended on a conciliatory if somewhat ironic note: "I have enjoyed writing them, however, and if the *Tribune* has not been the better for them I hope it has not been too much the worse."[6] Despite Reid's flexibility, James proceeded to treat this episode as his first full-fledged rejection by an unappreciative public, an assessment which he would cultivate and periodically reaffirm with renewed force in future years when he experienced more serious difficulties. In a letter to his father written two weeks later, he announced that "Whitelaw Reid has stopped off my letters to the *Tribune*—practically at least—by demanding that they should be of a flimsier sort."[7] Yet the manner in which James ignored the possibility of compromise suggests that he was, in fact, only too eager to sever his relations with the

Tribune. Writing for the newspaper-reading public could only have reinforced James's "mortal horror of seeming to write thin" and his contempt for the "vulgar" taste of the multitude. However, his relative success with and inescapable dependence upon the taste of the American magazine public made him unwilling to assume the inflexible posture which Flaubert and his cénacle maintained towards the taste of the common reader.

The young American novelist's divergence from the French school on this issue is well illustrated by his acount of "Emile Zola's catastrophe." As James related the amusing incident to Howells, Zola had "just had a serial novel for which he was being handsomely paid interrupted on account of protests from provincial subscribers against its indecency. The opinion [of Flaubert and his "following"] apparently was that it was a bore, but that it could only do the book good on its appearance in a volume." Given James's own repeated outbursts against the taste of the reading public in America, we might expect his reaction to be one of sympathy with Zola and disgust with the public rather than amusement; but James was much too pleased with his own recent success with American magazines to feel anything more than condescending pity for "poor Zola." As he somewhat smugly told Howells, he ran into Zola "looking very pale and sombre" while descending the stairs of Flaubert's apartment and "saluted him with the flourish natural to a contributor who has just been invited to make his novel last longer yet."[8] Popular success clearly remained one of James's chief ambitions. However, it was not just the pecuniary rewards which continued to attract him (though they *were* important). Throughout his career, James would regard the demand for and circulation of his work as a measure of his social significance and worth as a man of letters as well as a source of income and financial independence. If the money he received from the sales of his serials and books was income, it was also reassuring evidence that he was gaining and holding the attention of the general public. In this respect, the financial transactions of the literary life carried a double import: they represented the "vulgar" terms of James's trade, but they also confirmed the fact that he was not just being read and reviewed by a small and self-satisfied coterie of critics and friends.[9]

James's subsequent choice of England rather than France or America as a residence seems to have been, among other things, his way of trying to steer a middle course between the conflicting claims of the many and the few. England was a compromise, a vantage point from which James could observe the Anglo-American as well as the European social and literary scenes. It was also a convenient point of contact between two literary markets, the English and the American book trade. As he confided to his mother, "I am very glad I wasted no more time in Paris. I shall work here [London] much more and much better, and make an easier subsistence. Besides it is a comfort feeling nearer, geographically, my field of operation at home." (A subsequent generation of expatriate American writers would make the same choice—partly because of the language barrier and partly because they sensed, as did James, that "in England...Americans had advantages in being both within and without society.") In one sense, access to these two markets meant a wider measure of freedom, since it promised partial independence from the total conditions of either one; but it also posed the threat of double bondage. James would have to perform a delicate balancing act if he was to work both markets well enough to secure popularity as well as literary success on both fronts without alienating either audience. Having already made his mark on the American market, James now set out to conquer its English counterpart. Shortly after he took up lodgings in London during the winter of 1876, James became a subscriber to Mudie's, the British circulating library which was at the height of its power and prestige during this period of his career. He seems to have realized from the start that he would have to adapt himself in some degree to Mudie's conditions if he wanted to achieve success with the British public; and the guinea subscription fee may thus have figured to James as an investment in his career.[10]

Charles Edward Mudie, the proprietor of England's largest circulating library, began his long career lending books at his small Bloomsbury shop in 1842. By mid-century his "select" library was placing orders so large that publishers depended on Mudie's, a dependence which enabled him to exert a powerful influence upon the English book trade and, indirectly, upon English authors. "Select" referred to the fact that Mudie assumed responsibility for preselecting suitable, that is moral, novels which he deemed proper reading for the daughter of the family. Given the Victorian habit of reading novels aloud among family members, Mudie felt that it was necessary to establish standards which took account of the presence of the younger members of the audience, especially the female listeners. As Thackeray wrote in the *Cornhill*, "we shall suppose the ladies and children always present." The British circulating library shared part of the responsibility for the price as well as the content of new novels, for it cooperated (some said conspired) with the regular book trade in England to maintain a tight control (some said a stranglehold) over the publication and distribution of new books throughout the nineteenth century. By insisting that all new novels be issued in multi-volume format, the English book trade kept the price of novels extraordinarily and artificially high (31s. 6d. for a three-decker) and out of the reach of the general public, who were forced to borrow new books from the circulating libraries. This provided the libraries with a captive audience, in whose behalf they ordered 500 to 1500 copies of each three-decker they selected. The predictability of orders thus insured reduced the element of financial risk for English publishers and provided English authors with an unusually stable if limited audience. It was an arrangement which had several advantages for everyone concerned except, of course, those members of the reading public who could not afford the price of a subscription.[11]

The yearly fee of one guinea amounted to merely two-thirds the cost of a new novel and entitled the subscriber to unlimited borrowing. Even so, Guinevere Griest has recently estimated that only 60,000 at most out of Great Britain's 4.6 million families could afford to pay this in 1872, a figure which is compatible with reports that Mudie's could claim 50,000 subscribers by mid-century.[12] (Yet it is quite likely that each subscription represented multiple readers or listeners within the family unit.) Therefore, in spite of the fact that the size of the American first editions of James's novels usually ranged between 1500 and 2000 copies, roughly the same range as his English first editions, it is possible to speculate that the size of his English public (or at least those who read his novels in book form in addition to or instead of in serial form, as James preferred that they be read), was far greater in England than in America.

It is important to note that by the end of the eighteenth century, the circulating library had succeeded in taking books out of the control of an elite few, almost exclusively upper class and male, and into the marketplace, where they became a form of middle-class recreation and education, especially for women. The popular three-decker broke the once strict association between reading and the sanctity of the university, the study, and the gentleman's private library; and in some respects it resembled the American subscription book in its emphasis upon quantity. The pressure on writers to stretch their work into three-decker format frequently resulted in shameless padding in the form of long prefaces, wide margins, and enlarged type. Content was often effected as well: chapters were added, dialogue and description expanded, and authorial comment inserted, all to eke out the prescribed three volumes. Writers who wanted to circumvent this format or the censorship dictated by Mudie's as well as those who wanted to reach a wider audience were forced to attempt to publish outside the regular book trade. Dickens' publication of his works in monthly parts was one such attempt which, not incidentally, also reduced the risk of literary piracy. With the founding of *Macmillan's* and the *Cornhill* in the late 1850s, however, serialization drove out "part issue" because readers could get the serial plus other articles for roughly the same price.[13] Growing up in Europe and American in the 1850s and 1860s, Henry James had consumed enormous quantities of this type of fiction in his youth; and by the time he turned seventeen, he was unable to treat the conventional three-decker as anything but the subject of parody. Evidence of this can be found in an August 1860 letter to T.S. Perry which begins:

> Number one hundred and ninety Bongasse. The Fust of August: a Romance in 3 volumes. By 'Arry Jeames, alias G.P.R. author of the 'beacon beacon, beacon light' etc. Vol. I. Part I. Book I. Chap. I. The morning broke! High into the vast unclouded vault of Heving rose the Awb of Day, chasing before it the fleeting clouds that enshroud the slumbers of men.[14]

However, another development which helped to alter the British literary scene had a significant if unanticipated effect on the course of James's career. The "yellowback" was a new type of fiction designed to satisfy the British public's growing demand for literature which was both cheap and new. Yellowbacks were pirated foreign novels, frequently inferior in quality or "indecent" by Mudie's standards, which were published in an inexpensive one-volume format and sold through the book stalls of a railway library.[15] One such "library" was Ward, Lock, and Company; and, interestingly enough, it was this firm, rather than the prestigious Mudie's, to which James would owe his first popular success with the British public. Although it was certainly unethical, literary piracy did not become illegal until the passage of the international copyright law in 1891. Throughout the nineteenth century, authors on both sides of the Atlantic periodically pressed for the adoption of an Anglo-American copyright agreement, but until 1891 opposition from both governments and vested interests proved too strong. In America, most politicians and even some authors took the position that piracy represented the only means of keeping the price of literature within the reach of democratic readers. They conveniently ignored the fact that their refusal to grant protection to British authors often resulted in the exploitation of American authors by British publishers who practiced reverse piracy. As we have seen, James's first books were published in America by J.R. Osgood and Company of Boston in 1875. Although the apprentice novelist was already living in Europe by the end of that year, he had not yet established himself in London, nor did he possess a sufficient reputation to approach an English publisher. *A Passionate Pilgrim, Transatlantic Sketches,* and *Roderick Hudson* came out in American editions only, although they were imported to and distributed in London by Trübner and Company. Given this exposure, it was only a matter of time before James's work came to the attention of an enterprising railway library firm, as Ward, Lock, and Company proved when they pirated James's second novel, *The American,* just after its publication in America by Osgood in 1879.[16]

This unauthorized edition, with its "multicolored pictorial boards, lettering and illustration in blue, red, black, tan, and yellow" on the front cover and advertising on the back, was obviously designed to appeal to the taste of the multitude. The cover illustration, which portrayed Newman protecting Claire de Cintré while her brother holds a candle which illumines some unidentified danger, represented an attempt to exploit the melodramatic aspects of the plot and provided a striking contrast to the modest cloth binding favored by Osgood. There was an equally marked contrast in price as well. While Osgood's first edition, which numbered only 1000 copies, sold at $2 each and was offered for sale in England at 10/6, the pirated English version cost just 2 shillings. Although no figures are available for the size of the yellowback edition, it is reasonable to assume that both its popular price and format rendered it accessible to a much wider audience. James complained about this format to one correspondent, charging that the pirated edition was "vilely printed" and that whole paragraphs had been omitted. Yet his overall reaction to this first major experience with literary piracy was mixed and quite revealing. On January 13, 1878, he wrote elatedly to his mother: "Did I tell you it [*The American*] had been reprinted here by Ward & Lock, in the railway library with a wonderful picture on the cover?" And then, as if catching himself in the act of showing immoderate enthusiasm for this dubious source of newfound British popularity, James regained his professional self-control and added: "But this of course is a piracy, & I get no profit from it."[17]

The lesson of this experience was not lost upon James, who subsequently took advantage of an 1851 law which granted American authors the right to obtain copyright protection by applying on British soil. He was thus able to issue his next book, a collection of critical essays on French literature and culture, exclusively in London. The prestigious firm of Macmillan and Company had agreed to become his English publishers. Their willingness to take a chance on this all but unknown American critic suggests that James may have profited indirectly from the popularity of his pirated novel. James initially chose to present himself to this public in the guise of a cosmopolitan critic rather than an American novelist, perhaps to counteract his image as the author of a pirated and highly melodramatic international novel. Although bound copies of *French Poets and Novelists* were imported to America, the fact that James went through an English firm in 1878 indicates that he was using these essays (originally addressed to the American magazine public) to experiment with the English book trade and through it to approach the English reading public. In this context, it is worth noting that in the very same year, James agreed to let Osgood publish his first apprentice serial, *Watch and Ward*, in book form in America. James consented only because he needed the income; and although he revised the work for republication, he declined the opportunity to bring out an English edition. James obviously considered it to be of insufficient quality to merit the attention of the British public; and his decision not to seek simultaneous publication demonstrated his determination to approach the English market with care.[18]

James's next serial, *Daisy Miller* (1878), broke new ground in his effort to exploit the full opportunities of the English market and capture the attention of the British public. His friendship with Leslie Stephen, editor of the *Cornhill Magazine*, provided him with his first access to a new source of income, the English periodical. Prior serialization in England gave James the option of selling each of his works not twice but four times, first to English and American magazines, then to book publishers in both countries. This meant that if he was careful, he could enjoy three opportunities for revision as well as four sources of income. James's intention with *Daisy Miller* was to take advantage of his London residence in order to secure English copyright protection, while continuing to enjoy the copyright privileges of an American citizen by using advance sheets. These he usually sent to his father, who acted as a kind of unofficial literary agent and saw to it that his son's works were copyrighted in America. But because he did not act quickly enough, James experienced reverse piracy for the first time.[19] Before he could arrange for serial publication in America, unauthorized versions of *Daisy Miller* were printed in not one but two American magazines, *Littell's Living Age* and the *Home Journal*. Although these weeklies were not of the same caliber as Boston's *Atlantic Monthly* and its closest New York counterpart, the *Galaxy*, both of which had served as James's primary outlets in America, they presented James to a new audience and, in so doing, paved the way for his first and possibly greatest international success.[20]

In order to realize some profit from *Daisy* in America, James accepted an offer from Harper and Brothers to publish it in their Half-Hour Series, a format he in all probability would normally have detested. The Harpers issued it simultaneously in cloth and paper at 35¢ and 20¢ respectively. Although no precise information is available on the size of this edition, Leon Edel cites sales of 20,000 copies "in a matter of weeks." There is little doubt that at these incredibly low prices, *Daisy Miller* sold much better than any of James's other books.[21] It is also safe to assume that the paperbound Harper format added greatly to *Daisy's* circulation. The Harper Half-Hour Series was only one of several which flooded the American literary scene with cheap literature in the postbellum period. According to Frank L. Schick, between 1870 and the passage of the international copyright agreement in 1891, "the American public was offered some very good books in addition to dime novels and cheap literature, but at the expense of the quality of the physical book, the art of typography, and the foreign authors who received no royalties..." The Lakeside Library was the first to be established, and it was soon followed by the Seaside Library, the Riverside Library, the Home Library, and the Fireside Library. The names of these libraries are revealing: they generally indicate the place where their products were intended to be consumed. The two basic types were home (or domestic) libraries and libraries designed to be read on the way to, from, and during vacations, especially summer vacations by the water. The former functioned as a kind of democratic version of the English circulating library, while the latter type, obviously modelled on the English railway libraries, represented a successful attempt to profit from the growing amount of time devoted by Americans to travel and leisure.[22]

Physically, the cheap paperbounds were hardly books at all. They were usually printed in newspaper format on inferior paper with multiple columns, a mode of production which enabled their publishers to deal in large quantities which they then distributed through news companies. While some observers assumed that only the readers of the weekly story papers bought paperbounds, there were bookstore owners who insisted that they were also sold to people who had previously purchased novels at the regular prices in bookstores. It seems likely that both types of readers were taking advantage of these cheap books, thus simultaneously increasing the dimensions of the American novel-reading public while decreasing, at least temporarily, the distinction between the levels of taste of that public. Though these combined factors did not cause James's sudden breakthrough to popularity in America, they were a necessary precondition. I do not mean to imply that the notorious controversy over James's new invention, the international American girl, had no effect on *Daisy's* sales. The circumstances do suggest, however, that James's relative unpopularity in America prior to *Daisy Miller's* huge success may have been due at least in part to the way in which his books were published, priced, and distributed there. While it is certainly true that most of James's work was expensive in several senses of the word, $2 may have been quite literally too high a price for most Americans to pay for their literature, whatever their taste.[23] Although James lost money on the American piracy of *Daisy Miller,* the story's widespread circulation in the cheap Harper format on the heels of its serial appearance in three periodicals combined with the heated controversy over Daisy Miller's manners and morals to create a notable rise in his reputation on both sides of the Atlantic.

Daisy embodies all that was most attractive about the American girl; and, indeed, she has been regarded as representative of the American spirit itself with her frankness, energy, determination, and self-assurance. Yet her highly impulsive behavior, when measured by European notions of propriety, consistently appears to be in bad taste. Whether this type of behavior is the result of too much experience or merely uncultivated innocence proves to be immaterial to the American community in Europe, which seems to deem either attribute a crime. But it was this question which fascinated Daisy's Europeanized American suitor, Winterbourne, as well as her Anglo-American audience, thereby creating a renewed interest in and demand for James's work. As Howells put it to James Russell Lowell:

> There has been a vast discussion in which nobody felt very deeply, and everyone talked very loudly. The thing went so far that society almost divided itself into Daisy Millerites and anti-Daisy Millerites. I was glad of it, for I hoped that in making James so thoroughly known, it would call attention in a wide degree to the beautiful work he had been doing so long for so very few readers.[24]

Such popular success provided James with a fix on the taste of the Anglo-American reading public, but it also gave that public a fix on James. He was suddenly becoming typed as the creator of the international American girl; and the loyal readers he won when he patented this invention would become confused and angry when he attempted to depart from it later on in his career. Further evidence that James's reputation as a popular writer resulted from and was to become increasingly dependent upon the slight figure of the American girl came just a year later when *A Bundle of Letters* was pirated by an American publisher, Loring, who issued a 25¢ unauthorized paperbound version before James could take out American copyright. Composed in the form of private correspondence, this story (which begins and ends with letters written home from Europe by an American girl) succeeded in fulfilling James's obvious intention of appealing to *Daisy*'s public, for his father soon informed him that Loring's pamphlets were "selling like Wildfire." This was probably not much of an exaggeration; they were popular enough for the Seaside Library to publish a second unauthorized edition at the even lower price of 10¢. Unlike the "chastely 'gotten up'" Loring pamphlets, the Seaside edition spoke eloquently of the fate awaiting foreign literature during this period of cheap books, for it was issued in newspaper style along with *Sweet Nelly, My Heart's Delight* by Walter Besant and James Rice.[25] While this format could hardly have pleased James, he was now more concerned about his relations with the British public and the figure he cut on the English social scene. It was during this period that he claimed he had dined out 140 times in a single season; and so it was only appropriate that Daisy Miller made her first English appearance in book form in proper dress. She came out as a standard and expensive double-decker for the circulating libraries, despite her slim dimensions. James achieved the requisite length by presenting her in the company of two rather hastily written productions, *An International Episode* and *Four Meetings*. A one-volume cloth reprint followed after the necessary delay, a sign that Macmillan felt that English readers would now be willing to buy James's novels even without the cheaper prices of piracy.

Henry exulted in a letter to William over the warm reception which both he and *Daisy* were receiving in England:

> I am very glad that you were pleased with 'Daisy Miller,' who appears *(literally)* to have made a great hit here. 'Everyone is talking about it' etc., and it has been noticed in the papers. Its success has encouraged me as regards the faculty of appreciation of the English public; for the thing is sufficiently subtle, yet people appear to have comprehended it. It has given me a capital start here, and in future I shall publish all my things in English magazines (at least all the *good* ones) and sell advance sheets in America thereby doubling my profits.

In the same letter James makes an early reference to his dream of writing for the stage, which he envisions as "an open gate to money-making." He also discloses that he is working on a "great novel," one which deals with "the history of an *Americana*—a female counterpart to Newman." This letter suggests that the idea of a female version of Christopher Newman had its immediate origin in

James's desire to capitalize on the success of *The American* and *Daisy Miller*, although the end result, *The Portrait of a Lady*, would be far superior to both books.[26]

During 1878 James suddenly began to assume the character of the prolific novelist which he had sketched in his first review. A year earlier, he had responded to Howells' criticism of *The American* by promising that his next serial for the *Atlantic* would have a happy ending. The result was *The Europeans*, a serial designed to fulfill the terms which Howells and James had mutually agreed upon. As James candidly admitted to his friend Lizzie Boott in October of 1878:

> The offhand marrying in the end was *commandé*—likewise the length of the tale, I *do* incline to melancholy endings—but it had been part of the bargain with Howells that *this* termination should be cheerful and that there should be distinct matrimony. So I did [hit] it off mechanically in the closing paragraphs.

Although James here presents this serial as an act of overt accommodation to the limited taste of the *Atlantic*'s readers, the plot and especially the texture of *The Europeans* suggest that his relation with this public was not so passive. To begin with, the key flirtation in the novel does not culminate in marriage (as an anonymous *Scribner*'s reviewer pointedly noted).[27] In spite or rather because of her highly sophisticated scheming, the Baroness Eugenia scares off her intended prey, an extremely eligible but highly cautious New England bachelor named Acton. Eugenia's plotting is not entirely in vain, for she makes life interesting for her rather dull New England relatives, the Wentworths; and occasionally she even succeeds in making them interesting to herself and to James's readers as well. Like James, with whom she shares a cosmopolitan temperament and tone, the Baroness is quite aware that her skill at manipulating the response of her audience depends primarily upon her ability to sustain a highly entertaining style. However, her ambitions (which are not unlike her author's) plunge her into a dilemma of sorts when she perceives that this audience of New Englanders registers shock rather than amusement when confronted with the polished social performance which has made her so popular on the Continent.

As the Baroness's creator, James faced a parallel stylistic dilemma and for similar reasons. In his fascinating discussion of manners and theatricality in *The Europeans,* Richard Poirier suggests that "the style, like the comedy, is addressed to those of high and assured cultivation, to readers free from any provinciality. For all her theatrical foreignness, Eugenia does not bewilder us as she does Mr. Wentworth." While Poirier's observation may in fact have held true for James's English circulating library audience, it was precisely this kind of cosmopolitan sophistication which James suspected that most of his American readers lacked and refused to tolerate. The opening paragraph of the novel is a case in point. Poirier reads James's comic inflation of a "gloomy-looking inn" into "the best hotel in the ancient city of Boston" as an amusing joke between James and readers who obviously share the author's claim to "cosmopolitan superiority." Yet Poirier goes on to note that "the style is fancy to the point of being sarcastically periphrastic..." and asks: "What can be James's assumptions about the reader when he writes in this way?"[28]

Poirier attempts to answer this question by suggesting that James is using stylistic conventions here to entertain and amuse "us," to give us an "aesthetic pleasure in the enjoyment of the decorative for its own sake." While this may indeed be the general effect upon a modern reader (although the relative unpopularity of the novel among contemporary Jamesians hardly lends support to such a supposition), another answer to the question which Poirier has posed seems much more likely, especially when we remember James's early contempt for and lack of confidence in the taste of the American magazine public and his presentation of this serial as tailor-made to Howells' specifications. Poirier's analysis hinges to a large extent upon the existence of an ideal audience, for he constantly assumes and refers to an "us" whom James trusts with his intimacy and his jokes. It should be clear by now that this hardly matches James's conception of his own contemporaneous public.[29] In this context, James's decision to situate the action in this novel "upwards of thirty years" into the past can be seen as evidence of his lack of confidence in the tolerance and taste of his contemporaneous American readers. By carefully attributing the attitudes and events he describes to a prior generation of New Englanders, James distances and absolves his *Atlantic* readers from the provincialism which the novel will proceed to expose, subtly appealing to their vanity by encouraging in them feelings of comfortable superiority to the comically narrow taste and judgment of their ancestors. Yet while he plays to and upon the vanity of his American readers, James also manages to exhibit consistently the cosmopolitan tone and point of view which his European readers have already come to expect from him. Through his narrative voice, he entertains the latter while simultaneously attempting to accustom the former to a more worldly point of view. If, in spite of James's precautions, native readers reacted with hostility to his description of Boston, James could easily dismiss them as self-condemned provincials whose likes and dislikes were unworthy of the concern of the serious writer. In effect then, this strategy functions as a form of anticipatory self-defense in regard to the American segment of his audience.

James's narrator, like the Baroness, is thus called upon to perform a delicate balancing act in *The Europeans*. To the extent that his narrative voice is being modulated in the hope of reproducing the kind of discrimination which it displays, James's intent is clearly educative. However, the "sarcasm" of tone which Poirier aptly detects in the opening passages of the story betrays James's latent antagonism towards the American portion of his audience, readers whose taste he is alternately attempting to cater to and to cultivate. Neither the narrator nor the Baroness seems able to conceal an irritability which has as its origin their mutual suspicion that "the ancient city of Boston" and its inhabitants will not be able to sustain the weight of their respective plots. A further clue to the source of the narrator's irritability may be found in what Poirier refers to as the "fanciness" of James's prose. The first paragraph relies to some extent on the cheap and easy phrases of Victorian literature. "Mouldy tombstones and funereal umbrage" and "that blessed vernal season" describe a setting which the Baroness finds to be "the ugliest thing she had ever seen." The passage reads almost as if James were using Eugenia to pass judgment on the quality of his prose as well as the Boston scenery. This raises an interesting question. To what extent does the over-elaborate prose which James employs in such passages represent a concession to his Anglo-American audience's well-established taste for the cospicuously ornate and to what extent can it be said to constitute an effort to play what Poirier refers to as "pretentious and extravagant language" off against itself in the hope of undercutting and discrediting such excessive prose? Henry's eagerness to agree with William's subsequent criticism of the novel as "'thin,' and empty" and his later decision to exclude *The Europeans* from his collected edition suggest that he convicted himself of the former despite his desire to accomplish the latter. Perhaps he suspected that he had lapsed (or collapsed) into the cheap and easy while attempting to walk the very thin line between imitation and parody.

Whether or not *The Europeans* is a neglected literary masterpiece as Richard Poirier suggests, it deserves to be regarded as a piece of consummate literary diplomacy. English and American reviewers generally agreed that the novel's cleverness, subtlety, and "French" workmanship more than made up for its relative lack of plot and *Appleton's Journal* went so far as to pronounce the picture of the Wentworths, whom they dubbed a "typical American family," an "unmistakable achievement of genius."[30] James may have failed to please his brother and other more discriminating readers; but through his ability to produce *The Europeans* and other literary goods equally adapted to the taste of audiences on both sides of the Atlantic, he was rapidly achieving his goal of establishing an international reputation. However, such a project entailed many risks, as a subsequent incident soon demonstrated. John Morley had commissioned James to write a critical biography of Nathaniel Hawthorne for the English Men of Letters Series. James addressed this assessment of Hawthorne's career primarily if not exclusively to the British public, but committed the tactical error of arranging for Harper and Brothers to issue an American edition shortly after Macmillan and Company published the book in 1879. James's motive may have been purely pecuniary; *Hawthorne* had not been serialized prior to its book publication and he probably saw the American edition as a way to increase profits and forestall American piracy. Whatever

James's intentions were, the transatlantic publication of the biography triggered a minor international episode. His belabored insistence upon "the negative side of the American social scene," especially his much-quoted sketch of "the negative side of the spectacle on which Hawthorne looked out," became (and has remained) the subject of heated dispute. It is worth noting that several of the key phrases from the offensive paragraph on American culture (or rather America's lack of culture) appear in a notebook entry, where they are introduced by the phrase, "In a story, someone says—." This indicates that the passage was originally intended for a short story and may have even had its origin in James's habit of copying snatches of overheard conversations into his notebooks for later use. It is therefore possible that when James lifted this passage out of his notebook and into the biography he was tentatively trying on a fictional English persona and trying out a typically English tone and point of view rather than making a carefully considered cultural observation. As we shall see, once he came under attack he felt obliged to defend and even enlarge upon what he had written, thus entrenching the position of a writer who had only recently insisted upon his horror of generalizations and boasted of his super-subtlety, announcing: "Nothing is my *last word* about anything..."[31]

Although James probably assumed that he was minimizing the sting of this passage by casting his patronizing declaration about American culture in the past tense and distinguishing between the ante and postbellum character of the American mind, contemporaneous American readers were too offended by James's condescending attitude towards his native land and his American predecessor to notice his brief but flattering reference to the "good" and "critical" American whom the Civil War had helped to form. Their oversight is not surprising, given James's tendency towards overkill. His now famous list of the "paraphernalia" absent from American life reads as follows:

> No State... No sovereign, no court, no personal loyalty, no aristocracy, no church, no clergy, no army, no diplomatic service, no country gentlemen, no palaces, no castles, nor manors, nor old country-house, nor parsonages, nor thatched cottages, nor ivied ruins; no cathedrals, nor abbeys, nor little Norman churches; no great Universities nor public schools—no Oxford, nor Eton, nor Harrow; no literature, no novels, no museums, no pictures, no political society, no sporting class—no Epsom nor Ascot!

James added insult to injury when he insisted that "a good deal remains," only to identify his countryman's one "natural gift" as his "American humor' of which of late years we have heard so much." James's description of the postbellum American could hardly compensate for such abuse.[32]

Several contemporary critics have perceived that *Hawthorne* reveals as much about its author as it does about its subject, if not more. In this light the book has been seen as James's rationalization of his decision to expatriate himself. Given the fact that James had been residing in England since 1876, it seems more to the point to explore James's interpretation of the hostile fire leveled at his book by several American reviewers. The lesson of the "hubbub" emerged only as he attempted to justify the position he had taken to some of his literary friends in America. Even though Howells had been quick to disassociate himself from the pack of "contributing blood-hounds" who led the attack, he too had felt obliged to criticize James's over-use and application of the term "provincial." While in the privacy of their correspondence James proved eager to admit that he had overdone the epithet, Howells' protest against the passage in which James enumerated those things which were absent from American culture provoked a revealing if good-humored defense. James reacted by expanding his argument to include the present generation and insisted that America had yet to produce a novelist in the true sense of the word precisely because it lacked the proper paraphernalia. For the first time he cast his indictment of American culture in the present tense and even suggested that his own ability to write about the American scene was hampered by their absence.[33]

Less than three weeks later, the situation escalated. James was now prepared to take all the abusive notices as evidence of "the vulgarity, ignorance, rabid vanity and general idiocy" of the American public. In a letter to his friend T.S. Perry he concluded rather smugly:

> The whole episode projects a lurid light upon the state of American "culture," and furnishes me with a hundred wonderful examples, where, before, I had only more or less vague impressions. Whatever might have been my own evidence for calling American taste "provincial," my successors at least will have no excuse for not doing it.

The quotation marks around the word "culture" speak volumes. For James, the attack on his book was the best possible proof that American taste had *become* extremely provincial, even if it had not been so in Hawthorne's generation. The critical outburst which James had himself provoked served him well; it provided him with a retroactive justification of both the biography and his decision to pursue his career in England. He could now announce to Perry with a clear conscience that he had chosen "a higher civilization in literary respects. As I expect to be in London for the rest of my natural life, you must indeed come and pay me a visit..."[34]

James was equally adept at supplying retrospective motivations when confronted with criticism from a reader whose taste he respected. Henry had attempted to dilute the effect of William's displeasure with *The Europeans* by insisting that William regard the novel as "an artistic experiment" rather than as "a piece of conduct, to which one's life were somehow committed..." While he would later refine this strategy and apply it to his entire career in the Prefaces which he wrote for the New York Edition of his novels and tales, Henry's antidote to William's "painful reflection" on *The Europeans* was much less elaborate. It amounted to explaining that he considered the story to be one of several "experiments in form" in which he did not want to "run the risk of wasting or gratuitously using big situations." While this was true to some extent, as we have seen, it is important to note that Henry chose to undercut his elder brother William's criticism not by candidly acknowledging the made-to-order aspects of the story (as he had to Lizzie Boott) but by presenting himself as a fictional experimenter whose present work was essentially a form of intellectual self-financing. His exclusive emphasis upon his fear of "wasting or *gratuitously* using big situations" was a way of reassuring William (and perhaps himself) that his primary concern was with his intellectual balance sheet and his development as an artist, rather than with his pocketbook and his reputation as a popular writer.[35] James's picture of himself as holding his literary capital, the "big situation," in reserve carried the further implication that the serious work of art could not be produced on demand. It took time to mature, and so did its producer, the serious artist. His growing conviction that this was true, at least in his own case, is evident from the following prediction which he made to William: "But to these [big situations] I am coming now. It is something to have learned how to write, and when I look round me and see how few people (doing my sort of work) know how (to my sense,) I don't regret my step by step evolution."[36]

Curiously enough, James's big situation came in the not entirely original form of the European career of yet another young American female. On the surface at least, *The Portrait of a Lady* closely resembles James's previous work in terms of its heavy reliance not only upon this figure, which had become his personal trademark in the wake of the unprecedented success of *Daisy Miller*, but also upon the literary conventions established by popular writers and dramatists on both sides of the Atlantic. Isabel Archer, Ralph Touchett, and Caspar Goodwood are to some extent variations on several stock characters (the orphaned daughter, the pair of mutually attracted cousins, and the American businessman determined to secure the perfect wife) which had made prior appearances in James's earlier novels, notably *Watch and Ward, Roderick Hudson,* and *The American.* These Jamesian types were thus as familiar to his loyal readers as the stock character types of the provincial cousin, the English lord, the overbearing father, the scheming mistress, and the innocent *"jeune fille"* were to general audiences schooled in Anglo-American fiction and Continental drama. Furthermore the plot (which predictably "thickens" when Isabel Archer's unexpected inheritance of a magnificent fortune makes her the prey of an unscrupulous suitor) verges perilously close to the stock-in-trade of the cheap and easy novelists whose wares James had alternately ridiculed, parodied, and even imitated during his apprentice years. For example, William Veeder observes that Mrs. E. D. E. N. Southworth had treated the theme of the exploited heiress as a literary cliché as early as 1864, though she nevertheless proceeded to revive it in her novel *Ishmael.* However, the text of *The Portrait* displays a high degree of self-consciousness precisely in this regard, as when James makes the professional journalist, Henrietta Stackpole, refer to Ralph Touchett as an excellent specimen of "the alienated American" in order to give her the opportunity to note that this is a type for which "there is a great demand just now" in American periodicals. In similar fashion James has Isabel Archer observe that Pansy Osmond is "like a sheet of blank paper—the ideal *jeune fille* of foreign fiction," a page which she hopes will be "covered with an edifying text." Significantly, Pansy also reminds Isabel "of an ingenue in a French play." This provides her creator with the appropriate pretext he needs to remark upon and thereby call attention to the two other competing sets of conventions he is invoking: "Isabel had never seen a young girl of this pattern; American girls were very different—different too were the daughters of England." What distinguishes *The Portrait* from its literary and theatrical predecessors as well as from James's own previous work then, is precisely the degree to which its author overtly acknowledges his debt to Anglo-American and Continental traditions while covertly setting their respective conventions off against each other within the confines of a single text. In the process of doing so, James was to realize for the first time the full literary potential of his own invention, the international American girl.[37]

Ample circumstantial evidence to this effect can be found in an assessment of Zola's *Nana* which James published in February of 1880, shortly after *The Portrait* had made its transatlantic debut as a serial in both England's *Macmillan's Magazine* and the American *Atlantic*. The Anglo-American novelist turned this review into an opportunity to ventilate his displeasure with the unwritten laws of both the English and French fiction of his day. In a passage which previews the tack and tone which he would later take in his 1884 essay "The Art of Fiction," James suggested that French realism functioned as a welcome antidote to the prescribed timidity of conventional English (and presumably French) literature. But he pronounced *Nana* "unreadable" due to Zola's lack of taste and tact and warned:

> Nothing tends more to compromise it [realism] than to represent it as necessarily allied to the impure.... It takes a very good cause to carry a *Nana* on its back, and if realism breaks down, and the conventional comes in again with a rush, we may know the reason why.

He then charged that Anglo-American taste was vulgar and insipid, a state of affairs which he ascribed to the fact that in England and the United States "the storyteller's art is almost exclusively feminine, is mainly in the hands of timid (even when accomplished) women, whose acquaintance with life is severely restricted, and who are not conspicuous for general views." Ironically, when compared to their productions Zola's new novel came off quite well, for he at least had "a system, a passionate conviction, a great plan." James concluded this indictment of the Anglo-American novel with the familiar accusation that it "is almost always addressed to young unmarried ladies, or at least always assumes them to be a large part of the novelist's public," a system which he found (with a characteristically Jamesian turn of the screw) to be "a good thing for virgins and boys, and a bad thing for the novel itself..."[38]

It was but a short step from James's early prejudices against women writers and female magazine readers (as expressed in his apprentice reviews) to this broader and more serious criticism of the Anglo-American literary scene, but that step placed James on the French side of the literary border. Borrowing the persona of a French writer, he voiced his objection to the English novel on the following grounds: "Half of life is a sealed book to young unmarried ladies, and how can a novel be worth anything that deals only with half of life?" This assumption rests upon the traditional French view that marriage represented the primary and in fact the *only* form of initiation into life for women, a view which in turn rested upon the prior assumption, shared by both the fraternity of French realists and conventional French writers, that "life" meant sexual relations, especially for women. James would later challenge this view both explicitly in "The Art of Fiction" (where he evokes the example of "the young lady living in a village... upon whom nothing is lost") and implicitly in his treatment of central female characters in his fiction. In fact, *The Portrait* itself can be read as a brief for the case against just such a narrow view of the female character. But James uses this composite French point of view here to expose the arbitrary quality of the restrictions placed upon the English novel, a use which is characteristically undermined by his equally strong disapproval of the French realists' counter-tendency to rely upon the inevitable adulterous relationship and the conventional "brutal *fille*" as their literary stock-in-trade.[39]

James can be seen facing this dilemma squarely in *The Portrait*, a novel in which he committed himself to the project of escaping the limitations yet exploiting the opportunities of both sets of conventions. The undeveloped taste and character which James attributed to the American girl in his apprentice review of Nassau Senior's *Essays on Fiction* becomes a literary resource rather than a limitation in Isabel Archer's case, for her much-vaunted independence of mind sets both the Continental and the English notions of appropriate female behavior, embodied in the contrasting expectations which the residents of Gardencourt and the Palazzo Roccanera entertain in her regard, in vivid relief. This juxtaposition of norms takes on further complications as a result of James's justifiable fear that in his determination to avoid national clichés he would merely repeat himself. He was all too aware that his reputation relied almost exclusively on his notoriety as the author of entertaining international novels and tales, most notably *Daisy Miller;* and he was too shrewd an observer of literary phenomena not to realize that the Anglo-American public, which he continued to define as predominantly female, would be expecting more of the same. James attempted to address (but not capitulate to) the predictable expectations of his reading public by making these expectations a central focus of his fictional drama. The contrasting writing conventions to which he had objected in his review of *Nana* were, after all, only the expectations of the Anglo-American and Continental publics seen from the point of view of the producer rather than the consumer of fiction; they represented the other side of the literary tapestry, so to speak. Like his heroine, Henry James harbored an "unquenchable desire to please"; but like Isabel, he was also possessed by an equally strong determination to preserve his independence of mind and taste and his freedom to choose and act. Perhaps this helps to explain the curious fact, noted by several contemporary critics, that James reserves both his most deflating criticism *and* his highest respect for the heroine of his novel: she paradoxically represents both the strengths and weaknesses of her creator as well as the best and worst qualities of the women whom he assumed to be the majority of his potential audience.

These qualities are made explicit as Mrs. Touchett, herself an extremely shrewd if less attractive specimen of the type of the American female, describes Isabel to Ralph: "She thinks she knows a great deal of it [the world]—like most American girls; but like most American girls she is very mistaken." Though much more generous in his appraisal of his niece, Mr. Touchett has a penchant for making Isabel "chatter" which provides the narrator with an opportunity to remark:

> It was by this term that he [Mr. Touchett] qualified her conversation, which had much of the vivacity observable in that of the young ladies of her country... Like the majority of American girls, Isabel had been encouraged to express herself; her remarks had been attended to; she had been expected to have emotions and opinions. Many of her opinions had doubtless but a slender value, many of her emotions passed away in utterance; but they had left a trace in giving her the habit of seeming at least to feel and think, and in imparting, moreover, to her words, when she was really moved, that artless vividness which so many people had regarded as a sign of superiority.

The narrator concludes with a seemingly innocent but remarkably double-edged observation: "Mr. Touchett used to think that she reminded him of his wife when his wife was in her teens."[40] Were Isabel's uncle a totally reliable judge of character, the implication would be that Isabel was cut from the same pattern as her aunt and destined to follow the same eccentric lines of development. While James's emphasis here seems to be on qualities Mrs. Touchett has sacrificed over the years to (and through) her effort to remain an independent woman rather than on the possibility that Isabel will follow in her footsteps, this remark does little to alleviate the impression that Isabel is hardly a promising candidate for the demanding role of heroine in James's "big situation."

Yet Isabel's earnest effort to develop herself and improve her mind, which James usually treats as a mere pretension to culture in others of her sex and race, is here presented as one of the prime elements of her attractiveness as well as her claim upon the interest and sympathy of his readers. It is quite obvious from James's portraits of the other American women in the novel that he had not abandoned his condescending attitude towards the majority of American females, either as subjects or consumers of fiction. Nevertheless, the direction which his own carefully cultivated artistic development was taking called for a story which would attempt to make the most, rather than the least, out of the figure of one American girl. Like Isabel's cousin Ralph, both James and his contemporaneous audience entertain great expectations for Isabel and have a large stake in seeing to it that she not prematurely foreclose on her matrimonial career: their respective capacities for imaginative growth depend, at least in part, upon their ability to recognize (and Isabel's ability to realize) her similar potential.[41]

Even so, James proved unable to resist any opportunity to ridicule what he considered to be the American female's superficial (and even debilitating) relation to literature. We are told that although Isabel's paternal aunt, Mrs. Varian, has "a reverence for books," her large house has every amenity but a library, "and in the way of printed volumes contained nothing but a half dozen novels in paper..." Not surprisingly, her acquaintance with literature is limited to the *New York Interviewer,* a newspaper which she hides from her daughters, who read nothing at all! Much is also made of the predilection of another of Isabel's aunts, Mrs. Touchett, for communicating by means of highly inscrutable telegrams. "They say women don't know how to write them, but my mother has thoroughly mastered the art of condensation," Ralph notes wryly before treating himself, his father, his friend Lord Warburton, and James's readers to the highly entertaining yet strikingly emblematic spectacle of an exclusively male attempt to decipher Mrs. Touchett's first telegram: "Changed hotel, very bad, impudent clerk, address here. Taken sister's girl, died last year, go to Europe, two sisters, quite independent." The comedy generated by their collective inability to attach a definitive interpretation to Mrs. Touchett's text is intensified rather than dispersed with her arrival, for she defends herself from being pinned down by insisting that she herself never knows what she means by her telegrams, especially those she sends from America, obtusely (or cleverly?) adding: "Clearness is too expensive."[42]

The ironic tone is unmistakable in such passages; clearly James is having fun at the expense of both female readers and writers. Yet in the second instance, as in much of this novel, James's irony gradually reveals a more serious dimension as the novel progresses, for in retrospect this incident curiously prefigures and covertly signals the beginning of Isabel's protracted struggle to resist the various attempts of each of her fellow characters (especially the men) as well as her author to encroach upon what she considers to be her sovereign right of self-definition. Isabel's close friend and confidante, the comically patriotic Henrietta Stackpole, is one of several characters in the novel who overtly and unapologetically attempt to shape Isabel's career. Henrietta's well-meaning but simple-minded efforts to "save" Isabel from European "contamination" serve a double purpose: they provide James with a comic variation on one of his own most successful plot lines (used in *Roderick Hudson, The American,* and *Daisy Miller*) as well as an easy target for his prejudices against that "vulgar" modern phenomenon, the female journalist. Henrietta finances her travel to Europe by writing letters for the same newspaper which Mrs. Varian hides from her daughters; she also prefigures the principal character in the donnée of James's later satire on American journalism, *The Reverberator,* in her willingness to trample upon every vestige of personal privacy in order to get at the "inside story" concealed behind the gates of Europe's most exclusive estates. But her character, like that of Mrs. Varian and Mrs. Touchett, serves a more serious purpose as well. Each documents the narrator's insistence upon his heroine's relative though very real superiority and thus strengthens Isabel's claim upon the attention of his audience. Henrietta's opinions and conversational style in particular are consistently more rigid than Isabel's, though in the early chapters of the novel Isabel is not incapable of lapsing into "Stackpolese." By telling his readers that Isabel "was not a *regular* reader of the *Interviewer,*" James shrewdly implies both her susceptibility and her superiority to its style (or lack of it).[43]

Isabel proves to be much more susceptible to the cosmopolitan style of Serena Merle, the only woman in the book (except for the Countess Gemini, who serves as her comic foil) of whom it may be said that she is complete in the French sense of the word, that is—she has been both a wife and mistress. The seeming epitome of continental taste and tact, Madame Merle subtly presents herself to Isabel as an alternative model of accomplished femininity and impeccable propriety. Won over by this "exemplary woman's" convincing performance, Isabel believes that if Madame Merle has a fault "it was that she was not natural; by which the girl meant, not that she was affected or pretentious; for from these vulgar vices no woman could have been more exempt; but that her nature had been too much overlaid by custom and her angles too much smoothed." It is for this reason that Isabel finds it difficult to imagine Madame Merle except in her relations with others, though she manages to convince herself that her highly accomplished friend is not at all superficial:

> She was deep; and her nature spoke none the less in her behavior because it spoke a conventional language. "What is language at all but a convention?"... "She has the good taste not to pretend, like some people I have met, to express herself by original signs."[44]

Isabel fails to recognize the duplicity of Madame Merle's character, which has been forged by the pressure of intense social friction and poured into the fluted mould of social convention. The older woman's judgments about life are based upon a substantial fund of worldly and dearly-paid-for experience rather than on the dubious foundation of abstract philosophy and literature, though Gilbert Osmond does accuse his former mistress near the end of the novel of talking about revenge "like a third-rate novelist" and expressing herself "like a sentence in a copybook." (Madame Merle deftly parries this blow by turning the tables on Osmond: "You are more like a copybook than I. There is something, after all, that holds us together.")

The same accusation could be levelled with more justice at Isabel, at least as she is presented to the reader in the early portions of the novel; and, in fact, the narrator dwells upon the extent to which Isabel's character has been formed by and in terms of the large quantity and uneven quality of her reading. When we first meet her she is "trudging over the sandy plains of a history of German Thought"; and James goes to great lengths to stress the limited, over-protective nature of her American upbringing and to underline the degree to which her knowledge of the world is therefore confined to and dependent upon what she has read. In the space of several pages, we are told that as a child she had "uncontrolled use of a library full of books...," that young men generally feared her because of "her reputation for reading a great deal," that she was spoken of as "a prodigy of learning, a young lady reputed to have read the classic authors—in translation," and even that her aunt "once spread the rumour that Isabel was writing a book...and averred that Isabel would distinguish herself in print."[45] Almost with an audible sigh of relief, the narrator hastens to inform his readers that this last impression of Isabel is quite inaccurate: "the girl never attempted to write a book and had no desire to be an authoress." Although this is obviously a mark in Isabel's favor, the narrator makes it equally clear that Isabel betrays a disturbing and dangerous tendency to base her expectations of life upon what she has read in popular novels. Upon meeting her uncle, old Mr. Touchett, Isabel expresses doubt that she will ever feel at home among the English in terms which are indeed reminiscent of copybook language: "I don't believe they [the English] are very nice to girls; they are not nice to them in novels." Mr. Touchett wisely counsels her not to rely too much on the accuracy of novels, a warning based upon his own experience with a lady novelist who had "too much imagination." He explains that she published a novel which purported to represent him and reproduce his "Yankee" conversation, but it turned out to be "not at all accurate; she couldn't have listened very attentively."[46]

James had evidently listened attentively to the speech of American women, especially the young ones; and once again he seemed to be bent upon entertaining his audience, or at least its masculine component, at their expense and at Isabel's as well. Yet his larger intent with regard to Isabel and, by implication, her counterparts among the reading public is not so much parodic as it is educative. James wishes to subject what Isabel herself admits to be her "ridiculously active imagination" to the rigorous school of worldly experience. For Isabel that school is Europe and its classroom her disastrous marriage to the sterile aesthete, Gilbert Osmond. She graduates during her famous midnight vigil in chapter 42 when she finally begins to realize that "she had not read him [her husband] right." For James's female readers that school is the novel itself. Isabel's gradual transformation from a naive and inexperienced yet highly intelligent and imaginative young girl who judges people by what she has read in cheap and easy novels into a mature "lady" who pays, and pays heavily, for her hard-earned ability to "read" life with discrimination and perception is at once a criticism of and a corrective to the Victorian habit of novel-reading, at least as James feared it was commonly indulged in (especially by women).

By a similar logic, James's portrait of Gilbert Osmond (and, to a lesser extent, Ralph Touchett) exposes the less obvious limitations though more perverse and destructive qualities of another type of reader, the connoisseur. As the narrator pointedly notes:

> ... he [Osmond] was fond of originals, or rarities, of the superior, the exquisite; and now that he had seen Lord Warburton, whom he thought a very fine example of his race and order, he perceived a new attraction to this idea of taking to himself a young lady who had qualified herself to figure in his collection of choice objects by rejecting the splendid offer of a British aristocrat.

It is the very originality of Isabel's conduct which qualifies her as being sufficiently rare to figure as the worthy object of Osmond's matrimonial intentions (although such independent and unexpected behavior will predictably alienate Osmond from Isabel after they are married). He seems to be obliquely acknowledging this perverse attraction to originals while hinting at his ultimate preference for the most mundane proprieties when he confides to Isabel: "I had been putting out my eyes over the book of life, and finding nothing to reward me for my pains, but now that I can read it properly I see that it's a delightful story."[47] Quite appropriately, it is in his guise as the apparently expert and thoroughly initiated reader that Osmond presents such attractions to his future wife, for she believes that he above all other men will know best what to "make" of her—in all senses of the word. (The fact that Osmond has been brought up by "the American Corrinne," a horrible snob of a woman who had "pretensions to 'culture,' wrote descriptive poems, and corresponded on Italian subjects with the English weekly journals," adds a further level of irony to Osmond's artistic pretensions, Isabel's initial attraction to him, and her eventual fate at his hands.) Despite the fact that she appears to be her husband's diametrical opposite in terms of temperament, Isabel comes close to acknowledging strikingly similar predilections in her own character when she responds to Mr. Touchett's warning about the unreliability of novels by stating that she prefers the unexpected and is willing to forego success with the English if it means that she must be conventional. Her rejection of Lord Warburton's subsequent proposal makes good this claim, for Isabel explicitly recognizes that she has turned down an offer which "would have excited surprise on the part of the public at large" and which "nineteen women out of twenty" would have accepted "with extreme zeal." However, this incident goes beyond mere proof of Isabel's preference for the unconventional, for she has already refused a wealthy American businessman, Caspar Goodwood. Given her lack of means, a proposal from an English lord could only figure in and of itself as an unconventional gesture (as Warburton himself is quick to admit). It would seem that Isabel is possessed by a perverse desire to defy the expectations of all those who know her and whose constant speculation concerning her marital status begins prior to the opening of the novel proper and continues even after her marriage to Osmond.

In fact, it is precisely Isabel's willingness, even her eagerness, to defy the expectations of the public at large which generates James's admiration for her and his identification with her, for in this novel he is himself committed to a similar project. In a very real sense it is James's own desire to avoid a merely conventional plot line in the form of a typical international marriage which Isabel's rejection of Warburton's suit both reflects and achieves. Her determination to distinguish herself from the nineteen women out of twenty who would have accepted his offer on the spot realizes as well as displays James's superiority to the nineteen novelists out of twenty who would have permitted her to do so (much as her decision to marry the egotistical Gilbert Osmond is perceived by Osmond himself, and perhaps initially by the unsuspecting reader, as a confirmation of *his* innate superiority to her other suitors).

In effect, Isabel's career as an American girl is dominated by her fear of becoming merely one of a series, which is to say her fear of being reduced by the pressures of the plot (especially her sudden transformation from a penniless orphan into an heiress) to the status of a type character. As a type character, she would be worthy of a place only in a highly conventional novel, perhaps one of those standard English triple-deckers which chronicled the customary tale of the American girl who crosses the Atlantic in the hope of marrying an English lord. When we rephrase Isabel's situation in these terms, it becomes clear that it is precisely this fear of becoming merely conventional which links Isabel to her author and which forms the basis of his unusually intimate relationship with her. Were Isabel to collapse in this manner, so would the novel; and were the novel to become virtually indistinguishable from the three-deckers which stocked the shelves of the circulating libraries, James's identity as its author would become equally indistinguishable from that of the extremely conventional (if highly successful) producers of this commodity. James would, in effect, be reduced to the status and proportions of a mere manufacturer who grinds out countless variations on a well-established model, in this case his own patented invention—the international American girl.

However, it could not have been long before James realized that he would not be able to fashion an entire novel out of Isabel's repeated rejections of increasingly eligible suitors; and once this realization occurred, his interests became more compatible with Osmond than with his heroine. As Laurence Holland has convincingly argued, Madame Merle is ultimately working for and acting in Henry James's as well as Gilbert Osmond's behalf when she arranges Isabel's marriage, for in doing so she satisfies James's as well as her own "furious ambition." Serena Merle's plotting serves James well, for it introduces and incorporates the time-worn clichés and props of French literature and drama into the Jamesian novel, thereby enabling her creator to move beyond the confines of conventional Anglo-American fiction. James's complicity with Osmond and his former mistress is in turn made possible and mediated by a similar (if unwitting) complicity on the part of Isabel's cousin Ralph, the one man whose love for Isabel appears to be entirely selfless. Like James and Osmond, Ralph shares Isabel's preference for the unexpected. He is not at all disappointed when she refuses to marry his good friend Warburton, as he candidly admits when he tells her: "I shall have the entertainment of seeing what a young lady does who won't marry Lord Warburton." Contemplating the rest of her career, he even goes so far as to predict that his interest in her future and his fondness for the unexpected will be shared by a large audience of spectators, "and now that you have kept the game in your hands I depend on your giving us some magnificent example of it." (Here Ralph seems to be speaking of and for James's public, thereby implicating them—however indirectly—in the novel's plot.) Having paid an enormous price for his "ticket" to the performance of Isabel's life (he has not only provided her with a generous portion of his inheritance but has disavowed and dissembled his love for her), Ralph is only too eager to get his money's worth. It is for this reason that his deathbed interview with his cousin must include not only an open acknowledgment of his true feelings but also an indirect confession of the guilt he shares with James's less benign surrogate plotters: "You wanted to look at life for yourself—but you were not allowed; you were punished for your wish. You were ground in the very mill of the conventional!" Could James have addressed Isabel directly, he might have used the very same words.[48]

Earlier in the novel a not unsimilar interchange takes place when James makes Osmond admit to Isabel that he is not conventional but "convention itself." In retrospect this warning reads as if it, too, came directly from her creator, almost as if James had suddenly become aware in the process of writing the novel that she would eventually have to suffer the limiting consequences of his literary intentions and ambitions. No matter how independent he might like to see her remain, she would be obliged to work out her destiny within the formal confines, however originally interpreted, of the Anglo-American novel. Isabel characteristically ignores this timely double warning, but it comes back to haunt her as she gradually awakens to the true nature of her relationship with her husband. The link between James's and Osmond's interests is reinforced by the very striking terms in which she pictures her miserable domestic predicament, for these terms apply equally well to the significantly altered relationship which now exists between Isabel and her creator. In effect she seems to be reading her literary as well as her marital fate when she registers an eery sense of intolerable confinement in chapter 42, the famous meditation scene which James considered to be the best thing in the book. As she imagines herself the virtual prisoner of "Osmond's beautiful mind," an elaborate edifice which she only now perceives to be "the house of darkness, the house of dumbness, the house of suffocation," readers of the novel may be tempted to think of James himself and his own elaborate "house of fiction."[49] In this context the controversial conclusion of *The Portrait of a Lady* can be approached as a structural and thematic compromise. Isabel Osmond's rejection of what might be called the French solution—Goodwood's attractive offer of escape via adulterous love—only to return to Rome where she must once again face both her step-daughter's unhappy future and the matrimonial tyranny of her husband—whether temporarily or permanently we do not know—can be attributed in part to James's determination to escape the twin literary tyrannies of contemporaneous English and French fiction, the happy and the "indecent" ending. Although the conspicuous ambiguity of her motives projects and protects a saving (and seemingly inviolable) margin of inner freedom, Isabel's outward conformity to her marriage, that "magnificent form," is the price she must pay to salvage and preserve her originality as both a woman and a character in a work of fiction.[50]

Isabel's fate came full circle when *The Portrait* was published in book form in 1881 and became the first novel that Henry James had written which could claim the ambiguous distinction of making its original appearance as a three-decker for the circulating libraries. Its appearance in this format established James once and for all as the acknowledged master of the international novel and one of the Anglo-American scene's foremost literary lions; but James, whose ambition was of enormous proportions, considered himself capable of doing much better work. As he boasted to his friend T.S. Perry:

... the story contains the best writing of which I have hitherto been capable. But I mean to surpass it, *de beaucoup*. I mean also to "quit" for a while paying so much attention to the young unmarried American female—to stop, that is, making her the central figure: which is of necessity a limitation.[51]

One wonders if James suspected that in spite of his extraordinary precautions he, too, was in danger of being "ground in the very mill of the conventional."

3

"A Most Unholy Trade"

If, as many critics have observed, the achievement of *The Portrait of a Lady* signals the end of James's years of literary apprenticeship and his arrival as a highly successful Anglo-American novelist, it also marks the beginning of a prolonged period during which James's career was characterized to a large extent by a conspicuous (though infrequently remarked upon) amount of professional vacillation and uncertainty. Following James's lead in the Prefaces to the New York Edition of his novels and tales (1907–09), critics have usually searched for and found patterns of consistent artistic development during his "middle years"[1]; yet a close look at the publication history of James's post-*Portrait* period suggests that the literary vogue which he enjoyed in the early 1880s as the author of several well-received international novels and tales presented him with a distinct professional dilemma. The fundamental problem James seems to have been grappling with over and over again during these years is not so much the highly technical compositional one retrospectively suggested by the sequence of the novels as well as the content of the Prefaces to the New York Edition of his work—namely, how to develop the center of consciousness in a work of fiction—but the comparatively mundane and persistently troublesome question of subject matter. Should he continue to mine the profitable international vein or should he strike out instead for new but possibly treacherous literary territory? Both alternatives exerted unique attractions upon James at this stage of his career; but as he soon discovered, the former posed a serious theat to his development as a writer while the latter threatened to destroy his base of popular success.

Immediately following the publication of *The Portrait,* James began to show signs that he was dissatisfied with both the quality and the quantity of his recent transatlantic success. He seems to have been torn between the suspicion that it had been won too easily from a largely undiscriminating public and the realization that it was of insufficient proportions to satisfy his immense appetite for success. In February of 1881, while *The Portrait* was still appearing in serial form, James had agreed with his friend T.S. Perry's charge that literature was "going down" in America, explaining that "the stuff that is sent me seems to me written by eunuchs and sempstresses [*sic*]." "But," he continued, "I think it is the same every where—in France and in England. I suspect the age of letters is waning, for our time." James had very definite ideas as to what was taking its place. "It is the age of Panama Canals, of Sarah Bernhardt, of Western wheat-raising, of merely material expansion. Art, form, may return, but I doubt that I shall live to see them ... All the same, I shall try to make them a live a little longer!"[2] While the James who wrote this letter reacted with a dismay bordering on revulsion from what he perceived as the vulgarization of modern culture, there was another side of James which desired to play as significant a part in this spectacle as he could. The immense popularity of *Daisy Miller* had given James his first real taste of what this might be like; and so, appropriately enough, he turned once again to the slight figure of the international American girl, despite his recent prediction to Perry that he meant "to 'quit' for a while paying so much attention to the young unmarried American female." He had qualified that phrase by explaining that he meant to stop making her his subject, almost as if he were intent on assuring Perry that he was not paying too much attention to the taste of the women who made up such a significant portion of the American reading public. Coming as it does immediately after his exploration of the possibilities of this figure in *The Portrait*, James's decision to present Daisy, Isabel's less developed prototype, as the central character in a three-act comedy can only be regarded as a disappointing reversion to type, calculated to satisfy the expectations rather than develop the taste of the general public—even at the expense of his own artistic development.

James reworked the story into a play by enlarging upon its melodramatic possibilities. He sacrificed every note of subtlety, introduced several new and expanded characters, and even substituted a happy ending. The role of the scheming Madame de Katkoff, who comes across as a crude version of Madame Merle, is a heavy-handed development of the mere suggestion of a European-style relationship between Winterbourne and an older woman in the original story. In the play this character is blackmailed into conspiring with the even more villainous Eugenio, a courtier who schemes to marry Daisy off to Giovanelli in return for a share of her fortune. In striking contrast to the story, James sets this plotting into motion in the play in order to provide Winterbourne with the opportunity to rescue Daisy from their "evil" clutches and claim her as his wife! The extent to which James was willing to obliterate the subtle dimension that their mutual affection and distrust achieved in the original dramatized his own determination to win the approval and support of the theater-going public. This episode thus marks the opening of what is probably the most bewildering yet most fascinating chapter in James's career, his prolonged yet consistently unsuccessful attempt to turn himself into a popular dramatist. To James the professional, the theater represented not only a new market to conquer and a new audience to annex, but a significant extension of his social role and a confirmation of his impact on the English-speaking public. Far from satisfying his hunger for fame, fortune, and clout in the literary marketplace, his previous literary success seems only to have whetted his appetite. Perhaps, too, he was no longer content with being known and received in London society solely in his guise as the author of several charming international novels. He may even have feared that the British public would soon begin to tire of him in that entertaining but limited role. James needed a fresh entrée into Anglo-American circles if he was to maintain the participant-observer stance which he had worked so hard to achieve and which he needed to preserve if he was to continue to glean fresh material from the international scene. In short, like his American heroes and heroines, James had to pay his way into European society. Success on the English-speaking stage was one kind of currency, one way to keep himself as well as his books in constant circulation and demand.

If James's efforts to have *Daisy Miller: A Comedy* produced, first in England and then in America, were an attempt to capitalize on the age of Sarah Bernhardt, they also represented his desire to realize a private dream which had taken hold of him since early childhood. His earliest extant letter, written at the age of thirteen to a young friend named Eddy, reads: "As I heard you were going to try to turn the club into a Theatre And as I was asked w'ether I wanted to belong here is my answer. I would like very much to belong." The persistence of James's desire "to belong" to the world of the theater and to become a member of the exclusive "club" of successful playwrights, despite repeated rebuffs throughout his long career, suggests that writing for and being acted upon the stage represented a form of initiation and a variety of intimate interaction which he found lacking in the triangular relationship between a novelist, his publisher, and the reading public. It was as if James needed to feel the presence and hear the applause of the thousands who had been amused and even enlightened by the printed version of *Daisy Miller*. But his efforts to mount a stage version of *Daisy* failed; and in November of 1882, during a visit to America, James temporarily dropped his public mask of cultivated indifference and gave vent to both his bitter disappointment and his terrible fear of failure in the privacy of his notebooks:

> I needn't enter into the tiresome history of my ridiculous negotiations with the people of Madison Square Theatre, of which the proprietors behaved like asses and sharpers combined; this episode, by itself, would make a brilliant chapter in a realistic novel.

He had found this first direct contact with the conditions of production in New York and London "almost fatally disgusting and discouraging," yet he struggled to convince himself that though he was disgusted, he was not discouraged: "I simply cannot afford to be." James talks of investing one or two years in experimentation with the dramatic form, and determines to write nothing but short fictions during this time (a strategy which he did not actually pursue until the end of the decade). The entry ends on a remarkable note which, given James's impressive record of previous accomplishments, testifies to the incredibly high expectations which he entertained in regard to his career. James concludes: "I must make some great effort during the next few years, however, if I wish not to have been on the whole a failure. I shall have been a failure unless I do something *great!*XXXXX"[3]

As if to compensate for these private fears, James continued to maintain the public stance of a man who felt confident of his own success and sure of his own importance. In a letter written to his American publisher Osgood in 1883, he took the position that "the Editor of any periodical ought to be ready to take a short story of mine not because it has been described to him, but because it is mine." James followed this up with another letter to the publisher suggesting that he was doing Osgood a favor by offering him an opportunity which Houghton and Mifflin had just declined, the opportunity to publish *Daisy Miller: A Comedy* in book form after it finished its serial run the *Atlantic*. After pointedly reminding Osgood of the success of the original story, he attempted to soothe his wounded pride by making it a condition that the play "be printed in the manner of French comedies—that is, with the names of the characters *above* the speeches, and not on a line with them."[4] Osgood quickly agreed, probably much to the relief of the aspiring playwright; James wanted to salvage as much as possible from his first failure with "our unhappy English stage." These letters to Osgood indicate that as early as 1883, James may have been experiencing some difficulty placing his work in American magazines. How much trouble he was actually having is hard to tell. Although *The Portrait* had been rather well received in America, Frank Luther Mott insists that for years editors "had more or less forced James upon their readers and compelled them to like him." He also argues that during this period American magazines, which faced stiff competition from American newspapers as well as cheap literature, were becoming more responsive to the taste of the common reader. The competition had escalated when newspapers began issuing Sunday editions with "literary" supplements in the eighties, a blow against which the magazines retaliated by including more "solid matter"—articles on history, biography, economic and political issues—and less fiction. This shift left less room for purely literary material such as James's and served to lessen the distinction between newspapers and magazines in content, tone, and pace, a distinction crucial to James's ability to make assumptions about the quality of his magazine audience.

Furthermore, as advertising increasingly came to augment subscriptions as the economic base of the magazines, the distinction in price between newspapers and magazines also began to diminish; general magazines found themselves addressing a much wider, if less discriminating, public. These new readers, in turn, reacted upon the magazines and increased the already existing pressure to bring the magazines "down to the level of practical affairs," to use Mott's loaded phrase. Even in terms of editing, the magazines were becoming more and more like newspapers. There was an increased emphasis on word counts, and the leisurely pace of the magazine writer slowly began to give way to the more hurried tempo of the newspaper journalist.[5] Of course this process was a gradual one, and some of the magazines resisted it as long as they could; but the general shift in tone and format was irreversible and could not have gone unnoticed by James, whose hostility towards journalism grew rather than abated as his career progressed. In 1891 he would publicly claim that "the conditions of contemporary journalism" had forced the magazines to substitute "stuffed mannikins" for true criticism. "Periodical literature is a huge, open mouth which has to be fed—a vessel of immense capacity which has to be filled," wrote James in his essay, "Criticism." "It is like a regular train which starts at an advertised hour, but which is free to start only if every seat be occupied. The seats are many, the train is ponderously long, and hence the manufacture of dummies for the seasons when there are not passengers enough."[6]

Undoubtedly the illness and death of both of James's parents during 1882 and his duties as executor of his father's estate distracted him from his work; but in and of themselves, neither family responsibilities nor the publishing conditions discussed above can explain the irregular rhythm which now began to characterize his career. "The Siege of London," a new tale published in 1883, is a rather mechanical variation on James's patented theme, the international marriage. He managed to avoid "the young unmarried female" and entertain his readers by making his American widow's conquest of London society turn on her dubious status as a Western divorcée, but the half-hearted nature of his performance suggests that he had grown tired of (or even bored with) what he was soon to refer to as "the 'international' state of mind." It is worth noting that between the appearance of *The Portrait* as a triple-decker in 1881 and the commencement of *The Bostonians* as a serial in February 1885, James published several books—collections of short stories (new and old), essays, and travel sketches—but no novels. Macmillan and Company, his English publisher, did issue a fourteen-volume collected edition of his work in 1883, but the edition included no new full-length fiction. *The Portrait* led off, followed by *Roderick Hudson, The American, Washington Square, The Europeans, Confidence,* and the short stories, including *Daisy*. Macmillan was obviously relying on *The Portrait's* recent popularity to make the entire edition a success, but James was soon complaining to Macmillan about his "depressingly small" sales and royalties.[7] Although the collected edition was itself tangible evidence of the novelist's enviable current literary status, its disappointing sales must have reinforced James's uncertainty regarding his future course of literary production. Only one thing was clear: if he wanted to achieve an enduring reputation on the crowded Anglo-American literary scene, he would have to be willing to take the risks entailed in fictional experimentation and innovation. An opportunity to advance in this direction seemed to present itself in 1884, when Walter Besant issued a pamphlet (based on a lecture he had given) in which he claimed that fiction-writing should be granted the consideration of a fine art rather than a trade. Besant's essay provided James with the pretext he needed for turning what had become a private debate back into a public one. He attempted to resolve his professional dilemma by recasting it in terms of the larger contemporaneous controversy surrounding the career of the novel in Anglo-American culture. While James's response to Besant, his brilliant essay on "The Art of Fiction," has usually been read as a pioneering statement of impersonal novelistic theory, if we pay close attention we can hear James responding to his critics and announcing his future course of action. In so doing, he succeeded in calling into question those arbitrary conventions of English fiction which he had implicitly challenged in *The Portrait of a Lady* and to which he now refused, publicly, to give his assent.

James flatly denied that a novel ought to represent "virtuous and aspiring characters, placed in prominent positions," that it ought to have a happy ending (defined as "a distribution at the last of prizes, pensions, husbands, wives, babies, millions, appended paragraphs, and cheerful remarks"), that it ought to be "full of incident and movement," that it ought not to be "artistic." It was these last two unwritten "laws" of English-speaking fiction which seemed to trouble him most, probably because they were the source of frequent criticism of his own work. James slyly evoked the example of a reviewer who has criticized "certain tales in which 'Bostonian nymphs' appear to have rejected English dukes for psychological reasons," an obvious (if oblique) reference to criticism of the "impudent lack of incident (or of what is commonly understood to be such)" in *The Portrait*. He professed himself to be "utterly at a loss" to see why *Margot la Balafrée* was considered by that reviewer to be a story "when the rejection (or acceptance) of a duke is not, and why a reason, psychological or other, is not a subject when a cicatrix [a reference to a scar received by the heroine of the other novel] is." Turning the tables on his critics, James asked, "What *is* adventure...?" in order to suggest that "it is an adventure... for me to write this little article; and for a Bostonian nymph to reject an English duke is an adventure only less stirring... than for an English duke to be rejected by a Bostonian nymph." He then took issue with "the moral timidity of the usual English novelist," whose "cautious silence on certain subjects" James attributed, as in his review of *Nana,* to the English custom of addressing novels primarily to "young people." Once again, James evoked the example of the French realists, but his ultimate motive was not to substitute

French latitude for English caution but to free the field from *all* a priori restrictions. James concluded the essay on the following note of exhortation: "Remember that your first duty is to be as complete as possible—to make as perfect a work. Be generous and delicate and pursue the prize."

In publishing this list of everything that "condemns the art to an eternal repetition of a few familiar *clichés*" and "cuts short its development,"[8] James not only pledged his allegiance to the general cause of artistic freedom but committed himself to pursuing his own particular line of artistic development. Taken as a whole, "The Art of Fiction" amounted to an implicit challenge, addressed as much to himself as to his fellow professionals, to defy the conventional expectations of the English-speaking public. Perhaps he had concluded that he actually had more to gain than to lose by openly breaking with the international theme and exploring new subject matter as well as technique. Several of the short stories which James published in the same year as "The Art of Fiction" make it abundantly clear that he had indeed exhausted the international vein and even suggest that he was turning to the literary life itself as a potential substitute. "Pandora" aspires to be a very clever sequel to (and an affectionate self-parody of) *Daisy Miller*. Its self-reflexive humor carries the implied promise of continuous amusing variations on James's patented type, the international American girl—here rechristened "the self-made girl." Yet the story comes to an abrupt and somewhat disappointing conclusion when James rather mechanically marries Pandora off to a middle-aged American (to whom she has been engaged since her teens) instead of to the young and suitably titled German diplomat whose growing admiration for her forms the basis of the plot—a tacit admission that her creator had virtually run out of clever things to do with the unmarried female American. However "A New England Winter" and "The Author of 'Beltraffio,'" both published within months of "Pandora," break relatively new ground in their depiction of character for they introduce tentative portraits of the aesthete and the literary master into James's gallery of literary types. As his name suggests, Florimond Daintry of "A New England Winter" is a slight and conspicuously unimpressive version of an avant-garde artist, though James does attempt to give Florimond an air of current reality by telling his readers that he associated himself in Paris with "a little circle of 'naturalists'." An expatriated American who has "a great deal of eye" but pitifully little power of execution, Florimond is not given much to say or do in this transitional tale which, like the city of Boston in which it takes place, appears to be dominated exclusively by women and produces the impression of "a deluge of petticoats."[9] The unnamed first person narrator of "The Author of 'Beltraffio'" and Mark Ambient, the writer whose work the narrator admires to the point of worshipping, prove to be much more interesting and forceful specimens of this new type, the *raffiné* or aesthete, for the narrator's seemingly well-intentioned interference in the lives of his fellow characters turns out to have a distinctly perverse and even fatal effect. James implies that it is the masterful Mark Ambient's apparently admirable passion for form which breeds this contagious corruption in his young admirer, thus anticipating one of the most "super-subtle" themes of his late tales of the literary life. Set in England, this portrait of an explicitly avant-garde relationship between a master and a disciple clearly embodies James's continuing ambivalence towards the art for art's sake movement, at once playing upon the public's suspicions concerning the moral impropriety of the avant-garde while paying fascinated if reluctant tribute to the aesthetes' uncanny ability to elicit such intense devotion from their small but highly discriminating public.

James had ample opportunity to observe the latter phenomenon during his periodic visits to Paris; but from the mid-1880s on, he had begun to find himself in the novel and somewhat awkward (if highly flattering) position of having attracted a not unsimilar following of his own among the rising generation of transatlantic writers. These younger men and women not only admired James's work and shared his respect for the French realists but frequently sought his attention and advice by dedicating their own novels to him. Violet Paget ("Vernon Lee") and the French psychological novelist Paul Bourget (who would eventually attack naturalism in his 1889 novel *Le Disciple*) were among the first members of James's small but growing circle of youthful disciples. This extremely heterogeneous and widely scattered group gradually began to constitute an unconventional alternative public for James at a crucial moment in his career. They would be joined in the late 1880s and 1890s by other members of the emerging English-speaking avant-garde, a generation which included expatriate American writers and journalists such as Morton Fullerton (a Paris correspondent for the *London Times* who later became Edith Wharton's lover), Henry Harland (editor of the avant-garde *Yellow Book*), and Logan Pearsall Smith (one of James's most devoted if least talented disciples) as well as several rising British novelists who were destined to have a lasting impact on the modern literary scene—most notably Joseph Conrad, H.G. Wells, and Ford Madox Ford. Although it is difficult to pinpoint the precise date of the advent of the English-speaking avant-garde, Donald David Stone is one of several literary historians who argue that the crucial decade in the dissolution of Victorianism and the rise of the "modern sensibility" was not the 1890s but the 1880s (some place it even earlier, in the 1870s). James's "The Art of Fiction," George Moore's 1885 pamphlet "Literature At Nurse, or Circulating Morals" (an attack on the circulating libraries and their censorship of fiction), and the novels of Moore, Meredith, and Hardy are frequently cited by modern critics as key events in the transformation of English fiction. There is also sufficient evidence to testify to the fact that contemporaneous observers were quite aware that a change was taking place on the literary scene, although their response was extremely mixed and often quite hostile. William Dean Howells (whose qualified critical embrace of Continental realism loosely allied him with the English avant-garde) had only recently set off a transatlantic furor when he praised the French realists at the expense of Dickens and Thackeray, only to identify his good friend Henry James Jr. as the "chief exemplar" of the corresponding new school in Anglo-American fiction. Writing in the *Century* in November of 1882, Howells had enthusiastically referred to James's growing and "distinctly recognizable" following and further enraged Anglo-American critics (who subsequently charged both men with puffing each other's careers) by announcing: "It is the ambition of the younger contributors to write like him..."[10] Howells was probably guilty of over-stating the case. Unlike their French counterparts, the English avant-garde (though united by mutual admiration for the French realists, especially Zola, and their mutual distaste for conventional English fiction, especially the typical circulating library novel) never grouped themselves into a tightly-knit school—nor did they follow a single master. However, "The Art of Fiction" can be regarded and may well have been received as an English language version of and variation upon the literary manifestos issued by James's contemporaries among the French avant-garde, most notably Zola's 1871 preface to the Rougon-Macquart series and his recent collection of essays entitled *Le Roman Expérimental* (1880). And while James certainly did not regard himself as the acknowledged head of a new school of fiction, his correspondence as well as his subsequent literary production do suggest that he had decided to exploit and enhance his reputation as an experimental writer and cultivate his artistic development by adopting the role of the Anglo-American naturalist and adapting naturalism as a fictional technique.

In mid-January of 1884 (just ten days before he had addressed his mournful letter to Macmillan complaining about his disappointing royalties on the collected edition), James announced to his old friend Grace Norton that he had just begun a new novel for the *Century,* boasting that it would "mark a *new era* in my career, and usher in a series of works of superior value to any I have yet produced." A month later he could be found in Paris confiding to Howells that the recent success of Frances Marion Crawford's last novel "sickens and almost paralyses me," and admitting that he "would rather have produced the basest experiment in the 'naturalistic' that is being practised here than such a piece of sixpenny humbug." (He went on to charge that "work so shamelessly bad seems to dishonour the novelist's art to a degree that is absolutely not to be forgiven; just as its success dishonours the people for whom one supposes one's self to write.") Despite their "ferocious pessimism and their handling of unclean things," Daudet, Goncourt, and Zola were doing "the only kind of work" that James could respect. Read in conjunction with the two big novels James was to publish in 1886, these letters reveal that he was working hard at turning himself into "the great American naturalist" (a phrase he actually uses in regard to Howells). By the end of 1884, he had begun to play the part to perfection. As he proudly announced to T.S. Perry: "I have been all the morning at Millbank prison (horrible place) collecting notes for a fiction scene." Fearing that Perry might miss the point, he carefully dotted his i's and explained: "You see I am quite the Naturalist."[11]

James soon proved to be (almost) as good as his word. His next two novels, *The Bostonians* and *The Princess Casamassima*, were fictional experiments in adapting the principles of French realism to the Anglo-American novel. Together they constituted a sudden break with his established mode, the international marriage, and his most popular invention, the international American girl. To the extent that they each embraced the French system (especially its emphasis upon environment and heredity as shaping and debilitating forces and its endorsement of sexual frankness), these books violated the cardinal laws of Anglo-American fiction. To begin with, the characters in these two novels could hardly be described as either virtuous or aspiring, at least in any conventional sense. Verena Tarrant and Olive Chancellor in *The Bostonians* want to reorganize American society along lines of female supremacy while Hyacinth Robinson in *The Princess* (the illegitimate son of an aristocrat and the mistress who murders him) vacillates between an attraction to and revulsion from the means and ends of European anarchism. Not surprisingly, some of James's American readers would take offense at *The Bostonians* on the grounds that James presented English readers with an exaggerated (if not "libellous") version of the role which Boston reformers played in American life. In fact, while *The Bostonians* was still appearing in serial form in the *Century Magazine,* it aroused serious concern among members of James's family and Boston's elite. They feared that James had painted a little too closely from life when he created the figure of Miss Birdseye, the aging abolitionist and ardent women's rights activist who presides over the postbellum reform scene. Several readers, including Henry's elder brother, took Miss Birdseye to be an unkind satire on Elizabeth Peabody, a venerable reformer and sister-in-law of James's predecessor, Nathaniel Hawthorne. Speculation and resentment persisted, despite the fact that Henry firmly denied any such intention in a letter to William.[12] Furthermore, the fact that the *Century* was soon to enjoy a substantial success with its long-running series on Civil War battles suggests that by the mid-1880s, the American magazine public was waxing nostalgic over the Civil War and could hardly have been receptive to or amused by James's rather cold-blooded satire on the two reform movements most closely related to it, abolitionism and women's rights (whatever their attitude might be towards an allied movement, spiritualism).

Interestingly enough, H. E. Scudder, reviewing *The Bostonians* in the *Atlantic*, found Miss Birdseye to be "the one redeeming feature of the book, if one is considering its human aspects. The other persons are either ignoble, like the Tarrants [Verena's parents] and Mrs. Luna [Olive's sister], or they are repellent for other reasons..." As for the plot of the novel, the ever-present "young unmarried American female" which James's readers expected put in another appearance in the form of the slight presence of Verena Tarrant, but this time she was courted not by several glamorous Europeans but by a poor and somewhat dowdy young Southerner named Basil whose only serious competition for Verena's hand comes from his cousin Olive, a not-so-young spinster who dislikes men as a class and tries to convince Verena that her destiny lies not in marriage but in a life of public speaking in support of women's rights. The highly unconventional (and possibly "perverse") nature of this *menage à trois* was not lost upon Scudder, who expressed alarm over the "dangerous lengths" to which the details of the first interview between Olive and Verena... carry these young women" and complained that "we hesitate about accepting the relation between them as either natural or reasonable." For somewhat similar reasons Julia Wedgwood found fault with *The Princess Casamassima*. Dismayed and alarmed by the behavior of the title character, this British reviewer wrote:

> The Italian-American lady, whose portrait Mr. James draws so elaborately, may be intended by him to be a person of spotless character; but the account of her intercourse with the hero has recalled to our mind that of a fine lady in London with Tom Jones, and the coarseness of Fielding seems to us much nearer purity than the suggestive decorum of Mr. James....[13]

In effect Wedgwood, like her American counterpart, seems to be struggling to find a decorous way of warning her readers that Mr. Henry James's new novel broaches highly improper if not downright immoral subjects, but in a manner which makes it difficult to catch him in the act.

What Miss Wedgwood somewhat coyly refers to as James's "suggestiveness" (in part the result of his new commitment to literary naturalism) might have constituted his most serious threat to the code of the Victorian novelist. Yet it is clear that this violation was perpetrated in such a subtle and relatively tame manner that it went largely unnoticed by the majority of reviewers, who seemed to detect little change in his technique and whose main criticism of James remained the standard complaint that his novels lacked exciting incidents and suffered from abrupt and unhappy endings. English and American reviewers of both novels consistently remarked upon the length of the two novels and what they considered to be James's tedious manner. Many reiterated R. H. Hutton's assessment of *The Princess* in the *Spectator*: "... if it is a novel, it is one of a very unique kind. It has hardly any incident, unless the tendency of the whole network of circumstance and character to the tragedy with which the third volume abruptly closes, may be regarded as in itself constituting a single massive incident." (And this of a novel that ends with a suicide!) William James astutely put his finger on the problem when he wrote Henry to apologize for his own hasty condemnation of the serial version of *The Bostonians*. Though he insisted that he had enjoyed rereading the novel in book form after dinner each night for the past ten days, he added:

> One can easily imagine the story cut out and made into a bright, short, sparkling thing of a hundred pages, which would have been an absolute success. But you have worked it up by dint of descriptions and psychologic commentaries into near 500—charmingly done for those who have the leisure and the peculiar mood to enjoy that amount of miniature work—but perilously near to turning away the great majority of readers who crave more matter and less art.[14]

In this context it is worth noting that the essential plot-line of *The Bostonians* had already been handled in a relatively simple and straightforward manner in several previous works of American fiction. (James himself maintained that his model was Daudet's *L'Evangeliste,* a novel more in keeping with his desire to be regarded as a naturalist.) While critics have long been aware of James's indebtedness to both Hawthorne's *The Blithedale Romance* (1852) and his own earlier short story, "Dr. Fargo" (1874), in a recent study Howard Kerr persuasively argues that "*The Bostonians* recapitulated the patterns of magnetic romance and anti-reform satire which had characterized much of the American literary response to spiritualism since the early 1850s." As Kerr reveals, the novel owes elements of its plot and several of its character types not only to the antebellum tradition of reform literature but to *The Undiscovered Country* (1880) and *Dr. Breen's Practice* (1881), two of William Dean Howells' most recent productions. Given the fact that he had recently referred to Howells as "the great American naturalist" (though he had justifiably chided his friend for not going "far enough"), it is likely that the expatriated James regarded Howells' relatively realistic novels as an important source of information about the changing American scene and a necessary supplement to his own limited supply of first-hand observations (the sine qua non of naturalist theory, if not practice). It also seems likely that James chose to incorporate this type of social satire into his repertoire of popular modes as a practical means of getting back in touch with the American public and compensating them for the sustained departure from the international vein which the novel inaugurated. If this was the novelist's intention it failed miserably, for *The Bostonians* also inaugurated a peculiarly Jamesian version of a vicious circle. In choosing to begin his debut as a naturalist by trading in the conventions of American anti-reform literature, James could only have intensified his habitual fear of collapsing into the cheap and easy and reinforced his deep-seated tendency towards over-treatment and overly-elaborate analysis. He later confessed as much to William, explaining that he had "felt a constant pressure to make the picture substantial by thinking it out—pencilling and 'shading.' I was afraid of the reproach...of being superficial and cheap..." The result was that, as Henry himself admitted, the whole thing was "too long and dawdling."[15]

Another result of this vicious circle is the peculiar animus which characterizes the novelist's attitude towards his characters in *The Bostonians*. While James to a large extent sympathizes (and possibly even identifies) with Hyacinth Robinson in *The Princess,* Scudder was speaking for several generations of readers when he noted his own dislike of the characters in *The Bostonians* and attributed it to "the attitude which the author of their being takes towards them. He [James] does not love them. Why should he ask more of us?" (Interestingly enough, James had levelled a similar charge at Zola in his review of *Nana*.) Although James initially seems to endorse the manner and opinions of Basil Ransom (with whatever irony), he uses the reactionary Southerner primarily as a tool for exposing the weaknesses and foiling the plans of the Northern reformers, especially Olive. Modern critics who identify James's point of view with Ransom's have simply failed to note how thoroughly this character subverts the traditional (i.e., "masculine") values which he supposedly represents and to which he has pledged his allegiance. Over the course of the novel Ransom conspicuously violates his code of Southern chivalry (as when, for example, he rudely abandons Mrs. Luna at the Burrages' party in order to listen to Verena). His crude and selfish behavior culminates in the final scene of the novel when he tracks Verena down and wrenches her away from her obligations to Olive, her family, and her audience. Ransom succeeds in winning her for his wife, but only at the cost of the sympathy and respect (however qualified to begin with) of James and his readers.[16] Ironically it is Olive who, in her final impotence, her endurance of the loss of the one she loves, and her facing of the angry Boston audience, exerts a more legitimate claim upon the sympathy (if not the admiration) of her creator and his audience. (Furthermore, Olive's fastidious taste, her hatred of publicity, and her desire to convert Verena into a loyal disciple curiously prefigure some of the qualities of the fictional masters who people James's late tales of the literary life.)

The reception of the novel added an additional twist to the irony of this closing scene for James, too, was confronted—if less directly—with a disappointed and hostile audience. As if the strange triangle between Olive, Verena, and Basil was not enough of an affront to James's contemporaneous public, he had permitted himself to indulge in a long tirade against "the most damnable feminization of American culture." Through Ransom, James announced:

> The whole generation is womanized; the masculine tone is passing out of the world; it's a feminine, a nervous, hysterical, chattering, canting age, an age of hollow phrases and false delicacy and exaggerated solicitudes and coddled sensibilities, which, if we don't look out, will usher in the reign of mediocrity, of the feeblest and flattest and the most pretentious that has ever been.

In the mid-1850s, as we have seen, Hawthorne had expressed a similar disgust with his age in terms not unlike Basil's, but he had tactfully limited his outbursts to the confines of his private correspondence with his publisher. James tried to have it both ways. Through his narrative voice he attempted to preserve an ironic stance towards Basil's "narrow convictions" by explaining parenthetically that the rejection of these views by leading periodicals "was certainly not a matter for surprise." But judging from the hostile criticism which the story provoked both in serial and in book form, James's readers were not too coddled to know when they were being insulted. James's irony had been so double-edged that it self-destructed; and what had begun as "an attempt to show that I *can* write an American story" ended up as itself a rather nervous, hysterical attack on American culture.[17]

The novel ran into further difficulty as a result of publishing conditions. Osgood had been having financial problems for several years, probably the result of the heated competition from the cheap libraries as well as bad management. James had sold Osgood the serial and book rights to the novel for $5000; but when Osgood's firm failed in May of 1885, James lost the money Osgood owed him and was forced to renegotiate for the book rights with Macmillan, who offered him much less lucrative terms for both the English and American rights. Macmillan then brought the novel out in England as a three-decker in 1886, issuing only 5,000 copies in one-volume form which were divided between the English and American markets. For the first time in his career, James was deprived of a separate American edition of his novel. The same held true for *The Princess*, also published in 1886. Macmillan printed a one-volume edition of 3,000 copies to be split between the two markets following the appearance of the standard triple-decker for the circulating libraries.[18] Thus, due to an unfortunate combination of circumstances, James suffered the loss of his first and most consistent American publisher and alienated his American audience, jeopardizing two of his four customary sources of income, the American magazine and book trades, all in one blow.

As we have seen in chapter 1, *The Reverberator* was part of James's response to this blow. Published in 1888, this international comedy represented an obvious reversion to type and was designed to conciliate and reassure James's Anglo-American public. Although he did commence work in the same year on another non-international fiction, *The Tragic Muse* was for the most part a highly conventional novel in terms of both subject matter and technique. During the late 1880s, magazines had begun to note "the marvelous growth of public interest in theatrical matters."[19] Was it merely a coincidence that James began his first theatrical novel at the moment when this trend became especially evident in the increasing reliance of cheap magazines on pictures of actresses and on stage gossip? Once again, there seems to have been a considerable overlap between what fascinated James and what fascinated the general public. An avid student of the drama, James had schooled himself for years by attending the theaters of England, America, and France, most especially the Théâtre Français. In the past, this investment of time and attention had yielded several penetrating reviews in which James shrewdly evaluated the contemporaneous theatrical scene in all its aspects. Nothing had escaped his attention, for his definition of the theater embraced not only the actors and the play but "the audience, the attendants, the arrangements, the very process of getting to the playhouse." Now the public's growing interest in everything connected with the stage presented James with a new opportunity. He could transform his stock of observations into a novel which would attract readers by its inside account of life as it was lived behind the scenes. The public's willingness to pay for fictional glimpses of life on the other side of the theatrical curtain had been brought home to him as early as 1884, when his friend Mrs. Humphrey Ward achieved notoriety and large sales with the publication of *Miss Bretherton,* her thinly-disguised fictional portrait of a popular and controversial contemporary actress.[20]

Together with *The Reverberator, The Tragic Muse* dramatized the extent to which James was retreating from his commitment to literary realism, especially its emphasis upon sexual frankness. He had been forced to abandon his goal of becoming the great American naturalist, as he obliquely admitted when he assured Thomas Bailey Aldrich that the latter novel would not be "improper" despite its treatment of the "Aesthetic" world. Like the plays which would follow it, *The Tragic Muse* represented no significant threat to genteel Anglo-American proprieties (though the novel did take on politics, one of England's most highly venerated professions, implying that it was no more respectable than the arts). James's apparent willingness to conform to "the moral timidity of the usual English novelist" in the years immediately following the publication of his two naturalistic novels was not just a matter of economic necessity—it was a question of his very survival as a professional writer. If, as he had argued in "The Art of Fiction," the development of the Anglo-American novel (as well as his own artistic development) depended upon freedom from all a priori restrictions—most notably those which dictated a "cautious silence on certain subjects"—the prevailing literary climate of the late 1880s and early 1890s was actively hostile to that development, especially in England where public opposition to "corrupting" literature was reaching a peak. Goaded by the bold manner in which the publisher Henry Vizetelly openly boasted about the huge success of his English translations of French naturalists, particularly

Zola, the National Vigilance Association mounted an unprecedented and well-orchestrated campaign to suppress what they claimed was immoral literature. They began their attack first by pressing for a debate in Parliament (which took place in May 1888) and then by insisting that Vizetelly be brought to trial on charges of selling obscene literature. Although George Becker reports that the publisher voluntarily withdrew the books from circulation and agreed to plead guilty in order to mollify the hostile court and jury, he notes that Vizetelly got off with a fine and a suspended sentence only to be tried a second time in 1889. The court transcript further reveals that the unlucky publisher's willingness to submit to *prior* censorship of all of Zola's works did not prevent him from receiving a three-month jail sentence, in spite of his advanced age and bad health. Nothing short of imprisonment would satisfy his accusers, who obviously wanted to make an indelible impression upon the minds and future careers of the native writers, critics, and publishers who had defended or aligned themselves with the French school, no matter how tenuously. Almost every major newspaper editorially endorsed this new censorship and a few even advocated widening it to include "sensational stories of actual crimes" carried in their own pages. It is likely that James followed these disturbing developments with something more than a perfunctory professional concern, especially since Vizetelly had quoted favorable passages from James's review of *Nana* in the advertisements for his series of Zola translations (thereby reinforcing the link between the American and the Frenchman in the public mind). This helps to explain why the *Methodist Times* singled James out for attack in the aftermath of the trial, charging (correctly) that the international novelist was guilty of having "seriously contended" that "moral intentions" could be attributed to Zola's immoral work. It is also worth noting both that Vizetelly's firm had published Moore's 1885 pamphlet attacking the circulating libraries and that several of the newspapers drew a sharp distinction between cheap and expensive translations of French fiction, making explicit the true purpose of such censorship. Some of the allies of the National Vigilance Association were clearly more interested in class and sexual control than they were in social purity across class lines. (Fearing that immoral literature would corrupt and possibly stir unrest among the masses in general and women in particular, they favored expensive translations which would keep such material out of the hands of the lower orders and unmarried women. It was also argued that well-educated gentlemen would not suffer from a total ban on translations because they had the training and leisure as well as the right to read French literature and the equally "immoral" classics in the original—an aspect of the sexual double standard which James would later explore and expose in *The Awkward Age*.)[21]

James's willingness to forsake the art of the novel during the early 1890s as well as his determination to turn himself into a truly popular playwright must be approached—at least initially—in the context of this extremely repressive atmosphere. The intense hostility of the British public towards experimental fiction of any kind, especially French realism, had a chilling effect on English-speaking novelists, at least during the early years of the final decade of the century. Even fellow professionals such as Edmund Gosse who were not openly hostile to the cause of fictional experimentation began to announce that realism had run its course. Shortly after the Vizetelly trial Gosse published an article in the *Forum,* an American magazine, in which he probed what he called "The Limits of Realism." After identifying James as the inaugurator of the English language experimental novel (Zola's *La Joie de Vivre* and the early part of the middle of *The Bostonians* were cited as examples of international naturalism in its prime), Gosse charged that Zola had ceased to develop as a writer in recent years and that this theory had gradually broken down when put to the test of execution. He then proceeded to announce that the time was ripe for yet "another reaction," especially among "the younger men" in France (and presumably England) who were beginning to "escap[e] from the realistic formula." An intelligent and alert observer of international as well as domestic literary currents (he would soon help to translate Ibsen into English for the British stage), Gosse was indeed correct when he implied that Zola had recently suffered a serious decline in reputation, especially in his native France. In 1887 five self-proclaimed disciples of the French master had issued a vicious "Manifesto of Five Against *La Terre*" in which they publicly accused Zola of being guilty of almost every imaginable literary crime, from declining literary force and a betrayal of the true principles of his own naturalistic program (he was charged with laziness for having gathered "trumpery documentation" at secondhand and with "collapsing into repetitious and endless clichés") to "profound ignorance" of "things medical and scientific," an insatiable appetite for sales, and—worst of all—a "growing exaggeration of indecency in the use of dirty words..." (This last of the "aberrations of the Master" was crudely attributed to Zola's alleged difficulties with women and his incompetence as a lover!) Interestingly enough, only one avant-garde writer, James's female admirer "Vernon Lee," dared to speak out publicly in England on Zola's behalf during these years; however, her defense of "The Moral Teachings of Zola" (in which she presented the French naturalist as a social prophet) would not appear until 1893,[22] by which time the English-speaking avant-garde had regrouped and begun to counterattack in behalf of fictional experimentation.

While these developments certainly contributed to the strange shape which James's career was now assuming, it would be a mistake to view his sudden preoccupation with playwriting exclusively as a practical move designed to sidestep the censorship which threatened the English literary scene and capitalize upon the general public's curiosity regarding the theater world. James clearly recognized an opportunity of a much more distinguished nature.

He had often remarked in his reviews that although England had many theaters, it sadly lacked the drama. Now those years of observation and fascination were simultaneously pointing him in the direction of the English stage and warning him off. Would the British public understand or even welcome an attempt to supply this need? Based upon his knowledge of what gained popularity on the British stage, James had serious doubts. To complicate matters further, his contempt for reverberation in all its manifestations included the newspaperized world of the theater. He was forcefully repelled by the glare of publicity which surrounded the stage, yet at the same time he was propelled by an equally strong and unquenchable desire to experience life as it was lived behind the scenes and achieve popular success in the theater. Partly an attempt to exorcise these misgivings, *The Tragic Muse* embodied both James's attraction to and revulsion from the theater and signalled the beginning of his deliberate and systematic campaign to conquer the newspaperized world not as a novelist but as a playwright. But before James could assume this role, he had to come to terms with what he perceived to be the inflexible conditions of the English stage. In a well-known passage from the novel which echoes many of his theater essays, James squarely placed the blame for these impossible strictures on "the essentially brutal nature of the modern audience." We see through the words of the aesthete, Gabriel Nash:

> ...the population of a big commercial city, at the hour of the day when their taste is at its lowest, flockng out of hideous hotels and restaurants, gorged with food, stultified with buying and selling and with all the other sordid preoccupations of the day, squeezed together in a sweltering mass, disappointed in their seats, timing the author, timing the actor, wanting to get their money back on the spot, before eleven o'clock.

According to Nash, giving this audience its money's worth means that the modern playwright must write plays which can be performed during the time between dinner and the suburban trains, a condition which makes contemporary plays "less and less actable." Voicing the outrage of his author, the potential playwright, Nash demands: "What can you do with a character, with an idea, with a feeling, between dinner and the suburban trains?"[23]

Nash concludes his long condemnation of the contemporary British stage by stating his conviction that its crudity cannot compare with the subtle art of the novelist, a conviction which will become symptomatic of James's increasing tendency to project the most "vulgar" aspects of the literary life onto the theatrical enterprise for the remainder of his career. Yet other passages and more vivid presences indicate that James, like the young actress after whom he names the book, is quite capable of regarding these conditions as a challenge rather than as a barrier. (The character of Nash eventually disappears from the story and, in a Hawthorne-like manner, James makes Nash's portrait literally fade out of the book at one point.) Both James and his determined heroine,

Miriam Rooth, realize that they are infatuated with the stage and possessed by an over-riding ambition to achieve theatrical success on a grand scale, no matter what sacrifices and compromises such a course demands of them. As if two alter-egos were not sufficient instruments with which to explore his own ambivalence towards the theater and its public, James visited his dilemma upon two other central characters, Peter Sherringham and his cousin Nick Dormer. Peter's love for Miriam is kindled by her histrionic nature, yet he cannot accept the idea of being married to an actress; the very qualities which attract him to her make her unacceptable as a diplomat's wife. Nick must choose between an advantageous marriage to a woman who will almost certainly bring him public success in politics and a private dedication to the solitary art of portrait painting, a career with which she will have nothing to do. Although Nick's fiancée, Julia Dallow, thoroughly disapproves of the theater, in her fierce political ambition she bears a curious resemblance to Miriam: both women define success in terms of the response of the general public, the world at large. In entering the following description of Julia into his notebook sketch of *The Tragic Muse,* James was clearly projecting his ambivalence towards the theater onto Nick's vacillating courtship of Julia: "She appears soft, seductive—but in it all there lurks her *condition*—her terms. He is much *echauffé*—but he feels thus—feels the condition." Under the pressure of having to make a difficult choice about his career, each of these men becomes conscious (like Benvolio) of his "double nature." We are told of Nick that "there were two men in him, quite separate, whose leading features had little in common and each of whom insisted on having an independent turn at life."[24] It is this awareness of their own doubleness which links the two cousins, seemingly so unlike, both to each other and to their author, for James found himself in a similar predicament when, in the midst of writing the novel, he was approached by the actor-manager, Edward Compton, and asked to turn *The American* into a play.

In the pages of his notebooks, James attempted to resolve this dilemma, which had been brought to a head by Compton's request. James pointedly reminds himself that the theater has sought him out "in the person of the yet unseen, Compton," rather than vice versa. Mounting justification upon justification, James begins to envision his theatrical profits as an alternate mode of self-financing and the real source of artistic freedom: "it all hangs together (time, leisure, independence for 'real literature,' and, in addition, a great deal of experience of *tout un coté de la vie*)." On the basis of this passage and others like it, Leon Edel argues in his biography of James that the novelist's problem was exclusively financial: "Of his reputation as an artist, of his distinction in the literary world, there was now no question." To support this contention, Edel provides his readers with a brief summary of his subject's financial situation at this time.[25] While James himself repeatedly states in his correspondence that he is turning to the theater primarily in order to make money,[26] these admissions mask deeper motives which were more difficult for him to acknowledge. It is true, as we have seen, that publication problems surrounding *The Bostonians* and *The Princess* and the poor reception which they received did much damage to James's financial situation. This was brought home to him again and with renewed force in March of 1890 when Frederick Macmillan, who had lost money on both books, offered James a much smaller advance on *The Tragic Muse*. James refused Macmillan's offer of £70, instead of his usual £200 or £250, in a manner reminiscent of the *Tribune* affair, explaining: "I would rather not be published at all than be published and not pay—other people at least." Yet he also refused to consent to the fact that he was a failure "without trying, at least, as they say in America, to 'know more about it.'" He speaks of experimenting with other publishers and adds that unless he can "put the matter on a more remunerative footing," he will give up his English market and stick to the American. James's talk of confining himself to his American market was probably a bluff or an attempt to save face, for his position in the American market during this period was, if anything, less secure. But he did have an ace up his sleeve. He was already at work on the stage version of *The American* for Compton: a successful run would all but insure popular interest in a theatrical novel such as *The Tragic Muse*. Whether or not James used this well-kept secret as a bargaining point with Macmillan (or whether it was James who had called Macmillan's bluff by announcing that he would try another publisher) we do not know, but a compromise must have been reached. Macmillan and Company published *The Tragic Muse* in England in 1890, where it became the last of James's novels to appear as a three-decker. It was also the last novel he was to write until seven long years had passed.[27]

Without a doubt, then, money *was* a large factor in James's decision to write for the stage. Yet in his introduction to *The Complete Plays* Edel seems much closer to the truth when he speaks of James's terrible need to justify the theater venture, as if it were something abnormal. There is ample evidence to establish the fact that although James was indeed worried about his finances, he was primarily using pecuniary motives as a presentable pretext for pursuing a course of action which hardly squared with his avowed commitment to achieving literary perfection at any price and which therefore threatened to undermine his recently-established reputation among the emerging avant-garde public as one of the Anglo-American scene's most serious and dedicated literary artists. To begin with, it is interesting to note that James did not cut short his abortive assault upon the stage when his sister Alice died in 1892, even though she left him $20,000 and the income from some property in New York State which he had made over to her during her lifetime—enough money to mitigate the financial pressures about which he complained so frequently.

Furthermore, the sheer enormity of the novelist's theatrical ambitions went far beyond the confines of economic necessity or (as he had once put it to William) providing for his old age—especially given his status as a confirmed bachelor. He revealed the vast dimensions of these ambitions in characteristically pecuniary terms when he responded to his older brother's "hopeful enquiry about the great question" of theatrical profits. The would-be playwright cited Henry Arthur Jones's *The Dancing Girl* as an example of the kind of overwhelming success on the English-speaking stage which he obviously had in mind for himself: at £180 per week Jones could reasonably expect £10,000 from a year's run—"not counting his American or Australian profits, or the eventual country-tours of his play *by itself*..." (At the time he wrote this letter James's first play, *The American,* was being presented in repertory by the Comptons in the provinces on Fridays only—"the 'fashionable' night.") The prospect of big American proceeds constituted a special lure to James's overheated imagination, for he predicted that Jones could double his £10,000 if the play was a success in the United States. Another letter to William written later in the same year (1891) provides a further clue to the *non*-pecuniary motives which lay behind this obsession with theatrical success on a grand scale. Contemplating the possibility that *The American* would do well with London audiences, James predicted: "*That,* if it is the success I hope, will have a direct and immediate action on everything else; and consecrate and fix my theatrical position—the terms on which I may deal with the barbarous, the ignorant, the sickening race of managers, etc." Read simply in the context of the letter in which it appears, the phrase "a direct and immediate action on everything else" seems to refer only to the "*other* theatrical preoccupations" which James mentions in a preceding sentence. (Indeed, James had recently boasted to his friend Isabella Stewart Gardner that he had refused several "glittering American offers in order to elicit still more glittering ones on the basis of the triumph in *this* place.")[28] However, read in the context of his recent post-*Portrait* career, especially his humiliating dealings with Victorian magazine editors, publishers, and reviewers, this phrase suggests that his determination to achieve a stunning British theatrical success was the result of his compelling need to "consecrate and fix" his damaged social and literary position as a successful man of letters. Only popular (as opposed to "merely" artistic) success would enable him once again to dictate the "terms" on which he dealt with the men who wielded power in the literary marketplace. In other words, James hoped that success on the stage would grant him much-desired status in the exclusive world of the theater, restore his clout in the marketplace, and reestablish his once enviable literary reputation—at least among the conventional English-speaking public. (As we shall see, what such popularity might do to his reputation as a leader of the "experimental school" and his following among the Anglo-American avant-garde was clearly another matter.) That reputation rested, at least prior to the 90s, largely in the hands of critics for whom he had little respect. Only recently he had complained in a letter to Howells of "the imbecility of babyish critics"; and, with the exception of Howells himself, it seems quite unlikely that he felt he could rely on them. As for the members of the general public, James's relations with them had become increasingly worse; the distaste was mutual, as he knew all too well from the poor sales of his books. Despite the reverberation caused by *Daisy Miller* back in 1879, the public's memory was short; and *The Bostonians* was only four years behind him.

James undoubtedly realized that writing for the theater would bring him into a more direct contact with the general public than he had ever before experienced, but perhaps this is just what he had in mind when he wrote to Macmillan that he wanted to "know more about it." Once and for all he would assume the "masculine character" as Basil Ransom had described it in *The Bostonians*: "the ability to dare and endure, to know and yet not fear reality, to look the world in the face and take it for what it is..."[29] Face to face with this audience, James might read the answer to the mystery of his failure to regain the measure of popular success which he had lost during his middle years. If he observed carefully, he might even learn enough to achieve the kind of theatrical success which would spark a renewed interest in his recent fictional experiments, thus exposing them to a wider audience and providing both the novels and their creator with a second chance. We also know that James was irresistably drawn to the spectacle of the stage and that he saw in the theater the promise of an intimate experience of "*tout un côté de la vie.*" In other words, the theatrical venture represented a second chance of another sort—a chance to be initiated into a hidden side of life and an opportunity to extend his subject matter, motives which may also have figured prominently in his earlier efforts to gain access to Anglo-American theatrical circles.

Characteristically, there remained another part of James which continued to deplore the publicity of the modern world, which despised the "vulgarity" of popular taste and which thoroughly disapproved of the theater venture. This other man in James might be overruled, but he could not be permanently silenced; and before the aspiring dramatist could even begin to write, the other James expressed his contempt for the audience which his alter-ego had set out to conquer. As James contemplated transforming *The American* into a play for Compton, this other voice had seemed to mock him from the pages of his notebook: "Oh, how it must not be too good and how very bad it must be!" This phrase distinctly echoes the words which James had exchanged with Whitelaw Reid, the editor of the New York *Tribune,* back in 1876. Now, on the verge of trying once again to satisfy the appetite of the general public, James reminded himself of what he considered to be the lesson of that experience. In order to avoid another failure, he must deliberately write down to his audience. The voice continued to mock James by sarcastically invoking the highly conventional model of the well-made French play: "*A moi,* Scribe; *à moi,* Sardou; *à moi,* Dennery!" As Michael Egan emphasizes in his interpretation of James's theater years, this outburst was full of scorn. James knew quite well that "the *pièce bien faite* was a vehicle for the after-dinner amusement of the affluent middle classes," intended only as "frivolous entertainment." Egan concludes that James in effect condemned himself from the start to artistic mediocrity on the stage by choosing Scribe, Sardou, and Dennery as his models.[30]

Egan justifies this conclusion at least in part by emphasizing the fact that in 1889, the very year in which James entered these words into his notebooks, Henrik Ibsen had begun to break new ground on the English stage. He also points out that although James's initial critical reaction to Ibsen was one of hostility, by 1891 he had become "one of Ibsen's most prestigious supporters," largely as a result of seeing *Hedda Gabler* acted in London. Despite the fact that extreme ambivalence continued to characterize James's attitude towards Ibsen's work, his interest in and curious verbal identification with "our Northern Henry" (as he referred to Ibsen in conversation and correspondence with Eliabeth Robins, an actress who produced and starred in many of the English stage versions of Ibsen's plays) became increasingly intense. James's reviews of Ibsen's plays reveal just how quickly he realized that Ibsen provided quite a different answer to the question he had posed only recently in *The Tragic Muse:* "What can you do with a character, with an idea, with a feeling, between dinner and the suburban trains?" As Egan writes in *Henry James: The Ibsen Years:* "Ibsen showed James not only that the theatre *should* be used as a vehicle for serious social comment, like the novel, but that modern drama *could* sustain intense investigations of character and situation, of states of mind and soul."[31]

Just as there was a growing split within the Anglo-American literary scene between the conventional reading public and the English-speaking aesthetes or *raffinés,* so too was there an emerging gulf between the people who wrote and attended the conventional productions of the English theatrical establishment and the small but highly dedicated group of writers, critics, actors, and artists who campaigned vigorously for an avant-garde theater. Holbrook Jackson traces the beginning of this "dramatic renaissance" back to Charles Charrington's 1889 English production of Ibsen's *A Doll's House,* which he refers to as "the *Hernani* of the new dramatic movement in England." More than any other single figure, it was Ibsen who sparked this renaissance and who therefore enjoyed the support and commanded the respect of the theatrical avant-garde, a public which included the expatriate American actress Elizabeth Robins and her partner, Marion Lea, progressive theater managers, critics, and playwrights such as J.T. Grein, William Archer, and the young

George Bernard Shaw, the publisher William Heinemann, and respected literary men such as Edmund Gosse and of course, Henry James himself. (According to Jackson, the influential theater critic A. B. Walkley was "with them, but not of them..." and took a middle attitude towards these two extremes.) The "new drama" which they collectively fought so hard to produce and sustain was "in the main an occasional affair, highly experimental, and appealing only to a small and seriously-minded group of 'intellectuals' in London." As such, it was clearly not the kind of venture James had in mind for himself. Yet *Theatre and Friendship,* Elizabeth Robin's collection of the letters which James wrote to her during his theater years, not only documents his increasing fascination with and admiration for Ibsen, but also bears witness to the fact that members of the theatrical avant-garde tended to regard James as one of their own and view his attempt to turn himself into a playwright (at least initially) as part of their ongoing struggle to transform the English stage. To begin with, James's friendship with Elizabeth Robins was founded as much upon their mutual aversion to "the conditions of the existing Theatre" as upon their mutual admiration for Ibsen. James lent his public support to her attempt to escape from these conditions by attending each of her Ibsen productions and by choosing her to play Claire de Cintré in the London production of *The American* (a role which he hoped would provide her with a steady income but for which she was hardly suited, given her affinity for and history of playing Ibsen's forceful heroines). James's repeated (though unfulfilled) promises to Robins that he would write a play expressly for her further demonstrates that he was quite capable of thinking about himself as her avant-garde ally, though the plays which he actually wrote were hardly in keeping with the productions of Ibsen and his English-speaking disciples.[32]

Perhaps this helps to explain James's curious delusion that he had—"at last"—found his "*real* form" in the drama, a form which he was "capable of carrying far, and for which the pale little art of fiction" as he had practiced it had been "but a limited and restricted *substitute.*" The latter phrase reveals that James was becoming interested in the theoretical parallel (rather than the practical differences) between the art of fiction and the art of the drama, with the focus not upon the "vulgar" conditions of both marketplaces but upon the comparativey sublime question of their relative difficulty—a point of view from which the art of fiction did indeed seem to pale beside the more exacting art of the drama. The prolific artist who made his appearance in James's first published review had insisted that "the pains of labor" regulated and consecrated his fictional progeny: "If it were as easy to write novels as to read them, then, too, my stomach might rebel..." Now, almost three decades later, the novelist claimed that he found himself attracted to the drama—at least in part—precisely because of the "solid respectability" constituted by the sheer difficulty of the form. As he explained to William: "If it were *easy* to write a good play I couldn't and wouldn't think of it; but it is in fact damnably hard..." It was on these grounds that he saw a solid guarantee of his "*intellectual* self-respect" in the difficult art of the drama (which he persistently juxtaposed to the "barbarous" theatrical trade). Coupled with his growing support of and admiration for Ibsen, this new emphasis upon the drama's redeeming quality of sheer technical difficulty and the beauty of its formal perfection established a link between James's more distinguished literary and theatrical ambitions, at least on a theoretical level. (James's subsequent passion for "squaring" or achieving an almost mathematical symmetry between the fictional relationships he depicts in his work, a symmetry he frequently refers to in his notebooks as the result of applied structural "laws," was both a reflection and an extension of his highly theoretical habits of mind.) On this rather abstract level the drama (as opposed to the theater) was capable of appealing to James as a literary form which promised to reconcile his enormous respect for formal consistency and his equally powerful fascination with the spontaneous drama and suspense of the presented surface of life (a conflict which, as we have seen, was embodied in one of his earliest tales, "Benvolio"). Perhaps the successful sallies of the theatrical avant-garde had even convinced him that the time was indeed ripe for him to "conquer" this new "kingdom" (as he had recently put it to his friend, Robert Louis Stevenson).[33]

Although James's emphasis upon and esteem for difficulty and formal perfection in and of themselves was widely shared by members of the emerging literary avant-garde, it does not seem to have been a major preoccupation of their theatrical counterparts. Concerned as they were with attacking conventional morality and liberating both actors and playwrights from the tyranny of the actor-manager system (a system which depended upon expensive scenery, long runs, and the box office pull of popular matinee idols), the theatrical avant-garde did *not* tend to draw such distinctions between the theater and the drama. Furthermore, James's conspicuous silence on the question of theatrical subject matter as well as his willingness to tailor his own plays to the requirements of the powerful actor-managers who dominated the English stage ran directly counter to his own desire—shared with his friends and colleagues among the theatrical avant-garde—to provide England with the serious indigenous drama which it so sadly lacked. One obvious explanation for this curious disjunction is James's undeniable obsession with pecuniary profit and his desire for genuine popularity, two practical professional considerations which persistently undermined his conflicting theoretical commitment to perfecting his "real" form—the drama. If Ibsen and his followers were teaching James what the theater could be at its best, Ibsen's reception and reputation also demonstrated quite dramatically the consequences of refusing to satisfy the conventional expectations of London audiences. The avant-garde dramatist enjoyed the support and commanded the respect of unusually devoted and discriminating British spectators, but only at the cost of drawing down upon himself the hatred of the general public and the vilification of the press. According to George Bernard Shaw's study of Ibsen's reception and impact in England, *The Daily Telegraph* compared an 1891 production of Ibsen's *Ghosts* to "an open drain, loathesome sore unbandaged, a dirty act done publicly, or a lazar house with all its doors and windows open."[34] Such public abuse was evidently a price which James was unwilling to pay, for Leon Edel informs us that as a staged play, *The American* was a heavy-handed caricature of James's original novel, even down to the American pronunciations which James suggested, "the guiding principle of which seems to have been so speak everything 'a little from the nose.'" The fact that James provided the play with a happy ending and even considered renaming it *The Californian* suggests that he was quite willing to sacrifice the delicacy of his early work in exchange for the enthusiastic response of provincial audiences and the prospect of a London opening.

Further evidence to this effect came less than a month after the January 1891, opening of the play in Southport, near Liverpool, when Henry confided to William that he yearned for "a *London*, as distinguished from a provincial success. (You can form no idea... of how a provincial success is confined to the provinces.) Now that I have tasted blood, c'est une rage (of determination to *do*, and triumph, on my part)..."[35] In keeping with this determination, as *The American* went into strenuous rehearsal for its London opening, James the playwright supervised the building of new scenery (the furniture was imported from Paris) and the careful selection of new costumes, including a long chocolate-colored coat with huge buttons and blue trimming for Newman. As a theater critic James had repeatedly deplored the British public's fascination with elaborate costumes and unnecessary scenery at the expense of good acting and well-written plays, but now he relied upon Newman's accent and his comic appearance to do all the work: James was trusting nothing to his audience's imagination.[36]

Predictably, this strategy alienated some segments of James's theater public, especially the professional critics. Edel terms the opening night in London, September 26, 1891, "a dubious artistic success" but "distinctly a social one," reporting that the house (which included writers, painters, several millionaires, and even the American minister) received the play enthusiastically. The critics, however, proved harder to please. Their consensus seems to have been that Newman's costume and accent were overdone and that both the writing and the acting verged perilously close to melodrama, "with the local color laid on with a trowel..." As one reviewer summed it up: "We are as anxious as the critics of the newest school to hail the advent on our stage of literary men, but it is on condition that they bring their literature with them." The play did enjoy a respectable run, partly because the Prince of Wales lent it prestige by attending a performance. According to Edel, James did his utmost to extend the run by revising some of the scenes in light of the critics' comments and inviting them to attend a "second edition" on the fiftieth night, although Compton continued to wear the same coat and resort to the same tag-line, "That's what I want t'see." (In November of the following year he even went so far as to furnish Compton with "a completely rewritten and reconstructed [in a comedy-sense—heaven forgive me!] fourth act of The American" in order to keep the play in the popular actor-manager's provincial repertory.) Despite James's willingness to compromise the play's (as well as his own) artistic integrity, when *The American* closed after an "honorable run" of seventy nights, he could claim only modest earnings. To make matters worse, the theatrical venture threatened to damage James's relationship with and reputation among his friends and admirers in the avant-garde. As Henry complained bitterly in a letter to William, he was gradually getting used to the "intolerable" strain of theatrical authorship and production only to note that "friends—mostly—shun the subject like a dishonour. The thing has been a revelation to me of how queerly and ungracefully friends can behave. I shall only live, henceforth, for my *revanche*." He insisted upon blaming their avoidance of the theatrical subject exclusively upon the unfortunate fate of "the ill-starred play," implying that things would be different if only the play had been a big hit and deliberately ignoring the more likely possibility that at least some of those friends were dismayed and confused by his conspicuous and sudden willingness to compromise his reputation as a serious artist. Yet this combination of unfavorable responses did not cause him to reconsider or revise his plan, which called for him to write half a dozen plays during the next few years and short fiction rather than novels.[37]

Despite his highly theoretical regard for the drama, James persisted in approaching the theater primarily as a source of self-financing for his "true" work, the art of fiction. Back in July of 1890, Henry had responded to the disappointing sales of *The Tragic Muse* by insisting to William—in typically avant-garde fashion—that he was "quite divorced" from questions of circulation and popularity. His attitude was highly dignified and full of quiet resignation:

> One must go one's way and know what one's about and have a general plan and a private religion—in short have made up one's mind as to *ce qui en est* with a public the draggling after which simply leads one in the gutter. One has always a "public" enough if one has an audible vibration—even if it should only come from one's self.[38]

Although this appears at first to be a curious statement, to say the least, for a writer who was about to embark on a theatrical career, it squares quite easily with his subsequent course of literary production. Almost schizophrenically, James began to dramatize and adhere to this literary credo quite closely, not in his theatrical work but in the short stories, especially the tales of writers and artists, which he wrote during the theater years. This adherence formed the basis of his claim upon the continuing respect of his early admirers and the growing adulation of quite a different public, that circle of literary disciples (many of them from the younger generation) which had begun to follow his work in the 1880s.

This small but select and highly discriminating audience vibrated most sympathetically to James's stories of writers like "poor Dencombe," the dedicated and lonely artist in "The Middle Years" who despairs over the public's failure to grasp his literary intentions and pleads for "another go," an extension, a second chance. What Dencombe has in mind is the "happy notion of an organized rescue," the opportunity to write another book in which he can develop "a certain splendid 'last manner'" which will prove to be "the very citadel" of his reputation. Although Dencombe dies before he can write another novel, the promise of a second chance comes instead in the form of the influence he exerts upon "his greatest admirer in the younger generation," a young doctor whom Dencombe initially mistakes, ironically enough, for yet another obtuse reviewer. In the devoted and intelligent Doctor Hugh, who alienates a wealthy female patient in the course of trying to save the novelist's life and thereby sacrifices a possible inheritance, Dencombe finds not only a discriminating (though not "ideal") reader who will do his best to keep the master's reputation alive, but a sympathetic and responsive spectator to the solitary drama of his life.[39]

While several critics, including Leon Edel and Joseph Warren Beach, have stressed the importance of these tales—most of which were written in the very midst of James's trying theater years—to the development of his mature style (Edel even goes so far as to suggest that one of them, "The Coxon Fund," may mark the beginning of the emergence of James's late or so-called "third" manner), the contrasting nature of James's fictional and dramatic intentions with regard to his audience during these years has remained, for the most part, unexplored.[40] As the sole literary product of a period of intense theatrical experimentation and compromise, these tales were conceived and composed under unique conditions. The unprecedented extent to which they rely upon, create, and, in the case of the tales of the literary life, even describe an intimate relationship between a highly demanding writer and an equally discriminating reader suggests that, in some way, the very openness of James's bid for popular success on the stage was making him more aware of (and possibly even forcing him to acknowledge overtly) his need for a truly reciprocal relationship with an audience which was no less demanding but much more discriminating. It was as if James's experiences with the theater were enabling him to project what he perceived of as the more vulgar aspects of the literary life onto the theater, freeing him (temporarily at least) to treat his fiction almost exclusively as an art form rather than as a trade.

James's short stories of this period not only embody his enduring commitment to the possibility of a reciprocal relationship between literature and its audience but, to the extent that they were read sympathetically by his own avant-garde public, they also succeeded in eliciting and renewing the kind of subtle and intense writer-reader interaction which he had set out to portray in his tales of the literary life (and which he was conspicuously abandoning in the theater). On this level these stories functioned both as the artistic space within which James continued to develop his manner and the social space within which he created and preserved his emerging identity as "the master," for they projected and protected his vision of himself as a serious writer and an uncompromising artist. They thus made possible the very intimate relation between James and the Anglo-American avant-garde which was gaining shape and social reality through his continuing interaction with his most subtle readers—especially his disciples in the younger generation (some of whom had even begun to imitate or parody "the master's" epistolary and literary style).[41] This process came full circle in 1894 when one of James's youthful admirers, the expatriate American novelist Henry Harland, convinced him that he should contribute "The Death of the Lion," another of these tales, to the opening number of his avant-garde periodical, the *Yellow Book*. Associated as it was with "indecent" French novels, the color yellow had become the very symbol of aestheticism. Bound like a book with a daring yellow cover designed by the avant-garde artist Aubrey Beardsley, this pioneering quarterly succeeded almost instantly in becoming "a rallying cry, a term of opprobrium, a ventilator of the stuffy nineteenth-century literary air, and—briefly—an institution" during its relatively short life. Founded by Harland and publisher John Lane in 1894, the *Yellow Book* (which carried no advertising except for new book lists) was to fold in 1897, partly due to competition from the more aggressively avant-garde *Savoy* and partly as a side-effect of the Oscar Wilde scandal. (A yellow book which Wilde happened to have under his arm at the time of his arrest was mistakenly identified by outraged observers as the little magazine.) Although Stanley Weintraub has argued that "with the Jamesian Henry Harland as its literary editor, it shunned the post of an *avant garde* magazine," there is no doubt that the *Yellow Book* was perceived as an avant-garde periodical by many of its contributors as well as by members of the general public. And if, as Weintraub also contends, James's appearance in the first issue (as well as the editors' consistent refusal to include anything written by Oscar Wilde) was the result of Harland's desire to "establish a tone of prudence and respectability," it is also clear that the magazine's prospectus committed it to reconciling "a delicate, decorous and reticent mien and conduct" with "the courage of its modernness..." Determined not to "tremble at the frown of Mrs. Grundy," the editors took evident pride in publishing Aubrey Beardsley's unconventional and often sexually suggestive drawings, Hubert Crackanthorpe's attack on the "philistine bookselling tastes of Mudie and Smith," and the decidedly risqué stories of outspokenly frank women writers who adopted male pen names such as "George Egerton" (Mary Chavelita Dunne, the notorious author of *Keynotes* and *Discords*), "Vernon Lee" (Violet Paget, the female disciple of Henry James who had defended Zola in 1893), and "John Oliver Hobbes" (Mrs. Pearl Richards Craigie, a friend of James's whose attempt to divorce her husband on grounds of adultery and cruelty in 1895 would add a further aura of scandal to the little magazine). Morton Fullerton, Edmund Gosse, and Reginald Turner (a Jamesian whose story "A Chefd'Oeuvre" was at best a second-rate version of one of the master's tales of the literary life) as well as H. G. Wells (a future friend and temporary admirer of the master) were among the less controversial contributors to subsequent issues. (According to Weintraub, "No *Yellow Book* seemed to be without clear evidences of both the lessons of the Master and the winds from France.")

Attempting to combine what they regarded as the traditional and the new in their first issue, the editors had given "The Death of the Lion" the "place of honor for literature" in the opening number only to follow it with Richard Le Gallienne's poem "Tree-Worship" with its "adulterous nightengales." It is worth noting that although the majority of reviewers subjected most of the first number to "scathing condemnation," they did single out James's story for praise (though one warned him that he was keeping bad company). Despite or perhaps because of the extremely unfavorable reviews, the magazine sold so rapidly that the publishers could not keep up with the demand: a second edition had to be issued after the first one "vanished" in only five days. Katharine Lyon Mix reports that even the lending libraries and book clubs had waiting lists for the *Yellow Book,* which rapidly became "the conversation topic of the day."[42] This must have surprised the author of "The Death of the Lion," whose tale (like "The Middle Years") focuses upon an older writer who merits the devotion and requires the protection of a young admirer, largely because of the neglectful treatment he has experienced at the hands of the general public. Despite the strong autobiographical overtones in such tales, it must be stressed that they reflect James less as he already was than as the kind of artist he alternately hoped and feared he might become. It is important to remember that during these years James was obsessed with his dream of conquering the London stage and winning the approval of the multitudes. This helps to explain his ambivalence about appearing in little-magazine format. Although "The Death of the Lion" enjoyed what he acknowledged to be an unusual success in the *Yellow Book,* James insisted that his family not read it until it appeared in book form because "I hate too much the horrid aspect and company of the whole publication." He decidedly felt uncomfortable and out of place in the ranks of the English avant-garde, not only because of its association with moral impropriety (a theme he had treated, albeit ironically, as early as 1884 in "The Author of 'Beltraffio'"), but because of his own determination to continue his ardent wooing of its arch-enemy, the general public.[43]

Yet escape from the demands of the general public seems to have been one of Henry's primary though unacknowledged motivations for agreeing to supply another story, "The Coxon Fund," for the second number of the magazine. Although he claimed to William that he did so only "for the gold and to oblige the worshipful Harland (the editor)," writing for the readers of this avant-garde magazine provided him with a much needed relief from "the barbarous art of the actable drama" and the pressure of trying to please its undiscriminating audience. Late in 1894 James described this audience to a friend who also aspired to be a playwright, the publisher William Heinemann:

> In that art one must specify one's subject as unmistakably as one orders one's dinner—I mean leave the audience no trouble to disengage or disentangle it. Forget not that you write for the stupid—that is, that your maximum of refinement must meet the minimum of intelligence of the audience, in other words, of the biggest ass it may conceivably contain.

As he bitterly concluded: "It is a most unholy trade." No wonder James wrote in his notebooks of "the soothing, the healing, the sacred and salutary refuge from all these vulgarities and pains" which his "blessed and uninvaded workroom" provided.[44]

By then James had plenty of reasons for sounding so bitter. To begin with, he had learned the difficult lesson that a playwright's task continued long after the play was written. The hardheaded theater managers with whom he engaged in "vulgar" negotiations frequently demanded that he make numerous and time-consuming revisions: scenes had to be reconstructed, lines adjusted for or explained to particular actors and, even more disturbing, there were painful cuts which had to be made. To make matters worse, James could claim little pecuniary profit in exchange for all his patience and his willingness to compromise. He had been forced to confront the distressing (and embarrassing) fact that four of the plays which he had worked so hard to revise, *Tenants, Mrs. Jasper, The Reprobate,* and *The Album,* would never reach the stage; each had been rejected after long delays. Yet "rejected" is not really the correct term to describe the curious fate of *Mrs. Jasper,* a three-act comedy (later retitled *Disengaged*) which James had written expressly for the actress Ada Rehan and which Augustin Daly had agreed to produce. In December of 1893, a full year after he had accepted *Mrs. Jasper* for future production, Daly invited James to a preliminary reading of the play, but only after hinting to the already nervous playwright that the piece needed further revision if it was to have what he called "the elements of success." As James bitterly confided to

Elizabeth Robins, the actors' interpretations of their parts (especially in the case of Ada Rehan) struck him as so hopelessly inadequate that he could barely control or conceal his rage. He promptly fired off a pair of explosive letters to Daly in which he angrily withdrew the play, openly accusing the producer of having committed an extremely serious violation of "the code of relations between manager and author" when he deprived James "of the indispensable preliminary" of discussing his intentions and sharing his suggestions with the cast. Daly responded to the first letter in a cool and dignified manner by trying to convince James of his sincere commitment to the play, reminding the agitated playwright that he had already invested money in both the scenery and the costumes and assuring him that he would be "free and welcome" to correct the actors' conception of his characters and their delivery of their lines during subsequent rehearsals. Apparently unconvinced and even further outraged by Daly's composure as well as his willingness to leave the play's fate entirely up to the playwright (who might have secretly regretted his rash behavior and hoped that the producer would challenge his withdrawal), James escalated his attack. His second letter to Daly is extremely revealing, for he continued to charge not only that Daly had lost interest in *Mrs. Jasper* but that the entire company—especially Daly and Rehan—had conspired from the beginning in a plot against him. As in the case of his *Tribune* letters, James's response to what was, after all, not an outright rejection but an "editorial" correction was, in effect, to quit. But this time he could not resist taking a cheap parting shot at his adversary. James expressed his contempt for both Daly and Rehan in his characteristically indirect fashion by pointedly lamenting the inferior quality of the parts on which they had recently collaborated, sarcastically insisting that only his own play constituted an adequate "test" of her "great talent."[45]

It is little wonder that Henry experienced "a sense of relief and escape—escape as from a sinking ship" when he described this "horrid experience" in a subsequent letter to William (although he implied that the "sinking ship" was Daly's company and not his own artistic integrity). He had been unsuccessfully trying to play (and ignore the obvious conflict of interest between) two mutually exclusive roles—the practical man of the theater devoted primarily to pecuniary profit and the would-be master of the difficult art of the drama. Projecting his conflicting ambitions and intentions onto the split between the drama and the theater, he now insisted to his brother that "the whole odiousness" of the theater venture consisted in the connection between the two:

> The one is admirable in its interest and difficulty, the other loathesome in its conditions. If the drama could only be theoretically or hypothetically acted, the fascination resident in its all but unconquerable (*circumspice!*) form would be unimpaired, and one would be able to have the exquisite exercise without the horrid sacrifice.

It should be noted here that on previous occasions James had admitted that the difficulty of the drama consisted at least in part of—and was inextricably connected with—these very conditions. As this passage suggests, James's desire to see himself (as his admirers apparently saw him) as an uncompromising artist totally dedicated to perfecting the art of the drama was making it increasingly difficult for him to swallow his pride, bide his time, and accommodate (rather than resist) theater conditions, especially those imposed by "vulgar" actor-managers for whom he had little or no respect (he was by then privately referring to Daly as "that hopeless cad"). Yet at the same time he insisted upon clinging to his naive belief that commercial success would solve all of his problems (without creating new ones), as he revealed when he spoke of the fate of *Mrs. Jasper* as "an interesting illustration of what may happen, in the vulgar theatrical world, to one who is not *yet* cased in the only success there recognized—the success *not* of the Book." He optimistically added: "When once one is cased in that success, however, one's position wholly changes, and I think the *revanche* must be great and sweet." James may have lost a costly skirmish but he was not yet prepared to retreat from the theatrical battlefield. Giving vent to his "lively disgust and disappointment" over the prospect of such "a waste of patient and ingenious labor and a sacrifice of coin much counted on," he vowed:

> I mean to wage this war ferociously for one year more—1894—and then (unless the victory and the spoils have by that become more proportionate than hitherto to the humiliations and vulgarities and disgusts, all the dishonour and chronic insult incurred) to "chuck" the whole intolerable experiment and return and more elevated and more independent courses.[46]

This incident provides ample testimony to James's growing disgust with *himself* as well as with the "vulgar" conditions which he was stooping to meet. He had forsaken the art of the novel in order to regain social status and literary clout via popular success on the stage, only to experience the same kind of humiliating treatment in the theatrical marketplace that he had recently suffered at the hands of transatlantic editors, publishers, and reviewers. In and of themselves, theater conditions were probably no worse than those imposed by the representatives of the Anglo-American book trade. However, it was the *exposed* nature of the theatrical version of accommodation and resistance which seems to have made James so acutely uncomfortable. This discomfort is consistently demonstrated in his letters, which are punctuated by bitter complaints about the "bloody mutilations" which the theater managers insisted upon in the name of the public and periodic references to his "butchered" plays. In these outbursts James often sounds like a remorseful parent who is being forced to perpetrate violence on one of his own children. This was a new note for the businesslike professional who had once made the following statement to his friend Robert Louis Stevenson, in response to Stevenson's criticism of one of his novels: "Besides, directly my productions are finished, or at least thrust out to earn their living, they seem to *me* dead. They dwindle when weaned—removed from the parental breast, and only flourish, a little, while imbibing the milk of my plastic care."[47] Now it was as if the events of James's theater years were dramatizing not only his complex and often contradictory attitudes toward the reading public but his equally complex and even more covert relationship with the creations of his imagination. These outbursts against theater conditions amounted to an explicit if oblique acknowledgment of the fact that his determination to be successful masked deep reservations about the violence he was doing to both himself and his work. James's years of writing for the theater were making him realize that the umbilical cord which bound him to his work was not necessarily cut when a piece was completed.

Perhaps this is why James sought compensation of a psychological as well as a financial sort for the labor he had invested in the four unacted plays. When Osgood, now back in business in London, agreed to publish the plays in two handsomely printed volumes, James took the (for him) unprecedented step of reviving his parental connection with the plays by providing them with short prefaces. Ostensibly designed to explain why the playwright was willing to make such a public confession of his defeat, these prefaces actually represented James's effort to rescue his abandoned progeny and turn an overwhelming defeat into a modest victory. In the first preface, "the unacted dramatist" reveals that he regards publication as a consolation because it represents the possibility of an imaginary, a substitute performance:

> The covers of the book may, in a seat that costs nothing, figure the friendly curtain, and the legible "lines" the various voices of the stage; so that if these things manage at all to disclose a picture or drop a tone into the reader's ear the ghostly ordeal will in a manner have been passed and the dim footlights faced.

James makes the same plea to his readers in the preface to the second series of *Theatricals,* also published in 1894, where he employs a strategy which he will later expand in the Prefaces to the New York Edition of his work. He seeks to reconstitute his parental relationship with the plays and gain his readers' sympathy and attention by going behind the scenes to reveal the theatrical conditions which the plays were originally intended to meet. Once again, the published play, when offered as a substitute for the acted play, "itself grows mildly theatrical" under the paternal gaze of "the disconcerted author." In return, James clearly hopes that his readers will provide an equivalent to the "merciful curtain" for which the "naked text," which has been "dragged ashore only to stand shivering," now appears to plead.[48] The playwright is in effect urging his readers to "make-believe," to lend to these plays, printed in book form, a kind of dramatic attention which will match and complete his own dramatic intentions.

But James the practical man of business was not yet ready to confine his dramatic intentions within the covers of a book and entrust them to his reading public, nor was he really content to see his plays "theoretically or hypothetically acted." George Alexander, the successful actor-manager of the St. James's Theatre, had finally agreed to produce *Guy Domville,* a play which the Comptons commissioned but later rejected because of its unhappy ending. Despite Alexander's lack of "the larger imagination," he was a powerful ally: he combined the advantages of being a handsome actor who would look impressive in the period costumes which the play required and an efficient manager who would honor his pledge to produce the play without great delay. Perhaps most importantly, he was also popular enough as a performer and matinee idol to boast that his "fans" would fill the St. James's Theatre continually, no matter what he played in. (James himself had been part of Alexander's opening-night audience in February of 1892 when the actor-manager starred opposite Marion Terry in Oscar Wilde's "infantine" yet highly successful comedy, *Lady Windermere's Fan.*)[49] It is not altogether clear why Alexander agreed to play the role of Guy Domville, a young man from an eighteenth-century Catholic family who is torn between his desire to enter a monastery and his duty, as the last of his line, to marry and perpetuate his family name. James did his utmost to make the part attractive by providing the actor with a romantic involvement in the first act, followed by what he thought was a subtle but humorous drinking scene in the second act, all to be capped by a final moment of crisis in the third act when Guy renounces the woman he loves and forsakes the world for good. However, these practical concessions were undermined by James's intense identification with and sympathy for his otherworldly hero, a man destined to return "to the holy place he had forsaken" after a "misleading erratic episode." Guy's vacillation between his public responsibility to enter into marriage and take his place in the world and his personal yearning to retire into the priesthood and commit himself to a life of private devotion can be seen as yet another version of his creator's continuing professional crisis. Should James continue to court theater audiences and compromise with debasing theatrical conditions in an attempt to win fame and fortune or should he renounce this worldly and "most unholy trade" in order to devote himself exclusively to what he was increasingly coming to regard as his private religion, the art of fiction? (In many respects, Guy's dilemma is an extreme version of Nick's predicament in *The Tragic Muse.*)

While this is generally how the play has been interpreted,[50] if we approach it as an acting script rather than as a literary text we can discern a rather different and competing "plot." Although he had projected some of his own conflicting personal motives and vacillating professional ambitions upon his hero, James was not prepared to follow Guy's lead by renouncing either the world or worldly success. In *Guy Domville* we can watch James as he vacillates not between temptation and total renunciation but between two alternate strategies for manipulating and capturing the taste of the theater-going public. (This side of James is more closely allied with his extremely devious villain, Lord Devenish, whose melodramatic machinations literally set the plot in motion.) As we have seen, James the critic had been describing and analyzing international differences in that public since at least as early as 1872, when he published his first theater review, "The Parisian Stage." However, by the time he wrote *Guy Domville* in 1893, the aspiring playwright had become preoccupied with a domestic audience phenomenon, the dramatic contrast between the small avant-garde audiences (later referred to by James as the "*unusual*" public) which subscribed to Elizabeth Robins' productions of Ibsen and the "*usual* vulgar theatre-going public," the large audiences which provided popular actors such as Alexander and fashionable playwrights such as Oscar Wilde with full houses night after night. (James shrewdly identified Wilde's knack for flattering the vanity of his less discriminating public as one of the main sources of his popular appeal, noting that the pit and the gallery were so pleased to "'catch on' to four or five of the ingenious—too ingenious—*mots* in the dozen, that it makes them feel quite 'decadent' and 'raffiné' and they enjoy the sensation as a change from the stodgy.") After seeing Miss Robins act the part of Hilda in her production of Ibsen's *The Master Builder* in February of that year, James had singled out this curious new contrast for special comment when he insisted to her that despite its poor reception by the general public, the play "lives and makes its life felt on the consenting. The others were out of the account from the 1st." He went on to reassure her that "it is 'in theatrical circles'—or with the independent spectator that your own achievement will tell." James had originally counted himself as one of "the others," but he had soon found himself transformed into one of "the consenting" by "the hard compulsion" of Ibsen's "strangely inscrutable art." Most crucially, this compulsion became all the more potent on the stage. As James argued in his review of *Hedda Gabler*: "It immediately becomes apparent that he [Ibsen] needs the test [of representation, of production] to show his strength and the frame to show his picture. An extraordinary vivification takes place..."[51] Ibsen's plays thus underlined a contradictory lesson for James. While the work of a playwright who refused to compromise was likely to generate a split in contemporaneous audiences, James's own encounter with Ibsen, especially the inspired productions which Elizabeth Robins mounted, had demonstrated that consent could be compelled as well as courted.

James obviously realized that although his loyal friends and fellow artists would do their part to make *Guy Domville* a social success by attending the play on opening night, they were far too few in number to give the play the long run and financial success he so desired. Yet given both the subject matter of the play and its unhappy ending, either of which was enough to affront the taste of conventional audiences, we can only conclude that after several years of one-sided compromise with the stage, James was determined to find out to what extent he could impose his own measure of subtlety upon the theater-going public. He seems to have been gambling that general audiences could be made to swallow the bitter pill of Guy's ultimate renunciation if they were given popular actors in elaborate costumes and a classic French drinking scene to wash it all down. Some aspects of the play would cater directly to the undeveloped taste of the usual theater-going public, but all the while James would be attempting to manipulate their taste as part of his effort to transform that mass of "others" into a circle of "the consenting," an effort which in some respects paralleled the international balancing act which he had perfected in apprentice novels such as *The Europeans*.

James was so nervous on opening night, January 5, 1895, that he avoided the St. James's Theatre altogether by attending a performance of Oscar Wilde's *An Ideal Husband*. His subsequent comments about the evening reveal that he focused his attention not so much on the play itself but on the way its fashionable audience responded to the witticisms of his popular competitor. As he insisted (after the fact) to William, the enthusiastic reception granted Wilde's play precluded the possiblity of an appreciative response to *Guy Domville*. He remembered asking himself: "How *can* my piece do anything with a public with whom *that* is a success?"[52] In light of *Guy Domville's* actual reception, it would be all too easy to follow James's lead and blame the fate of the play entirely on the "vulgar" taste of the British theater public. Yet it is possible that James might have returned to the St. James's Theatre later that night as a moderately successful playwright, if only the second and third acts of *Guy Domville* had been written and acted in a manner consistent with the first act. While James was watching spectators at the Haymarket respond warmly to Wilde's consistently well-timed epigrams, his own audience at the St. James's was having great difficulty accepting the crudely executed and poorly motivated shift in tone, character, setting, and costume between the first and second acts. As George Bernard Shaw later testified, James's "rare charm of speech" captivated the audience in the first act. "Unfortunately, the second act dissolved the charm rather badly; and what was more, the actors felt it."[53]

Judging from the reviews, the first act demonstrated James's masterful ability to capture the attention and win the approval of the pits and the gallery as well as the stalls and the boxes. The same sources suggest, however, that the next act provided ample proof that James was quite capable of alienating his entire audience in a single blow, for it jarred the sensibilities of the anonymous spectators as well as the well-dressed celebrities and the critics. The mock drinking scene, which called on Guy to repeatedly dispose of his drinks in a flower pot, exhausted the patience of everyone, including Alexander's loyal fans; and thus it destroyed the good will of the very portion of the audience which it was presumably designed to placate. To make matters worse, the awkward attempts of one of the actresses to cope with her over-elaborate hat in the second act shattered the theatrical illusion. Contagious coughing gave way to tittering among the gallery and the pits, diminishing the conventional distance between actors and audience and making it increasingly difficult for both the cast and the audience to preserve the proper actor-spectator relationship. Finally, a voice from the vicinity of the pits yelled out, "Where did you get that hat?" The spell which James had cast in the first act had now been audibly broken, and the actors became visibly shaken.[54]

Guy's final transformation from the "didactic puritan" of the first act and the "fine generous blade" of the second act to "that impossible, noble, iron-grey Mr. Alexander" in the third act provided further strain to the credibility of even a well-disposed spectator like H. G. Wells, then a fledgling drama critic. So it should hardly come as a surprise to learn that Alexander's climactic speech in the third act did not go over well with the gallery. Guy's announcement of his final decision to remain "the last, my lord, of the Domvilles!" evoked the unwelcome response of a frustrated spectator: "It's a bloody good thing y'are." Although the curtain fell soon after, the performance was not yet over. The frame of the play had been violated; and James was unfortunate enough to arrive on the scene just in time to become a participant in this extended drama, which by now absorbed the audience as well as the cast. Perhaps out of malice, Alexander led the playwright onto the stage in response to calls for the author. Face to face with the audience which he had alternately attempted to please and to conquer from behind the scenes, James unwittingly became the "leading man" in a sequel to *Guy Domville*.

The "first act" of this sequel took place then and there. As Henry somewhat melodramatically described it four days later in a letter to William, "a brutal and ill-disposed gallery which had shown signs of malice prepense from the first...kicked up an infernal row at the fall of the curtain." In response to "the hoots and jeers and catcalls of the roughs," "all the forces of civilization in the house waged a battle of the most gallant, prolonged and sustained applause..." In his "nervous bewilderment" Alexander "lost his head" and responded to these jeers by coming out on the stage and making a brief speech during which he apologized for the play. Although this won him a final round of applause from the "obstreperous gallery," Henry assured

William that Alexander had since suffered "universal reprobation" and was "signally ashamed" of his behavior.[55]

While Leon Edel is anything but blind to the defects of the play, he seems to be following James's cue when he implies that the playwright was an innocent casualty of this "war between the intellectual elite, the friends, the well-wishers, and the rowdies to whom the applause [for James] was an act of defiance." Edel also insists that the entire episode was merely "a strange and peculiar theatrical brawl" rather than one of those "battles over artistic ideologies such as occur with interesting regularity in Paris theatres." Neither formula precisely describes or illuminates the post-opening-night drama as it continued to unfold, both in the privacy of James's rooms and in the public glare of the theater sections of the London papers. The reviews as well as James's correspondence suggest that social and artistic ideologies *were* at issue. Although even the most sympathetic critics readily conceded that the second act was a failure, Edel informs us that "by and large Henry James had an excellent press."[56] It seems that in spite of the fact that the entire audience shared the impatience which only isolated spectators had given voice to at the time, the unprecedented act of voicing that common sentiment while the play was still in progress split the audience in two. The jeering which greeted James's appearance on the stage forced all of the spectators who disapproved of treating a playwright in this manner to join ranks behind him in order to repudiate and disassociate themselves publicly from such behavior. Whatever they may have thought of the play itself and whatever doubts they might have harbored regarding the appropriateness of James's theater venture, the critics, artists, celebrities, and "respectable people" who made up this extremely heterogeneous coalition were not disposed to endorse such a blatant violation of theatrical *and* social convention. Furthermore, the sympathetic reviews of drama critics such as Shaw, Wells, Walkley, and (to a lesser extent) Bennett can only be understood in the context of the ongoing battle for an avant-garde theater, for their qualified praise of *Guy Domville* betrays little genuine enthusiasm for the play itself. Their defense of the play and the playwright reflected instead their support for the theatrical avant-garde (which considered James one of their own, whether rightly or wrongly) and the anger generated by James's rude treatment at the hands of the gallery and the pits.

The critics' confusion about what they had witnessed and why it had occurred was well illustrated by George Bernard Shaw, who praised the acting of the lead characters and insisted that "the cultivated majority," himself included, unanimously applauded James. This assessment, combined with Shaw's attempt to write off the unappreciative as a mere "handful of rowdies," contradicted his own uncomfortable admission that he found the play to be lacking in passion. Somewhat reluctantly, he revealed that he was not himself "in Mr. James's camp," mainly because the play offered a version of life known only to "cultivated ladies and gentlemen" who "live on independent incomes or by pleasant artistic occupations." Still, Shaw seems to have felt compelled to come to James's defense. Perhaps this is why he insisted that although James did not depict life "as imagined by the pit or gallery, or even by the stalls," this did not mean that James's dramatic authorship was not valid (probably a covert self-reference since Shaw himself sat in the stalls that night). He even attempted to draw a moral from the incident by concluding that *Guy Domville* proved his contention that audiences had no right to dictate the laws of the drama to playwrights, or to drama critics, for that matter. In his *Pall Mall Gazette* review, entitled "A Pretty Question," H. G. Wells betrayed a similar confusion. He began by observing that "the play was received with marked disapproval by a considerable section of the audience," yet he defended James's delicate workmanship and placed most of the blame for the play's failure on "the imperfect appreciation of the actors." In effect, then, either the actors or the spectators in the pit and the gallery (objectified as a "handful of rowdies") diverted attention from and took most if not all of the blame for the consequences of the playwright's vacillating intentions. This attitude is epitomized by an extremely revealing passage from A. B. Walkley's review which Edel thoroughly endorses. In this "most balanced appraisal of all," James is presented as a kind of martyr for the theatrical avant-garde who gathers "the enemy's spears into his heart" in order to make "a gap through which his successors will be able to pour in triumph."[57] Needless to say, this self-sacrificing role is hardly what James himself had in mind, but it fitted all too neatly into the emerging legend of the master. This helps to explain why the incident brought Henry James more "fan mail" than he had ever before received. Many people came in person to console him. Ellen Terry asked him to write a play for her, and *Guy Domville* lasted four weeks at the St. James's, a feat which James attributed to the fact that many loyal friends and admirers had gone to see it three and even four times.

Although it is not my intention to minimize the effect which this incident had upon both James's reputation and his own perception of his career, one must be wary of the assumption, fostered by Edel, that the traumatic events of that evening virtually crushed James and caused him to regress into a childlike passivity. While he certainly experienced an understandable desire to retreat from so much unpleasant reverberation, James must have secretly enjoyed the unprecedented quantity of quite audible vibration which now came to him from an unexpectedly wide variety of sympathetic friends and new and old admirers, many of them strangers. After insisting to William that his play was "over the heads of the *usual* vulgar theatre-going public," he boasted that "it's altogether the best thing I've done" and immodestly added that it had been well received by "the only two drama critics who count, W. Archer and Clement Scott." "Meanwhile," he continued, "all *private* opinion is apparently one of extreme admiration—I have been flooded with letters of the warmest protest and assurance.... Everyone who was there has either written to me or come to see me—I mean every one I know and many people I don't."[58]

James had failed in his attempt to manipulate and conquer the "usual" theater public, but this failure was to have unforeseen compensations. As Henry revealingly put it in another post-opening night letter to his brother, the play had been "a rare and distinguished private success and scarcely anything at all of a public one": "...every *raffiné* in London (I mean of course only the people who *don't* go to the usual things)" had been to see it. When Mrs. Edward Compton (the wife of the actor-manager who had declined to produce *Guy Domville* because of its unhappy ending) even went so far as to ask James to write her husband another play, her sudden show of confidence in him (in spite or perhaps even because of the play's "distinguished" failure) was a telling symptom of the playwright's newly-established appeal.[59] Ironically the strange fate of *Guy Domville* not only rallied the support of "people with taste" who might otherwise have questioned his ability as a playwright but reinforced the loyalty of old friends and new disciples who may have harbored serious doubts concerning the wisdom and appropriateness of James's experiments with the drama.

As an immediate consequence, "this little drama" (was he referring to the play itself or to his own appearance on the stage of the St. James's Theatre that night?) brought James "in two or three weeks twenty-five times more letters than a career of *refined literary virtue* has brought (about my books) in twenty-five years." The long-term effect upon his reputation and career would be no less dramatic, as he himself began to sense when he shrewdly observed that "my 'position' is much more 'distinguished' in consequence of *Guy Domville,* than before—is in fact very distinguished." By this time, almost a month after the opening-night fiasco, the playwright had begun to take his cue from the reviewers: he was now finding fault with Alexander's treatment of his part, which he privately condemned as having proven "fatal" to the "mutilated brutally simplified, massacred little play." Evidently re-infected by a temporary renewal of his theatrical "fever," James was capable of believing that the play itself was not the problem and that *Guy Domville* would have survived the initial attack of the London "roughs" if only it could have held out until "the Season." Then his American compatriots "would come in their hundreds" to the rescue, keeping "the thing on a couple of months longer—or some weeks at least..."[60] Coached by James's retrospective presentation of himself in the Prefaces and elsewhere as an artist who was totally divorced from questions of popularity, most critics have assumed that his "distinguished" failure to turn himself into a popular playwright was a foregone conclusion. Yet it is interesting to speculate upon the question of what effect "vulgar" success on the London stage would have had on James's contemporaneous and posthumous reputation as well as his subsequent development as a writer. Quite conveniently for James, his opening-night treatment at the hands of "those yelling barbarians" constituted the presentable pretext he needed for flagrantly abandoning (rather than beating a hasty retreat from) the "debased" and "debasing" world of the theater, thus establishing his artistic position once and for all, especially among the increasingly influential avant-garde. The entire incident came close enough to re-enacting the plot of several of his own tales of the literary life (as well as the climax of *The Bostonians*) to fulfill all his old fantasies of brutal rejection by a philistine public, thereby supplying him with both a story of his own and a highly sympathetic audience. In effect, then, the disastrous opening night served James well, for it retroactively justified his contempt for the general public while providing him with a dramatic and highly dignified and diplomatic exit from the theatrical scene (probably much to his private relief).

James had originally envisioned the theater as his own version of a second chance; but the possibility of another chance had come in a totally unexpected way, as in the case of "poor Dencombe" of "The Middle Years." James's virtually self-induced ordeal before the footlights at the St. James's Theatre lent him the same unique aura of public failure and private success which he had managed to confer upon his fictional writers. In combination with his emerging final manner, it entitled him to play the part which he had created and celebrated (however ambivalently) in his stories of writers and artists. Only now could he rightfully lay claim to the avant-garde title of "the master."

4

"The Larger Latitude"

The third act in the extended drama which began with James's appearance on the stage of the St. James's Theatre took place in the letters, the notebook entries, and ultimately the fiction which he wrote in the remainder of the nineteenth century. Although he was to consolidate his literary position by perfecting his emerging final manner during this period of his career, the next five years would eventually figure to James as "years of darkness" which gained shape and justification only retroactively in terms of the triumphs of his major phase, the "years of light." A more immediate effect of the theater venture, especially the strange fate of *Guy Domville,* was to rekindle and reinforce James's commitment to pursuing his own artistic development. In an effort to renew his earlier challenge to debilitating transatlantic literary conventions regarding subject matter and form, he would inaugurate a series of remarkable fictional experiments; but as we shall see, the resulting novels in turn inaugurated what can best be described as an extended reign of terror among his fictional progeny. Yet while the post-opening-night controversy continued to rage, James found himself the victim of his own terrible fear of having lost his literary bearings as well as his vision of his career as a novelist. We can listen to the master as he attempts to assess his location on the contemporaneous literary landscape and plot his future course of literary production in his delayed response to a letter which William Dean Howells had sent him in December of 1894 (a letter which he had postponed answering, perhaps intentionally, until January 22, 1895, when the fate of *Guy Domville* and his theatrical career had been decided). Howells' letter had "soothed" and "cheered and comforted" James because, as it now struck him, "You put your finger sympathetically on the place and spoke of what I wanted you to speak of." It was as if Howells had anticipated not only James's ordeal but the precise nature of his friend's subsequent need for encouragement when he set out, well in advance of the St. James's première, to reassure James about the strength of his literary reputation. Now, in language very similar to that which he had used back in 1888 (when he expressed his worst fears to Howells concerning the failure of *The Bostonians* and *The Princess*), James once again confessed to feeling that he had "fallen upon evil days—every sign or symbol of one's being in the least *wanted,* anywhere or by any one, having so utterly failed." Curiously enough, he attributed this to the fact that "a new generation, that I know not, and mainly prize not, has taken universal possession. The sense of being utterly out of it weighed me down, and I asked myself what the future would be."

This complaint sounds somewhat disingenuous, to say the least, since the younger generation (in the form of the avant-garde) had clearly begun to embrace him, if not as their acknowledged master then as one of their most influential older allies (though it is true that he did not feel entirely comfortable in either role). James's sense of being utterly unwanted probably had more to do with his uneasy relations with literary men in his own and Howells' generation, for it was rooted in his old fear, dating back to the pre-theater years, that "periodical publication is practically closed to me—I'm the last hand that the magazines in this country, or in the U.S., seem to want." He pretends to be convinced that production is the only remedy and expresses pleasure at finding that Howells has recommended the very same course. "It is exactly, moreover, what I meant to admirably do—and have meant, all along, about this time to be into the motion of," he writes, perhaps rereading his past intentions in the light of present realities. James's literary future begins to take on even more definite shape when he decides that "'production'... means production of the little *book,* pure and simple—independent of any antecedent appearance...." He insists that he has "always hated the magazine form, magazine conditions and manners, and much of the magazine company" and reveals his dislike of "the hurried little subordinate part that one plays in the catchpenny picture-book—and the negation of all literature that the picture-book imposes." Suddenly everything falls into place. "It is about the distinctness of one's *book*-position," James concludes, "that you have so substantially reassured me; and I mean to do far better work than ever I have done before." Triumphantly, James proceeds to announce that he is "bursting with ideas and subjects—though the act of composition is with me more and more slow, painful and difficult. I shall never again write a long novel, but I hope to write six immortal short ones—and some tales of the same quality."[1]
The pretext provided by this letter to his old friend and literary advisor helped James launch his effort to make the difficult psychological re-entry back into the Anglo-American literary establishment from which he had temporarily departed. As we read this reply to Howells, we can watch James as he attempts to recover not only his balance but his sense of direction. When we hear him ask Howells to forgive "the cynical egotism of these remarks" and then qualify that request with the sly parenthetical observation, "the fault of which is in your own sympathy,"[2] we know that he has succeeded in restoring, at least for the moment, the characteristic playfulness and self-confidence of his epistolary

voice. The project of recovering, or rather discovering, his characteristic narrative voice and presence was to become his most sustained and difficult task during the remainder of his career.

James's sense of being "utterly out of it" can also be attributed, at least in part, to the marked changes which the traditional literary scene had undergone during his absence from it (at least in novelistic form) during the previous five years. To begin with, proponents of an international copyright agreement had finally succeeded in getting legislation passed in July of 1891 which made Anglo-American literary piracy illegal. Their success closed off one of the main sources of cheap books in England as well as in America, thus adding to the increasing pressure (now being exerted upon the regular book trade as well as the circulating libraries by both the ever-expanding British reading public and a growing number of authors) to dispense with the mandatory multi-volume format for the novel. While novel-readers resented the three-decker largely because of its inordinate price, literary producers, led by George Moore, were coming to regard it as an artificial format which obstructed the development of the novel as a genre and inhibited technical experimentation. In June 1894, the libraries capitulated to the mounting pressure by issuing circulars which stipulated that on January 1, 1895, new regulations would be enforced, regulations which, in effect, signalled the demise of the three-decker. Under this escalating assault, the number of triple-deckers published in England had already fallen from almost 200 in 1884 to 52 in 1895; and by 1897, only 4 new three-deckers would be issued. As Holbrook Jackson emphasizes, the collapse of the three-decker represented more than the demise of a format, it constituted "the capitulation of a type of novel."[3]

James's position on the question of international copyright was quite clear. He had taken the issue seriously enough to address a letter to the American Copyright League in November of 1887 urging the speedy passage of copyright legislation. Referring to the false and dishonorable position of the American reading public with regard to pirated British authors, he wrote: "It is precisely because we *are* a universally reading public that it is of the greatest importance there should be no impediment to our freedom." Such an impediment was the lack of a copyright agreement, he argued, since we forfeit our right of frank criticism when we don't pay for our "bargains."[4] James's attitude towards the triple-decker is more difficult to ascertain. In her account of the extremely rapid disappearance of the three-decker and the gradual demise of Mudie's, Guinevere Griest notes that "serious writers like Henry James" had generally remained silent and suggests that "although he [James] recognized and used the form, he did not rely on the libraries as the popular writers did." This statement is somewhat misleading, for it implies not only that James was never a popular writer but also that he was not dependent upon the circulating libraries *because* of this lack of popularity. As we have seen, James's cosmopolitan literary ambitions as well as the size of his English editions had been inextricably interwoven with the English circulating library system up to, if not during, his period of experimentation with the drama. In fact Clarence Gohdes, in his study of British interest in American literature, found that as late as 1896 James ranked second only to Howells when judged by the number of titles listed in Mudie's catalogue.[5] For James the British public *was* primarily, though certainly *not* exclusively, the clientele of the circulating libraries. During his first thirty years as a writer, he had not only recognized and used the three-decker format, but had more or less relied upon Mudie's to insure a stable (if not sensational) sale as well as constant (if not wide) circulation for his novels in book form. James's lack of direct comment on the three-decker's demise thus becomes somewhat problematic, though it can be attributed (at least to some extent) to his immersion in the world of the theater during these years and his preoccupation with his own difficulties. Yet he seems to have been indulging in his characteristic mode of exaggeration when he referred to himself as "utterly out of it," for his vow that he would "never again write a *long* novel" reflected an acute awareness of the altered conditions of his trade. (He may also have been attempting to solicit Howells' professional advice and assistance, however obliquely.)

Perhaps this helps to explain why, in the very month in which the much-publicized ban on three-deckers took effect, James entered into his notebooks a brief outline for another tale of the literary life, "a mate to 'The Death of the Lion,'" which would focus upon these altered conditions. "The Next Time" turns on the contrast between Ray Limbert, an artist who repeatedly fails to write a popular novel, and his sister-in-law, Jane Highmore, a writer who repeatedly fails to produce anything *but* highly successful three-deckers. In combination with the finished story the original sketch, penned just weeks after the opening night of *Guy Domville,* not only sheds important light on James's knowledge of and attitude towards the evolving literary scene, but reveals the way in which he perceived its relation to both his recent experience with the London stage and his own more remote past. James begins by objectifying himself as "the poor man, the artist, the man of letters, who all his life is trying, if only to get a living—to do something *vulgar,* to take the measure of the huge, flat foot of the public." He then recalls his own "frustrated ambition ... how, already 20 years ago, when I was in Paris writing letters to the *N.Y. Tribune,* Whitelaw Reid wrote to me to ask me virtually *that*—to make 'em baser and paltrier, to make them as vulgar as he could, to make them, as he called it, more 'personal.'" The novelist even implies that his entire career may be summed up by this single story when he laments: "Twenty years ago, and so it has been ever, till the other night, Jan. 5th, the *première* of *Guy Domville.*"[6] When James identifies the possibility of "a small tragedy of the *vie littéraire*" in Limbert's failure to make "a sow's ear out of a silk purse," he is appropriating for fictional purposes an inverted proverb which he had used only recently in a letter to William describing his own failure as a dramatist: "And yet I had tried so to meet them [the British public]! But you can't make a sow's ear out of a silk purse." Henry was to repeat this bit of homespun philosophy in the completed tale, where he has the narrator utter it in response to "poor Limbert's" unsuccessful attempts to turn himself into a popular novelist. However, in "The Next Time" what began as a retrospective self-assessment now has the force of prophecy. In this transformation we may find a clue to James's complex and somewhat contradictory attitude towards both the altered literary scene and his own future as a professional novelist.[7]

In this tale of the literary life, James obviously endows Ray Limbert with some of his own artistic ability and pecuniary ambition (perhaps obsession would be a better word); and most commentators have duly noted that when James describes Limbert's reaction to being "sacked" by periodicals not once but twice on what amounts to a charge of insufficient vulgarity, he is drawing upon his own experience with both the *Tribune* and the London stage (or rather his own version of these two "failures"). While the master predictably expresses nothing but contempt for the reading public and their failure to appreciate Limbert's subtle artistry, he strikes a new note in his ironic portrait of Mrs. Highmore, a manufacturer of three-deckers who yearns to be "an exquisite failure" like Limbert, "but of course only once." While the figure of Jane Highmore is rather mechanically drawn (and may therefore reflect James's growing tendency to construct his plots around pairs of opposites as much as his carefully cultivated habit of observing changes in the literary and social scene), she does represent a new type of literary producer, one who recognizes the *non*-pecuniary advantages and possibilities of a novel which fails to sell. Mrs. Highmore astutely realizes that there are members of the contemporaneous public (of which the narrator is an excellent example) who regard success as "vulgar" and "prosaic" and whose esteem can be won only at the cost of pecuniary failure, precisely because pecuniary failure represents rejection by the usual (i.e., the "vulgar") fiction-reading public. As she shrewdly notes: "There was something a failure was, a failure in the market, that a success somehow wasn't." While James does have his anonymous narrator qualify Mrs. Highmore's logic by pointing out that theoretically "a book sold might easily be as glorious as a book unsold," his own contempt for things that have "done well" merely reinforces her conviction that "a failure *now* could make—oh, with the aid of immense talent of course, for there were failures—and failures—such a reputation!"[8] In several interesting respects, James's contrast between these two members of "poor Limbert's" public is a variation on the theme of "The Death of the Lion," a tale in which another narrator (a perceptive and presumably loyal reader of Neil Paraday) unsuccessfully (or ineffectively?) seeks to protect the great writer from the exploitative adulation and reverberation of Mrs. Wimbush and her fashionable circle of literary lionizers. In both tales the pressure of the stupid or (as James preferred to call it) "babyish" public constitutes an overtly hostile and ultimately fatal factor. In "The Death of the Lion" this pressure is embodied by the threat posed to Paraday's artistic conscience and consciousness by the superficial adulation of a voracious public looking for ever-newer forms of sensation and titillation (although there is a slight hint of negligence if not outright complicity on the part of the young disciple who narrates the tale). However in the later story, James shifted his focus in order to examine a distinctively modern literary phenomenon, the plight of an artist who is caught between the conflicting demands of the general public and its archenemy, the literary avant-garde.

The more subtle seductions of this elite public are represented by the super-subtle critic who narrates "The Next Time." He is perhaps the first full-blown example in James's work of the type of reader who prizes commercial failure almost as much as he values artistic talent and who withholds literary recognition from any writer tainted with anything so vulgar as pecuniary success. As he disarmingly reveals: "I had cultivated the queer habit of seeing nothing in certain celebrities, or seeing overmuch in an occasional nobody, and of judging from a point of view that . . . mostly remained perverse and obscure." The avant-garde criticism which the narrator writes for "a little magazine" is part of "the great reaction," an aesthetic "protest against the chatty" which was gaining strength in England at precisely this time and which had itself become fashionable enough to inspire the kind of pseudo-avant-garde enterprises which James satirizes when he sketches Mr. Bousefield. Bousefield is the proprietor of a "high-class monthly" who hires Limbert as his editor because he sees "the great reaction coming" and wants to get on the bandwagon of "true literature." However, Limbert's failure to please Mr. Bousefield's subscribers qualifies the extent to which the public at large is really willing or able to assimilate "true literature" and "real criticism."[9] The mutual antagonism between these two audiences, *"le gros public"* and the avant-garde, is expressed on the one hand by the narrator's contempt for the circulating libraries and their triple-deckers and, on the other, by the damaging effect which his praise ironically has upon the sales of Limbert's novels. (Appropriately enough, it is Limbert's refusal to stop publishing the narrator's criticism in the monthly which determines Mr. Bousefield to sack him.)

Running throughout the tale are two corresponding and mutually exclusive definitions of literary success. As Limbert defines the "vulgar" version: "When a book's right it's right . . . When it sells it sells—it brings money like potatoes or beer. . . . Success [in the artistic sense] be hanged!—I want to sell." Limbert's fate, however, is to enact the avant-garde version of the typical success story, for in spite of his protracted efforts to the contrary, "The Major Key," his valiant effort to woo the general public, ironically amounts to "merely" another "great performance" rather than a "great success." One cannot help thinking of *Guy Domville* when reading that this novel "converted readers into friends and friends into lovers; it placed the author... but it shrank to obscurity the account of sales eventually rendered." (It is interesting to note that this passage distinctly echoes the prospectus of the *Yellow Book* in which the editors had promised: "It will be a *book*... that every book-lover will love at first sight; a book that will make book-lovers of many who are now indifferent to books." In fact, it is possible to read the entire story as a thinly-disguised satire on this little magazine and its editor, the worshipful Henry Harland.) As in James's own case, everyone agrees that Limbert's position is "quite assured"; and we may even hear an echo of William Dean Howells' comforting remarks when Mrs. Highmore, that "repository of knowing hints" and "esoteric learning" about the market, periodically reassures her brother-in-law about the quality of his reputation (if not the quantity of his sales): "You stand alone, dear Ray; you stand absolutely alone!"[10] The ironic tone in which this bit of information is reported by the narrator suggests that James could not resist the opportunity to comment, however indirectly, on Howells' ability to afford (in all senses of the word) such an elevated point of view.

Both the narrator and Mrs. Highmore can thus be seen as embodiments of the categories of readers most likely to be appreciative of James and his work, for together they represent an ironic composite portrait of James's own highly mixed contemporaneous audience. She evokes three types: the popular writers and sympathetic readers whose literary aspirations outpaced their actual abilities and the loyal readers who remained faithful to "the master" primarily due to friendship or family ties rather than because of any innate affinity with his artistic intentions. (As we have seen, all three varieties of readers had rallied quickly to James's side during the *Guy Domville* incident with assurances regarding his "distinguished" literary position.) The narrator, by contrast, is a highly discriminating and intensely individualistic spectator, the very type, at least in James's work, of the elite (and possibly even the "perverse") avant-garde reader who considers public failure a necessary precondition for (though not a definition of) private or genuine artistic success. As James's post-opening-night letters testify, this point of view had become extremely seductive to him: it not only coincided with his longstanding distaste for reverberation but provided him with a convenient rationale for his humiliating failure to achieve popularity on the stage. Yet there is a subtle suggestion of complicity on the part of the narrator in regard to Limbert's failure and even his death, a suggestion rooted in the critic's apparently innocuous admission that they had once loved the same woman—now Limbert's wife (whom he is desperately trying to support). The discriminating reader thus has ample ground for suspecting the narrator's possible perversity of motive when he greets each of Limbert's productions as yet another new masterpiece, thereby dooming them to pecuniary failure. In this highly indirect manner James was able to dramatize and express his own inability to rid himself of suspicion towards the avant-garde and his refusal to endorse thoroughly this new literary phenomenon. The fact that "The Next Time" was itself published in a little magazine, the *Yellow Book,* adds an extra dimension to the levels of irony in the tale, especially when we recall that James had experienced acute discomfort in regard to appearing in this avant-garde format just a year earlier. On the basis of his letter to Howells, we can surmise that he agreed to this reappearance in the *Yellow Book* at least in part because he feared that other magazine outlets in both countries would be closed to him. Yet unlike "The Middle Years" or even "The Death of the Lion," both previously published in little-magazine format, "The Next Time" strikes a new note and suggests that James now saw himself as being faced with dangers (as well as opportunities) on two literary fronts. Although he continued to worry about being ignored or misunderstood by the "babyish" novel-reading public, he began to betray an increasing ambivalence in regard to the possibility that his work (as well as his reputation) might be appropriated by the English-speaking avant-garde. (James himself tended to use the French term *raffinés,* though they were commonly called aesthetes.)

Later that year, in October of 1895, James entered into his notebook a preliminary sketch for another tale of the literary life which focused almost exclusively on the latent antagonism not between an unpopular author and *"le gros public"* but between a super-subtle author and three equally subtle readers, two of whom are professional reviewers. Following James's lead in the Prefaces and supported by the notebook entries themselves, most critics (including F. O. Matthiessen and Leon Edel) have interpreted "The Figure in the Carpet" as a "plea for mature criticism" in the face of what James later referred to as the Anglo-American public's "so marked collective mistrust of anything like close or analytic appreciation."[11] James's sense of himself as an utterly misunderstood author is usually taken so for granted that it tends to obscure those elements in this notebook entry, amplified in the completed tale, which suggest that James was fascinated by (and perhaps even trying out) a unique variation on this role, that of the novelist who prefers *not* to be understood, at least in any conventional sense. Although James begins his notebook sketch by emphasizing the critics' general inability to apprehend the secret which "pervades and controls and animates" Hugh Vereker's novels (a subject in which James sees a "lovely chance for fine irony on the subject of that [critical] fraternity"), he soon becomes more interested in an entirely different phenomenon: the *effect* which the revelation of the existence of Vereker's "secret" intention has upon the career and the consciousness of three particularly astute (if not ideal) readers.[12]

In the completed tale, we quickly learn that the two male readers are journalists employed by *The Middle,* a weekly of sufficiently "vulgar" quality, and that the precocious female reader, Gwendolen Erme, has published a triple-decker at the tender age of nineteen. Yet in spite of the fact that they are initially presented in the character of mere literary hacks, all three readers are converted (in the language of "The Next Time") if not into lovers then into singularly obsessed friends (two of them actually do marry in the course of the tale). The subject of their mutual obsession and the agent of their conversion is not (as in James's previous tale) the publication of a new novel by their author but their passionate desire to penetrate his mysterious secret. Vereker himself is thoroughly implicated in their strange transformation. The literary master's uncanny ability to pique the narrator's curiosity through his calculated decision to divulge the existence, but *not* the content, of his secret intention belies his own carefully cultivated pose of indifference towards the reading public. Interestingly enough, a careful reading of this tale reveals that, contrary to regarding himself as a failure, Vereker sees himself as a writer who has unexpectedly achieved a significant degree of success independent of "popularity." As the narrator discovers, Vereker has suddenly found himself in an extremely awkward position: he has become "in a manner the fashion; the critics at least had put on a spurt and caught up with him."[13] Although the narrator's version of Vereker's assessment of his literary position is certainly open to questions of reliability, it is precisely the younger man's confidence that he has "unveiled" Vereker's mystery (in a review of his "latest") which stimulates the author's somewhat perverse desire to (re-)mystify his aggressive reader. We may well begin to wonder whether James had recently found himself in the novel (and extremely uncomfortable) position of having to receive similar assurances from his own disciples in the younger generation. In this context it is worth noting that one of them, Jonathan Sturges, was staying with James when he entered the first sketch for this tale into his notebooks on October 24th, and that James records no objective donnée for the tale, an omission which often indicates an autobiographical origin. (However, it was during this very visit that Sturges provided James with the donnée for his late masterpiece, *The Ambassadors.*)[14]

Vereker's insistence upon the existence of a figure in the fictional carpet which is his life's work becomes the tempting bait in the ensuing critical chase, much as James's similar insistence throughout his New York Edition Prefaces would later inspire a veritable industry of James criticism. Whether or not such a secret actually exists, the conception of its existence serves Vereker well: it provides him with an irresistible claim upon the attention of his rapt audience of three (to the exclusion of almost everything else) and brings out their latent and highly contagious potential for super-subtlety. As Vereker puts it to the narrator: "You're anything but a plain man yourself, and the very *raison d'être* of you all is that you're little demons of subtlety."[15] By creating a felt need in these three readers which only he can satisfy, Vereker not only transforms reading into an elaborate rite of initiation but also creates a unique demand for his work which makes up in the quality of its intensity for what it lacks in quantity. The very keynote of his appeal is its secret, its exclusive, its "initiated" quality. Thus Vereker's second chance comes not in the form of another novel, a "second manner," or a fashionable failure, but in the ability of his fictional secret to generate, restore, and protect his "mystery," his aura of inexhaustible meaning.

Such were the rarified rewards (both personal and professional) if James was prepared to confine himself to an elite avant-garde audience; but he appears to have been unable to scale his literary ambitions down to fit this tempting but limited role. As had been the case with Flaubert and his circle in the 1870s and 1880s, there were many points of convergence between James and the Anglo-American aesthetes of the 1890s: their elevation of art to the status of a private religion, their emphasis upon literary form and style, their distaste for the merely conventional, their transformation of the habit of reading into an act of initiation, and (most importantly) their opposition to the taste of a reading public which consumed quantities of historical romances, mistook journalism for literature, and liked all its i's dotted. James seems to have realized that it was precisely this sense of shared opposition which made him so appealing to the younger generation; yet this awareness did not prevent him from continuing to woo the taste of the general public, however ineptly. Once again, it was not merely a question of his unwillingness to sacrifice the pecuniary rewards which only popular success could guarantee, although making money was to continue to figure as one of his prime acknowledged motives for his incredible rate of literary production. (It became especially important after 1897, when he purchased Lamb House in Rye and began furnishing it as his home.) James's continuing reluctance to identify himself exclusively (or even primarily) with the literary avant-garde testifies instead to the fact that he refused to give up a lingering faith, however shaken, in the possibility that he could capture the attention and educate the imagination of the *un*initiated, the public at large. Yet given the reception of both *Guy Domville* and the short stories which he had been publishing, often in little-magazine format, during and immediately after his theater years, James had good reason to fear that his work might be perceived as addressing itself exclusively to the super-subltle ranks of the *raffinés,* thereby isolating him from the attention (and blocking his access to the imagination) of the more traditional segment of the Anglo-American reading public.

Over the years, James had come to expect that his novels would be criticized for their tendency towards psychological analysis, their emphasis upon execution at the expense of incident and plot, and their difficulty; but one wonders how he reacted when, in the nineties, some reviewers began to attribute these characteristics not so much to his personal stylistic idiosyncracies or to his unique conception of the novel as to his enlistment in the ranks of the "decadent" Anglo-American avant-garde. As early as 1893, one reviewer had responded to the publication of a collection of James's short stories, *The Real Thing,* with the complaint that the style was artificial and dilettantish, "the very flower of the *fin de siècle* conventionality..." In his review of *Essays in London,* published in the same year, another critic suggested that James's actual (if not intended) audience was restricted to his fellow professionals, for his was "a style which only writers could fully savor and enjoy." When James collected his tales of the literary life and combined them with several other short stories for publication in book form, the reaction ran along similar lines. For one reviewer in the *Atlantic,* the four stories in *Terminations* (1895)—"The Death of the Lion" "The Coxon Fund," "The Middle Years," and "The Altar of the Dead"—confirmed his sense of James's implicit disdain for the common reader as manifested in "his utter disregard of his reader's time..." Furthermore, when "The Figure in the Carpet," "Glasses," "The Next Time," and "The Way It Came" appeared together under the title *Embarassments* in the following year, the favorable notices were punctuated by several reviews which explicitly classed James as a "decadent." (According to Stanley Weintraub, it was *Terminations* which converted Logan Pearsall Smith, "a young Oxonian of Quaker background," into one of James's most devoted disciples.)[16]

Perhaps this helps to explain why, in February of 1896, James decided to turn one of his unpublished plays into a fictional potboiler. Possibly at James's suggestion, his friend Mrs. W. K. Clifford had approached Clement Shorter, editor of the *Illustrated London News,* and indicated that the author might be willing to adapt himself to Shorter's journalistic conditions. When Shorter expressed interest in publishing such a serial, James quickly accepted all of the editor's terms—except for the fee. Yet James's discomfort with this bargain found indirect expression in his inability to resist the distancing gesture of using quotation marks when he coupled his request for more money with his assurance that the story would be "energetically designed to meet your [Shorter's] requirements of a 'love story.'" By serializing this first post-theater novel in an illustrated periodical which made such an unabashed appeal to the lowest common denominator of the taste of the British public, James may have been trying to reassure himself as well as the fiction-reading public that he had not joined the ranks of the avant-garde. In was also an easy way to make a quick £300.[17]

When it is not totally ignored by those contemporary critics who have studied James's post-theater novels,[18] *The Other House* is usually pointed to as an example of Ibsen's influence upon his work; and it is interesting to note that the book version of the serial was brought out in England by William Heinemann, James's theater friend and fellow Ibsenite. Heinemann had also issued *Terminations* and *Embarrassments* and was to remain James's primary British publisher during the closing years of the nineteenth century. While Michael Egan charitably refers to this novel as Henry James's "first full-blown Ibsen tragedy," Leon Edel's appraisal of it as "an Ibsen play without Ibsen's morality—or his insight" seems much more balanced.[19] James had fulfilled his promise to Shorter ("I shall endeavor to be thrilling") by combining the elements of a love story with those of a murder mystery. Although he provided his readers with some powerful dialogue and toned down the melodramatic aspects of the plot by substituting an "off stage" drowning for poisoning as the mode of Effie Bream's death, violence remained the keynote of the plot, effectively giving away the book's identity as only James's latest (and one of his least subtle) attempts to give the public what he thought it wanted.

Measured by this intent, *The Other House* was a relative success, for Matthiessen and Murdock point out that despite Shorter's claim regarding the serial's unpopularity, *The Other House* went through two editions in book form in 1896 and 1897. However, measured by James's promise to himself (as recorded in his first post-opening night notebook entry) to "take up my *own* old pen again—the pen of all my old unforgettable efforts and sacred struggles,"[20] to dip, in short, into the ink of art, *The Other House* was a failure. During the preceding five years, the theater (as opposed to "the drama") and its audience had provided James with an alternate target at which he could aim (and towards which he could channel) his growing animosity towards the conventional reading public and the self-contempt which he experienced when he tried to meet its taste. James's plays had suffered accordingly, for the proportion of his ambition and the intensity of his determination to succeed under such conditions had left the characters in his plays little or no room in which to live and breathe and move freely. Thus James was hardly an entirely innocent party to the murder of "the sacrificed little play," as he referred to *Guy Domville* in a letter to William;[21] and on some level, he bore as much responsibility for the "butchering" of his plays as the theater managers and their "vulgar" audiences (though there is no evidence that he ever directly confronted or openly acknowledged the fact of his own complicity).

When, in *The Other House,* James makes Tony Bream acknowledge his responsibility for the death of his daughter Effie (even though Bream knows quite well that Rose Armiger has actually committed the murder of the "butchered," "tortured" child), it is almost as if James himself, in the very midst of wreaking further violence on his work and his own fictional progeny, were indirectly confessing his personal guilt in regard to *his* "butchered" children. Appropriately enough, Bream's confession is prompted by his realization that

Rose has sacrificed the child in order to provide him with a second chance at love by enabling him to marry her; though he also recognizes that Rose's motives are hardly altruistic.[22] (He had promised his dying wife in Rose's presence never to remarry as long as their daughter, Effie, lives.) This outright violence, which is uncharacteristic of James's post-theater work (the suicide in *Watch and Ward* and the deaths of Roderick Hudson and Hyacinth Robinson are early precedents), can be explained partly in terms of James's intended audience: he had endeavored to be thrilling. However, the mechanical way in which he rendered this scenario for a play into a sensationalized serial was itself an act of violence; and, as such, it could only have intensified his own sense of guilt and complicity. In making this scenario serve as a makeshift bridge between the theatrical scene and the literary marketplace, James unwittingly carried over some of the most unpleasant psychological baggage of the past five years to his own "other house," the house of fiction.

But there is ample evidence that James was also attempting to bridge the gap between the two "houses" in a less mechanical and more innovative manner. His notebook entries of this period, many of which record the germs of what would later become the novels of his "major phase," are punctuated by several moving passages of self-communion and retrospection which dramatize his intense desire not only to get back into relation with the art of the novel but also to discover the meaning and the moral of the theater years. He had complained to William about the precious time he wasted during those years, "a pitiful, tragic bankruptcy of hours that might have been rendered retroactively golden" if only *Guy Domville* had been successful with London theater audiences.[23] Yet in the privacy of his notebooks, we can watch the novelist as he tries to render these years "retroactively golden" in a sense other than the pecuniary one, which he had used repeatedly as a justification to William for his theater venture. Perhaps the most striking example of such a passage occurs in an entry made on February 14, 1895. Initially addressing himself to the question of how to handle "the adulterine element" when writing for an American magazine *(Harper's)*, James encourages himself to begin a full scenario of the action. At the mention of the charged word "scenario," "compensations and solutions" suddenly seem to appear. James is moved to ask himself:

> Has a *part* of all this wasted passion and squandered time (of the last 5 years) been simply a precious lesson, taught me in that roundabout and devious, that cruelly expensive, way, *of the singular value for a narrative plan too* of the (I don't know *what* adequately to call it) divine principle of the Scenario?

James's search in this entry for "the moral of the whole unspeakable, the whole tragic experience" and his determination to convert "my infinite little loss into an almost infinite little gain" by treating "the divine principle of the Scenario" as "the thing to live by"[24] has inspired several modern studies which treat the novels that he wrote in the remaining years of the nineteenth century primarily (if not exclusively) as experiments in technique, attempts to apply this single principle and realize his dramatic intentions. Indeed, passages such as the above give ample license for these endeavors and provide contemporaneous evidence to support James's own retrospective treatment of *The Spoils of Poynton, What Maisie Knew,* and *The Awkward Age* in the Prefaces to the New York Edition of his work as formal experiments, efforts to apply his knowledge of dramatic technique to the art of the novel.[25]

Yet James's eloquent remarks regarding this "divine principle," remarks which are reminiscent of his theoretical (and largely impractical) distinction between the theater and the drama, may have served the more immediate purpose of temporarily disguising and distracting him (and, ultimately, contemporary scholars as well) from another highly experimental aspect of his post-theater fiction—"the adulterine element." As a comparison between his subsequent notebook entries and his completed novels reveals, despite all James's talk about (and reliance upon) the use of a detailed written plan or "scenario" for his fiction, he often ended up by deviating markedly from his original intentions.[26] Quite significantly, many (if not most) of these deviations occur as a direct or indirect result of the "delicate" subject matter which he now began to broach in his fiction; and, approached as a group, the novels themselves suggest that the question of how to *handle* such subject matter had become the most perplexing one for James during this period in his career. Most critics have been struck by the "preoccupation with houses and children," especially female children, which pervades James's post-theater fiction; and in his biography of James, Leon Edel even describes this entire series of novels as "a terrible world of blighted houses and of blighted childhoods—of little girls—and a strange world of female adolescence" in which James himself assumes "the protective disguises of girlhood." However, Edel does not attempt to explore or explain the link between this preoccupation and James's experiments with form. Because he is looking for a pattern of psychological regression, Edel insists upon a Freudian reading of James's evident fascination with the figure of the young female, contending that James assumed "the disguise of femininity" as part of a post-theater retreat from the harsh realities of the adult world and out of a desire to escape the psychic risks of assertive masculinity. Edel's psycholanalytic bias makes it difficult if not impossible for him to reconcile his own recognition of (and admiration for) James's "technical progress" during this period with his equal insistence upon his subject's psychic "regression." He is thus forced to posit a curious split in the novelist's consciousness: "His mind moved forward—his feelings returned to childhood hurts."[27]

This analysis fails to take note of a much more obvious possibility, namely that James's preoccupation with houses and children was a direct result of his renewed commitment to artistic freedom in general and his own artistic development in particular. It seems quite likely that the conspicuously experimental nature of these novels is inextricably tied up with the theme of providing for the young precisely because this problem, exemplified by the figure of the unmarried female, represented for James both the past limitations upon and the future possibilities of his career as a novelist in a literary scene which assumed her presence and a culture which treated her as both the representative and arbiter of the taste of its reading public. Only four years earlier in his influential essay, "Criticism and Fiction," William Dean Howells had defended this social and literary convention, forcefully reminding Anglo-American writers that the English-speaking novel, unlike its continental counterpart, had to be acceptable reading for the "Young Girl." Likening American magazine proprieties to the "sacred laws" which governed the profession of "a physician or a priest," he had nevertheless gone on to predict that "if by some prodigious miracle, any American should now arise to treat [guilty love] on the level of Anna Karenina or Madame Bovary, he would be absolutely sure of success, and of fame and gratitude as great as these books have won for their authors."[28] In this context, James's sudden fictional interest in young children, especially girls, and his simultaneous experiments with "delicate" subject matter can be seen as an attempt to fulfill Howells' prediction as well as a resumption of his own ongoing struggle to subvert those Anglo-American reading conventions which he had challenged implicitly in many of his earlier novels and explicitly in "The Art of Fiction."

In that essay James had called upon his fellow novelists to liberate the Anglo-American novel from all a priori strictures, insisting that any subject could be made suitable for and interesting to the English-speaking public, if only it were handled in the proper manner. As he pointedly noted, nowhere was the freedom of the English novel more proscribed than on the question of sexual relations. Given this fact, it is worth remembering that only under the double pressure of James's intense desire to redeem the wasted labor of the theater years and his need to come to terms with what he now referred to (somewhat in the manner of a scientist) as "the adulterine element" when writing for an American magazine did the scenario begin to *appear* as "the key that, working in the same *general* way fits the complicated chambers of *both* the dramatic and the narrative lock."[29] Ironically, it was to be adultery (or "guilty love," to use Howells' chaste phrase), one of the most conventional of theatrical subjects, which would eventually bridge the gap between James's dramatic and literary intentions. However, it would take him several years to develop a strategy which would enable him to handle that subject in a manner that was acceptable to the traditional Anglo-American public yet unconventional enough to satisfy even his most avant-garde readers. As James had already acknowledged, the question of "delicate" subject matter was really a problem of audience, and it would have hardly surprised him to learn that Howells had followed his rosy prediction with a sobering question: "But what editor of what American magazine would print such a story?" The highly respectable American editor had answered his own question in the negative, concluding that the novelist "must again submit to conditions. If he wishes to publish such a story (supposing him to have once written it), he must publish it as a book."[30]

Perhaps because he had submitted so thoroughly (if not altogether willingly) to "vulgar" theatrical conditions, James now seemed bent upon declaring his literary independence by forcing the American magazine public to accept fiction which did not conform to their conventional expectations. Yet if James's post-theater works can thus be approached and understood as blows struck for the freedom of the novel, they must also be viewed as victims of their creator's continuing obsession with the drama and casualties of his running battle with the fiction-reading public; for the novels of the late 1890s, like the plays which preceded them, would to some extent be sacrificed to their author's unfulfilled theatrical ambitions and would be treated by James as laboratory cases upon which he could experiment. Just as he had tried (unsuccessfully) to turn himself into a popular dramatist, James now set out to transform the house of fiction into a theater and the reading public into a substitute audience. And, whether or not it directly provided him with an experimental compositional structure and technique (as several critics have argued), the "dramatic analogy" did supply James with a suitable formal motive for stationing his central characters, most of them female, in a strategic position between his authorial imagination and his readers. This sleight of hand would conveniently minimize the substantial risks of authorial exposure which such a project entailed, for James sensed that if he wanted to defy the expectations of the magazine public, he would need to shield himself behind the protective screen of his characters' consciousness. Intentionally or not, he would in effect deny his post-theater characters the kind of authorial protection which only his immediate narrative presence could afford. In so doing, he was to succeed in introducing "delicate" subject matter into his fiction, but only at the cost of prolonging the violence of the theater years, for he would expose and even abandon them, however unwittingly, to the limited (and limiting) imagination of what he had only recently denounced as a vulgar and brutal public.[31]

In this light James's next novel, *The Spoils of Poynton* (1897), figures as the transitional link between his plays, the stories of writers and artists which he wrote during the theater years, and his post-theater experiments with officially taboo subject matter. Although this work does not deal with adultery, its sustained defiance of literary convention altered James's relationship with his fictional progeny, initiating a reign of what he himself would later refer to as "terror without pity." The novel begins by focusing on Mrs. Gereth, a widow who has made a "career" out of collecting fine old things. Mrs. Gereth's revulsion from Waterbath (the home of the vulgar Brigstocks) and her fear of having to surrender Poynton (her own magnificent house and the precious collection of objects which it contains and protects) to a product of Waterbath, Mona Brigstock, is in many respects a projection of her creator's horror at the prospect of having to serve up the first real fruit of "his own old pen" and his new "scenic system" to a Philistine reading public which had never demonstrated any ability to appreciate the more subtle creations of his imagination. Not unlike the aging novelists and youthful disciples in James's tales of the literary life, this middle-aged widow and her young friend, Fleda Vetch, are drawn to one another in the opening scene of the novel by a mutual horror of British Philistinism (embodied here by Waterbath) and "their common need to escape" its systematic ugliness. James's sympathy with Mrs. Gereth takes the practical form of providing her with Fleda (an observer and confidante whose sympathy mirrors his own) and endowing her with a determination to resist "the cruel English custom of the expropriation of the lonely mother" (which in turn takes the form of a plot to prevent her son Owen from marrying Mona Brigstock). In return, Mrs. Gereth's determination to resist this vulgar *social* convention not only promises James an opportunity to defy *literary* convention by focusing on a type other than the ever-present "young unmarried female" but also provides him with a plot and theme which circumvents (and indeed subverts) that equally vulgar convention, the love story.

Buoyed up by her idea of transforming Fleda into an ideal daughter-in-law, a wife for Owen who will appreciate the quality of Poynton's contents if not its somewhat obtuse owner, the masterful Mrs. Gereth proceeds to "initiate" Fleda, a young person "whose only treasure was her subtle mind," into the aesthetic pleasures of Poynton. The plot, at least as Mrs. Gereth conceives of it, hardly has the makings of a conventional love story, for she takes Fleda up with the rather perverse idea that her subtle young friend will be willing to marry her "stupid" son not out of love or even affection but in order to inherit and protect Poynton and its precious objects. Mrs. Gereth's maternal emotions, such as they are, appear to be directed almost exclusively towards her "old things"; like "poor Dencombe" in "The Middle Years," her only passion is for her work. In this respect, her "career" exhibits marked parallels with that of her creator and his fictional artists. All suffer in a strikingly similar way at the hands of the British public, here represented by the Brigstocks and their tasteless daughter (Mona's oversized feet even recall James's notebook reference to his own vain efforts "to take the measure to the huge flat foot of the public").[32] It is also worth noting that James has Mrs. Gereth describe her inability to choose between her precious old things in nautical metaphors which distinctly echo his own reaction, recorded in the Prefaces to his published plays, to the prospect of having to make odious cuts in his plays. ("It was true that when after their return from Ricks they tried to lighten the ship, the great embarrassment was still immutably there, the odiousness of sacrificing the exquisite things one wouldn't take to the exquisite things one would.")[33]

James's desire to shield himself from the disapproval of the reading public by using Mrs. Gereth as his stand-in and buffer in this novel thus resulted in a rather curious substitution. However unintentionally, he was beginning to transform the Jamesian novel by replacing the conventional types and themes of Anglo-American fiction with the character-types and themes which he had developed in his stories of writers and artists—with one crucial exception. Instead of making his central figure a male and an artist, in *The Spoils* (as well as the two novels which immediately follow it) James began to cast females in the central roles. As *The Spoils* opens, its "plot" hinges on Mrs. Gereth's reluctance to relinquish her authority as well as her life's work (Poynton is referred to as "the record of a life") to a younger generation which, like James, she ostensibly "knows not and mainly prizes not." Her plan to supplant Mona Brigstock with Fleda Vetch, her own carefully trained disciple, makes her a reflection of as well as a surrogate plotter for her author and establishes their identity of motive. Similarly, Fleda's initial devotion to the mistress of Poynton and her appreciation of Poynton's contents distinctly recalls Dr. Hugh and other sympathethic readers in James's tales; but the resemblance soon begins to break down. If Fleda can be viewed as Mrs. Gereth's disciple, she must be seen as a decidedly independent version of that type, for she quickly begins to sense that her "master's" genuine and touching devotion to her fine old things masks a chilling relish for the sheer exercise of power and the collection and manipulation not only of furniture but of people, herself included. While Fleda's growing recognition of the darker side of Mrs. Gereth's passionate devotion to the spoils represents a willingness on James's part to probe and acknowledge the potential for exploitation inherent in any master-disciple relationship (as when, for example, he has Fleda reflect quite early in the novel that Mrs. Gereth's "ruling passion had in a manner despoiled her of her humanity"),[34] James prefers to dramatize this recognition (and in effect contain it) by presenting it in terms of Fleda's growing (and rather improbable) love for the obtuse Owen. In this safe and highly conventional guise, Fleda's intransigent opposition to Mrs. Gereth's manipulations of her fellow characters comes to occupy center stage and demand the reader's attention.

It is impossible to determine whether James also intended Fleda's unrequited love for Owen to act as a modest bribe for the attention of the presumably feminine public of the *Atlantic Monthly*, where the novel was to

"The Larger Latitude" 115

appear in serial form. What we do know from the notebooks is that in the process of working out the scenario for this overgrown short story which was fast becoming a novel (and which James feared that Scudder, the editor of the *Atlantic,* would no longer want), he found his material taking an unexpected turn. James's notebooks record his caution to himself "against the drawback of having, in the course of the story determined on something that I had not intended—or had not expected—at the start." He reveals that he has intended "to make Fleda 'fall in love' with Owen, or, to express it *moins banalement,* to represent her as loving him." Yet he also admits that it was *not* his intention to make Owen reciprocate this feeling. "Now, however, I have done so; in my last little go at the thing ... it inevitably took that turn, and I must accept the idea and work it out."[35]

The above passage suggests that from this point on in the composition of the novel, all would depend upon James's ability to *handle* the relationship between Owen and Fleda in an unconventional manner if he was to realize his experimental intentions and fulfill his commitment to artistic innovation. In the notebook passage which immediately follows, it becomes clear that James will call upon Fleda to bear the brunt of this burden. After sketching the outline of a confrontation between the two lovers at Ricks (the modest home of Mrs. Gereth's deceased maiden-aunt which has become her asylum) and noting that the scene will shed a new and negative light on Mrs. Gereth, James observes that

> the whole idea of my thing is that Fleda becomes rather fine, DOES something, distinguishes herself (to the reader), and that this is really almost all that has made the little anecdote worth telling at all. It gives me a lift—an air—and I must make it give me as much of these things as it ever possibly can.

James goes on to map out the events through which he can exert an "irressitible pressure" upon Fleda in order to provide her (and ultimately himself) with a chance to distinguish herself to the reader by exhibiting what amounts to a super-subtle fineness.[36] In the final version of this scene between Fleda and Owen as it appears in the completed novel, Fleda's distinction takes the form of evoking, only to renounce, the cheap and easy opportunity to satisfy her passion which would be virtually guaranteed her were she the creation of a French realist. As she senses for the first time that Owen may reciprocate her love, Fleda is reminded of novels she has read "about gentlemen who on the eve of marriage, winding up the past, had surrendered themselves for the occasion to the influence of a former tie." James informs us through his narrator that Fleda recognizes "something in Owen's behavior now, something in his very face, that suggested a resemblance to one of those gentlemen. But whom and what, in that case, would Fleda herself resemble?" When we learn that "she wasn't a former tie, she wasn't any tie at all; she was only a deep little person for whom happiness was a kind of pearl-diving plunge,"[37] we know that she has begun to shoulder the burdens of Jamesian super-subtlety.

This is only one of several occasions where the novelist makes use of Fleda's acute consciousness of her predicament to dismiss, deflate, or even subvert the clichés of French realism as well as conventional fiction and drama.[38] In a similar fashion, her dialogue is often made to serve the same purpose, as when, later in the novel, Mona's mother melodramatically announces her intention of pleading with Fleda over Owen, only to have Fleda respond, after the slightest of hesitations, "As if I were one of those bad women in a play?"[39] Of course, Fleda must pay a price for the opportunity to enact such an original part in James's unconventional fictional drama. In exchange for being endowed by her creator with an exquisite sensibility and a highly active imagination (not entirely unlike his own), it is her fate to have to *handle* Owen (as well as his mother) in such a manner as to insure that he will go through with his marriage to Mona Brigstock (whom he no longer cares for), despite her own acknowledged love for him (and her unwillingness to become his mistress). This line of behavior understandably strikes Mrs. Gereth (as well as many readers of the novel) as bordering on the perverse; but it is precisely Fleda's rigorous refusal to manipulate others for her own benefit which justifies her creator's confidence in her character. Fleda's sustained performance repays James's investment in her character with interest, for it becomes not only the subject of but the means of focusing (and therefore controlling) his readers' attention. Whether "heroic" or "perverse," Fleda's consistency provides James with a highly original "story" and saves him from the two most vulgar literary conventions, the "indecent" liaison and the happy ending (which his *Atlantic* readers were sure to expect).

Not surprisingly, when Heinemann brought the novel out in book form in 1897, it was greeted with a strange mixture of reluctant praise and ridicule reminiscent in many ways of the peculiar combination of grudging respect and latent resentment which James's two collections of tales, *Terminations* and *Embarrassments,* had recently provoked from Anglo-American critics. The source of this resentment is not difficult to identify. Reviewers felt compelled to acknowledge and pay homage to James's technical mastery and his reputation as an unparalleled literary craftsman (perhaps in an attempt to distinguish themselves from mere journalists and to avoid the reproach of Philistinism). At the same time, most reviewers obviously found the task of reading (and writing about) James's work to be an extremely difficult and time-consuming operation which was further exacerbated by the absence of those usual compensations to the conventional reader of novels (and reviews), the fast-moving plot, the thrilling incident, and the pointed moral. As one anonymous reviewer commented somewhat schizophrenically in the *Bookman*: "One almost maligns the worth of *The Spoils of Poynton* in mentioning the frivolous structure on which it supports nearly three hundred pages." He categorized the work as a "decorous farce," the highlight of which was "the vigorous shoving onslaught" of the Philistine Brigstocks and the resistance of "the bold marauder" (presumably Mrs. Gereth). This same reviewer found Fleda to be "but a poor ally" whose "subtle virtue and refinement" were "so much beyond the needs of the case" that her "little tragedy" came "perilously near to spoiling" the reader's fun.[40]

Another anonymous critic marched straight up to the problem and boldly identified it when he made the following pronouncement in the *Academy*: "Mr. Henry James writes for the few, and belongs to the very few. It is, indeed, almost a pity that so many dunces have been banged, bullied, and frightened into saying that they like the work of Mr. Henry James, but that he is really too subtle." However, he then proceeded to charge that the real problem with James was his insufficient subtlety! "Mr. Henry James is subtle enough to work out the difficult sum [of his characters' difficult choices] correctly; but not subtle enough to rub out the workings on his slate; and leave only the effective answer." Such a strained accusation betrays this critic's fear of sounding like one of James's Philistine detractors, despite the fact that he obviously resents what he considers to be the unrelenting pressure on critics to praise James. The possibility that the process of perception might itself be a subject for the novelist seems never to have crossed this reviewer's "subtle" mind; yet he does manage to put his finger on one of the novel's unique qualities, its characters' seeming perception that they are being watched closely by their creator. The characters in *The Spoils*, observes this reviewer, do "live, and move, and have their being, but they *know all the time* that Mr. Henry James is looking..."[41] Even a somewhat hostile reader could detect the existence of (if not the intent behind) the extreme pressure which James was now beginning to exert upon his characters, especially his central ones.

James was, in effect, attempting to protect his flanks while waging his continuing battle with the taste of the reading public by passing the burden and the risks of exhibited super-subtlety and fineness on to his central characters. But in executing this extremely complicated defensive maneuver (designed to conceal his own highly manipulative presence behind the fictional curtain) James only succeeded in attracting the increasingly perplexed gaze of his audience. His relationship with his characters underwent a similar transformation as a direct result of this determination to make them serve as his substitute combatants. In his effort to equip them with sufficient subtlety and imagination to wage war vicariously for their author, James found (apparently much to his own surprise) that he had endowed them not only with the capacity to recognize their strange fate but with the ability to register a variety of responses to it, ranging from intense curiosity to acute awkwardness. On future occasions, some of these abundantly endowed characters would even betray a distinct reluctance (or even an outright unwillingness) to "live and move and have their being" on such terms. As Charles Feidelson has shrewdly commented: "Undoubtedly, an author like this is enough to drive his characters crazy. They have very good reason to turn to him and tell him that *he* is crazy, as one of them virtually does in *The Sacred Fount.*"[42]

James's next two novels, *What Maisie Knew* (1897) and *The Awkward Age* (1899), are a case in point, for in both novels curiosity and awkwardness not only become predominant thematic and structural concerns but distinguishing characterological traits as James struggles to come to terms with his authorial responsibility to both his readers and his characters. It is no accident that both of these novels (and, indeed, all of the full-length fiction which James was to write up to the time of the New York Edition of the novels and tales) deal with adultery, although neither book is "about" adultery in any conventional sense. James could hardly have been unaware of the fact that by choosing to broach this officially taboo subject in the polite company of the English-speaking novel, especially at this moment in his career, he was placing himself (as well as his characters) in an intensely curious if not conspicuously awkward position in relation to the Anglo-American reading public. Yet he now found it impossible to accept the conventional justifications for what he perceived as "the moral timidity of the usual English novelist." As James had pointed out in "The Art of Fiction":

> In the English novel (by which or course I mean the American as well), more than in any other, there is a traditional difference between that which people *know* and that which they agree to *admit* that they know, that which they *see* and that which they *speak* of, that which they *feel* to be a part of life and that which they *allow to enter into literature.*

If this sentence provides us with a thread to guide us through the difficult maze of *What Maisie Knew,* a novel which treats of divorce and multiple adulterous relationships from the revealing yet concealing point of view of the precocious daughter of two of the principals, then the observation which immediately follows it could serve equally well as an admirably concise epigraph to *The Awkward Age,* a study of sexual innocence and experience which James conceived of as a novelistic version of a play and executed almost exclusively in terms of dialogue: "There is a great difference, in short, between what they *talk of in conversation* and what they *talk of in print.*"[43] It should be noted that in this key passage from the essay, James artfully manages to evoke the spectre of everything unspoken of (and unspeakable?) in the nineteenth-century English novel without specifying (as he does elsewhere) the particular kind of experience excluded from Anglo-American fiction. By carefully avoiding here any explicit reference to sexual relations and, in effect, by leaving the matter entirely up to his reader's imagination (or, hopefully, his or her *lack* of that quantity in the case of young persons and unmarried women), James the critic easily succeeded in challenging this novelistic taboo without ever having to violate it. But in the post-theater fiction which this passage seems to prefigure, James the novelist faces a much more difficult and dangerous task, for he has set out to discover and perfect a strategy which will enable him to present sexual relations in general, and the "adulterine element" in particular, as a legitimate subject for the Anglo-American novelist. In this context, *Maisie* and *The Awkward Age* can be viewed as the product of James's unacknowledged yet quite systematic attempt to apply pressure to the flexible contours of the Anglo-American novel and stretch the form to its utmost limits by experimenting with subject matter (as well as with form and technique).

In the period immediately preceding and following the composition of *What Maisie Knew* and *The Awkward Age* (a period during which James was recording in his notebooks the données for the three novels of his "major phase"), there is ample circumstantial evidence to suggest not only that he considered the question of how to deal with sexual relations in the novel to be primarily a problem of handling one's audience, but also that he now regarded the restrictions against dealing with this aspect of human relations as the supreme obstacle to the artistic development and maturity of both the English novel and the Anglo-American novelist, himself included. In November of 1894, after entering the germ for what would later become *The Wings of the Dove* into his notebook, James set himself to the task of working out the latent dramatic elements in the "little idea of the situation of some young creature (...preferably a woman...), who, at 20, on the threshold of a life that has seemed boundless, is suddenly condemned to death..." He envisions a young man, "entangled with another woman," who has the imagination and kindness to want to give this young girl "the chance to live and to be loved." No sooner does James imagine this situation then complications begin to appear of a sort which would frighten off "the usual English novelist." He notes that the sick girl has nothing to give the kind young man in return: "no life and no personal, no physical surrender, for it seems to me that one must represent her as too ill for *that* particular case." It is not at all clear here whether James feels he must picture her as being too ill to have intercourse with her suitor more on grounds of personal taste or on the general grounds that such a relationship would be inherently unsuitable for and unpresentable to his conventional Anglo-American public. Although he does confess that the idea of physical possession ("the brief physical, passional rapture which at first appeared essential to it") bothers him and that he personally finds the possibility of the man's " 'having' a sick girl" to be ugly, incongruous, and nasty, James also maintains that "such a remedy for her despair—and such a remedy only" (or, as he more vulgarly phrases it at one point—" 'Oh, she's dying without having had it? Give it to her and let her die' ") strikes him as "sufficiently second-rate," a phrase which suggests that he was equally determined to avoid the literary clichés of the French realists.[44]

James's dilemma becomes clearer as he projects the story first as a rather conventional variation on a sentimental Anglo-American love story—"let her think that they might have loved each other *ad infinitum* if it hadn't been too late"—and then as an equally conventional French ménage à trois: "If I were writing for a French public the whole thing would be simple—the elder, the 'other,' woman would simply be the mistress of the young man, and it would be a question of his taking on the dying girl for a time—having a temporary liaison with her." After this direct acknowledgment that his dilemma is essentially a problem of audience, James adds: "But one can do so little with English adultery—it is so much less inevitable, and so much more ugly in all its hiding and lying side," a state of affairs which he attributes to the fact that "it [adultery] is so undermined by our immemorial tradition of original freedom of choice, and by our practically universal acceptance of divorce."[45] In this entry we find James, the international novelist, vacillating once again between English and French literary *and* social conventions regarding adultery, much as he had done years before when composing *The Portrait of a Lady*. James had ended that novel on what many readers considered to be an unsatisfactory note; and he would continue to disappoint his readers in this respect each time he attempted to treat adultery as a serious theme in his fiction until 1904, when he arrived at the unique strategy and structure of *The Golden Bowl*.

Although he did not actually write *The Wings* until after the turn of the century (by which time he had experimented with this compositional problem with varying degrees of success in four full-length works of fiction), James did return to this donnée periodically over the next few years. On one such occasion, February 14, 1895, the master reread his long note on the subject of the dying girl under the pressure of wanting to do a "short 'International' novel" for the Harpers, only to be reminded of yet another recorded donnée in which the problem of how to handle adultery had loomed large. Reflecting on the germ for what would eventually become *The Golden Bowl,* James realized that "the idea of the father and daughter (in Paris, supposably), who marry—the father for consolation—at the same time, and yet are left more together than ever, through their respective *époux* taking such a fancy to each other" had the makings of an "intensely international" story; and his fingers seemed to "itch for it." Yet he was caught up short by the perception that "*Everything* about it qualifies it for *Harper* except the subject—or rather I mean, except the adulterine element *in* the subject." As we have seen, it was precisely at this moment in his career (when James confronted the question of how to *handle* the adulterine element before the American magazine public) that the compensations and solutions of the "divine principle of the Scenario" seemed to appear. Whether this "divine principle" actually presented James with a temporary evasion of the problem instead of (or as much as) a solution to it is open to question, for the passage ascends rather abruptly from an essentially hardheaded (if sophisticated) assessment of the terms of James's trade to an extremely moving (though somewhat melodramatic) vision of his personal destiny as an artist. It is worth remembering here that although James would enter the germ for *The Awkward Age* into his notebook less than two months later,[46] he turned to the less threatening donnée of *The Spoils* for his subject matter on his first attempt to apply his so-called "scenic system." Perhaps he was not yet prepared to risk such a serious challenge to conventional expectations regarding proper novelistic content.

If this is true, it is likely that James may have been testing out the waters when, in December of 1895, he began work on "the little subject of the child, the little girl, whose parents are divorced..." in order to fulfull his promise to Henry Harland for a 10,000 word piece for the April *Yellow Book*.[47] Although James nowhere states an explicit intention to use this serial as an opportunity to experiment with subject matter traditionally forbidden to the Anglo-American novelist, there is good reason to believe that he was taking advantage of "the larger latitude" enjoyed by the contributors to and readers of this avant-garde periodical in order to do just that. James retrospectively hints at this freedom of content as well as length in his reminiscences regarding the *Yellow Book* in the Prefaces as when, for example, he coyly contrasts the "perversity" of Aubrey Beardsley's pictorial and literary contributions to the *Yellow Book* with his own "comparatively so incurious text."[48] Appropriately enough, James's first fictional treatment of what he referred to (with no little irony) as "the larger latitude" had itself been addressed to and reserved for that magazine's select and presumably sophisticated public. James had incorporated into "The Death of the Lion" (the tale of the literary life which appeared in the opening number of the little magazine) a highly comic exchange between the super-subtle narrator and one Mr. Morrow, a vulgar and obtuse reporter who wears gloves that are "violently new." In this interview James had poked fun at a growing trend among avant-garde writers— especially the women—who frequently assumed pen names of the opposite sex in order to increase the freedom, authority, and even the popular appeal of their narrative voices. Mr. Morrow confuses the narrator with his talk of Guy Walsingham, a woman writer who insists on "the larger latitude" in spite (or rather because) of her sex, and her popular competitor, Dora Forbes, the mustachioed author of *The Other Way Round*. The confusion subsides when we learn that "he [Dora Forbes] goes in for the slight mystification because the ladies are such popular favorites," but not before the narrator finds himself further bewildered by the awkward possibility that his interlocutor is referring to three sexes! At the end of this tale, Neil Paraday (a parody of?) the truly great author, lies dying upstairs while the author of *Obsessions,* Miss Collop (alias

Guy Walsingham), entertains her hostess' callous house guests with an "inédit" reading of her (presumably racy) manuscript. Only too aware that this reading is not intended for a promiscuous (i.e., sexually mixed) audience, Dora Forbes quite maliciously intrudes his very unsettling masculine presence into the drawing room, intentionally producing a "disconcerting drop" in his celebrated rival's public manner. The narrator leaves the house at this juncture, but not before dryly noting that "she [Guy Walsingham] must have been in the midst of the larger latitude."[49]

Quite predictably, James's attitude towards "the larger latitude" in this story is conspicuously urbane and his tone highly ironic; his avant-garde readers would have been shocked by anything else. Yet as we have seen, he was quite capable of being as repelled by the (even wider) latitude of the French realists as he was disgusted by the rigid censorship enacted in behalf of the Anglo-American magazine public. In his own writing, James had worked hard to avoid either extreme, not only for reasons of personal taste but out of an unwillingness to cut himself off from either the most sophisticated or the most provincial segments of the English-speaking public. But late in 1895 an incident occurred which may have confirmed James's sense of the necessity of moving further in the direction of French latitude than he had ever gone before. Just as he was beginning to flesh out the scenario for *What Maisie Knew*, the story of the abandoned child of divorced parents which he had promised the editor of the *Yellow Book*, James received a request from Robert Underwood Johnson, editor of the *Century Magazine*, for an article reminiscing about Dumas *fils*, who had recently died. As Matthiessen and Murdock admirably summarize the article in their commentary on the notebooks:

> James' chief contention about Dumas is that the Frenchman's concern with "bad cases" should not distract us from perceiving that he was above all else "a professional moralist." To illustrate the difference between Dumas' "determined observation" and its absence in certain of "our innocent writers ... innocent even of reflection," James noted: "One of his great contentions is, for instance, that seduced girls should under all circumstances be married"— by somebody or other, failing the seducer. "This is a contention that, as we feel, barely concerns us, shut up as we are in the antecedent conviction that they should under no circumstances be seduced."

When Johnson rejected the article in February of 1896 on the grounds that it was unsuitable for a "family magazine" like the *Century*, James simultaneously registered his disgust and tried to contain it by working up the incident in his notebook as a germ for yet another "little ironic, satiric tale" of the literary life. He quite rightfully insisted that "the wondrous matter is their [the magazine's] conception, their representation of their public—its ineffable sneakingness and baseness," for the *Century* editorial staff seemed to be bent upon denying their readers "any indication of the ground on which he [Dumas] is worthy of their attention." What they really wanted, James concluded, was "an *intimate picture*" of an artist who is famous "because he wrote certain things which they won't for the world have *intelligibly mentioned.*"[50] Never one to miss an opportunity to make money, James soon succeeded in placing the article in both the *New York Herald* and the *Boston Herald* (February 23, 1896) after which it promptly appeared in England in the *New Review* for March of 1896. According to James's biographer, the article was presented to the American newspaper public as if it were "a shocker." The oversized headlines read: "[Dumas] Reputation for Immorality due to Alien Judgment" and "Life to Him Appeared Wholly a Fierce Battle Between Man and Woman."[51] Such headlines justify James's classification of the *Century* incident as "illustrative of the whole loathsomely prurient and humbugging business" and support Johnson's initial concern as well. Evidently the editor of the *Century* was only too familiar with the appetite of the American reading public.

It was a lesson James was soon to put to good use. In choosing a young though precocious pre-adolescent girl for his central character in *What Maisie Knew,* James was clearly attempting to exploit the social convention which characterized the young girl an innocent, plastic, and desirous to please and the literary convention which made her character both the representative and measure of the taste of the Anglo-American reading public. Although James submerges Maisie in the corrupt medium of her parents' adultery and her stepparents' liaisons, he skillfully avoids having to provide his readers with a direct representation of that "corruption" by limiting himself primarily (though not exclusively) to Maisie's consciousness, a consciousness which is ever-developing but whose terms are themselves limited, at least initially, by her sex as well as her age. Because of these limitations Maisie's point of view is an ideal buffer, admirably suited to the task of protecting her creator by deflecting the hostility which such a breach of the proprieties—however tentative and indirect—would be sure to provoke from the conventional reading public. At the same time, only to the extent that Maisie's consciousness is reflective and capable of development can her point of view function as an effective vehicle for an author intent, as James seems to have become, upon carefully probing and cautiously transgressing the sexual boundaries of Anglo-American fiction by directing the attention of the novel-reading public to the debilitating disjunction between what it knows and what it agrees to admit that it knows, what it sees and what it speaks of, what it feels to be a part of life and what it allows to enter into literature.

Under these conditions, the precise degree of Maisie's knowledge becomes for James an extremely acute structural and thematic concern. Make her know too little, and where was her danger and his story; yet make her know too much, and the sexual corruption of her innocence would lead him into the twin abysses of French realism, excessive latitude regarding sexual relations and pessimism. In an instructive article entitled "Henry James and His French Contemporaries," W.C.D. Pacey offers an interesting contrast between James's actual handling of the theme of *Maisie* and the treatment it probably would have received at the hands of a nineteenth-century French novelist. Pacey observes that "for the latter, the interest of the story would have resided either in the person of Mrs. Beale Farange [Maisie's mother] or in her first husband, perhaps in both, and their adulteries." He also suggests that, handled in the French manner, the novel would have become "an account of their attempts to hoodwink one another and ensnare other victims..."[52] Such a treatment would, in effect, have reduced James to the status of a mere imitator, a disciple of the French realists rather than a master in his own right. Maisie's character was all that stood between James and this fate; but if Maisie was to "save" her creator, he would have to "save" her by protecting her exposed innocence and cultivating in her a "moral sense." This complex mutual dependence between character and creator served to intensify their respectively awkward situations. Having voluntarily relinquished much (though not all) of the traditional prerogatives of authorial omniscience and omnipotence when he chose to interpose Maisie's limited point of view between himself and his readers, James found himself unable, without sacrificing his consistency of point of view, to offer her the kind of protection and even the overt affection which the figure of an abandoned female child would have traditionally received from an Anglo-American novelist. Largely for the same reasons, he was hardly in a position to use his narrative presence to intervene directly with his readers on her behalf. Maisie responds to this extraordinarily awkward predicament by consistently exercising a "deep diplomacy" designed to make it appear as though she does not "take things in." Although she succeeds in convincing her parents that she is extremely stupid, James's narrator and his readers know better; and when, quite early in the novel, Maisie suddenly achieves "a complete vision, private but final, of the strange office she filled,"[53] it is as though she were not only referring to the pressures of the plot but foreseeing the strange burden which she will be called upon to bear in her creator's behalf.

James does attempt to lighten Maisie's unprecedented burden and relieve the extraordinary pressure on her slight figure by employing Mrs. Wix, a rather dowdy old governess, to watch over her in his stead and by empowering Mrs. Wix to exercise a pedagogical and even a parental concern for this child of his imagination. Walter Isle is one of several commentators who have noted the frequency with which Mrs. Wix expresses herself in clichés, a tendency that has struck some critics as particularly jarring in a novel which, for the most part, is so conspicuously experimental. If, as Isle and others have observed, Mrs. Wix looks, sounds, and even acts at times suspiciously like a character out of an old-fashioned English novel (Dickens is most frequently suggested),[54] it is because

James has engaged her services as a governess on the express terms that she provide the naive and simple-minded yet sincere and sustained interest in protecting Maisie's innocence which a conventional English novelist would have exhibited and attempted to reproduce in his readers and which James, in marked contrast, was not only unable to express but unwilling to evoke, at least in its uncomplicated and unsubtle original form.

As the last and the most faithful of a series of governesses and guardians, Mrs. Wix figures as the true tutor of what she refers to as Maisie's "moral sense" and the primary guardian of Maisie's innocence. But save for the lesson of her own exemplary yet extremely conventional moral sense, Mrs. Wix's efforts to remedy Maisie's highly irregular education are, at best, inept. In fact, quite the reverse occurs: Maisie's curious predicament, her status as a bone of parental contention and her function as a sort of "go between" and pretext for her stepparents, promotes the equally irregular "education" of both her somewhat shabby yet highly respectable old governess and her more stylish elders (who are hardly proper to begin with). Maisie herself seems to have "a dim discernment of the queer law of her own life that made her educate to that sort of proficiency those elders with whom she was concerned." But her sense of herself as having "promoted, as it were, their development" only complicates the delicate question of precisely what Maisie knows, for she seems to be either oblivious of or worse—undisturbed by—the extremely awkward possibility that their development may not have been for the better. This is stating the situation rather euphemistically, especially in the case of Maisie's divorced stepmother and former governess, Mrs. Beale.

At the same time, the preceding passage sets the stage for Maisie's virtual ascension, a few sentences later, to an awesome state of knowledge which verges on omniscience and thus threatens to introduce into the novel the very type of consciousness which James has had to deny himself from the start:

> As she [Maisie] was condemned to know more and more, how could it logically stop before she should know Most? It came to her in fact... that she was distinctly on the road to know Everything... She looked at the pink sky with a placid foreboding that she soon should have learnt All.

James himself is clearly only too aware that he is running the risk of permanently alienating the traditional English-speaking public when he attributes such comprehensive knowledge to a female character, especially a young one, in a novel which abounds in corruption (sexual and otherwise). In the scene which immediately follows, as elsewhere in the book, James anticipates and caricatures his more conventional readers while attempting to placate them by making Mrs. Wix repeatedly register and express in highly melodramatic terms the shock and fear of a traditional reader. "Have I lost all delicacy, all decency, all measure of how far and how bad? It seems to me mostly that I have, though I'm the last of whom you would ever have thought it," confesses poor Mrs. Wix, who is clearly terrified by the thought that she may have "had to pay" with her own innocence for clinging to Maisie. While the climax of the novel (which takes place, appropriately enough, in "immoral" France) appears to justify Mrs. Wix's faith in the persistence of Maisie's "moral sense," James's readers are still left, much like Mrs. Wix, with plenty of "room for wonder at what Maisie knew" when the two cross the Channel back to England. The book closes on this deliberately ambiguous note as part of James's determination to educate his readers by undercutting and complicating their repertoire of stock responses.[55]

Judging from the reviews *Maisie* elicited when it was published simultaneously in England (by William Heinemann) and in America (by Herbert S. Stone) in 1897, James seems to have seriously overestimated the Anglo-American public's willingness or capacity to be so educated. According to Richard Foley, the book was poorly received in America, where the *Times* warned its readers that "there is no lesson... no information, no edification; only deftness..."[56] Although an anonymous reviewer in the *Academy* fiction supplement did praise *Maisie's* "supreme delicacy" and its author's loyalty, despite his repeated failure to achieve popular success, "to a literary conscience that forbids him to leave a slipshod phrase, or a single word out of its appointed place," the general objection to James's subject matter marked the English-speaking public's failure to recognize the nature and intent of James's technical innovations. One reviewer in the *Spectator* virtually grasped the key to the structure of the novel only to throw it away. After remarking that the novel "reminds us of nothing so much as a beautifully dressed child making an elaborate mud-pie in the gutter" and observing that "the mud-pie is a regular work of art, and the child continues to keep its own hands and dress unsoiled," this writer paused only long enough to announce that "when all is said and done, the result is only a mud-pie and nothing more" before reverting to a highly conventional synopsis of the plot of the novel. His review ended with the predictable complaint that Maisie's figure had been robbed "of its intended pathos."[57]

A critic in the *Literary World* proved himself to be less sympathetic and even more predictable when he opened his review of the novel with the statement that "*What Maisie Knew* is of a quality incredible in a writer whose work has heretofore been, morally, beyond reproach." He went on to charge that "in what it says, still more in what it suggests, it ranks, except for a terrible underlying dullness, with the worst schools of French fiction." After summarizing the plot and labelling it "inconceivable," this reviewer voiced a complaint which deserves to be quoted at length, for with minor variations and rare exceptions, it would be levelled at James's authorial pressence, his style, and his work for the remainder of his career by the great majority of common readers (and no small number of professional critics). According to this line of argument:

> [James] exhibits not one ray of pity or dismay at this spectacle of a child with the pure current of its life thus poisoned at its source. To him she is merely the *raison d'être* of a curiously complicated situation, which he can twist and untwist for purposes of fiction. One feels in the reading that every manly feeling, every possibility of generous sympathy, every comprehension of the higher standards, has become atrophied in Mr. James's nature from long disuse, and that all relation between him and his kind has perished except to serve him coldly by way of 'material.'
> It goes without saying that the style of the book is jerkily incoherent. The characters, Maisie included, converse in vague innuendoes, and, as no answer is promised 'in the next number,' the readers of the story—may they be few—will probably never understand exactly what any one concerned said or did or meant. This is just as well, for what little one is able to understand is alike repellent to taste and feeling, to law and gospel.[58]

The obtuse reception which *Maisie* suffered at the hands of the critics and the general public might have been enough to deter most writers from continuing to experiment with the handling of sexual relations in their work. Such unpleasant reverberation could only have intensified James's desire to retreat from the (by now bewildered) gaze of the English-speaking public; and, in fact, James did retreat in quite a literal sense when, during the fall of 1897, he signed a twenty-one year lease which entitled him, for the first time in his career, to enjoy the privacy and protection of his own home. (Lamb House, a venerable red brick structure dating back to the time of George the First, was situated in a cozy corner of Rye, a charming town on the southeast coast of England. In the late 1890s several avant-garde writers, including Ford Madox Ford and Stephen Crane, would establish residences in nearby towns and become James's neighbors and occasional visitors.) Yet during the very same summer in which James had discovered and contemplated moving to Lamb House, he had also attended a social and literary event which may have encouraged him to intensify his assault upon the conventions of Anglo-American fiction. The event was an Oxford University lecture on Gustave Flaubert delivered by James's friend and admirer, Paul Bourget. According to Leon Edel, the prospect of Bourget (himself a French novelist of dubious repute in the English-speaking world) being asked by conservative, classical "old Oxford" to lecture on Flaubert, the author of the "immoral" *Madame Bovary,* "teased James's sense of paradox and irony." As Edel also points out, the timing could only have added to James's sense of the irony of the whole affair, for this lecture was delivered on 23 June, just one day after the celebration of Queen Victoria's Diamond Jubilee.[59] Edel is equally on target when he suggests that James attended what he was later to refer to as this "faint convergence" as "the exponent of the 'modern' novel at a time when the novel—a century and a half old—was still regarded as an upstart in English literature," though Edel could have removed the qualifying phrase from his description of the event as "a convergence of staid Oxford with what was *almost* a kind of nineteenth-century avant-garde." However, as we have already seen, James's affinities with the avant-garde in general and with the French realists in particular were continually being undercut both by his own highly idiosyncratic sense of literary propriety and by his inability to embrace wholeheartedly their posture of cynicism in regard to questions of circulation and popularity. So it should come as no surprise to learn that James experienced extremely ambivalent feelings in response to this strange interaction and declaration of truce between "the seat and habit of the classics" and the Continental exponents of the "modern."[60]

James attempted to exorcise his misgivings not once but twice, initially by making them the subject of one of the literary letters he was writing for *Harper's* and later by separating out the conflicting elements and projecting each aspect of his mixed reaction onto the characters in his next full-length novel. This novel would be entitled, appropriately enough, *The Awkward Age*; but first James penned a curious tale about yet another English governess (young, but seemingly old-fashioned) who fights to save her young charges from what amounts to the "French" corruption of rival guardians. In "The Turn of the Screw," a "ghost story" referred to by its author as a mere "potboiler"[61] (yet praised by many contemporaneous and modern readers as a masterpiece of terror), James once again immersed his fictional children in a conspicuously corrupt medium, though this time he employed several structural devices designed to keep his readers wondering whether the governess is really the victim or the source of her charges' corruption.[62] Interestingly enough, one of the formal devices which James employs to manipulate his readers towards this effect is an opening scene or frame for the serial. This frame enables him to present his story as a manuscript which the governess wrote and passed on to a young man who had fallen in love with her subsequent to the events she describes (and who may or may not have had a sexual relationship with her). The young man, now middle-aged, is clearly reluctant to read the mysterious manuscript aloud until he has gotten rid of some of his literal-minded female house guests, a touch which simultaneously works his audience up and makes them "more compact and select" (and, not incidentally, enables James to make the opening frame self-reflexive in regard to the dubious propriety of telling such a tale before *his* own sexually-mixed magazine public). Furthermore, James doubles both the frame and his distance from his readers by having "The Turn of the Screw" narrated not by the original owner of the governess' manuscript but by one of the house guests, a sympathetic and acute male auditor who informs James's audience that he has been entrusted with the manuscript after "poor Douglas'" death.[63]

James also went to elaborate lengths to increase the distance between himself and his audience in *The Awkward Age,* his next production, for he was once again experimenting with handling the "adulterine element" when writing for the American magazine public. This novel ran as a serial in *Harper's Weekly* between October of 1898 and January of 1899, following by only four months the serial appearance of "The Turn of the Screw" in *Collier's Weekly.*[64] Although *The Awkward Age* reads in many respects like a sequel to *Maisie* and might just as well have been entitled *What Nanda Knew,* there are significant differences in theme, texture, and structure between the two works. To begin with, unlike its predecessor *The Awkward Age* was conceived of and executed as an Anglo-American treatment not only of a modern "French" subject, but of a conspicuously French (though decidedly *un*-modern) form, the *"roman dialogué"* in the manner of Gyp and Henri Lavedan. (James would later present it in his Prefaces as a frankly experimental attempt not only to write a dramatic novel but to cash in on the English-speaking public's voracious appetite for dialogue.)[65] Although *The Awkward Age* does proceed largely by means (and in terms) of dialogue, it is worth noting that he does maintain a minimal (though at times highly conspicuous) narrative presence in the novel. Walter Isle has called attention to the fact that James intrudes upon occasion in order to indicate the tone of speeches, unspoken but "visible" reactions, and the placement and movement of figures on stage. Yet he rather complacently concludes that "the careful notations of tone, gesture, and response are little more than ideal acting would give to the dialogue," without exploring either the cause or the effect upon James's characters (and readers) of this all but total abdication of the prerogatives and responsibilities of traditional narrative.[66]

As has been previously suggested, this abdication can be seen as both the symptom and the result of James's desire to avoid sustained and direct contact with his audience, especially when handling the "delicate" subject of sexual relations. This tendency, evident in all of James's post-theater novels, is carried to new extremes in *The Awkward Age*; and once again, the result is that James is forced to exert an enormous pressure upon his fictional characters (as well as his readers). This pressure in turn amounts not only (as Isle serenely infers) to an authorial demand for nothing less than ideal acting from his characters, but to a similar demand for ideal reading—or rather ideal spectatorship—on the part of his audience. As was the case in *Maisie,* James appears to be calling upon his characters to act in his behalf, to challenge the timidity of the English-speaking novelist and liberate the Anglo-American novel by undermining the "great difference ... between what they [the English-speaking public] talk of in conversation and what they talk of in print." And once again this burden threatened to fall most heavily upon the character who, according to conventional wisdom, was least equipped to bear it—the slight figure of the young unmarried female. The character of the young girl was, ideally, to be quite intentionally formed and educated in a manner which would guarantee that she remain oblivious to this very disjunction and innocent of the implications, sexual and otherwise, of this literary convention. In turn her state of sustained and carefully cultivated ignorance regarding sexual relations in life and in literature was, according to this unwritten law, to be remedied and compensated for by marriage and marriage alone. Such a system makes the awkward career of Nanda Brookenham, an unmarried nineteen-year-old girl, at once an exceedingly appropriate and an immensely risky vehicle with which to explore the flexibility and extend the freedom and scope of the English novel.

By choosing as his germ "the note one had inevitably had to take of the difference made in certain friendly houses and for certain flourishing mothers by the sometimes dreaded, often delayed, but never fully arrested coming to the forefront of some vague slip of a daughter," James thus placed himself in a kind of double jeopardy, for he was experimenting with the effect of Nanda's presence not only upon her mother's super-subtle circle but upon his own more heterogeneous transatlantic audience and the particular house of fiction of which he was master, the Anglo-American novel. If the "sitting downstairs" of this "merciless maiden" could only now "be felt as a crisis" for a sophisticated modern English mother like Mrs. Brookenham,[67] her presence had long figured as a protracted literary crisis for her fictional creator, a novelist and critic who had ridiculed the cultural pretensions of the feminine component of his public in his very first review and spent an entire career trying to take the measure of the huge flat foot of a transatlantic public which exhibited the character of the young unmarried female as both its representative and its most valuable production. This calculated parallel or doubling informs the structure and texture of *The Awkward Age* and helps to explain the curiously reversed pattern of intimacy which characterizes James's relationship with the fictional mother and daughter in this novel. Although he consistently keeps his distance from all of the characters in this drama, in marked contrast with his obvious dislike for Maisie's mother Mrs. Farange, he is moved to present Nanda's mother (or rather to allow her to present herself) as an extremely attractive woman, highly skilled in the art of conversation and genuinely concerned about her daughter's awkward descent from the schoolroom to her drawing room (although she quite wisely avoids the pretense that her motives are unselfish). Like James, Mrs. Brook is seriously perplexed about how to *handle* Nanda's arrival on the scene; and perhaps this is why James seems so sympathetic with her artful attempt to artificially prolong Nanda's childhood. When this fails, they join forces in candidly presenting Nanda's exposed state to their respective audiences as a conspicuously awkward and regrettable situation, a tactic intended to anticipate and defuse predictable charges of maternal (and authorial) neglect and admirably suited to the task of concealing the very real agitation and fear which is triggered by Nanda's inevitable intrusion upon the scene. Both James and Mrs. Brook are disturbed by the possibility that Nanda will appear in the character of an eager sexual competitor, entering the field as a dangerous rival for Vanderbank's affection. This constitutes an extremely awkward situation for both mother and author, the obvious remedy for which would be to get Nanda "safely married" as soon as possible, preferably (from Mrs. Brook's point of view) to a wealthy man, namely Mitchy. But this solution is blocked and the situation is made increasingly dangerous and awkward by the fact that both mother and daughter are in love with the same man, Vanderbank.

Of course, there is always the neat though somewhat easy Continental solution of an arranged marriage; and the Duchess not only represents but endorses this remedy with respect to both Nanda and her own niece, "little Aggie." James initially manipulates the Duchess' maternal solicitude towards her niece and Agnesia's Pansy-like docility and plasticity in order to reveal Mrs. Brook's contrasting selfishness and highlight Nanda's relative intractability. In marked contrast to Nanda's haphazard exposure and her highly irregular education, Aggie has been amply protected and provided for (her education has included Mr. Garlick's class in Modern Light Literature). But James soon begins to "work" this contrast at the expense of the Duchess and Aggie in order to justify and marshal sympathy for Mrs. Brook (and, by implication, for himself), a sympathy which is given almost miraculous (and perhaps not quite convincing) presence and expression in the closing scene of the novel by Nanda herself when she virtually exchanges roles with her mother and begs Van, almost maternally, not to abandon Mrs. Brook—in part because "she's so fearfully young."[68]

Nanda's magnanimous stance towards her mother and her admirable performance during her final "scene" with Van serve two purposes. First, it is James's characteristically indirect mode of compensating Mrs. Brook not only for having placed her in a set of muddled British social conditions (and before a modern audience) which are analogous to the muddled literary conditions in which he found himself at the time, but for having endowed (or burdened?) her with his own Anglo-Saxon unwillingness (or inability?) to avail himself of the easy and conventional French solution by which both mother and daughter would have been permitted to share the same lover. The Duchess' relation with James is precisely the reverse: she initially profits from his admiration for Continental manners and is endowed with an exaggerated version of his preference for "les situations nettes—je n'en comprends pas d'autres," a point of view from which she grandly condemns the English with their "eternal English false positions."[69] Although at first James seems to be endorsing the Continental double standard of permissiveness regarding *"jeunes filles"* and *"femmes"* when he permits the Duchess to take a lover with seeming impunity, he protects himself in good Anglo-Saxon fashion first by making her a widow rather than a married woman and then by making her pay, and pay heavily, for the favor by losing her lover Lord Petherton to her niece shortly after Aggie marries Mitchy. Furthermore, in marked contrast to Aggie's post-marital eruption, Nanda's consistent performance, culminating in her final gesture of renunciation, is intended to exonerate retroactively both her mother and her creator from the charges of moral irresponsibility and even outright malevolence which could be levelled at their parallel interest in and attitude towards both her character and her marital career.

James's curious distance from and seeming lack of affection for Nanda, the ostensible heroine of the novel, is both the symptom and the result of his identity of motive with her mother. Like her younger prototype, Maisie Farange, Nanda suffers doubly from virtual abandonment at the hands of her parents as well as her creator; yet in *The Awkward Age,* neither Nanda's character nor her fate, in and of themselves, is sufficient to make her worthy of the role to which she lays claim, that of the central character or consciousness in an experimental James novel. In marked contrast with Maisie, around whose point of view James structured an entire novel, Nanda does not even make an appearance in *The Awkward Age* until the second "scene" of the third of the novel's twelve "books," by which time all of the other major characters have long since been introduced. Like her predecessor, Nanda does prove to be extremely knowledgeable; but unlike Maisie, she is not a precocious child but an unmarried girl of marriageable age. Her exposure to her mother's circle only confirms the effect, for good or for bad, of her previous exposure to unhappily married women like Tishy Grendon and the "indecent" French fiction which her mother has left lying around their home. By the time the novel opens Nanda is already, in effect, "damaged goods"; and this complication not only drives down her value on the marriage market but threatens to deprive her of any claim to the protection of her family (or her creator) as well as her claim upon the sympathy and affection of her fellow characters and her audience. While Van admits that his ultimate unwillingness to accept Nanda on these terms represents his anachronistic allegiance to the traditional and probably outmoded English social definition of a "nice" girl, his rejection of Nanda's love also suggest his (and James's?) allegiance to a related and equally traditional though more resilient literary convention which made it difficult, if not impossible, to imagine an unmarried woman of "advanced" age as either an object of desire or the prime subject of a novel (for where, after all, did the British public draw the line between an unmarried girl of a certain age and that stock supporting character of English novel, the spinster?).[70]

As in the case of Maisie, James felt moved and obligated to provide Nanda with a substitute guardian in recognition of and compensation for such a cruel fate. But given Nanda's advanced age, James could hardly supply her with a governess; and so he hit upon the solution of Mr. Longdon, an upright and elderly English gentleman who, like Mrs. Wix, looks, talks, and acts like a character out of an old-fashioned English novel. But unlike Mrs. Wix, Mr. Longdon (and all the other super-subtle characters in this novel) *knows* it. Immediately after he is introduced to both Van and James's readers, Longdon confesses to feeling "quite out of it" and tells Van that he has "accepted this queer view of the doom of coming back."[71] However, like Mrs. Wix (his less discriminating and less self-conscious prototype), Mr. Longdon performs a double service for his creator. Quite conveniently for James, on the pretext of noting a curious resemblance between Nanda and her grandmother (the one great love of his life) Longdon conceives a growing affection for her and develops the kind of paternal interest in her fate which a traditional novelist would be expected to exhibit and elicit from his readers. Longdon befriends Nanda, watches over her, and worries about what she does or does not know. After trying, unsuccessfully, to arrange for her to marry Van, the man she has loved from afar since her nursery days, Longdon even adopts her. At the same time, he also functions as a stand-in for and friend to James's more traditional readers, for he dislikes Nanda's mother intensely (as much as Mrs. Wix dislikes Mrs. Farange) and registers a comparable shock, though in a much less melodramatic manner, at the talk and tone of Mrs. Brook and her highly sophisticated (decadent?) circle.

One also senses that in *The Awkward Age,* as in the case of *Maisie,* Mr. Longdon's old-fashioned distaste for Mrs. Brook and her super-subtle circle of friends is shared to some extent by his creator. At times James even seems to be trying to use this elderly outsider to exorcise his lingering doubts and express his own persistent reservations concerning Mrs. Brook's highly dramatic presence and her extremely manipulative brand of "authorship." While Longdon can thus be seen as an author-surrogate reminiscent of Mrs. Wix, he clearly lacks both the high personal manner and the masterful skill as a "playwright" and "stage manager" necessary to complete the analogy in a dramatic fiction like *The Awkward Age.* In keeping with his character, Longdon's one attempt at "plotting" is quite conventional and would be equally appropriate to a traditional English novel, French play, or even a fairytale. (Mrs. Brook makes this convergence explicit when she notes that there is something in Longdon which "suggests the *oncle d'Amerique,* the eccentric benefactor, the fairy godmother.")[72] None of the characters has any difficulty guessing at Longdon's "secret" attempt to "bribe" Van to marry Nanda—in fact, the Duchess even has to help him conceive this plan, which his fellow characters seem to agree in regarding as touchingly old-fashioned. Despite the fact that all of the characters in this novel display considerable abilities as actors, only Mrs. Brook consistently exhibits a dramatic skill which successfully combines the art of the actress with the art of the dramatist. As the acknowledged inspiration and stage manager of her fellow actors, she is also in an ideal position to vicariously exercise and display the dramatic skills of her creator, the author/playwright.

Mrs. Brook fully demonstrates her skill as well as James's in book 8 of the novel. Here in one extraordinary scene, the "complicated chambers of *both* the dramatic and the narrative lock" do seem to line up and the self-reflexive analogy between character and creator becomes all but explicit. Interestingly enough, the purpose of this *tour de force* on the part of both dramatist/author and actress/character is to expose Nanda deliberately before their respective audiences by means of one of the most conventional props of literature and the stage, the "indecent" French novel. Reunited after Aggie's marriage to Mitchy on the occasion of a dinner party at the home of Tishy Grendon (Nanda's unhappily married friend), the new and old "recruits" to Mrs. Brook's circle group themselves around Mitchy after Mrs. Brook gives them their cue by declaring, almost in incantatory fashion, "Mitchy's silent, Mitchy's altered, Mitchy's queer!" James then provides the following stage directions:

> Tishy was nearest Mr. Longdon, and Nanda, still flanked by Mr. Cashmore, between that gentleman and his wife, who had Harold [Nanda's brother] on her other side. Edward Brookenham [Nanda's father] was neighbored by his son and by Vanderbank, who might easily have felt himself, in spite of their separation and given, as it happened, their places in the group, rather publicly confronted with Mr. Longdon.

This grouping, in turn, provides Mrs. Brook with the opportunity to ask " 'Is his [Mitchy's] wife in the other room?'... " What ensues may be best described as a drama within a drama, to paraphrase James's assessment of Ibsen, for Mrs. Brook manipulates the conversation with the intent of directing her fellow characters' attention first to the absence of Aggie and Lord Petherton, who are "playing" in the next room, and then to "the extraordinary way she [Aggie] has come out," all as part of her (and James's) effort to freight the encounter which will follow with sufficient dramatic intensity and significance to force their audience to confront the awkward problem of what Nanda knows and pose the difficult question of whether it is "good for her."[73]

Just as the "prints" on Aggie's arms are the only visible signs of the "struggle" she has put up to keep Petherton from gaining his "trophy," the French novel, so the hesitations in Nanda's voice are the sole audible registers of the wounds she bravely sustains when her mother forces her, by means of a perverse sort of catechism, to admit not only that she has written Van's name on the blue cover of this compromising work (which he had lent to her mother), but that she has read it herself before pronouncing it unfit reading for her married friend Tishy because of its "awful subject." Mrs. Brook recovers the volume, holds it behind her, and then tosses it into an empty chair upon being forced to admit that she, too, has read it. She then exacts her revenge by challenging her daughter once more, this time with the express purpose of destroying any lingering doubts in Van's (or the reader's) mind concerning the "damaged" state of Nanda's innocence: "Have you read this work, Nanda?" Nanda's understated response, her simple "Yes, mamma," only complicates matters, for the truly initiated reader will realize that her refusal to lie, even with Van's affection and esteem hanging in the balance, implies that, at the very least, it is not so easy to judge whether a girl (or a novel) is "good" or "bad."[74]

Mr. Longdon, like the reader, has been a silent spectator to this scene; and his abrupt departure, which signals the end of both the scene and the eighth book, is James's way of anticipating and accommodating the possible desire of the more squeamish members of *his* audience to "walk out" as it were on such an unpleasant performance, or at least to put the novel down for a brief intermission. In the two books which remain, James attempted to contain and forestall the probable revulsion of his conventional public with respect to such an ugly exposure of his characters by making Mrs. Brook acknowledge "the smash." Though Mrs. Brook's display of such "total candor" appears to be directed towards *her* now alienated circle of spectators (especially Van), one senses that James is desperately working this display of candor to dazzle and disarm his own audience. Perhaps he needs to divert *his* spectators' attention from the awkward possibility that this collision is a self-reflexive commentary not only upon modern British society but upon his own artistic procedures. By presenting the smash (and implicitly, the entire "plot" of the novel) primarily as a pretext for eliciting such an extraordinary performance from his troup of actor/characters, James attempts to anticipate and undercut potential critics. This strategy dominates the final book of the novel and amounts to an effort to justify (and possibly even redeem) its bleak conclusion, for James returns Nanda to her own old room, where she is "free" at last to receive male visitors alone while her mother continues to do so downstairs. Although he makes every effort to furnish Nanda with a high style comparable to her mother's in partial compensation for her cruel exposure and the loss of Van, her voice sounds conspicuously strained and she seems to be not quite able to withstand the incredible pressure to which James continues to subject her. When Mitchy arrives to profess his continuing adoration for Nanda, he insists that she is "almost as good for husbands as Mrs. Brook is for wives...," an obvious reference to Nanda's unwitting responsibility for his own unhappy state. Mitchy is succeeded by Mr. Longdon, who not only has provided Nanda with an ample supply of good books (including a twenty-three-volume set of standard English works) but who now pledges never again to leave her in spite (or rather because) of all that he has witnessed. Yet this attempt to "bribe" Nanda and James's readers does not quite come off; and James candidly if covertly admits this failure when, in the closing pages of the novel, he permits Nanda to break down momentarily under the pressure and "collapse, on the spot, into the nearest chair, where she choked with a torrent of tears." Although Nanda quickly recovers herself "with an effort worthy of her fall,"[75] her tears amount to an eloquent non-verbal response to (and commentary upon) the violence with which her creator has foreclosed on her fictional future—and all in the name of the future of the novel. Nanda's collapse was to prove prophetic.

5

A Second Chance

Henry James would eventually do his utmost to redeem the suffering of his fictional children, but not until one of them openly confronted him and challenged his artistic procedures. Out of his subsequent awareness of the highly unsatisfactory nature of his complex relationship with his characters, there would emerge an implicit commitment on James's part to improving the terms of intercourse between them while continuing his effort to expand the repertoire of the English-speaking novel and educate the taste of the fiction-reading public. This commitment would take the form of a determination to develop literary devices and a fictional structure designed to facilitate mutual cooperation and insure mutual protection between the author and his central characters. In turn, James's determination would become the very key to his attempt to transform himself from an essentially egotistical and self-protective fictional experimenter, whose most distinctive authorial manipulations were often exercises in self-defense, to the almost paternal and ultimately benign master of the major phase, whose most devious artistic maneuvers would be conceived and employed primarily—though not exclusively—as practical measures taken to protect the vulnerable children of his imagination.

But as the penultimate year of the nineteenth century opened, James became preoccupied not with the violence which he was doing to his characters but with his intellectual balance sheet. Although he had several recent novels to his credit (*The Awkward Age* had just completed its serial run in *Harper's* and he was busy correcting the proof for its appearance in book form), we find him confessing in his notebook that "*the* thing, the desire to get back only to the *big* (scenic, constructive 'architectual' effects) seizes me and carries me off my feet: making me feel that it's a far deeper economy of time to sink, at *any* moment, into the evocation and ciphering out of *that,* than into any other *small* beguilement at all." Under the combined pressure of publishing conditions (short things, he knew, were easier to place) and what seems to have been a largely self-imposed economy of rigorous restraint with regard to "big" effects, James began to find himself yearning "... once more, to let myself go! The very thought of it soothes and sustains, lays a divine hand on my nerves, and lights, so beneficently, my uncertainties and obscurities."[1]

Furthermore, the notebook entry which immediately precedes this one (dated January 22, 1899) suggests that James's nerves had only recently become unsettled because George Alexander had just requested his permission to produce *Covering End,* a play which James had reworked into a story and published as one of *The Two Magics* in 1898. While he made a point of stressing "the obstacles and objections" to Alexander, James could not help noting privately "how this little renewal of contact with the vulgar theater stirs again, in a manner, and moves me." Characteristically, he immediately corrected himself by insisting that he found this renewed contact with the theater to be as "strangely odious" as ever: "it's the contact with the DRAMA, with the divine little difficult, artistic, ingenious architectural FORM that makes the old pulses throb and old tears rise again." The effect of this renewed touch of "the blended anguish and amusement" of his theater experience proved so unsettling to James ("the divine unrest again touches me") that he even tried to contain his unrest and quiet his nerves by converting his initial eagerness to do "a *fresh* one-act thing" for Alexander into the determination to write a one-act short story instead, arguing to himself that it was "very much the same trick!"[2]

James's eagerness to "get back only to the *big*... effects," as voiced in his notebook, can thus be seen as yet another indirect expression of his desire to achieve dramatic "effects" on an even larger scale, in this case by continuing to impose his dramatic intentions not on the short story but on the novel and its audience. But before he could "let himself go," James was treated to yet another painful lesson regarding the response which these intentions evoked from the Anglo-American reading public, or at least its professional representatives, the critics. During the spring of 1899, *The Awkward Age* was attacked on two fronts by the majority of critics on both sides of the Atlantic. As might be expected, they were quick to charge that James's subject matter was highly improper and his manner exasperating and tedious, if not perverse. An anonymous British reviewer in the *Spectator* insisted that the "external suavity" of James's style was the only feature which distinguished him from the modern school of "naturalistic realists" who move in an "atmosphere of mental and moral squalor." According to this conventional line, *The Awkward Age* was the result of "that misguided opinion, by which so many modern writers of fiction are obviously actuated, that normal or wholesome themes being exhausted, a novelist can only display originality or achieve artistic results in the delineation of the detestable." An unsigned review in the May issue of *Saturday* magazine went even further. In a confidential tone designed to impress upon its readers the sobering fact that there were limits of literary propriety which even famous American authors should not be allowed to transgress, this periodical warned:

> Mr. James will imperil his vogue if he is not careful. We have grown to look upon him as a dainty, dapper, well-groomed author, who, despite some Transatlantic eccentricities, could be introduced to our friends of both sexes. But every year he grows more careless of his literary person, his epigrams are more flashy, his innuendoes are less clean-shaven, until in his present presentation he may almost be denied admittance as shabby-genteel.

The characters in the novel were likewise pronounced guilty of parodying "the precocity of the most unnatural French creations." After complaining about the overabundance of dialogue in the novel and quoting a description from it which he found to be reminiscent of "a shilling shocker," this reviewer dismissed James's "story" completely by likening its significance to that of "the needy knife-grinder..."[3]

The novel fared little better in American periodicals where, according to Richard Foley, "disappointment and bewilderment seem to have been the prevailing reaction of the critics."[4] The *Nation,* which had published many of James's early apprentice reviews, found *The Awkward Age* to be an especially difficult dose to swallow. Its reviewer broached the question of subject matter only reluctantly and with such timidity and indirectness as to suggest that this stately periodical was eager to divert the attention of its own sexually mixed audience to the safer question of James's obvious technical dexterity. Yet even the novel's style was found wanting because of James's "trifling, yet peculiarly irritating" defects of manner. The *Nation* could only conclude, with obvious discomfort, that "to think of these frankly inquiring minds and untrammelled spirits united with bodies would be to picture to ourselves an uncommonly bad lot, much worse than we have any right to suppose Mr. James has ever wished to introduce." However, magazine proprieties failed to silence a less squeamish reviewer in the *Literary World* who insisted upon calling attention to the "grosser" aspects of James's fiction. "His observation and knowledge seem to grow keener with each new novel. But where will they end...?" wondered this alarmed critic. "Will they swamp themselves finally in pessimism and unpleasantness and horrors?" Another reviewer openly charged that the dialogue, "with its scrupulous avoidance of candour, its wealth of sinister suggestiveness, is a marvel of enigmatic insinuation." Still another found the repartee inventive but not enough so to compensate the reading public for "the relentless *longueurs*" of the novel. "A frankly discursive book offers continual reliefs; but we feel here that nothing is purely episodical, that every chapter is conscientiously designed to bring the *dénouement* infinitesimally nearer..." huffed and puffed this reviewer in *Literature.*

Aside from concern with and shock over James's subject matter, then, strain, worry, boredom, fatigue, and annoyance seem to have been the most frequent responses which James's fictional drama evoked from the majority of professional readers. A reviewer in the *Academy* stands out as one of the few who perceived that "Mr. Henry James is the wonderful artistic outcome of our national habit of repression" (although he did express bewilderment regarding the novel's title). By insisting upon treating James's tendency towards understatement and indirectness in the context of his willingness to represent subjects which bordered so closely on vulgarity (if not outright perversity), this critic was able to perceive and insist upon the intimate connection between "the proprieties, the conventions of this land, the genius for repression, which have created that need for a new realism," and *The Awkward Age,* which he interpreted as James's "so satisfying" response to this felt need.[6]

When Howard Sturges, James's young friend and disciple, wrote a letter praising the novel, he was therefore expressing a minority opinion, as the master himself was quick to recognize and point out. In James's reply to Sturges (dated May 19, 1899) we find him admonishing his friend in the face of all the adverse critical reaction to the book to "*be* one of the few! I greatly applaud the tact with which you tell me that scarce a human being will understand a word, or an intention, or an artistic element or glimmer of any sort, of my book." As he wryly noted: "I tell *myself*—and the 'reviews' tell me— such truths in much cruder fashion. But it's an old, old story—and if I 'minded' now as much as I once did, I should be beneath the sod."[7] Despite such periodic disclaimers, James obviously continued to "mind" the obtuseness of his critics; for, as we have seen, he had proven to be neither willing nor able to divorce his estimate of literary success from the question of the quality (and sometimes even the quantity) of the response which his productions elicited from the reading public. And, while he had never confronted his critics directly (or publicly taken issue with the reception granted any of his novels), James had attacked his reviewers' conventional assumptions in several pointed essays, most notably "The Art of Fiction" (1884) and "Criticism" (1891). Now, as the nineteenth century drew to a close, he decided to make use of an essay commissioned for "The Universal Anthology" in order to respond, however indirectly, to the assumptions behind the critical reaction to *The Awkward Age.* Unwilling to offer either an overt defense of his own recent experiments with subject matter or an explicit justification of his highly idiosyncratic artistic procedures, James preferred to argue the issues involved on the most general grounds possible and to treat the occasion as yet another opportunity to delineate and defend the freedom and flexibility of his chosen genre. The resulting essay, written in December of 1899, not only surveyed the past role of the novel in Anglo-American culture but prophesied its future career. It was entitled, quite appropriately, "The Future of the Novel"; but it might as well have been entitled "The Future of Henry James," for it projected, however covertly, the role which he himself hoped to play in the novel's continuing development.

James began by reiterating his by now quite familiar complaint that "the larger part of the great multitude" which constituted the English-speaking public was composed of "boys and girls; by girls in especial, if we apply this term to the later stages of the life of the innumerable women who, under modern arrangements, increasingly fail to marry—fail, apparently, even, largely to desire to." When James identified the type of literary product which addressed itself to this segment of the reading public as "the 'story'," he revealed the obvious contempt in which he held this article of commerce, representing as it did "the side of the whole business of fiction on which it can always be challenged," the side of the "mere unsupported and unguaranteed history;" the *inexpensive* thing, written in the air, the record of what, in any particular case, has *not* been..." Retracing the familiar ground of "The Art of Fiction," James stated that in this form, the "prolonged prose fable" had "never philosophically met the challenge, never found a formula to inscribe on its shield, never defended its position by any better argument than the frank, straight blow" of its immense popularity. He then implied that this failure of self-consciousness could be attributed to the fact that the Anglo-American novel was addressed to young people in general and to women in particular. But at this point in his argument, James abruptly changed tactics by endorsing, at least initially, the position taken by an "admirable minority of intelligent persons... for whom the very form itself has, equally at its best and worst, been ever a vanity and a mockery." Instead of launching a direct defense of the novel as an art form, James slyly alluded to the growing alliance between what one might call old-fashioned novel-haters and "a different circle altogether, the group of the formerly subject, but now estranged" people (presumably like himself) who "have loved the novel, but who actually find themselves drowned in its verbiage, and for whom... it has become a terror they exert every ingenuity, every hypocrisy, to evade." However, by a clever sleight of hand this apparently more devastating criticism was transformed into yet another version of James's earliest justification of the genre, for it was precisely this great variety of response to the contemporaneous novel (exhibited by three classes of readers, the "indifferent," the "alienated," and the "omnivorous") which testified, according to James, to the incredibly wide range of "man's general appetite for a picture" and "his eternal desire for more experience." This was an appetite and a desire which only the novel, with its ability to "stretch anywhere" and "take in almost anything" and its quantity of "abundant yet various" experience, could satisfy.[8]

But James was not content to rest his argument here, for he went on to sketch a scenario covering the career of the novel which turned on the very fact of the novel's awkwardness "in the presence of the ladies and children—by whom I mean, in other words, the reader irreflective and uncritical." Curiously enough, James proceeded to characterize the "so precarious" current footing of the novel, "its undefended, its positively exposed state..." in terms unmistakably similar to those with which he had described the plight of Maisie Farrange and Nanda Brookenham, those super-subtle young females who figured as the putative "heroines" of his own most recent fictional experiments. Once again, James's sense of both the worst limitations and the best possibilities of his chosen medium and its public found shape and expression in female form. Meditating on the future of the genre, James focused upon the female character in its least developed form as the representative of the most vulgar aspects of the contemporaneous literary scene, while at the same time he delighted in exhibiting it in its most developed form as the very image of the novel's inexhaustible appeal, its perpetual margin of "individual freedom." Borrowing an analogy from his friend and fellow-professional, Robert Louis Stevenson, between the "trap set by the artist" and "the offer of her charms by the lady," James likened the successful appeal of a novel to infatuation and attributed the lady's "precious secret," her "plasticity" and "elasticity" of character, to "the prose picture." Like this particular type of "lady" (one suspects that, like Nanda and Maisie, she has little in common with the typical "nice girl"), the novel "has the extraordinary advantage... that, while capable of giving an impression of the highest perfection and the rarest finish, it moves in a luxurious independence of rules and restrictions." As he went on to insist: "Think as we may, there is nothing we can mention as a consideration outside itself with which it must square, nothing we can name as one of its peculiar obligations or interdictions."[9]

This analogy, in turn, provided James with a renewed vision of his own future as a professional novelist and his unique artistic destiny. Only by assuming the character of the "great artist yet to come" could he personally rise to this occasion and save both himself and his chosen genre from their two gravest dangers, "superficiality" and "timidity." As James slyly admitted: "One almost, for the very love of it, *likes* to think of its appearing threatened with some such fate, in order to figure the dramatic stroke of its revival under the touch of a life-giving master." Having thus (covertly) established the necessity for his own continuing presence upon the literary scene, cast in the role of the "life-giving master," James was able to muster up the courage to convert this general (and therefore relatively safe) defense of the freedom of the novel into a clever attack on the "respectable tradition of making it defer supremely, in the treatment, say, of a delicate case, to the inexperience of the young." He gingerly prepared his readers for what was to come by alluding to a prior state of English-speaking society, one characterized by frankness and freedom "about the incidents and accidents of the human constitution," in which "the novel took the same robust ease as society." According to James this ease, which produced Richardson and Fielding, had been supplanted by "a mistrust of any but the most guarded treatment of the great relation between men and women," or, as he put it with great circumspection, "the constant world-renewal." However obliquely, James was unmistakably engaged here in responding to and dismissing the criticism which had been levelled at his own recent experiments with subject matter when he asserted that this mistrust, in its turn, was in the process of being superseded. "The novel is older," James insisted, "and so are the young" in whose name so much had been "kept out" of the novel. Deftly turning the tables on his critics once again, he quite accurately presented the coalition between women and the young as the very public which was currently registering the most vociferous objections to the neglect of "many sources of interest" and education by the contemporaneous novel. Casting women in the role of leaders of this growing avant-garde reaction, he noted that "nothing is more salient in English life today... than the revolution taking place in the position and outlook of women—and taking place much more deeply in the quiet than even the noise on the surface demonstrates..." He even went so far as to warn (in a tone which evokes the image of raised eyes) that when, as novelists, "women do obtain a free hand they will not repay their long debt to the precautionary attitude of men by unlimited consideration for the natural delicacy of the latter."[10]

With these words, James signalled the fact that he was speaking once again in the guise of the prescient and somewhat amused observer of the evolving Anglo-American literary scene, for what had begun as a Thackeray-like indictment of the traditional custom of addressing novels to "mixed company" and a rather old-fashioned tirade against "the tyranny of the young girl" was here transformed, by a characteristically Jamesian turn of the screw, into a sophisticated commentary upon the dominant role which the "New Woman" (with her taste for "the larger latitude") and the English-speaking avant-garde (with their distaste for "forms at once ready-made and sadly the worse for wear") were playing (and would continue to play) on the modern literary scene. As had been the case with "The Art of Fiction," these literary observations and predictions were ultimately geared as much (if not more) to James's hopes and fears regarding his own literary career than they were to his concern over the past, present, and future career of the novel. But when, in the closing passage of the essay, James concluded by calling upon novelists to "rekindle the fire of fiction" and restore the element of "mystery" to his craft, his tone was no longer that of an "estranged" and "deceived" lover of fiction or a subtle and detached observer of the current literary scene. His was the voice of a devoted ministrant who was himself once again in the process of preparing to "really approach the altar."[11]

Yet in spite of all this extensive private and public self-prompting, James seems to have remained unwilling or unable to approach the altar directly and, as he so revealingly phrased it, "let himself go." In the early days of 1900, he did begin work on a scenario for what he hoped would emerge as the vehicle for an "international ghost," but he soon ran into difficulty over the problem of how to achieve the particular kind of effect he was after. He wanted to create "the *revealed* effect of 'terror'," which he defined in his notebook as "the fact of the consciousness of it [terror] as given, not *received,* on the part of the central, sentient, person of the story." While he privately confessed that he found the idea "damnably difficult," James persisted in treating the difficulty he was experiencing as if it were purely a structural problem which could be solved by manipulating the narrative point of view:

> When I think of the expedient of making the narrator's point of view that of the persons outside—that of one of them—I immediately see how I *don't* get that way, the presentation by the person who is the source of the 'terror' of *his sense of being so.* On the other hand I don't, if I tell the thing from his point of view *in* the '1st person' get, easily, that I can see, the intense simplification.

While it is true that the limited word counts which magazine editors now imposed upon James's stories made "simplifications" a (seemingly unachievable) necessity, James's vacillation regarding the best means of achieving this particular effect in his ghost story (which had been christened *The Sense of the Past*) may have had a much deeper and more intimate source. His uncertainty suggests that he harbored suppressed doubts and anxieties regarding the precise nature of the authorial presence which he should maintain and the fictional procedures which he should employ at this stage of his artistic development.[12]

Indeed, James seemed to be positively relieved when he learned from Howells that Doubleday, the publisher who had originally commissioned this tale of "terror," had withdrawn the request. He abruptly stopped work on *The Sense of the Past,* announcing to Howells that he was "laying it away on the shelf for the sake of something that *is* in it"; but he also confessed "the ungraceful truth" that his "tale of terror did, as I was so more than half fearing, give way beneath me. It *has,* in short, broken down for the present." As in his notebooks, James presented this "breakdown" to Howells primarily as a technical affair, though he did admit that "preoccupied with half a dozen things of the altogether human order now fermenting in my brain, I don't care for 'terror' (terror, that is, without 'pity') so much as I otherwise might." James even professed himself to be ready to provide his friend with "'a neat little *human*—and not the less international—fifty-thousander consummately addressed to your more cheerful department... in other words, an admirable short novel of manners, thrilling too in its degree, but definitely ignoring the bugaboo.'" Almost with an audible sigh of relief he continued, "*that* card one has always, thank God, up one's sleeve, and the production of it is only a question of a little shake of the arm."[13]

Why was James suddenly so willing to drop his "Monster" (as he now referred to *The Sense of the Past*) and commit himself to producing an intensely "human" story which would appeal to Howells' "cheerful department"? A clue to this seemingly abrupt change of heart and mind can be found earlier in the same letter to Howells, which was actually begun on August 9, several days *before* he received Howells' letter of August 4 announcing that Doubleday no longer wanted the tale. In this portion of the letter, James had described his mounting excitement over *The Sense of the Past* in the following terms:

> [W]hat the case involves is, awfully interestingly and thrillingly, that the 'central figure,' the subject of the experience, has the terror of a particular ground for feeling and fearing that *he himself* is, or may at any moment become, a producer, an object, of this (for you and me) state of panic on the part of others. He lives in an air of *malaise* as to the malaise he may, woefully, more or less fatally, find himself creating—and that, roughly speaking, is the essence of what I have seen.

James presents the attempt to represent such a case as a daring "experiment" in "the supernatural and the high fantastic," only to reveal that he has "just finished, as it happens, a fine flight ... *into* the high fantastic, which has rather *depleted* me, or at any rate affected me as discharging my obligations in that quarter." The book to which he is referring here is *The Sacred Fount*, a novel which was to produce a state of bewilderment, if not outright panic, in several generations of readers from the time it was published (without prior serialization) in 1901. A closer look at both *The Fount* and James's explicit linking of it with *The Sense of the Past* may therefore shed new light on both the work itself and James's evident fascination with a case which he found so intrinsically difficult to handle.[14]

James began *The Sacred Fount* as a short story which, like "The Figure in the Carpet," was to be told from the point of view of an obsessed narrator. And, as was the case with Hugh Vereker's fictional secret, the central idea (which expanded under treatment to novel length) depends upon and at times seems designed to stimulate the public's latent potential for super-subtlety. To the extent to which this was James's conscious intention, the novel may be judged at least a partial success, for when it has not been totally ignored or dismissed by James's contemporaneous and posthumous critics, *The Fount* has elicited readings which are truly remarkable, even in Jamesian criticism, for the degree of ingenuity which they sustain and exhibit. Although the authors of these interpretations arrive at quite diverse conclusions regarding what James was "really doing" in the novel, their critical voices ultimately tend to sound the same because each has been manipulated by James into developing a degree of super-subtlety (perhaps over-subtlety would be a better word here) and displaying an obsession similar to that of the narrator of the novel. In other words, James has presented his audience with a first person narrator who not only exhibits an uncontrollable passion for "squaring" every relationship which he observes or imputes on the part of his fellow characters but who is capable of inducing an identical compulsion in those readers who attempt to analyze *his* self-exhibitory behavior on its own super-subtle terms.[15] Interestingly enough, James appears to have achieved this effect largely by anticipating it and incorporating it into the "plot" of the novel itself, which dramatizes the contagious effects of exhibited super-subtlety in terms of the narrator's evolving relationship with Mrs. Briss, a character who rises to the narrator's bait presumably as part of her effort to protect herself from his penetrating and hyperactive imagination. Such an interpretation of what James was ultimately "up to" would be consistent with the line taken by defenders of the novel who insist, along with Leon Edel, that "an author who planned his works as carefully as Henry James and endowed his narrators with special and consistent 'points of view,' not only knew what he was about, but was actually constructing a puzzle, a maze, a labyrinth, with diabolical ingenuity." Yet there is ample circumstantial evidence to suggest that Edmund Wilson's point was well-taken when he argued that James "was not clear about the book in his own mind."[16]

To begin with, for all James's reputation as a careful planner, he originally intended the donnée of *The Fount* to serve as the idea for a short story, only to find, as in the case of *The Spoils* and *Maisie,* that he was unable to develop the idea within his prescribed space. In a letter to his literary agent, James B. Pinker, James even confessed that he was experiencing great difficulty bringing the novel to a conclusion, though he immediately tried to cover his tracks by presenting the problem as one of revision rather than composition: "I have found it a more protracted matter to *end* it—I mean finish and super-finish it— than I expected at the moment I originally wrote you about it..." As he was later to admit to Howells, James had so much trouble with this novel that he almost failed to complete it at all:

> I remember how I would have "chucked" *The Sacred Fount* at the 15th thousand word, if in the first place I could have afforded to "waste" 15,000, and if in the second I were not always ridden by a superstitious terror of not finishing, for finishing's and for precedent's sake, what I have begun.

A further clue to the nature of James's dissatisfaction with this book, a dissatisfaction so strong that he decided to exclude it from the Collective Edition of his life's work, can be found in his late preface to *The Ambassadors,* a novel that he began immediately after *The Fount*. In this preface James justifies his use of a third-person central consciousness by insisting that "the first person, in the long piece, is a form foredoomed to looseness" and "the terrible *fluidity* of self-revelation," but in this context "self-revelation" rather than "fluidity" becomes the key term.[17] Despite occasional moments of deliberate self-parody in *The Fount*, James seems to have experienced great difficulty not only in exerting his customary control over the characters in this novel but in maintaining his customary distance from them, especially in the case of the super-subtle narrator.

There are several possible explanations for this. In the first place, James appears to have been unwilling or even unable to establish the kind of distance between himself and his audience which he had gone to such great lengths to achieve in *Maisie* and *The Awkward Age;* and this in spite of the fact that, to an even greater degree than its predecessors, *The Fount* turned on the question of "the adulterine element" or "the delicate case" (as James had termed it in his most recent essay). Conspicuously lacking in both the structural screens and the thematic safeguards which he had previously found necessary when handling this sensitive subject matter before the mixed company of the Anglo-American public, James's treatment of "the great relation between men and women" in *The Fount* is not only less dramatic than in *The Awkward Age* but more direct than in *Maisie*. Although he continued to rely heavily upon extended dialogue and circumlocutive diction as protective devices (the title is a euphemism for an exploitative variety of sexual intercourse), James's tendency towards the indirect exhibition of his own super-subtlety threatened to collapse into mere self-exposure. For the first time, he found himself addressing the novel-reading public not only in the first person but from the point of view of an adult male, thus depriving himself by a single stroke of both the objectivity of the third person and the relative protection which he had achieved by exploring and exploiting the novelistic conventions regarding the limited character and consciousness of the young girl. When he exchanged the presumably limited central consciousness of the young girl for that of the conspicuously super-subtle and highly egotistical narrator of *The Fount*, a man who may himself be an artist and who admits to being ridden by his imagination, James unwittingly made himself—in the character of the narrative "I"—the exposed object of his characters' intense speculation and the overt focus of his readers' bewildered attention. His donnée, with its suggestion of sexual "vampirism," thus took a dangerous and seemingly uncontrollable turn. It became the germ of a rather bizarre variation on his stories of writers and artists, thus completing the process which had begun in *The Spoils* by which James had substituted the character types and themes of his tales of the literary life for the conventional types and themes of the novel.

In an excellent article on *The Fount*, Norma Phillips suggests that the vampire/sacred-fount theme which the narrator expounds can be applied to his relationship with Mrs. Briss, even if it cannot be proven that it corresponds to the sexual relations which they observe or impute. Discussing the second interview between these two characters, Phillips writes: "The terms of their collaboration are plain enough: this is in every way a discussion between a superior and an inferior, a mentor and a pupil." If the narrator is "in command" at this point in the novel, by their third interview Mrs. Briss emerges as a theorist capable of rivalling him; and during their fourth and last interview, she virtually takes over control of the scene. As Phillips concludes, "the vampire theme of fruition and depletion, far from being illusory or superficial, is fundamental to the whole conception of the novel in that it is the very means by which the collapse of the narrator is effected," for Mrs. Briss has "filled her receptacle at the sacred fount of *his* acute consciousness."[18] If we rephrase Phillips' argument in terms of the character types which James had been developing in his tales of the literary life, we can see that the relationship between the narrator and Mrs. Briss bears an obvious resemblance to the many collaborations between super-subtle writers and their equally subtle readers which characterize those tales. But there are several crucial differences. Nowhere in James's previous work is the "master" a male whose primary and most gifted "disciple" is an adult female, and in none of James's tales is discipleship so explicitly presented as a mutually exploitative relationship and a potentially depleting experience for the master. (Although the older artist in the story "The Lesson of the Master" can be said to have exploited his young disciple, the exploitation theme is not reciprocal; and in "The Middle Years," for example, discipleship is presented as a form of mutual devotion and affection.) While the theme of depletion is latent in "The Death of the Lion" as well as in "The Next Time" and "The Figure in the Carpet," it finds full expression only in this novel, where it suggests a dawning consciousness on James's part of the moral and artistic consequences of his uncanny ability to elicit intense and super-subtle responses from both his characters and his readers—especially among the avant-garde. (In this context it is worth noting that in its original form, the donnée treats a vampirish relationship between age and youth, but James immediately began to wonder whether its terms could be "altered to the idea of cleverness and stupidity."[19] Given the recent example of Emile Zola's much-heralded "decline," one cannot help wondering whether James feared a similar "depletion" at the hands of some of his own most ambitious disciples.) If the raffinés of James's short stories can be seen as embodiments of the very type of both the super-subtle character *and* his own super-subtle readers, they are unaware of their unique double status and thus enjoy a saving margin of unconsciousness. But this does not hold true for Mrs.

Briss: for her prototype we must look not to the ostensibly devoted disciples of the tales but to the "prodigious" and quite devious Mrs. Brook.

Nanda's mother and Mrs. Briss share not only a shortened nomenclature and a highly dramatic manner but a common fictional predicament: both are characters whose attempt to conceal a secret of a sexual nature (the intimate figure in the carpet of their private lives?) is threatened by another character (or characters) ultimately acting in their creator's behalf. Yet unlike either the mutual devotion displayed by some of the writers and readers in the tales or the one-sided loyalty and affection which Nanda manages to sustain throughout *The Awkward Age,* Mrs. Briss's continuing collaboration with the narrator of *The Fount* constantly threatens to degenerate into mutual hostility. As if sensing that she is at once something more than just a super-subtle reader and something less than a traditionally drawn character with conventional (and plausible) motivation, Mrs. Briss becomes an increasingly intransigent and rebellious disciple who is also a resentful and uncooperative character. She seems to delight in making things difficult for her creator (as well as for the narrator) by taking advantage of her unprecedented fictional predicament to register her discomfort with and disapproval of the very terms on which she and her fellow characters, including the narrator, are forced to exist. In the closing scene of the novel, her collaboration with the narrator finally does collapse into overt conflict, precisely because their complex relationship lacks the protective propriety of a conventional fictional pretext, whether of literary discipleship or parental concern. When she turns the tables on her ostensible mentor during this final scene, simultaneously denying the validity of his method while exhibiting a superior ability to apply it, she is not only displaying an implicit consciousness of her imposed duplicty but serving notice that she will no longer continue to play this curious double role.

It could even be argued that, in a highly convoluted sense, Mrs. Briss and James's narrator are never more in secret collaboration than in this crucial scene, where both covertly work together to turn the tables on James. All along, their interviews have provided the narrator with a convenient opportunity to indulge in his favorite (and almost sole) occupation, boasting about the rigors of his own merciless method and the perfections of his indirect manner of dealing with his fellow characters. But by constantly insisting upon calling attention to his own manner—which bears an unmistakable resemblance to that of his creator—the narrator has gradually managed to subvert his ostensible role, that of a fictional screen behind which James can conceal his own awkward and highly embarrassing curiosity regarding the most intimate affairs of his characters. Thus instead of diverting attention from his creator, the narrator becomes an all too obvious surrogate for and reflection of James who, during the course of writing the novel, seems to have gradually become aware that his narrator was bent upon achieving this measure of covert revenge. If so, James's sporadic attempts at deliberate self-parody may be regarded as part of an unsuccessful attempt to anticipate and make the best of a bad situation. Although he realized that his obsessed and egocentric narrator was functioning as a disquieting and unflattering reflection of (rather than as a screen for) his authorial presence, James's determination to see the novel through to completion in effect committed him to providing his characters with a unique opportunity to register and enact in his immediate presence the acute discomfort, bordering on terror, which he produced in them.

Evidence to support this line of interpretation can also be found by focusing on the changing nature of the narrator's relationship with Mrs. Server, the supposed partner to one of the liaisons whose inner workings he is so tenaciously observing and so vigorously trying to expose. Under the mounting pressure of the narrator's merciless scrutiny, Mrs. Server desperately attempts to avoid him, a maneuver which he gleefully takes to be a tell-tale symptom of her efforts at concealment. Upon finally cornering this exhausted character, the narrator quite cruelly continues to watch her in James's behalf. In language evocative of a backstage interview with a hardworking actress who is vainly trying to rest between scenes, the narrator notes that "she had folded up her manner in her flounced parasol, which she seemed to drag after her as a sorry soldier his musket." When Mrs. Server begins to flutter "like a bird with a broken wing" under his ever-watchful eye, he decides, not without condescension, to "reassure and soothe and steady her," for he suddenly recognizes that this creature, whom he has pushed to the verge of a total collapse, is on (and in) his hands. As he somewhat scientifically and inhumanely puts it, "the mere mechanism of her expression, the dangling paper lantern itself, was now all that was left in her face." Yet his "most pitiless curiosity" is still not completely satisfied; and he insists upon pushing her to the very brink by asking her, point blank, what has happened to her. Only at this crucial juncture does the narrator finally recognize in Mrs. Server the terrible ravages of a "consuming passion," though he symptomatically fails to recognize that passion as his own. In the manner of a detached scientist examining an exotic specimen, he notes that Mrs. Server reminds him "of a sponge wrung dry and with fine pores agape. Voided and scraped of everything, her shell was merely crushable. So it was brought home to me that the victim could be abased, and so it disengaged itself from these things that the abasement could be conscious." Mrs. Server's only response, her mute but conspicuous consciousness of her abasement, serves as a most telling reproach to James as well as to his narrator, for with this passage the narrator, who is acting on behalf of his creator, reaches new heights (or depths) of human cruelty and callous exposure in his treatment of his fellow characters. The fact that this ugly truth has itself been "brought home" to James can be seen in both the narrator's immediate change of tactics (he belatedly decides that he must "protect" Mrs. Server) and his ultimate acknowledgment, however contained, of the sensation of a novel emotion: "It was as if, abruptly... I had wished to unthink every thought with which I had been occupied for twenty-four hours."[20]

After repudiating this opportunity to terminate abruptly the narrator's obsessive quest, James found his subsequent efforts to contain the narrator's cruelty ineffectual, for he was learning that conscious cruelty, like super-subtlety, could be highly contagious. This becomes clear at the moment when even a minor character like Lady John (whom the narrator has previously considered to be unworthy of his attention) can manage, when pressed, to draw herself up, marshal her manner, and defend herself on his terms and at his expense. As Lady John aptly puts it, he should "give up... the attempt to be a providence," because you "can't be a providence and not be a bore." With remarkable acuteness, she succeeds in aiming her parting shot at her creator's artistic procedures as well as at her interlocuter's tortuous method: "A real providence *knows*; whereas you... have to find out—and to find out even by asking 'the likes of' me." The narrator is thereby forced to come to terms with the effect he has on his fellow characters, admitting "that as it was I who had arrested, who had spoiled their unconsciousness, so it was natural they should fight against me for a possible life in the state I had given them instead." This leads him, in turn, to his ultimate insight and perhaps the ultimate lesson of the novel: "I had spoiled their unconsciousness, I had destroyed it, and it was *consciousness alone* that could make them *effectively* cruel."[21] James might as well have made the same confession to *his* characters (as well as to his audience). Speaking through his first person narrator precisely from the point of view of "the central, sentient, person," he was at last able to realize and acknowledge the fact that it was *he* who was both the "producer" and the "object" of all the terror in his post-theater novels, because it was he alone who had made his characters (and some of his readers?) conscious enough to be effectively cruel. Only after seeing this highly unflattering fictional reflection of himself in the mirror of *The Fount* did James confide to Howells that he was not only eager to drop *The Sense of the Past* but no longer able to care for "'terror' (terror, that is, without 'pity')..." He now perceived that in his convoluted effort to screen himself from the displeasure of the conventional reading public he had, in effect, cruelly substituted and sacrificed his characters, his fictional children, in his place.

What is more, James was then forced to swallow the fact that this sacrifice had been perpetrated in vain. In July of 1901, shortly after *The Fount* made its appearance, the editor of the *Bookman,* an American periodical, summed up James's post-theater career in a review which was as blunt as it was brief.

"Henry James is beyond all question in a bad way," pontificated Harry Thurston Peck. Peck went on to charge:

> He became morbid and somewhat decadent several years ago, when he wrote *What Maisie Knew* and *In the Cage*; but even so, he was interesting, and one could read him through. When he wrote *The Awkward Age* we thought that it was only a temporary lapse; but now that he has produced *The Sacred Fount* he really seems to be sinking into a chronic state of periphrastic perversity.

Given the intense (if highly idiosyncratic) propriety of James's repeated efforts, both in his fiction and his critical essays, to convince the Anglo-American public that the acceptance of the larger latitude would ultimately assure them of a healthier fictional diet, there was no little irony in Peck's formulation of James's "decline," a formulation which endorsed and reiterated the increasingly widespread image of James as a writer whose works could no longer be deemed safe for public consumption. The immediate effect of both this image and *The Fount* was to decrease further the sales of James's books and to wreak new damage on his already strained relationship with the general public, and this precisely at a time when the demand for native American fiction was reaching new peaks.[22]

Ever an acute analyst of the literary marketplace, James had publicly taken note of this unprecedented demand for American fiction in an 1898 article entitled "The Question of the Opportunities." Focusing his attention on the present state of the American literary scene, he had found himself face to face with "the huge, homogeneous and fast-growing population from which the flood of books issues and to which it returns..." From this vantage point, American fiction could only appear to be a literary commodity designed to meet the needs of a public "of proportions that no other single public has approached, least of all those of the periods and societies to which we owe the comparatively small library of books that we rank as the most precious thing in our heritage." James the critic made no attempt to conceal the fact that the pressures exerted by the "great common-schooled and newspapered democracy" figured as a dire threat to this precious literary heritage, if not a fatal blow to the cause of future literary production. However, near the end of the article James proved himself to be quite capable of approaching this situation from an entirely different point of view. Deftly slipping out of his role as critic and into the guise of "a novelist interested in the general outlook of his trade," James began to speculate on the direction which the American novel should take. Temporarily turning his back on the problem of audience, James redirected his attention to the central role of "Business" in American life; and, once launched on this tack, it became clear to him that the "business man" was the typical American figure. The relation between this representative American type and "his wives and daughters... his social substitutes and representatives" contained elements which struck the literary producer "as only yearning for their interpreter," for it presented "the further merit of melting into the huge neighboring province of the special situation of women in an order of things where to be a woman at all—certainly to be a young one—constitutes in itself a social position." This opportunity led James back (albeit by a circuitous route) to his original point of departure, the question of the quality and quantity of the new mass public, for he concluded by insisting that it was women who made up the majority of the American reading public:

> Whether the extraordinary dimensions of the public be a promise or a threat, nothing is more unmistakable than the sex of the largest masses.... Both as readers and as writers on the other side of the Atlantic women have, in fine, "arrived" in numbers not equalled even in England, and they have succeeded in giving the pitch and marking the limits more completely than elsewhere.[23]

The conditions as well as the opportunities of the American literary scene seem to have resolved themselves for James into a single theme, that of the role of women in American culture. Considered as potential characters, women not only presented the English-speaking novelist with a way of "getting at" the American business man but with an interesting situation of their own which demanded treatment. However, considered as potential readers, these same women represented the enormous pressure which the mass public could exert upon the English-speaking novelist in the form of conventional expectations which demanded to be satisfied.

As we have seen, James had hit upon the double aspect of the young unmarried woman as a highly regarded literary and social type in early novels such as *Daisy Miller* and *The Portrait;* and, more recently, he had developed structural devices to exploit these conventions in the post-theater novels which treated adultery. But, as we have also seen, such an artistic procedure placed terrible demands upon all of his fictional characters, especially the young girls. Mrs. Briss might have been speaking not only for her fellow characters but for James's disaffected female readers as well when she confronted him (through his first-person narrator) near the end of *The Sacred Fount.*[24] The very baldness of this confrontation had finally brought home to James, as mere reviews never could, the violence that he was doing to his relationship with both the traditional reading public and the fictional children of his imagination. And he had candidly, if obliquely, acknowledged as much when he put aside *The Sense of the Past* in order to begin work on a "lovely—human, dramatic" scheme addressed to Howells' "more cheerful department." As he projected it here, the fruit of James's reaction against the "terror" of *The Fount* was to be both international and "exquisitely 'pure'"—in short, it would be a novel designed to meet the expectations of Howells' clientele, the women and men who made up the public which he had described in "The Question of the Opportunities." Though its publication was to be delayed for several years, *The Ambassadors* would indeed go far towards meeting those expectations and would do much to restore James's reputation in the eyes of the novel-reading public.[25]

Both the structure and the theme of this novel reveal that James had become intent upon reestablishing a measure of reciprocity in his dealings with both his characters and the general public, a reciprocity which, as he seems finally to have recognized, had all but disappeared from his fiction during the post-theater years. Such reciprocity could take many forms for James, but each of these forms was predicated upon his willingness to trust the intelligence and imagination of his audience. James's lack of such a trust had manifested itself in his plays which were, for the most part, attempts to give the usual theater-going public what he thought it wanted, and in his experimental post-theater fiction, novels in which he relinquished authorial prerogatives, abdicated from the responsibilities of traditional narrative, and placed the burden of exhibited super-subtlety almost entirely upon his characters. We know that faith in the imagination and taste of the general public was obviously not an easy commodity for James to come by, especially given his interpretation of his failure as a playwright and the renewed testimony of his failure to sell. But we also know that he had developed and protected a vision of reciprocity between writers and readers in his tales of the literary life, tales which were read and valued by the English-speaking avant-garde. Thematically and structurally, *The Ambassadors* suggests that James was willing and even eager to give the more traditional reading public another chance to realize this vision, another opportunity to demonstrate that a masterful artist could indeed *make* them grow more imaginative. The possibility, in fact the necessity, of such a transformation had captured his imagination from far back. While still in his twenties, he had written a review of the novels of George Eliot in which he focused upon the essential role played in any novel by "the sympathetic reader." As he had then observed:

> In every novel the work is divided between the reader; but the writer makes the reader very much as he makes his characters. When he makes him ill, that is, makes him indifferent, he does no work; the writer does all. When he makes him well, that is, makes him interested, then the reader does quite half the labor.

James insisted that there was a way to get the reader to do "his share." "It is perhaps a secret," he conceded, "but until it is found out... the art of story-telling cannot be said to have approached perfection."[26]

Many of James's stories of writers and artists had dramatized his vision of and desire to achieve just such a division of labor between writer and reader. Like Ralph Limbert's masterpiece in "The Next Time," these tales had helped to convert "readers into friends and friends into lovers." Their success with the Anglo-American avant-garde must have reinforced James's confidence in his ability to establish just such a relationship, albeit with a highly select audience. During the post-theater years, James had gradually substituted the themes and, to some extent, the character types which he had developed in these stories of literary discipleship for the conventional themes and types of the Anglo-American novel. Whether James was conscious from the start of the possibility that such a substitution might provide him with the solution to two of the fictional problems which most preoccupied his attention—namely the question of how to handle "the adulterine element" before a sexually mixed audience and how to make the reader do "his share"—is extremely doubtful. However it does seem likely that the post-theater novels in general and *The Fount* in particular gradually forced him to come to terms with the moral and artistic consequences of the strange hybrid which he had been developing. *Maisie* and *The Awkward Age* had dramatized the sacrifices entailed when the figure of the young unmarried girl was made to bear the primary burden of exhibited super-subtlety in a novel which treated adultery. On the other hand, *The Fount* had demonstrated equally well the consequences of attempting to treat "a delicate case" without the protective screen of her limited and limiting consciousness. James's next novel can be seen as a conscious effort to revise and exploit this fictional substitution *without* having to depend upon and sacrifice the female young. In other words, *The Ambassadors* represents James's determination to develop an artistic strategy which will enable him to "make" his audience "handle" adultery without permitting either himself or his characters to lapse (or collapse) into conscious cruelty.

This would not be an easy task. After several years spent in superimposing the super-subtle motifs of his tales of the literary life on the more conventional concerns of the traditional novel, James had arrived at a fictional dead end. Now, the necessity of providing Howells with a "pure" serial addressed to his "cheerful department" gave James an opportunity to return to and revise his old invention, the international novel, in light of his post-theater fictional experiments. In this context, it is not difficult to see in Strether a strong resemblance to both Mr. Longdon, Nanda's "oncle d'Amérique" in *The Awkward Age,* and Mrs. Wix, who gazes at her young charge through a pair of perpetual "nippers" in *What Maisie Knew,* both of whom perform the role of substitute guardians whose putative task it is to "save" a younger character from sexual corruption. But James cleverly took advantage of the international aspects of his plot to undercut and disguise such similarities between Strether and his post-theater prototypes. His strategy involved dramatizing and juxtaposing the expectations of the two reading publics among which his reputation had been made, the conventional Anglo-American and the English-speaking avant-garde. He began by embodying the taste, tone, and limitations of the former in the figure of Mrs. Newsome, Chad's mother and the widow of an American business man. Contrary to typical American social and literary conventions as described in "The Question of the Opportunities," Mrs. Newsome herself would not make a personal appearance in the novel but would be represented instead by her social substitute and fiancé, Lambert Strether. Appropriately enough, James chose to define Strether's professional identity in terms of his career as the editor *not* of a newspaper (or a little magazine) but of the *Woollett Review,* a highly respectable periodical with a "lovely" green (rather than a "decadent" yellow) cover which is backed by his future wife. The self-reflexivity of this aspect of the plot becomes clear when we recall not only that the original donnée for the novel had concerned William Dean Howells, perhaps the most prominent American magazine editor of the day, but also that it was Howells who made it possible for James to have the work published serially in America by the *North American Review,* the prestigious American journal which, like its fictional Woollett counterpart, was chiefly known for its economic, political, and ethical commentary.[27]

In direct proportion as Strether represents and speaks for this "green" journal, he characterizes himself as limited by the infantile proprieties of the American magazine public. Indeed, James decided to anticipate and undercut the conventional expectations of his American serial audience by caricaturing those expectations in the form of the cheap and easy story line which Strether and Mrs. Newsome jointly propose as an explanation for Chad's prolonged absence in Europe. Reduced to its simplest terms, their hackneyed version of the "plot" rests on a vision of Chad as a typically innocent American who needs to be rescued (or "saved") from the corruptions of Europe as embodied by the horrible woman who has seduced and "kept" him in Paris. This "vulgar" plot serves James well, for Strether's initial willingness to see himself as Mrs. Newsome's ambassador not only provides him with a plausible and even an honorable motive for interfering in Chad's affairs but characterizes his imagination as limited (or "ridden," to use James's terms) by his "New England conscience."[28] In turn, only the motive provided by Mrs. Newsome's melodramatic vision of Chad's plight and the limitations of Strether's provincial New England conscience set him apart from the narrator of *The Fount,* who confesses that he is "ridden" by his hyper-active imagination and who conspicuously lacks a justifiable human pretext for meddling in what is, after all, none of his business. However, from the very outset of the novel, Strether also displays a readiness not only to reconsider and revise ("edit"?) Mrs. Newsome's version of the plot but to adopt a new one better suited to the actualities of Chad's case. James was clearly faced with a structural and thematic dilemma here not unlike the one he had faced in *Maisie.* If he made Strether imagine "too much," he would revert back to the cruel (and unpopular) super-subtlety of his post-theater fiction, most notably *The Sacred Fount*. Yet make Strether imagine "too little" and the plot of *The Ambassadors* would collapse into Mrs. Newsome's highly conventional version, a collapse which would seriously undercut and undermine his efforts to make more conventional readers do their share of the work. James attempted to resolve this problem on two levels. Thematically, he developed a contrast and exploited the conflict between Strether's relative freedom of imagination and Mrs. Newsome's inability to do anything but adhere inflexibly to her old terms. Strether's attempts to soften her position, both a sign and a consequence of his gradual rejection of her brand of imaginative rigidity, not only provide one of the key elements of "suspense" (and humor) in the novel but dramatize James's desire to elicit a similar imaginative openness and flexibility from his magazine public. And, in turn, Strether's recognition that such "deep diplomacy" could cost him "everything" expresses James's own awareness that he is incurring a similar risk should he fail in *his* attempt to reshape his audience's expectations.

Given these risks, it becomes easier to understand why James now chose to readopt and revise a rather traditional fictional device, the confiding narrator. Though he would candidly reveal his reliance upon a traditional theatrical device, the confidant or *"ficelle,"* in the preface which he later wrote for the New York Edition of the novel, James cleverly throws dust in his readers' eyes regarding his use of and dependence upon the narrator of *The Ambassadors*, perhaps because he disdained the idea of being caught by his avant-garde public in the act of using so old-fashioned a novelistic aid to understanding. Yet as John E. Telford has recognized, James makes frequent appearances in *The Ambassadors* as "the editorially omniscient author," speaking frankly in the first person and referring to his central character by turns as "our hero," "our friend," and "poor Strether." Telford considers James's use of a first-person narrator in this novel to be part of a devious "tiptoe technique, in which James patters quietly back and forth between authorial omniscience and Strether's point of view" in order to conceal shifts in point of view.[29] While Telford's analysis of James's motives for developing this strategy may, in fact, appear to be quite accurate in light of the retrospective emphasis James placed in his Prefaces upon maintaining consistency of point of view, his willingness to resume a more or less traditional narrative presence and voice at this point in his career can also be seen as a strategy designed largely to placate his more conventional readers and thereby reduce the above-mentioned risks. By resuming direct communication with his readers while covertly controlling their perceptions through Strether's limited and limiting consciousness, James could attempt to regain their confidence. The narrator's use of such familiar epithets as "our friend" and "poor Strether" were meant to convince James's audience that far from being a calculating and manipulative behind-the-scenes master (which he, in fact, was), Strether's creator was a trustworthy and respectable author who cared about what happened to his characters (which was also ultimately quite true). At the same time, the narrator's confidential tone and his use of such old-fashioned (and sometimes condescending) modes of reference to Strether aided James in his effort to establish in his readers a sense of the limitations of his hero's consciousness, a sense which had to be evoked and sustained if there was to be any chance for James to develop and maintain a sympathetic bond between Strether, himself, and the novel-reading public.

This structural concession to the undeveloped portion of James's audience was complimented and to some extent paralleled by his use of yet another structural device, the *ficelle,* this one aimed primarily (though not exclusively) at James's avant-garde readership. As James presents her in his preface, Strether's confidant is a thoroughly subordinate character whose sole duty it is to act as the reader's "friend" via her conversations with Strether. But James does not let his audience in on the fact that this confidant, Maria Gostrey, is playing a characteristically Jamesian double role, for she functions as her creator's "friend" as well. If Strether's limitations are largely established and recorded by the narrator (who is constantly telling his readers what Strether does *not* know or will only find out *later*), it is primarily (though not exclusively) Strether's conversations with the super-subtle Miss Gostrey which reveal and stimulate his potential for imaginative growth. During these conversations Maria gradually makes Strether aware of both his own limitations and his author's expectations, a recognition on his part which signals his fitness to play (and her willingness to prepare him for) the demanding role in the unconventional drama which is to follow. From the moment Strether lands in England, this highly cosmopolitan guide for Americans in Europe begins to tutor his (and the common reader's) imagination in behalf of James and his avant-garde audience. Unwilling to exhibit or exert his own super-subtle imagination directly through his narrative voice, James chooses instead to preside over the joint initiation of Strether and his audience from behind the screen of Maria Gostrey's presence. He clearly expects her sympathetic appreciation of cosmopolitan ways to have a contagious effect on Strether (and, through him, on the traditional Anglo-American public). In her guise as Strether's guide and mentor, Maria educates not Strether's moral sense, which is already highly developed, but his imagination; and until he (and the "babyish" reader) is ready to "toddle" alone, she holds herself ever-ready to "bear him up" and "see him through." Half oracle and half dialogue coach, she pays Strether a flattering kind of attention which indirectly expresses his creator's affection for him as well as their mutual confidence in his ability to play his appointed part in the international drama, a performance whose substance and texture bears little resemblance to Mrs. Newsome's melodrama of redemption.

Strether repays the compliment precisely by showing that he is susceptible to this kind of subtle "bribe" to his imagination. And so when, after finally meeting Chad—an event which takes place, appropriately enough, in Maria Gostrey's box at the theater—Strether expresses his astonished sense of his young friend's apparent mastery of the art of living, his cautious acknowledgment of Chad's altered state is a demonstration of his ability to respond to Chad's situation in a way which is neither unimaginative nor ungenerous rather than a symptom of his possible perversity of imagination (as was the case with the narrator of *The Fount*). While Strether's preparation for this initial test of his character has been essentially the work of Maria Gostrey, James deliberately downplays her role by framing Strether's response to Chad in familiar international terms. Strether's stated fondness for continental fiction legitimizes and makes presentable his revised "reading" of Chad's relationship to Madame de Vionnet, which he now perceives as a variation on the continental social and literary convention which deemed it permissible (and even desirable) that a young man be initiated into the art of life by an older woman. However, quite in keeping with his professional identity as an American editor bound to (and by) the taste of the magazine public, Strether initially needs to imagine an "edited" version of this familiar French plot, one which will conveniently cloak or muffle the sexual aspects of such a relationship. James anticipates and attempts to accommodate this need with the help of Chad and his super-subtle friends, a charming circle of highly cosmopolitan "raffinés" who conspire to act as though Madame de Vionnet has formed the young American not for herself but for her young daughter, Jeanne. Their convincing performance—especially during the key scene in Gloriani's garden where Madame de Vionnet and Jeanne make their first appearance in the novel—enables Strether to view Chad's relationship with Marie de Vionnet as a "virtuous attachment," for they have successfully presented it to him as a magnificent practical example of the "innocent" art of initiation.

While this interpretation, in turn, leaves Strether free to meet and pay tribute to Chad's teacher, the woman whose subtle arts have made him what he is (or appears to be!), it also demonstrates the fact that Strether's own initiation into the art of reading life is far from complete. If, acting in James's behalf, Maria has prepared Strether (and James's readers) to respond imaginatively to Gloriani's collection of *"gros bonnets"* and *"femmes du monde,"* a much more varied range of social types than the provincial ladies and gentlemen who populate the Woolletts of Victorian America (and England), it is now up to Marie de Vionnet and her fellow characters to present her relationship with Chad in such a manner that Strether (and James's conventional audience) will not be obliged to confront directly the depths of intimacy which form its basis. With this in mind, she acts the part of the eager mother so effectively during her first private interview with Strether that their encounter immediately strikes him as a safe relation. Indeed, Strether soon finds himself responding to the Countess' appeal for help by promising to save her, though he does not yet know what his words mean. Ten days later, on the night of his young friend's dinner party, Chad's super-subtle friends, Little Bilham and Miss Barrace, continue Strether's education by revealing what this promise may entail.[30] Even young Jeanne de Vionnet participates in the initiation process, for her presentation of herself as the very type of the innocent *jeune fille* effectively prevents Strether from questioning her closely about her true feelings towards Chad. By this time, his initiation has proceeded far enough for him to realize that Jeanne's delicate character has not been formed to bear any such pressure; and, in a distinct reversal of the motifs of the post-theater fiction, Strether successfully appeals to Jeanne's mother, asking her not to sacrifice her daughter by trying to find out how much she likes Chad. Significantly, Strether's willingness to make such a request (and Madame de Vionnet's willingness to comply with it) marks a new stage in their developing intimacy. Instead of maintaining a diplomatic distance from Marie de Vionnet, Strether has connected himself to her by putting himself in her dept. Only at this point does Little Bilham strategically disclose the potentially damaging information that it is Madame de Vionnet, not Jeanne, whom Chad cares for, even revealing that she cares more for him than he does for her. Just as the raffinés have hoped, Strether by now regards himself as morally obligated to honor his promise and repay his debt to Madame de Vionnet. He does this by insisting that Chad ought not to give her up, an insistence which amounts to an outright rejection of Mrs. Newsome's version of the plot and announces his willingness to function in a capacity which bears little resemblance to his appointed role as her ambassador. Strether's initiation is almost complete.

All too aware of the false position in which he has now placed himself, Strether decides to seek refuge from the pressures of his position in the Cathedral of Notre Dame, only again to meet Madame de Vionnet. There, under the influence of the scene and the spirit of Victor Hugo (whose seventy bound volumes he has just purchased), Strether decides to give her a sign that he is finally ready to accept and appreciate her on her own terms—as a wonderful example of her type, the *femme du monde*. This sign consists of taking her to an early lunch at "a delightful house of entertainment on the left bank—a place of pilgrimage for the knowing" (to which Chad has never "initiated" her) and telling her that he considers her to be worth saving. Strether senses that this intimate yet seemingly innocent Parisian lunch marks the distance he has travelled since an earlier pre-theater dinner in London when— highly conscious of Maria Gostrey's "cut down" dress and her exposed shoulders and bosom—he had been preoccupied by the overwhelming contrast with Mrs. Newsome's perpetually ruff-encircled throat. Now it is the implied contrast between Miss Gostrey and the even more seductive (though quite chastely attired) Countess de Vionnet which makes him feel that he has, at last, "let himself go" and "touched bottom." Having intentionally absented herself from the novel since Gloriani's party in order to insure that her function as Strether's "friend" and tutor will be silently divided up and taken over by Chad and his circle—most notably by Marie de Vionnet herself—Maria returns to Paris shortly after this scene. Satisfied that her absence has helped him, she indirectly acknowledges both the success of this substitution and the near completion of Strether's education by pronouncing him ready at last to "toddle alone."[31]

But just as Madame de Vionnet has covertly replaced Maria as Strether's tutor, so too has Strether's intransigent friend, Waymarsh, silently taken over his duties as Mrs. Newsome's European ambassador. Through Waymarsh's continuing presence in the book, James is able to preside over the transformation of Strether's consciousness while maintaining his ability to anticipate and accommodate the conventional response of those resisting readers who, like Mrs. Newsome herself, are constitutionally unable either to participate in or appreciate that transformation. A constant reminder and loyal representative of the willfully uninitiated and permanently unsympathetic portion of James's public, Waymarsh sounds the alarm to Woollett, bringing down the wrath of Mrs. Newsome in the form of a second delegation of ambassadors composed of her formidable daughter Sarah Pocock, Sarah's ineffectual husband Jim, and her charming niece Mamie. During a subsequent meeting between Mrs. Newsome's two ambassadors which takes place in Sarah's Paris hotel room, Strether repays Maria's confidence in him by seizing the opportunity not to save himself but to make good his promise to "save" Madame de Vionnet. Under the watchful eyes of Mrs. Pocock, Waymarsh, and Madame de Vionnet, he rises to the occasion by imagining that they are all "gathered for a performance, the performance of 'Europe' by his confederate [Madame de Vionnet] and himself." He then proceeds to live up to this imaginative conception of his situation by coming to the aid of his confederate, who is struggling to present herself to the suspicious Sarah Pocock in the respectable guise in which she initially appeared to Mrs. Newsome's first ambassador—that of the eager mother (rather than in her true identity as Chad's unhappily married mistress). "You may think me indiscreet," she announces with a candor which is intended to disarm Sarah, "but I've *such* a desire my Jeanne shall know an American girl [Mamie] of the really delightful kind." Even Waymarsh gets into the act by responding: "Yes, Countess, the American girl's a thing that your country must at least allow ours the privilege to say we *can* show you. But her full beauty is only for those who can make use of her." When Madame de Vionnet turns to Strether, pleading for him to "speak of us in such a way!—" he dutifully picks up his cue and completes her thought with the words "as that something can't but come of it?" While on the surface Strether's refusal to disavow Madame de Vionnet's motives and dissassociate himself publicly from her merely amounts to good taste and fidelity to his promise, he goes beyond mere duty and virtually invites Sarah to regard them as co-conspirators when he adds "Oh something *shall* come of it! I take a great interest!" To give added emphasis to his words he escorts Marie de Vionnet to her carriage, their joint exit a further testimony to their community of interest.[32]

Quite characteristically, it is not until he visits Madame de Vionnet at her home a few days later that Strether realizes just how completely, under Sarah's very eyes, the Countess has "pulled him into her boat... They were in it together this moment as they hadn't yet been, and he hadn't at present uttered the least of the words of alarm or remonstrance that had died on his lips at the hotel." Acutely conscious of the fact that both Sarah and Waymarsh regard him as a traitor, Strether prepares himself for a final confrontation with his replacement. This scene takes place at his hotel, where he asks Sarah point-blank whether "You don't, on your honor, appreciate Chad's fortunate development?'" His very directness gives her the precious opportunity she has been waiting for all along and she proceeds to make a good old-fashioned scene:

> "Fortunate?" she echoed again. And indeed she was prepared. "I call it hideous." Her departure had been for some minutes marked as imminent, and she was already at the door that stood open to the court, from the threshold of which she delivered herself of this judgement...

If Sarah's melodramatic reply, emphasized by her subsequent exit from the novel with her husband, her sister-in-law, and Waymarsh in tow, amounts to a final attempt on James's part to anticipate and accommodate the response of those intransigent readers who remain resolutely unsympathetic to Strether's point of view, her departure is an invitation to those readers to follow suit by putting down the equally "hideous" novel for good. "She passed out as she spoke and took her way straight across the court... and the manner of her break, the sharp shaft of her rejoinder, had an intensity by which Strether was at first kept in arrest."[33]

However, Strether's imagination still has one further hurdle to clear before James can pronounce him "complete." "Poor Strether" acknowledges his sense of this impending test when he admits to Miss Barrace that he feels as if all his fellow characters are "knowing and watching and waiting." To which she replies: "We know you as the hero of the drama, and we're gathered to see what you'll do." The climax of this much more subtle drama occurs off-stage, as it were, in a lovely village outside of Paris. Here, in a "small and primitive pavilion" on the edge of a garden by a "full grey-blue stream," Strether sees "exactly the right thing" to satisfy his imagination and make the picture "compose"—"a boat advancing round the bend and containing a man who held the paddles and a lady, at the stern, with a pink parasol." But when the "young man in shirt-sleeves" and the "young woman easy and fair" turn out to be none other than Chad and Marie de Vionnet, this charming "picture" suddenly becomes "a sharp fantastic crisis" for Strether. Eager to avoid another unpleasant "scene," Strether hesitates a few seconds before giving them a sign that he has recognized them. He immediately forms an impression, "destined only to deepen, to complete itself, that they had something to put a face upon, to carry off and make the best of, and that it was she who, admirably on the whole, was doing this." Sensing that Marie de Vionnet's sudden reversion to her native French is an artful effort to simulate "an overflow of surprise and amusement" and get "somewhat away from him," he even begins to worry that they might secretly suspect him "of having plotted this coincidence, taking such pains as might be to give it the semblance of an accident," though he quickly dismisses this somewhat perverse thought. Instead of reacting to and thereby exposing the "*lie* in the charming affair," the revealed truth of the couple's sexual intimacy, Strether justifies the confidence of James and his sympathetic readers (who have become, along with Strether, embarrassed spectators to this potentially "violent" scene) by aiding Madame de Vionnet in her effort to maintain the illusion (reality?) that her relationship with Chad is, nevertheless, a "virtuous attachment." Brought face to face with their profound intimacy, Strether insists upon regarding her not as that comparatively vulgar type, the scheming mistress, but as a consummate comic actress whose extemporaneous performance had been "wonderful for readiness, for beautiful assurance, for the way her decision was taken on the spot, without time to confer with Chad, without time for anything." While Strether's willingness to focus retrospectively not on the revealed "lie" but on Madame de Vionnet's "wonderful" manner is clearly meant to serve as a cue to James's initiated audience, who were expected to do the same, the master magician gives the situation one final turn of the screw by making Strether perceive that he himself is responsible for the aspect of "the show" which most disagrees with his "spiritual stomach"—"the quantity of make-believe" involved. "Could he, literally, quite have faced the other event? Would he have been capable of making the best of it with them?" wonders Strether, only to confess that he "had dressed the possibility" of their sexual intimacy "in vagueness, as a little girl might have dressed her doll."[34] (These terms clearly evoke and link him to his youthful female precursors, especially Maisie.)

Recognizing "at last that he had really been trying all along to suppose nothing" and worrying that "his labor had been lost," Strether feels the need to talk things over with his friend Miss Gostrey, who he fears will ask him "'What on earth—that's what I want to know now—had you then supposed?'" But once he is again in her presence, Strether comes to quite a different realization. She has shrewdly counted all along on his not supposing anything:

> It came out for him more than ever yet that she had had from the first a knowledge she believed him not to have had, a knowledge the sharp acquisition of which might be destined to make a difference for him. The difference for him might not inconceivably be an arrest of his independence and a change in his attitude—in other words a revulsion in favour of the principles of Woollett.

Seeing that "the shock" has descended but that Strether hasn't, "all the same, swung back" to Mrs. Newsome, Maria feels justified in announcing at last that he is finally "complete." Yet Strether's "completeness" turns out to have unanticipated consequences for the super-subtle women who have made him what he now is. When Maria dutifully informs him that Madame de Vionnet thinks that they "might at any rate have been friends," a covert way of hinting at a possible future intimacy between them. Strether readily acknowledges this (previously unthinkable) possibility, but only to disavow it: "That's just ... why I'm going." Perhaps anticipating the fact that Strether will respond in a similar manner to her own veiled offer of a deeper intimacy than they have yet enjoyed, Maria is moved to exclaim "I'm sorry for us all!"[35]

The key to Strether's determination to pass up even Maria's highly tempting offer "of exquisite service, of lightened care, for the rest of his days..." is his fear that Chad may already have "forsaken" the magnificent Madame de Vionnet, if not for the considerable financial "bribes" of the "art" of advertising then for the comparatively vulgar sexual attractions of some other woman. Faced with the example of Chad, whose initiated state has rendered him capable of such refined "criminality," Strether can only come to terms with and justify his own initiation by falling back upon his New England conscience, which dictates that he should "not, out of the whole affair," have gotten "anything" for himself.[36] Although he has clearly rejected "the principles of Woollett" as represented by marriage to Mrs. Newsome, Strether remains unable or unwilling to embrace "the larger latitude" in the form of a continuing relationship with Marie de Vionnet or Maria Gostrey. Caught between the conventional demands of old-fashioned novel readers and the super-subtle expectations of the "raffinés," James's "hero" ends up disappointing both. Though Strether and his creator had each forsaken the literary and social conventions of Woollett, neither was ready to turn a serious flirtation with the avant-garde into a permanent liaison.[37]

6
A Substitute Performance

Most critics agree that *The Ambassadors* marks the beginning of a new phase of James's career, for in that novel, as well as in the two major novels which follow it, *The Wings of the Dove* and *The Golden Bowl,* he returned to the international scene and theme after a protracted absence of almost twenty years. James's biographer, Leon Edel, has gone so far as to argue that in these three final novels James in effect rewrote his literary past. According to Edel, *The Ambassadors* amounts to "a return to *The American* in which the writer at fifty-seven redreamed in his maturity what he had written at thirty-four." Similarly, Edel considers *The Wings* and *The Golden Bowl* to be mature "retellings" of James's early masterpiece, *The Portrait of a Lady.*[1] The importance of these early international novels to the development of the character types and themes which dominate the fiction James produced in his third or final phase should certainly not be underestimated. However, the elaborate structure and strange texture of the major novels can best be accounted for by noting the covert but unmistakable family resemblance which they bear to both the non-international fiction and the tales of literary discipleship which James produced during and immediately following his theater years. As we have seen, although James went (and would continue to go) to great lengths to disguise the similarities between *The Sacred Fount* and *The Ambassadors,* the latter was in effect a reaction to (and a revision of) the former. James had to confront the terror inspired by his narrative presence and exorcise the contagious cruelty bred by his artistic procedures in *The Fount* before he could compensate for and redeem them in *The Ambassadors.* It is almost as if the master's highly complex and convoluted late manner, which is generally regarded as a revised version of his earlier style, had reached a stage of development at which he could only function effectively by treating an entire novel as the dry run (or discarded "scenario") for its successor.

Not totally unlike George Dencombe, the fictional master of "The Middle Years," James seemed to regard himself as an artist who "had ripened too late and was so clumsily constituted that he had to teach himself by his mistakes." To adopt Dencombe's overstated and somewhat melodramatic terms, his development as a writer "had been abnormally slow, almost grotesquely gradual," perhaps because—like Ralph Limbert—he had continually found himself torn between the conflicting demands of a public which he perceived as split into antagonistic factions: male versus female, cosmopolitan versus provincial, avant-garde versus conventional. To put the case more positively, the master who presided over Strether's successful "completion" as both a character and a reader in *The Ambassadors* was, in effect, enacting "poor Dencombe's" dream of literary immortality, for he was having "another go," a "second age" during which he could return to the materials accumulated over a lifetime devoted almost exclusively to the art of fiction and revise them in the light of his "splendid 'last manner.'" James obliquely endorsed such an exaggerated version (and strictly retrospective vision) of his own development in a letter which he wrote to his old friend, Grace Norton, near the close of 1902. Having just completed *The Wings of the Dove* and not yet begun work on *The Golden Bowl*, he confided his belief that "it takes one whole life...for some people to learn how to live at all, which is absurd if there is not to be another in which to apply the lessons."[2] The particular lessons James had learned from *The Ambassadors* can be inferred by comparing this novel to its successors, *The Wings* and *The Golden Bowl*, especially in terms of his handling of the adulterine aspect of the plots and his treatment of the international American girl. In both *The Fount* and *The Ambassadors* James had to some extent departed from the pattern of his post-theater fiction by choosing an adult male to play the demanding role of central consciousness in novels which treated adultery. Mamie Pocock, the American girl, and Jeanne de Vionnet, the French *jeune fille*, had each played only a minor part in James's first mature international drama. In marked contrast, the master returned to the figure of not one but two young unmarried females in *The Wings*, one American and the other English, as if he were indeed attempting to rewrite or revise not only *The Portrait of a Lady* but those post-theater novels—most notably *The Awkward Age*—which challenged Anglo-American literary conventions regarding the depiction of sexual relations.

Evidence that the significance and consequences of these conventions were still very much on James's mind during this period can be seen not only in the comic treatment which they receive in *The Ambassadors* but in observations upon the international literary scene which appear in an article he published in the *North American Review* just two months before commencing work on *The Wings*. Although he began by indulging in one of his customary castigations of the "conspiracy of silence" imposed upon Anglo-American novelists and followed this up with his familiar charge that the conventions regarding the representation of sexual relations had "blighted" the English-speaking novel, James publicly began to wonder where the "free exercise" of the art of the novel might lead in the absence of such a "system." Claiming that a decisive change was occurring on the Anglo-American literary scene (a change which he himself had described and endorsed in "The Future of the Novel"), he once again observed that as writers and readers of fiction, members of the younger generation—especially women—were "emancipating" themselves from conventions, both in and out of literature. Yet for the first time in his career, he found himself arguing that "the new force thus liberated" would produce what he could only conceive of as "a new kind of vulgarity," the kind which resulted from the absence or outright defiance of convention. The career of the Neapolitan woman novelist, Matilde Serao, provided James with the "precious example" he needed in order to illustrate this disturbing phenomenon and demonstrate "what might with a little time become of our fiction were our particular conventions suspended." Insisting that all of Serao's "novels of passion" illustrated a signal lesson for producers of Anglo-American fiction, he warned:

> The effect, then... of the undertaking to give *passione* its whole place is that by the operation of a singular law no place speedily appears to be left for anything else; and the effect of that in turn is greatly to modify, first the truth of things, and second, with small delay, what may be left of them of their beauty.

In other words, the price to be paid for this new freedom from convention would amount to nothing less than "an exposure... to a new kind of vulgarity," a quantity of which the Anglo-American world already had, according to James, "kinds enough." This prospect moved him to conclude that "the absence of the convention throws the writer back on tact, taste, delicacy, discretion, subjecting these principles to a strain from which the happy office of its presence is, in a considerable degree and for performers of the more usual endowment, to relieve him." Unrelenting strain or outright vulgarity thus appeared to be the only alternatives to convention; and faced with the usual English-speaking novelist's inability to sustain the former, James found himself at the end of the essay in the novel position of turning "round again to the opposite pole" and laying "a clinging hand on dear old Jane Austen."[3]

While James explicitly attributed his alarm and this extraordinary public about-face to the recent appearance of a new type of fiction, "commonly identified as the 'sexual'" (which, as he correctly claimed, was predominantly the work of "the female hand"), the evident conviction in his voice when he spoke of the extraordinary strain placed on the artist's "tact, taste, delicacy, [and] discretion" in the absence of convention had a more intimate source than his familiarity with newspaper notices regarding the "salience" of "sexual fiction."[4] His own repeated experiments with the novel of passion (most notably *The Ambassadors*) had made him only too aware of the dangerous and unanticipated consequences of emancipation from Anglo-American literary conventions regarding sexual relations. While it is true that James had neither ignored these laws nor defied them outright in the post-theater fiction, in his most recent novel he had largely succeeded in subverting them by making them the primary focus of both his central character and his audience. The resulting potential for the new kind of vulgarity which James identified in his assessment of Serao's novels had indeed surfaced, however briefly and belatedly, in book 12 during Strether's final scene with Madame de Vionnet. By this point in the novel, Strether's initiation into "the larger latitude" of the avant-garde has reached completion. As a direct result, he realizes for the first time the sheer depth of the Countess' consuming passion for Chad and recognizes at last that she is "afraid for her life." Distraught at the idea that Strether now sees her as she really is and as she must take herself, Marie bursts into tears, momentarily "giving up all attempt at a manner." Although she recovers her customary control almost immediately, this consummate actress is temporarily reduced in both Strether's and the reader's eyes from "the finest and subtlest" of creatures to the time-worn category of an aging mistress whose devious arts can no longer conceal the fact that she is "as vulgarly troubled, in very truth, as a maid servant crying for her young man."[5] This sudden collapse into vulgarity, however temporary, could only have figured as an abject warning to an author about to embark on the treatment of not one but two "delicate cases." As James had obliquely admitted and predicted in his essay on Matilde Serao, even "an eminent individual" (presumably like himself) might have to supplement his unusual endowment of tact and taste with a reliance on literary convention if he was to give passion its place in the English-speaking novel without sacrificing either the truth of things or their beauty.

In this context it is worth noting that although he seemed to see the heroine of his scenario for *The Wings* "perhaps as an American," projecting her "*homme d'affaires*" as "a good American comedy-type," James's designation of her nationality can be explained in terms of his desire to cater to the taste of conventional theater audiences by following up on the modest success of the stage version of *The American*. There is nothing else in the original donnée which would qualify it as international or necessitate making its central figure an American girl. Yet James ultimately chose to cast Milly Theale, the American "heiress of all the ages," in the extremely demanding role of the "young creature... who, at 20, on the threshold of a life that has seemed boundless, is suddenly condemned to death (by consumption, heart disease, or whatever) by the voice of the physician."[6] Unfortunately, no further notebook entries survive regarding the subsequent transformation of this scenario for a play into a novel seven years later; but circumstantial evidence does suggest that James began this process by attempting to modify the strategy of exploiting Anglo-American magazine conventions which he had adopted in *The Ambassadors*. As he later confided to his friend H. G. Wells, by then one of the most successful English novelists of the rising generation, James had prepared a preliminary statement for *The Wings* and addressed it to the editor of an American periodical in the hope of having the novel serialized there. In a letter to Wells written shortly after the publication of the novel, James insisted that he destroyed these "detailed and explicit plans" after the "unconvinced and ungracious editors" rejected his overture. Although he boasted that the book "was then written, the subject treated, on a more free and independent scale," he remained deliberately vague about the precise nature of the ostensible changes in plan which followed upon his emancipation from magazine restrictions and conditions. He went on to claim that the possiblity of his addressing any other such "manifesto to the dim editorial mind" was highly unlikely, explaining that "in the first place they will none of me, and in the second the relief, and greater intellectual dignity, so to speak, of working on one's own scale, one's own line of continuity and in one's own absolutely independent *tone,* is too precious to me to be again forfeited."[7] Given James's frequent complaints to his literary agent about his inability to "work down" as well as his continual private exhortations to himself to "let himself go," it seems quite likely that the freedom of scale resulting from this failure to achieve serialization did figure to him as a welcome relief. However, given his recent reappraisal of the value of literary conventions regarding sexual relations, it is equally likely that the prospect of total freedom of "line" and independence of "tone" struck him as an added difficulty rather than as a long-awaited opportunity. Nor does the avant-garde point of view which he adopts in this letter to Wells square with the fact that, as his unpublished letters to his literary agent reveal, James was to make repeated though unsuccessful attempts to place his subsequent novel, *The Golden Bowl,* in an American periodical.[8] This posture of conspicuous disdain for magazine conditions and proprieties is quite what one would expect to find in a private exchange between the master and an admirer from the younger generation; but it should be regarded as a carefully cultivated pose which may have been intended, in this particular case, to deflect Wells' attention from the more conventional aspects of the novel and to deny James's private frustration at being blocked from using serialization as a presentable pretext for returning once again to seemingly outmoded international themes and clinging to conventions which he had publicly challenged and previously disavowed.

Interestingly enough, James did not consider the final product to be an unqualified success. Although he would eventually insist in his preface to *The Wings* that the novel suffers from a strictly structural flaw—namely "my regular failure to keep the appointed halves of my whole equal"—his references to a "makeshift middle" and "alternations" from one "successive centre" of consciousness to another suggest considerable authorial vacillation, vacillation which may be the direct result of his continuing attempt to steer a middle course in his treatment of the "delicate" case between the conflicting expectations of the usual novel-reading public and the literary avant-garde.[9] James has two audiences to woo in both *The Ambassadors* and *The Wings,* but in the latter novel he tries to meet and modify their contrasting expectations not by transforming one central consciousness which is capable of appreciating and responding to both but by shuttling back and forth between the point of view of two competing heroines, one conspicuously American and the other conspicuously super-subtle.

As was the case with the casting of Lambert Strether as an American magazine editor in *The Ambassadors,* James's presentation of Milly Theale in the old-fashioned guise of the quintessential American girl, the international "heiress of all the ages," originated as a bid to gain the attention and maintain the sympathy of his more traditional Anglo-American readers. It was also part of his sustained attempt to compensate for and counterbalance his unconventional treatment of the passionate relationship between Kate Croy and Merton Densher. Instead of providing the orphaned and unprotected Milly with a good American comedy-type in the form of an "*homme d'affaires,*" James supplemented her pure and innocent presence by amplifying and reflecting it in the consciousness of her confidante and travelling companion, Susan Stringham, a New England authoress who contributes her stories only "to the best magazines" and who tries to guide and protect her young friend, however ineffectively. In marked contrast to these two very respectable and highly conventional international types, James's other heroine, Kate Croy, is a modern and thoroughly super-subtle unmarried woman whose selfish and manipulative Aunt Maud bears an uncanny resemblance to the mothers of James's post-theater novels. Not unlike an older version of Maisie and Nanda, Kate finds herself having the kind of "adventure" which is (as James would soon describe it with tongue-in-cheek circumlocution in a preface) "so perversely and persistently but of a type impossible to ladies respecting themselves." Like this kind of lady, whose respect for herself and social proprieties prevents her from having adventures of her own, the American girl as a type was so rooted in the conventional "reserves and omissions and suppressions of life" that she could only appear quaint and touchingly out of date if she remained in character. Indeed, the emphasized purity of Milly's character is such that while she is quite capable of eliciting rare performances from others, she herself can neither exhibit nor acquire sufficient subtlety of motive to sustain "a human, a personal 'adventure,'" of her own.[10] However, this fatal flaw qualifies Milly to enact the transcendent role of the exquisitely pure dove whose final flight of selfless generosity is intended to redeem the vulgarity which it rises above and whose wonderful wings can spread wide enough to conceal the gilded ugliness from which it flies.

It is Kate rather than Milly who possesses and displays the dramatic presence which establishes, largely determines, and all but totally dominates the tone and texture of the novel, a presence which is admirably equipped to satisfy the super-subtle expectations of James's avant-garde readers but hardly calculated to reassure (or appeal to) the more traditional members of his public. From her first appearance as the stunningly handsome but "penniless girl" who offers to give up everything for her father in the opening scene of the novel to her final exit as the jealous lover who delivers her last lines with an eloquent shake of her head, it is Kate Croy rather than Milly Theale who bears most of the burdens of exhibited super-subtlety in James's international drama. Although she proves herself to be a highly versatile actress who is capable of playing any part which comes her way by turning almost every obstacle to her happiness into an opportunity to perform, she is ultimately doomed to fail. James himself, in the guise of Kate's ne'er-do-well father, sets the tone and stage for the ensuing drama when he rejects her initial presentation of herself as a dutiful and loving daughter, in effect forcing her to embrace a devious double role. Abandoned by her creator (like her post-theater prototypes), Kate signs what amounts to a run-of-the-play contract with her wealthy Aunt Maud, another of James's fictional surrogates, who insists that she perform the part of the "brilliant" and highly marriageable niece (even though she knows quite well that Kate is passionately in love with a poor but promising journalist, Merton Densher). What Aunt Maud does not know is that Kate has secretly agreed to enter into a long-term engagement to Densher as his fiancée. Recognizing the obvious incompatibility of these two roles, Kate tries to stall for time until she can come up with a plan that will enable her to enjoy Densher's love and her aunt's money without having to sacrifice either one for the other. As she alternates back and forth between these two competing parts, depending upon who her immediate audience is, Kate, like her creator, seizes upon Milly Theale's dove-like character as a solution to their mutual dilemma.

Milly enters upon the scene in the character of the immensely rich but mysteriously doomed American girl; and her presence in this character inspires Kate to come up with a scenario which she hopes will please both Aunt Maud and Densher. Presenting herself in yet another guise, Kate offers to appear in the supporting role of "the wondrous London girl" appointed to wait upon her leading lady, the "American princess," in return for Densher's promise that he will continue to keep their engagement a carefully guarded secret by playing the part of the jilted lover on the rebound. Kate clearly relies on Densher to perform this role so convincingly that he will gain access first to the American heiress' sympathy and affection and then to her vast wealth. The conspiracy of silence which cloaks the two lovers' mutual passion is ostensibly calculated to exploit Milly and deceive Aunt Maud, for they count on the possibility that the American girl will fall hopelessly in love with Densher before she dies and generously leave him a sum large enough to repay them for their efforts and make them financially independent enough to defy Aunt Maud and give up "acting" for good. However, this conspiracy was directed at James's two publics as well: it amounted to a convenient if makeshift screen between conventional readers and the new vulgarity while constituting a sufficiently original (perverse?) plot to satisfy even the most super-subtle raffiné.

Unlike Densher, a reluctant and somewhat intransigent performer who must constantly be coached and eventually even be bribed by the accomplished Kate in order to stay in character and keep their secret, Milly offers herself to James and her fellow players from the start as an aspiring but woefully inexperienced actress, a novice at the game of life who is only too eager to learn what is expected of her. She is willing to work and work hard, not for the money (which she obviously doesn't need) but for the experience which she so sadly and conspicuously lacks. While James and the others do their collective best to help Milly experience "life," this "mere little American, a cheap exotic, imported almost wholesale," finds herself hopelessly out of her native element and helplessly in over her head from the moment she makes her first appearance on the English scene at Aunt Maud's dinner party. As a Jamesian literary type, the American girl had repeatedly demonstrated sufficient "appetite for motive" to qualify her to figure as "the heroine" of an old-fashioned international novel such as Mrs. Stringham (or the young James) might produce. But both Milly and her creator sense that she is hardly equipped to keep up with the clever leading lady in his distinctly modern international drama. James persistently attempts to remedy this imbalance first by providing Milly with a confidante who would do "anything" for her and then by surrounding her with a strong and suitably admiring supporting cast; but his efforts consistently fail. Milly's relative lack of motive and manner make her feel "dead, dead, dead" in the company of her fellow actors, a troupe of super-subtle performers who (with the exception of Mrs. Stringham) all know how to act as if they were "made for great social uses." As Milly herself recognizes during the famous Bronzino scene in book 5, there is a strong family resemblance between herself and the lady in Lord Mark's "mysterious portrait," with "her slightly Michaelangelesque squareness" and "her eyes of other days." This likeness symbolizes the essentially static nature of Milly's character, for unlike Kate, who knows that she must rely on her ability to constantly readjust the impression she produces (whether in the glass over the mantle of her father's flat or in the reflection she sees mirrored in the gaze of a spectator), Milly's value as a character resides precisely in her recognized beauty and purity of type, a beauty which has been captured, preserved, and permanently frozen within the frame of the old-fashioned portrait (a covert reference to James's early masterpiece, *The Portrait of a Lady*?). "I shall never be better than this," she suddenly insists, as if acknowledging that her very goodness (as both a character type and a human being) limits her capacity to develop and her ability to act, in every sense of the word.[11]

James attempted to diagnose and treat Milly's fatal "illness" by reintroducing himself into the novel in the scene which immediately follows, where he appears in the guise of Sir Luke Strett, an eminent London physician who specializes in difficult cases. Unable to dissemble the highly unconventional aspects of Sir Luke's more than professional interest in his patient's strange predicament, James allows him to develop and display an almost paternal relationship with the orphaned American girl. (Together with Susan Stringham, he thus represents a kind of substitute parent or guardian, a further link between this novel and the post-theater fiction which presented readers with characters such as Mrs. Wix and Mr. Longdon.) Milly recognizes at once that Sir Luke, like the childless Susan Stringham, is offering himself as a "straight friend," in other words as a character who can and will provide her with behind-the-scenes aid and comfort in the form of direct access to her creator's sympathy and authorial intentions. "Half like a general and half like a bishop," Sir Luke thus becomes a sort of combination acting coach and father confessor, someone before whom Milly can let down her guard and express her fears and from whom she can derive much-needed instructions, however vague, as to how she is supposed to act. When she rather wishfully claims to Sir Luke that she can do exactly as she likes, he urges her to oblige him "by being so good as to do it," adding only one qualification—that she should get out of London. This remarkable exchange between author and character is followed by subsequent interviews of a similar nature during which James, through Sir Luke, gives Milly her "marching orders" and attempts to persuade her "to take the trouble to live." Yet in spite of their combined promptings as well as Milly's best efforts in her own behalf, Milly's very identity makes it virtually impossible for her to live "by option, by volition." As she fully recognizes, Sir Luke is treating her "as if it were in her power to live; and yet one wasn't treated so— was one?—unless it came up, quite as much, that one might die."[12] Thus even this highly unconventional attempt to try to help Milly act merely serves to direct her and James's readers' attention to her fatal inability to do so. In effect, Milly's acute self-consciousness regarding her unprecedented predicament becomes the most that can be expected from the traditional figure of the unmarried American girl; and though this form of consciousness is intended to serve her as an effective weapon, it cannot equip her to take offensive action in the battle for Densher's love which ensues.

Only when James's technical difficulties are recast in these terms can we understand what he really meant when he deviously referred to the novel as a partial failure in his preface. It was precisely Milly's identity as an international American girl, a national identity which had to be established and maintained if he was to invoke traditional Anglo-American themes as part of his appeal to conventional readers, which made her incapable of adequately filling out the role of a central consciousness in such a subtle drama. Her one great moment to act occurs in Venice at the end of book 9. There Milly is given a unique opportunity to equal and outperform her rival: she is put in the position of having to present herself as a dying girl who refuses to try to save herself because she is unwilling to pressure the man she loves into denying the suspicion of infidelity that is killing her. But James is reduced to asking his audience to take this performance on trust, for he never renders the scene at first hand. The departure of Aunt Maud and Kate from Venice shortly before this interview occurs becomes essential because James needs to insure that Densher will be the sole spectator to this potentially magnificent but inherently unrepresentable scene. However, Densher's surprising willingness to linger in Venice in the absence of his fiancée, who is also his acting coach, must be bought and paid for. He insists that he will remain behind and see his part through to completion without further prompting by Kate only on the condition that she come to his rooms and consummate their growing intimacy by spending the night with him. While it is certainly not difficult to believe in Kate's willingness or ability to rise to this challenge, such a scene is equally unrepresentable—though on entirely different grounds than the ones which spare Milly the terrible strain of trying to pull off her final performance. Given the expectations of James's mixed audience as well as his personal objections to "the new vulgarity," the directness and increasing sexual explicitness of the avant-garde was never a real possibility for him.

As a result it is Merton Densher's character, consciousness, and subsequent behavior which must ultimately bear the heaviest burden in the novel—that of registering the enduring effects of these two scenes. Not only must both performances be presented indirectly and retrospectively through the protective screen of Densher's memory, but their intensity can only be registered and measured after the fact by the effect which they (allegedly) produce upon his consciousness, which is to say the dramatic change in the subsequent quality of his relationship with Kate and Milly. Densher's altered mental state and his strange behavior upon his return to London, a performance which culminates in his final confrontation with Kate, thus amounts to a desperate attempt on James's part to coerce his readers (both conventional and avant-garde) into believing in the American girl's virtuoso performance—her ability to establish a profound kind of intimacy with Densher, an intimacy so intense that he would feel compelled to sacrifice his longstanding passion for Kate rather than compromise Milly's memory. Even under Kate's close questioning, Densher must remain curiously but conveniently vague (and therefore arguably unconvincing) regarding the details of his last interview with Milly: James simply could not risk the direct representation of a scene which, in all truth, was probably difficult if not impossible for him to imagine the American girl as actually having carried off.[13]

The net result of James's desire to meet his more traditional readers halfway was thus a work which he refers to in his preface as a partial failure but which many of his critics greeted as "a partial recovery." F.M. Colby used this phrase in the *Bookman,* where he insisted upon the difference between the novel and its immediate predecessors, *The Sacred Fount* and *The Awkward Age.*[14] Though he was quick to admit that James's "unsociable way of writing continues through *The Wings of the Dove,*" Colby argued that "it comes nearer than any other of his recent novels to the quality of his earlier work." Similarly, an anonymous British reviewer writing in the *Times Literary Supplement* detected a new "element of grave and penetrating tenderness" and praised James for the "humanizing" note in his portrait of Milly. James's old friend, William Dean Howells, echoed both of these views when he compared Milly Theale with Daisy Miller in a lengthy appraisal of "Mr. Henry James's Later Work" which he addressed to readers of the *North American Review.* After describing Milly as being perhaps "too good, too pure, too generous, too magnificently unselfish," he denied that he was suggesting that James had consciously offered her as "an atonement to the offended divinity of American womanhood for Daisy Miller." But then he deviously added, "... if it were imaginable the offended divinity ought to be sumptuously appeased, appeased to tears of grateful pardon such as I have not yet seen in its eyes." Howells went on to assert that "the ideal American rich girl" had never really been done before, "and it is safe to say that she will never again be done with such exquisite appreciation."[15] Yet James set out to "do" or rather re-do her one last time when he began work on *The Golden Bowl,* a novel based on the donnée whose adulterine element had appeared so difficult to handle when he first entered it into his notebooks back in 1895, shortly after the disastrous opening night of *Guy Domville.*[16] It was as if he were determined to find a way, once and for all, that would enable him to endow this figure from his literary past with the ability to live, which is to say act, on the same super-subtle terms as her post-theater counterparts without sacrificing either the redeeming aspects of her type and presence or her fictional future. The lesson James learned from *The Wings* was that if the American girl was to hold her own and possibly even triumph in a novel of passion, she would have to become more interesting and more initiated. For as one shrewd reviewer noted, Kate Croy had "nearly supplant[ed] her intended victim in tragic and intellectual interest."[17]

Like Milly Theale, Maggie Verver is conspicuously American and conspicuously rich; but unlike her doomed predecessor, whom Howells had correctly identified as the representative of "an extinct New York ancestry," the motherless Maggie enjoys the attention, affection and protection of her adored and adoring father, a fabulously wealthy collector of fine art objects who exerts his "rare power of purchase" in behalf of his only child by securing an impoverished but charming Italian prince as her husband. Although she is type cast in the role of James's inevitable international American girl, Maggie makes her first appearance in *The Golden Bowl* not as the last of a distinguished line, an orphaned and ailing heiress desperately seeking to "live" and to love, but as an innocent and over-protected daughter who is about to open a new chapter in her life by taking on the character of a wife. Though Maggie and her father have "everything," the one thing they seem to lack is cleverness; and this clearly puzzles and worries the Prince, a master of super-subtlety. As he candidly (and disarmingly) warns his future wife, neither she nor her father really knows anything about him:

> There are two parts of me...One is made up of the history, the doings, the marriages, the crimes, the follies, the boundless *bêtises* of other people...Those things are written—literally in rows of volumes, in libraries; are as public as they're abominable...and you've, both of you, wonderfully, looked them in the face. But there's another part...which, such as it is, represents my single self, the unknown, unimportant—unimportant save to *you*—personal quantity. About this you've found out nothing.[18]

Maggie's limited ability to recognize that she has yet to fathom this personal, this most intimate side of her Italian mate is signalled by her naive eagerness to identify her future occupation with just such a project; but the entire first book of the novel consists almost exclusively of a dramatization of what she doesn't know about the Prince and a demonstration of the consequences of her continuing failure to remedy this serious gap in her education, even after their marriage takes place.

What Maggie doesn't know is not only that the Prince had once been on intimate terms with her best friend, Charlotte Stant, but that Charlotte has expressly journeyed to London on the eve of their marriage to bear witness to her continuing passion for him and obliquely signify her willingness to resume their old relation where it left off, should he so desire. Although she too is the child of American parents and refers to herself as a single woman, Charlotte has little or no affinity for her native land and bears even less of a resemblance to that conventional Jamesian type, the international American girl. Born and bred in Florence and educated in a convent, this charming "polyglot" girl has a "strange sense for tongues" and a pronounced cleverness which have captivated the Prince's imagination from far back (much as her prototype, Kate Croy, had captivated Merton Densher).[19] Yet there is no conscious conspiracy in *The Golden Bowl,* for Charlotte and especially the Prince manage to restrain themselves admirably until Maggie unwittingly tempts them beyond their control, first by encouraging her widowed father to marry her best friend and then by assiduously devoting herself to the happiness of her father, a devotion so all-absorbing that it not only invites but virtually forces her husband and her stepmother to console themselves by resuming their former intimacy. Book 1 largely focuses on this gradually renewed intimacy between Charlotte and the Prince and culminates with its consummation during an extended country weekend which they spend away from their respective spouses. In turn this event, which Maggie seems dimly to sense, inaugurates the onset of her painful initiation into the truth of the affair, which is to say the complexities of life, an initiation which makes for the substance and suspense of book 2.

Maggie begins the second book of the novel by imagining her unprecedented domestic situation as "some strange tall tower of ivory, or perhaps rather some wonderful, beautiful, but outlandish pagoda" around which she has walked and walked "but never quite making out, as yet, where she might have entered had she wished." For the first time she realizes how odd it is that she has never before tried to gain access to this structure, a signal that she is beginning to recognize and grow restive under the limitations of her character, limitations entailed by her fidelity to her identity as the international American girl. In effect, then, Maggie finally begins to perceive her own case as one of arrested development. In the words of Fanny Assingham, the Ververs' close family friend and the woman who has helped to make Prince Amerigo's marriage, something "disagreeable" has to happen to Maggie in order to "make her decide to live." As Fanny remarks near the end of book 1, "her sense will have to open... to what's called Evil—with a very big E: for the first time in her life. To the discovery of it, to the knowledge of it, to the crude experience of it... To the harsh, bewildering brush, the daily chilling breath of it."[20] It is highly appropriate that this description of Maggie's case should come from Mrs. Assingham, herself a somewhat overgrown American girl, for Fanny is credited by her friends in the younger generation with having discovered, along with her British husband, "a kind of hymeneal North-West Passage" in the form of their own international marriage.[21] Furthermore, Mrs. Assingham's childless state qualifies her interest in her fellow characters as vaguely maternal and essentially benign, rather than merely meddlesome (although, like Maggie, one of her most salient features is her dangerous naiveté). Fanny's strongest sympathies initially seem to lie with Charlotte and especially with the Prince (of whom she is admittedly enamored), yet in book 2 she becomes Maggie's sole confidante and support, as if James were covertly prompting his heroine to act independently of her father by compensating her for the fact that she can no longer confide in him or seek his paternal protection. (By the same stroke James also succeeds in subjecting Fanny's imagination to a course of rigorous instruction.) In a curious reworking of the post-theater motif of abandoned and unprotected children, it is precisely Maggie's desire to shield her father from the knowledge of their spouses' infidelity which becomes the key with which she successfully gains access to the "outlandish pagoda" and her primary motive for acting once she enters upon this stage of her development.

In this manner Maggie's motive and her strategy virtually become one, for her determination to protect her father necessitates that she bring an end to the adulterous affair without acting in a way which will call his attention to her newly awakened and highly agitated state. For this reason, though she privately confronts the Prince with her knowledge of his infidelity near the beginning of book 2, the Princess never publicly breaks with her husband and even finds herself in the unprecedented situation of following his super-subtle cue when she conceals this knowledge from his mistress, despite repeated opportunities to seek relief or revenge. Indeed, James structures the second book of the novel around these very opportunities, for they constitute a series of tests which Maggie knows she must pass if she is to succeed in saving her father and her marriage (and which James needs her to pass if he is to preside over her successful initiation into super-subtlety and save his novel from the twin dangers of the new vulgarity and old-fashioned melodrama). As Fanny puts it, Maggie must consistently refuse to act "with the blind resentment with which, in her place, ninety-nine women out of a hundred would act; and by so making Mr. Verver, in turn, act with the same natural passion, the passion of ninety-nine men out of a hundred."[22]

Maggie rises to the occasion and her creator's expectations not only by showing admirable restraint but by learning to lie well, a devious skill which one associates with the super-subtle types James developed in his post-theater fiction but not with Milly Theale nor with the heroes and heroines of his early international novels. Yet mastering "the difficulties of duplicity" becomes the central task of the Princess' education, an education which must be completed if she is to bridge the gap convincingly between James's literary past and present. As Maggie pictures the developing situation to herself:

> Humbugging, which she had so practised with her father, had been a comparatively simple matter on the basis of mere doubt; but the ground to be covered was now greatly larger, and she felt not unlike some young woman of the theatre who, engaged for a minor part in the play and having mastered her cues with anxious effort, should find herself suddenly promoted to leading lady and expected to appear in every act of the five.[23]

The quantity and quality of effort demanded from James's new leading lady is nowhere more evident than in two highly dramatic scenes which take place at Fawns near the conclusion of book 2. The first of these crucial scenes begins with an after-dinner bridge game between the Ververs, the Prince, and Fanny Assingham, with Maggie looking on from a property sofa in the wing, "much in the mood of a tired actress who has the good fortune to be 'off,' while her mates are on..." As she watches "her father's wife's lover facing his mistress," Maggie invokes only to dismiss the melodramatic scene which she knows she could provoke simply by breaking out in "a single lurid sentence" and spoiling the "high decorum" of the moment:

> It was extraordinary: they positively brought home to her that to feel about them in any of
> the immediate, inevitable, assuaging ways, the ways usually open to innocence outraged and
> generosity betrayed, would have been to give them up, and that giving them up was,
> marvellously, not to be thought of.[24]

Yet her willingness to resist this obvious and comparatively vulgar temptation and her ability to accept the unconventional burden of easing the "actual present strain," a burden which her fellow players tacitly count on her to bear, must be subjected to a much more demanding test if she is to demonstrate her mastery of her role and thereby earn and justify James's promotion of her to the position of leading lady. Maggie must not only refuse to play the outraged wife, she must foil her stepmother's subsequent attempt to upstage her by pretending that there is absolutely nothing wrong between them. When Charlotte follows her out onto the terrace with the express intention of pressing her on this very issue, Maggie responds at first by trying to hide but finally manages to muster enough dramatic manner to convincingly deliver the following denial: "I accuse you—I accuse you of nothing." This "conscious perjury" is sealed by a kiss which is witnessed by their fellow characters, an attentive audience which confers a sense of "high publicity" on the consummate performance of these two actresses.

Such "humbugging," as Maggie calls it to herself, represents nothing new on Charlotte's part, for it is the stock-in-trade of her avant-garde repertoire. But for Maggie it amounts to nothing less than an implicit rejection of her identity as a mere American girl and an extension of the terms of her education to include an embrace of the larger latitude, for she perceives that "the right" now takes the (for her) unprecedented form of "not, by a hair's breath, deflecting into the truth." By a characteristically Jamesian turn of the screw, it is precisely this interpenetration and transformation of the Princess' moral terms which allows her to continue to protect her father and which aligns her for the first time with her husband in a conspiracy of silence, a form of complicity which constitutes for them the beginning of a profound, if extremely unconventional, kind of marital intimacy. "They were together thus, he and she, close, close together—where Charlotte, though rising more radiantly before her, was really off in some darkness of space that would steep her in solitude and harass her with care."[25]

By the time the second such test of Maggie's manner occurs, the Princess has begun to regard herself as a "far-off harassed heroine—only with a part to play for which she knew, exactly, no inspiring precedent." She knows only that she wants to go directly to Charlotte, who is by now conspicuously alone and harassed, in order to "make somehow, for her support, the last demonstration." Realizing that she lacks a presentable pretext for this act, Maggie finds one in the form of an old three-decker novel which she has brought down to Fawns and in which Mrs. Verver has previously expressed an interest. Charlotte has left the house "helplessly armed" with the second rather than the first volume of this novel in an effort to seek refuge in the garden. Equipped only with "the right volume" and "the bravery of her general idea," the Princess pursues her husband's mistress not out of any petty desire to corner or humiliate her but in a generous effort to "succour" her—a benign gesture which admittedly affects Maggie as a conscious "turning of the tables on her friend" but which is clearly intended by James to strike his audience as further proof of the former's evident superiority of type (rather than as evidence of her conscious cruelty or egotistical self-righteousness, as some modern readers have insisted). During this scene, which amounts to a repetition and revision of the evening on the terrace, Maggie gives the performance of her life, for she proves willing and able to play the fool by acting as if she were a jealous daughter instead of a jealous wife. When Charlotte deviously accuses her stepdaughter not only of loathing her marriage to Adam but of having worked against her, the Princess meekly responds: "What does it matter—if I've failed?" Twirling her sunshade on her shoulder with evident pride, Charlotte insists upon pressing the point: "You recognize then that you've failed?" Upon which Maggie waits, looks at the two books on the seat, puts them together in their right order, and simply says "I've failed." For the discriminating and alert members of James's audience, this stage business is clearly ironic and self-reflexive. It mutely calls attention to the fact that the Princess' pretension to failure paradoxically signals her achieved success in making "right" a situation which has been wrong from the start.[26]

At this point in the novel, the Princess correctly concludes that she has "done all," presumably an admission that she is conscious of having done everything within her power to protect her beloved father. But in doing so, she has also succeeded in capturing the imagination and affection of her husband and satisfying the needs and expectations of her creator (whether wholly intentionally or not, we simply do not and cannot ever know for sure). Maggie's consummate performance, capped by the scene in the garden, also makes it possible for her husband's mistress to salvage her pride as well as her ostensible identity as Mr. Verver's devoted wife, for Charlotte now has a presentable motive for taking Adam back to America (a plan which Mrs. Verver deviously claims to be her own but which her husband has already insisted upon in private). In turn, only this painful and "definite break" between father and daughter can bring the drama to its "proper" conclusion. The Ververs' joint exit both constitutes and signals the completion of Maggie's initiation (she is ready to "toddle" alone) while indirectly acknowledging the existence of a genuine intimacy between the Princess and the Prince. As we last see Maggie and her husband, they are alone together virtually for the first time in the novel, and precisely at the moment when he is most aware of her acquired talent for living, her demonstrated superiority to Charlotte, and his growing passion for her.

Like the stillness which reigns at the end of the novel, in which whatever takes place is "foredoomed to remarkable salience," their mutual passion is "not so much restored as created"; and this creation—however fragile—crowns the triumph of Henry James. After years of experimentation, frustration, and failure, he must have believed that he had finally managed to succeed, once and for all, in writing a novel of passion without callously exposing and cruelly sacrificing his literary progeny, the children of his imagination.[27]

Although the ending of *The Golden Bowl* is certainly not a happy one in any easy or conventional sense and some critics have angrily protested that Charlotte's fate is unnecessarily harsh, it is worth noting that father and daughter explicitly part in the light of Charlotte's demonstrated greatness, her absolute value to his achieved plan. Thanks to Charlotte, Adam has managed to succeed as a devoted parent, albeit quite deviously, by presiding over his daughter's transformation into a wife and—more importantly—her initiation into passion (thereby providing for her future as well as that of his grandchild). By the same logic Charlotte has Adam (and James) to thank (or to blame, as some critics would have it): even though she has entered the novel as a homeless and penniless girl on the verge of becoming an "old maid," she manages to exit with her dignity and her magnificent manner intact as the wife of a wealthy and indulgent man who knows what to make of her and who will put her exquisite taste to good use. In James's defense, it should also be remembered that unlike her predecessors (Fleda, Maisie, Nanda, and, to a lesser extent, Kate), each of whom serves in her creator's behalf only to suffer the abrupt foreclosure of her fictional future, Charlotte has not and will not be "wasted," as Adam pointedly assures Maggie at the close of *The Golden Bowl*. Just before the curtain falls, Mrs. Verver is permitted to make one last appearance before James's audience: as she sits regally enthroned between her hostess and her host, Charlotte's proud bearing suggests that she is only too conscious that she has been allowed to act out her destiny by playing the very best role of her career. To paraphrase James's contemporaneous comments on Balzac's relationship with *his* fictional characters, the truth of the master's love for Charlotte and her fellow actors lies precisely in his ability to appreciate and enjoy "their communicated and exhibited movement... their standing on their feet and going of themselves and acting out their characters... It was by loving them—as the terms of his subject and the nuggets of his mine—that he knew them; it was not by knowing them that he loved."[28]

Indeed, James had succeeded in endowing all four central characters in *The Golden Bowl* with a dramatic presence and a depth of subtle intention and significance virtually unparalleled in any of his previous productions. Nowhere is this more true than in the case of Adam Verver, the mysterious author of Maggie's being. Although his role in the novel at first seems to be a secondary one vaguely akin to that of the various substitute parents and guardians of

James's post-theater fiction (Mr. Longdon and Sir Luke come most readily to mind), Adam's unique relationship with his fellow characters as well as his retroactive willingness to take on the burden of responsibility for the novel's plot (as well as credit for its ultimate success) covertly align him with his creator. In fact, upon close inspection the strange shape which their respective careers gradually assume appears to be remarkably similar. Like Henry James, Adam Verver comes to realize that his "years of darkness had been needed to render possible the years of light." And like Verver, James had finally begun to come to terms with and accept the inescapable fact that "he had wrought by devious ways"—though "his plan" had "all the sanctions of civilization . . . " In the case of both careers, only retrospectively did it appear that "a wiser hand" than either at first knew had kept them "hard at work at acquisition of one sort as a perfect preliminary to acquisition of another, and the preliminary would have been weak and wanting if the good faith of it had been less." Their "comparative blindness had made the good faith, which in its turn had made the soil propitious for the flower of the supreme idea."[29]

Adam Verver's "supreme idea," ostensibly a plan to turn American City into a national museum, is actually the magnificent museum of international types and themes which is constituted by the novel itself. His creator's supreme idea turned out to be even more ambitious. James's plan for a collective edition of his life's work had begun to take shape during the composition of *The Golden Bowl*, which he completed early in 1904; and it was to gel during his subsequent return to his native land. Through his literary agent, James B. Pinker, the master had successfully completed negotiations with Charles Scribner's Sons (the American publisher of *The Sacred Fount*, *The Wings of the Dove*, and *The Better Sort*, a collection of short stories) to bring out *The Golden Bowl* as a handsome two-volume novel, something which he ironically failed to do in the case of the English edition, which Methuen and Company insisted upon issuing as one long and cumbersome volume.[30] Encouraged by the reception and sales of *The Better Sort* as well as by the "additional sale" which they hoped would accrue to *The Golden Bowl* as a result of James's proposed trip to America, Scribner's also expressed an interest in the novelist's plan for a definitive edition of his novels and tales. James's much publicized and long delayed return to America commenced in August of 1904; and, just as he and his American publisher had hoped, once there he became the focus of what was, for him, an unprecedented amount of reverberation. This publicity was primarily the result of a series of lectures (later published in book form as *The Question of Our Speech/ The Lesson of Balzac*) which he delivered across the country to audiences composed largely (though not exclusively) of women.[31] Addressing his literary agent from Cambridge, Massachusetts, in the spring of 1905, the master temporarily dropped the mask of indifference with regard to questions of sales and popularity which he so effectively wore in social interaction with his young disciples and admirers like Wells. Assuming the identity of a shrewd and calculating man of business, he boasted to Pinker that *The Golden Bowl*

> has done very much better here, clearly,—*ever* so much—than any book of mine has ever done: which is so much to the good, and gives, I think, somewhat the measure of my having been well inspired, in respect to such consequences, to one's prosperity in general etc., in coming over.[32]

A few days later James again wrote to his agent, this time enclosing a card announcing that his lecture, "The Lesson of Balzac," would be given the next evening to the Contemporary Club of St. Louis. The master gloried not only in the size of his audiences (which he put down as 600-700 people per lecture) but also in the amount of his pay. As he pointedly noted in a postscript:

> Let this P.S. put it most frankly and crudely that I *have* done very well, for my material, my "literary" situation & representation, by my presence here these last few months. That is very clear indeed. In fact it is sadly clear that if I were but to come back & abide I should find things probably profitable enough to enable me to live in (comparative!) affluence: my being here makes such a difference.

(However, with characteristic vacillation, James quickly added that he "would rather *starve* at Lamb House than abide there.")[33]

According to Richard Foley, these lectures received more attention as delivered performances than as printed speeches. Newspaper reporters proved to be interested primarily in the master's appearance and platform personality, his delivery, the type of audience he attracted, and their reactions. Although some found him lacking as a lecturer, others insisted that "hearing him was excellent training in reading him aloud and helped to explain some of his 'novelistic caprices.'" When we learn that at this period of his life, James sometimes dressed "with a certain extravagance of color," sporting "tight check trousers, waistcoat of a violent pattern, coat with short tails like a cock sparrow—and none matching" and that he struck one observer as a figure of vaudeville only to remind others of a lawyer, a banker, or a priest, we might feel justified in finding in him more than just "the suggestion of an actor" which his biographer attributes to his costume as well as to his speech.[34] In his public presentation of himself during this lecture tour, James seems to have achieved almost as much success in anticipating and adapting himself to the expectations of his American audiences as he had previously experienced in his more private interaction with the ranks of the English-speaking avant-garde. The evident pride which he took in this carefully orchestrated dose of self-advertisement was merely the flip side of the conspicuous disdain for popularity which he displayed when dealing with his ever-growing circle of disciples and admirers among the rising generation, a generation which included not only avant-garde writers and artists but a new type of professional reader who was just beginning to emerge on the Anglo-American literary scene, the academic critic of the modern novel. However, largely as a result of the crucial role played by this latter group in the formation and preservation of James's literary reputation, the disdain has consistently been over-emphasized at the expense of the pride.[35]

It is in this context that the master's supreme idea, the definitive and selective edition of his life's work, must be reevaluated, for following the lead of James (as well as his contemporaneous disciples and admirers), most modern critics have tended to view this edition and the eighteen prefaces which were written to accompany it as the labor of an author whose entire career could and *should* be regarded as the fulfillment of a single exemplary intention. Though disagreement certainly persists as to what specifically constitutes that intention, this segment of James's audience has been lured into and prepared for just such an interpretation of the master's career by the experience of reading the Prefaces in conjunction with the fiction, most particularly the novels of the major phase and the tales of the literary life. Goaded and trained by stories such as "The Figure in the Carpet," in which the fictional artist Hugh Vereker insisted that "there's an idea in my work without which I wouldn't have given a straw for the whole job," James's avant-garde and academic readers have been only too eager to search for a similarly unified pattern in "the order, the form, the texture" of the New York Edition, especially when prompted to do so by the Prefaces themselves. Somewhat tongue-in-cheek, Vereker had delighted in describing his "exquisite scheme" as being "as concrete as a bird in a cage, a bait on a hook, a piece of cheese in a mouse-trap. It's stuck into every volume as your foot is stuck into your shoe. It governs every line, it chooses every word, it dots every i, it places every comma." Yet several generations of Jamesians have, for the most part, risen to this bait by taking fiction for fact and reading such passages as literal descriptions of James's artistic intentions. (The master's habit of "baiting" both the youthful disciples in these tales and his own avant-garde public makes his use of the term "supersubtle fry" in the Prefaces extremely appropriate—especially when we remember that "fry" not only refers to young fish but connotes offspring or children.)[36] The result is a veritable industry of James criticism which tends to praise (or condemn) the supposed consistency between his fictional theory and practice while stressing the allegedly unbroken continuity of his artistic development, thus promoting and perpetuating a seriously skewed image of the novelist as a literary master who was preoccupied from the start almost exclusively with technical problems.

James's disciples and admirers helped to establish this myth and inaugurate this phenomenon when they hyperbolically hailed the publication of the Prefaces and the New York Edition as "an event, indeed the first event" in the history of the novel. Adopting the central metaphor of "The Figure in the Carpet" to describe the edition as a whole, Percy Lubbock was to observe that "[w]e have to deal... with a densely-woven tapestry, in which style, line, color, and composition are all of a piece, all inherent, all part of one process." After identifying James's key achievement as his having "disengaged from a hundred misconceptions the question of form," Lubbock went on to insist that the entire corpus of the master's work should be regarded as "[t]he gradual solution of the problem" of form, with each novel showing "the answer carried a little further than in its predecessor." From this suitably elevated point of view, the Prefaces appeared to have the distinctly disinterested function of "impartially indicating merits and defects," while James's development from the "easy finished lightness" of his apprentice years to the "packed elaboration" of his final novels struck Lubbock as quite natural and even inevitable. The admiring disciple concluded his *Times Literary Supplement* review by announcing the master's unqualified triumph and predicting that his "influence, already so conspicuously marked, will more and more dominate..." Not surprisingly, James would warmly praise this review as "the most appreciative and *fine* tribute I have ever received." In fact, he himself paved the way for and did much to foster this highly idealized version of his own career. In a well-known passage from a letter to Howells (which another Jamesian, R.P. Blackmur, quotes approvingly in his introduction to *The Art of the Novel*, his collection of all eighteen prefaces), the master described the Prefaces as "a plea for Criticism, for Discrimination, for Appreciation on other than infantile lines—as against the so almost universal Anglo-Saxon absence of these things; which tends so, in our general trade, it seems to me, to break the heart..." He went on to suggest that collected together, they ought "none the less, to form a sort of comprehensive manual or *vademecum* for aspirants in our arduous profession." What is less well known is that these remarks immediately follow James's admission that one of his prime motives for writing these introductions was to help the edition sell "two or three copies more!" As he candidly admitted:

> They will have represented much labour to this latter end—though in that they will have differed indeed from none of their fellow-manifestations (in general) whatever; and the resemblance will even be increased if the two or three copies *don't,* in the form of an extra figure or two, mingle with my withered laurels.[37]

Interestingly enough, a careful reading of James's published correspondence, as well as the Prefaces themselves, reveals that the collective edition had a double meaning and purpose for him from the start. As the second passage from this letter to Howells implies, the New York Edition represented yet another opportunity to sell his books, a second chance for an author who remained genuinely perplexed and dismayed by his relative unpopularity in an age of best sellers and stubbornly obsessed with the idea of achieving commercial success. In this context, the project may have been viewed by James in terms not unlike those which Adam Verver applies to his grand plan for American City. Designed as "a gift, primarily to the people...," Verver's museum was to resemble "a house from whose open doors and windows, open to grateful, to thirsty millions, the higher, the highest knowledge would shine out to bless the land." But at the same time, as the former passage to Howells suggests, the master also intended this selective edition to be an offering to the faithful, "a monument to the religion" which he, like Adam Verver, wished to propagate, "the exemplary passion, the passion for perfection at any price."[38] To the extent that it took this latter form, the edition would ironically look like a forbidding edifice which only the most initiated of readers could appreciate and gain entrance into.

Even the structure of the New York Edition reflects this doubleness of intention. As his biographer has noted, James could have filled at least thirty-five volumes at this time (and over forty by the time he died) had he chosen to do so; but just before he returned to England in the summer of 1905, he informed Pinker of his decision to limit himself to twenty-three volumes, partly (according to Edel) in emulation of Balzac's definitive edition. Although he was to present the edition publicly as a collective one, the master seems to have had multiple reasons for being selective as well. While Edel argues that James "banished" only those novels and almost all of the tales with an exclusively American setting in order to present himself as a cosmopolitan and international novelist, the actual list of seven rejected novels plus several contemporaneous letters suggest that other factors also entered into this decision.[39] This list not only includes such early novels as *Watch and Ward, Confidence, The Europeans, Washington Square,* and *The Bostonians,* all of which are indeed set exclusively in America, but also *The Other House* and *The Sacred Fount,* two relatively late novels which take place in England. Since James chose *not* to omit *The Tragic Muse* and his other post-theater novels, none of which are international in setting or theme, a supplement or alternative to Edel's explanation must be found. It is possible to speculate that *Watch and Ward* (James's first serial), *Confidence, The Other House* and, to a lesser extent, *The Europeans* and *Washington Square,* were each rejected because they were regarded by James as partial or total failures, mere apprentice works or potboilers which had done little or nothing to further his reputation with either conventional or avant-garde readers. These novels would have required enormous amounts of revision in order to even begin to figure as the work of a literary master (or as producing the "singular unity of effect" which the

Scribner prospectus boasted of and committed him to representing). As James confided to Robert Herrick:

> The *raison d'être* (the edition's) is in its being selective as well as collective, and by the mere fact of leaving out certain things (I have tried to read over *Washington Square* and I *can't*, and I fear it must go!) I exercise a control, a discrimination, I treat certain portions of my work as unhappy accidents. (Many portions of many—of all—men's work are.)

He then went on to add in a somewhat mysterious (and perhaps a deliberately provocative) vein: "From that it is but a step further—but it is 1 o'clock a.m. and I've written seven letters and I won't attempt to finish that sentence or expand my meaning." Yet he quite perversely proceeded to write more about the edition, explaining that if he had planned "not to re-touch—that is to revise closely—I would have reprinted *all* my stuff and that idea is horrific."[40]

Contrary to Edel's speculation that James "hoped for addition and amplification later but wanted the 23 volumes to be the main building," this last phrase implies that he was looking for a presentable pretext for *not* having to include all of his work when he hit upon the idea of adopting the example of Balzac's twenty-three volume *Comedie Humaine*. This letter also provides a clue as to why James chose to exclude *The Sacred Fount* and *The Bostonians*. As we have seen, both were extremely unpopular novels—though for very different reasons—which he would be very likely to want to dismiss and disown as "unhappy accidents."[41] More importantly, the former represented the master's one unfortunate violation of his own implicit rule (soon to become explict in the preface to *The Ambassadors*) against using a first-person narrator in a long fiction, a violation which resulted in an unprecedented loss of authorial control, while the latter struck him as "tolerably full and good" but so out of step with his subsequent development that it would "take, doubtless, a great deal of artful re-doing—and I haven't, now, had the courage or time for anything so formidable as touching and re-touching it."[42] In other words, from treating certain portions of his work as "unhappy accidents," it was but a short step to passing off the remaining canon as if it were the result of "an absolutely premeditated art."[43]

Combined with the Prefaces, the very sequence of this collective edition was meant to reveal and emphasize this "fact," really the master's grandest fiction. By silently omitting *Watch and Ward* and departing from strict chronological order,[44] James was able to accomplish two things. His misrepresentation of *Roderick Hudson* as his "first attempt at a novel," when followed by *The American* and *The Portrait,* made it possible for him to present himself as having made his initial entrance and continuing mark upon the literary scene exclusively in the character of an international novelist, a one-sided version of his literary past designed primarily to reawaken the interest and recapture the sympathy of his more conventional readers.[45] At the same time, beginning with the preface to *Roderick Hudson* and running through virtually all the subsequent prefaces to volumes containing novels rather than collected tales (especially the prefaces to *The American, The Tragic Muse, The Spoils, Maisie, The Wings, The Ambassadors,* and *The Golden Bowl*), James focused on the function of the "centre" or central consciousness as a crucial "principle of composition" and offered the question of how to maintain consistency of point of view as perhaps *the* key technical problem which he faced over the years. When viewed in the context of the silently altered sequence of the novels, such a recurring emphasis on sheer technical difficulty enabled James to appear from the first in the guise of an unusually dedicated writer who regarded fiction as an art rather than a trade, who devoted himself to repeated formal experiments during the course of his career, and who achieved increasing success in solving this structural problem, thereby expanding the possibilities of his chosen medium.[46] It was, of course, in this latter guise that James aimed to satisfy the super-subtle expectations and win the enduring loyalty of his avant-garde public, the only segment of his audience which could be relied upon to keep his reputation alive among subsequent generations of writers and readers.[47]

The Prefaces have proved remarkably effective in this last respect. Regarded as one sustained performance (rather than as mines of critical theory or individual acts of practical criticism), they tell an exemplary tale of a highly successful literary life, a type of tale which James professed to find inherently unrepresentable. As he insisted in his preface to *The Tragic Muse*:

> Any presentation of the artist *in triumph* must be flat in proportion as it really sticks to its subject—it can only smuggle in relief and variety. For, to put the matter in an image, all we then—in his triumph—see of the charm-compeller is the back he turns to us as he bends over his work. "His" triumph, decently, is but the triumph of what he produces, and that is another affair.... The privilege of the hero—that is of the martyr of the interesting and appealing and comparatively floundering person—places him in quite a different category, belongs to him only as to the artist deluded, diverted, frustrated or vanquished...[48]

The last three prefaces which introduce the novels of James's major phase are especially important in this regard, for together they form the climax of the triumphant success story which constitutes his unprecedented literary career. By substantially revising the early novels and tales which he included in the edition (*Roderick Hudson, The American,* and *The Portrait*) in order to bring them in line with the manner of these late novels, James managed to create an illusion of almost unbroken artistic development, an illusion which he sustained by presenting *The Wings of the Dove* between the volume of short stories which featured *Daisy Miller* and the four remaining volumes, which contained *The Ambassadors* and *The Golden Bowl*. This arrangement had two important advantages. First, it neatly bridged and concealed the gap between his apprentice years as the chronicler of the international American girl and his super-subtle major phase, the period during which he returned to and revised this figure in light of his post-theater fiction—fiction written during and following his "years of darkness." Secondly, it enabled him to appear as if he had progressed confidently and triumphantly from the partial failure of a technically ambitious and sophisticated novel like *The Wings* to the undisputed success of *The Ambassadors,* the novel which he proudly pronounced "the best, 'all round,'" of his productions (instead of vice versa).[49]

The net result of this subtle maneuvering was that it allowed James to continue to figure in the accompanying prefaces in the double role in which he had cast himself, that of the consummate artist who had thoroughly mastered not only the complexities of the international scene and theme but the super-subtle secrets of the art of fiction, thus satisfying the contrasting expectations of his traditional and avant-garde readers. This rather devious strategy also enabled him to sustain a unique kind of intimacy with his highly mixed audience, an intimacy which becomes most marked in the preface to *The Golden Bowl.* This novel—whose second book is in effect a revised version of its first half—is ironically such a successful revision of both *The Portrait* and *The Wings* that James can say very little about its composition without giving the entire show away. Thus the preface which introduces it becomes not so much the story of James's story as the story of how the New York Edition itself came into being. After discussing the relatively "minor" question of the illustrations which photographer Alvin Langdon Coburn helped provide for the collective edition, the master goes on to tackle the "major" issue at hand, the general question of revision as it applies to his own case. With an apparently straight face he brazenly insists:

> To re-read in their order my final things, all of comparatively recent date, has been to become aware of my putting the process through, for the latter end of my series (as well as, throughout, for most of its later constituents) quite in the same terms as the apparent and actual, the contemporary terms; to become aware in other words that the march of my present attention coincides sufficiently with the march of original expression; that my apprehension fits, more concretely stated, *without an effort or a struggle,* certainly *without bewilderment or anguish,* into the innumerable places prepared for it.[50]

This is nothing if not a presentation of the artist in triumph; yet it curiously escapes the fate of flatness which James had predicted, for it is a masterful performance which is taking place right before our very eyes, a truly remarkable sleight of hand in which we—the amused spectators—are invited to participate.

As this final preface draws to a close, James's by now bedazzled (or thoroughly baffled!) audience finds itself in the seemingly unprecedented position of being asked to lend his prose a *"viva-voce* treatment." According to the master, the only "act and process of apprehension" which will "infallibly" guarantee his readers their utmost enjoyment is neither skimming nor "'quiet' reading" but "the closest pressure... the pressure of the attention articulately sounded."[51] Although he thus represents this plea for reading out loud as a necessary operation which the audience must perform in order to secure full payment or compensation from his productions, this ultimate test of the quality of James's prose constitutes a devious last chance for a writer committed to eliciting, measuring, and—most importantly—developing certain qualities of subtlety and discrimination in them as readers. (As his 1905 lecture "The Question of Our Speech" reveals, the master also hoped to use the spoken language itself as a means of educating his audience—especially its female members—and transforming them into more subtle and discriminating performers on the scene of life.) At the very least, this mode of reading would slow readers down and prevent them from skimming and skipping, one of James's chronic complaints against the usual Anglo-American public. At its best, a *vivâ-voce* treatment might even serve James's less developed readers as a welcome point of entry into his elaborate house of fiction. As H.G. Dwight, one of the master's American admirers in the younger generation, had pointedly noted in his contemporaneous analysis of James's success as a lecturer, it had become the fashion to exaggerate the difficulties of the late style. Yet once James's late manner was recognized as a speaking manner, the difficulty greatly diminished (although it certainly did not totally disappear). While he readily agreed that James's novels demanded more attention "than many readers think a mere book deserves," Dwight shrewdly observed that "the clauses, the parentheses, the intonations of daily life are of course familiar enough to our ears; but they still have a strangeness for eyes accustomed to the telgraphic brevity of the newspaper."[52] Perhaps James had learned this crucial lesson as a result of his positive reception by the audiences of common readers who flocked to hear him lecture during his tour of America.

If the difficulty of the master's late manner is regarded as a kind of verbal fence designed, at least in part, to protect James and his fictional progeny from the careless or inattentive reader, then his plea for reading out loud in this final preface can also be seen as a partially open gate in that fence, especially in light of the fact that the Victorian habit of reading *en famille* was well developed in Anglo-American culture. Furthermore, when we recall that this habit produced the existence of a "read-to" as well as a reading public, we might even be justified in viewing this plea as the ingenious ploy of a frustrated dramatist who remained bent on gaining belated compensation for his dramatic intentions in the form of a substitute performance for his works. Such a performance would partially realize his unfulfilled theatrical ambitions by recasting his readers as a troupe of substitute performers and covertly transforming his read-to audience from a group of potentially passive spectators into a circle of "the consenting"—neatly bridging the gap (at least temporarily) between his two publics and thereby undercutting and partially healing the split between his initiated and his undeveloped readers.[53]

As the master suddenly realizes in the final pages of this preface, he has hit upon this unique solution to the complex problem of audience only because he has managed to overcome his fear of "tidying up" his "uncanny brood" and revive his parental connection with them. Their plea for "exemplary damages, or at least for poetic justice" has become his presentable pretext not only for the act of revision but for writing the Prefaces and assembling the collective edition itself, since their reappearance strikes him as "unimaginable save for some inheritance of brighter and more congruous material form, of stored-up braveries of type and margin and ample page, of general dignity and attitude, than had mostly waited on their respective casual cradles... " Thus for James to pretend to anything less than artistic "conduct with a vengeance... conduct minutely and publicly attested," would be to violate the terms of his "delightful bargain" with these previously neglected literary progeny, who have asked only that their creator "actively believe" in them. Like Maggie Verver, the master has had to learn how to lie convincingly, but not so much for his own sake as for the sake of his literary productions: all the "hocus pocus" of the edition has been made necessary (and can be retroactively justified if detected) by his sincere desire to provide yet another chance for the children of his imagination.[54] Of course, this rather belated display of parental concern may be cynically dismissed as merely the last in a series of extremely shrewd and self-serving tricks. But like Hugh Vereker, Henry James undoubtedly assumed that his avant-garde readers would expect him to try to cover his tracks. James may even have counted upon the possibility that those "little demons of subtlety" would try to pierce his fictional secret and unveil his authorial mystery (if only to sharpen their own skills at his expense). Perhaps he even wanted them to recognize and savor (if not expose) the uncanny family resemblance between the ostensibly impartial "critic" who narrates the Prefaces and the professional literary men who are implicated in the frequently perverse plots of the short stories which they narrate. If so, he had once again misjudged his audience, for his avant-garde public as well as subsequent generations of detractors and admirers within the academic world have tended to approach the Prefaces as the impersonal statement of a technically masterful theoretician instead of the "exemplary" performance of a prodigiously entertaining artist who never relinquished his dream of popular success.[55]

In a final turn of the screw, it was the commercial failure of the New York Edition itself which served to complete and helped to cap the extremely seductive legend of the master, thereby insuring James's longevity on the modern literary scene and providing yet another chance for his fictional progeny—though once again in a totally unexpected way. As the "voluminosities of Proof" for the New York Edition kept rolling in and covering his desk "like the convolutions of a vast smothering boa-constrictor," James took note of the small royalty checks which he received from Scribner's, a sign of the edition's poor sales, and began to sense the sad truth that his supreme idea for a second go would not succeed (at least not in the sense in which he had envisioned it). Though he tried to assure his literary agent that he was capable of recovering "the perspective and proportion of things," the severe and prolonged depression that he subsequently experienced (as well as his brief attempt to return to the theater) suggest that James never fully recovered from the edition's "disconcerting failure" to sell.[56] The master was still brooding about the edition's commercial failure more than three years later when he wrote to Pinker thanking him for a royalty check of £52.8.8, but expressing the fact that he was "disturbed and rather dismayed" at the way that source of income appeared to be shrinking. "I was hoping for so much better things!" And as late as August of 1915, he could write to his friend Edmund Gosse:

> The Edition has been, from the point of view of profit either to the publisher or to myself, practically a complete failure; vaguely speaking, it doesn't sell... I am past all praying for anywhere; I remain at my age (which you know), and after my long career, utterly, insurmountably, unsaleable.[57]

James's worst fears about being unpopular and unread, originally projected in the tales of the literary life which he wrote during his theater years, finally seemed to be coming true. Indeed, most of his works were out of print when he died in 1916. Like Ray Limbert, the fictional master in "The Next Time," Henry James's strange fate was to enact repeatedly the avant-garde rather than the popular version of literary success, no matter how hard he tried to alternate between or combine the two. Luckily for the real life master, however, modern critics have largely tended to share the taste and point of view of the narrator of that story, a super-subtle reader who regards popularity as vulgar and prosaic and whose esteem can be won only at the cost of pecuniary failure. To paraphrase another character from this tale of the literary life, a failure now can "make—oh, with the aid of immense talent of course, for there are failures—and failures—such a reputation." Leon Edel reports that James had to await rediscovery until the mid-twentieth century, by which time "his books were in print in great numbers, as many as five editions in paperback of *The Ambassadors* alone. His letters were saved in quantities that would have astonished him, and became expensive autographs. He became a word, an image, a symbol long after his death." This new demand for paperback editions of James's fiction largely reflects the introduction and rapid growth in the middle of this century of college level and graduate school courses dealing with American literature, courses which were frequently inaugurated and taught by the New Critics and their followers, often the direct literary descendents of James's avant-garde disciples. Thus as we enter the final decades of the twentieth century, the master's posthumous reputation and sales continue to receive an unanticipated extension, at least within the walls of academia, for in an unforeseen twist worthy of James's most ironic stories of writers and artists, his works have become required reading for most students of American literature and the modern novel.[58] Unfortunately, these students know him primarily if not exclusively in his guise as the triumphant master and are usually kept ignorant of the many compromises that helped to shape his actual working life—humanizing facts which make up the fascinating story of his long and highly uneven career, a more moving tale of the literary life than any James himself would actually ever write.

Notes

Introduction

1. This situation is currently being remedied to a large extent by scholarship on popular and neglected women writers as well as reprints of their work, such as the Feminist Press's reprints of Rebecca Harding Davis' *Life in the Iron Mills* and Charlotte Perkins Gilman's *The Yellow Wallpaper*. Another case in point is Kate Chopin's 1899 novel, *The Awakening,* which is now being taught as a "lost classic" of American literature in many undergraduate survey courses.

2. William Veeder, *Henry James—The Lessons of the Master* (Chicago: University of Chicago Press, 1975), p. 1. This information is valuable for the way in which it testifies to the unsuspected breadth of young James's reading experience as well as for what it can tell contemporary scholars about the lack of such breadth in our own literary experience of this period. Marcia Jacobson has recently extended Veeder's approach by applying it to the novels of the 1880s and 1890s. In *Henry James and the Mass Market* (University, Alabama: University of Alabama Press, 1983) she reconstructs the literary context of these years in order to argue that James continued to make "repeated attempts to work within the best-selling genres of the period in a way that would yield a probing examination of the society that gave them birth." Yet her illuminating discussion of the literary marketplace in these last two decades is undermined by her tendency to overstate the differences and ignore the parallels between the ante- and post-bellum best seller. On these points see Jacobson, pp. 3-10 and 15.

3. Henry Nash Smith, *Democracy and the Novel* (New York: Oxford University Press, 1978), pp. 128-129. Cushing Strout has taken a refreshing tack by probing what he calls James's "vocational conflict" (rather than his erotic life) and its effect upon a late story, "The Jolly Corner." Although Strout accepts the rather hackneyed idea that the writer's life is a "passive" one, he does an admirable job of exposing and exploring the dimensions of James's ambition and his desire for popularity. See Strout, "Henry James's Dream of the Louvre, 'The Jolly Corner,' and Psychological Interpretation," *The Psychohistory Review,* vol. 8, nos. 1-2 (Summer-Fall 1979), pp. 47-52.

4. On these two points see Smith, pp. 143-144 and 160, respectively.

5. See, for example, Smith's implicit endorsement of the commonly held view that by 1897 (if not earlier), James "was prepared to sacrifice wide appeal for a mass audience in order to address himself to a self-conscious elite." Smith, p. 152.

6. Henry James to James B. Pinker, 6 January 1910, Collection of American Literature, Beinecke Rare Book and Manuscript Library, Yale University; hereafter cited as Beinecke. All quotations from the James-Pinker correspondence are copyright, 1985, by Alexander R.

James. The majority of these letters have not yet been published, though some have appeared in Leon Edel and Percy Lubbock's editions of James correspondence and Edel does draw upon them to a limited extent in the concluding volumes of his biography of James. As far as I can ascertain only two other scholars have made significant use of this material, a symptom of the tendency of modern critics to ignore or underestimate the role played by the literary marketplace in the careers of canonized writers. In the early 1960s, Alan B. Donovan noted with some surprise that "of the Yale collection of four hundred and eighty letters from James to Pinker, only four have ever been published..." He also observed that "...the most enlightening part of the Pinker letters is the exact business relationship between author and agent which they delineate." See Donovan, "My Dear Pinker: The Correspondence of Henry James With His Literary Agent," *Yale University Library Gazette*, 36, no. 2 (Oct. 1961), pp. 78 and 88. I would stress that this relationship is important not only in its own right but because of the way in which it illumines James's attitude towards both the reading public in general and his particular following among the rising generation of novelists, some of whom were also Pinker's clients. In regard to this latter point, Elsa Nettels has recently made excellent use of the James-Pinker correspondence in her effort to document the master's attitude towards Joseph Conrad and his work in "Master and Confrere," the first chapter of her comparative study of *James and Conrad* (Athens: The University of Georgia Press, 1977). However, her extremely useful analysis of their personal relations is flawed by her assumption that the question of possible influence (both personal and literary) necessarily applies only to James's impact upon Conrad, rather than to *both* sides of this complex relationship.

7. This phrase appears in Pound's *Little Review* essay on the master, which was later reprinted in a collection edited by another highly influential American expatriate, T.S. Eliot. See *Literary Essays of Ezra Pound*, ed. T.S. Eliot (London: Faber and Faber Limited, 1954), p. 216.

8. Pound also asserted that despite his limitations, James "HAS written the MOST obscene book of our time, Puritan or no puritan." "Letter to H. L. Mencken," 28 November 1917, *The Letters of Ezra Pound: 1907-1941*, ed. D.D. Paige (New York: Harcourt, Brace & World, Inc., 1950), p. 125. Pound's essay on James suggests that this is a reference to "The Turn of the Screw." See Pound, *Essays*, p. 326. The issue of James's alleged obscenity is treated in chapters 4 through 6 below.

9. Henry James, *The Art of the Novel*, introd. by R. P. Blackmur (New York: Charles Scribner's Sons, 1962), p. 223.

10. Henry James to James B. Pinker, 20 May 1914, Beinecke, emphasis mine; and Henry James to James B. Pinker, 1 August 1914, Beinecke.

11. Henry James Jr. [son of William James] to James B. Pinker, 5 April 1913 and 6 August 1917, Beinecke. For their part, Scribner's (the American publisher of the New York Edition) seem to have anticipated poor sales from the outset. As Charles Scribner wrote to Pinker: "We never expected a rapid sale; indeed, we were never too sanguine of a paying sale, but I believe that the sale will continue." This letter reveals that Scribner's published the Edition primarily for prestige rather than for profit, indirectly justifying Henry Jr.'s suspicions regarding the probable effect of more aggressive and innovative advertising. Charles Scribner to James B. Pinker, 6 October 1908, Beinecke.

12. Pound, *Essays*, p. 297. James's rather different view of what he was doing and why is described by Leon Edel in *The Master* (New York: J.B. Lippincott and Co., 1972), pp. 528-532. James had his literary agent place a formal statement regarding his reasons for adopting British citizenship in the London *Times*, where it provoked what Edel justifiably refers to as a

"distorted" response from the American public. In a letter to Pinker, James refers to this statement as "attest[ing] my fullest responsibility for the act," noting that it has "a sort of 'exemplary' value which I shall rejoice in any degree to have established." Henry James to James B. Pinker, 17 October 1915, Beinecke. James had obviously misjudged his American audience.

13. Perhaps the most famous of these attacks is Van Wyck Brooks's *The Pilgrimage of Henry James* (New York: Octagon Books, 1972), a study which was first published in 1925. Pound's predictable distaste for this book, which criticized James's fiction precisely on the ground of the (supposedly) detrimental effect of his expatriation, surfaced in an unpublished letter which he addressed to Morton D. Zabel in 1935. Congratulating Zabel on a James essay he had published, Pound could not resist chiding him for having "... miss[ed] a chance to shit on the head of that damn idiot and worse than public nuisance Van Wyke [sic] Brooks. Jheezus, there is a bedbug that ought to be disinfected." Quoted in Alan Holder, *Three Voyagers in Search of Europe: A Study of Henry James, Ezra Pound, and T.S. Eliot* (Philadelphia: University of Pennsylvania Press, 1966), p. 169. Holder's valuable study of these three expatriates not only reveals the master's importance to the two younger writers as both a literary influence and a role model but also documents the pivotal role each played in shaping and maintaining James's posthumous reputation.

14. Richard N. Foley, *Criticism in American Periodicals of the Works of Henry James from 1866 to 1916* (Washington: The Catholic University Press, 1944); *Henry James: The Critical Heritage*, ed. Roger Gard (New York: Barnes & Noble Inc., 1968); and Leon Edel, *The Middle Years* (New York: J.B. Lippincott and Co., 1962) and *The Treacherous Years* (New York: J.B. Lippincott and Co., 1969). Fortunately, Edel's edition of the letters James wrote during the theater years sheds new and important light upon James's state of mind during this period of intense compromise as well as upon the intensely sympathetic response he evoked in the wake of the *Guy Domville* fiasco. See *Henry James Letters*, ed. Leon Edel (Cambridge: Harvard University Press, 1980), III, especially pp. 315-521. A highly condensed version of my formulation of the crucial role played by James's theater experience in the evolution of both his career and his reputation can be found in my essay reviewing this volume of James's correspondence. Anne T. Margolis, "The James Family," *American Quarterly*, vol. 34, no. 5 (Winter 1982), pp. 566-569.

15. James B. Pinker became Henry James's literary agent in 1898 after the novelist terminated a brief and not very successful relationship with the firm of A.P. Watt. Pinker (who numbered several of James's younger colleagues among his clients, including Joseph Conrad, Stephen Crane, and H.G. Wells) was to function as James's agent for the remainder of the novelist's career and would gradually emerge as one of the master's most trusted friends and confidants. For more information on the James/Pinker relationship, see Donovan, "My Dear Pinker..." and Edel, *The Treacherous Years*, pp. 337-339.

16. In several key instances (most notably *The Portrait of a Lady*, *The Wings of the Dove*, and *The Golden Bowl*), my treatment of the novels simply cannot do full justice to my own sense of their ability to generate an aura of virtually inexhaustible mystery and meaningfulness. I have tried to compensate by directing the reader's attention, either in the text or in the notes, to a few of the many fine critical studies which explore the subtleties of the text under discussion and analyze its uniqueness (though the existing body of secondary material on James is so vast that I have had to be extremely selective).

17. James's unfinished three-volume autobiography, first published between 1913 and 1917, compliments, completes, and enlarges upon the Prefaces by retrospectively presenting the master's entire life (including his earliest childhood experiences) as the story of his more or

less deliberate preparation for his unprecedented literary vocation. See Henry James, *Autobiography*, ed. and introd. Frederick W. Dupee (New York: Criterion Books, 1956).

18. James not only acknowledges but *celebrates* the fictional aspect of his Prefaces in the concluding paragraph of the final preface to *The Golden Bowl*, where he implicitly invites his initiated readers to emulate this "vital" performance. Henry James, *The Art of the Novel*, pp. 347-348. R.P. Blackmur's penetrating and eloquent Introduction to *The Art of the Novel* is the classic modernist reading of the Prefaces. The influence of this 1934 essay upon the course of twentieth-century James criticism can hardly be overestimated. Blackmur apotheosizes James as a fictional master who "had to elucidate and to appropriate for the critical intellect the substance and principle of his career as an artist... with a consistency of part with part that amounted almost to the consistency of a mathematical equation, so that, as in the *Poetics*, if his premises were accepted his conclusions must be taken as inevitable." Blackmur, Introduction to *The Art of the Novel*, p. vii. D.W. Jefferson explicitly takes issue with Blackmur's reading of the Prefaces and presents modern readers with a refreshingly different (though equally one-sided) emphasis in the first chapter of *Henry James and the Modern Reader* (New York: St. Martin's Press, 1964). There he downplays the difficulty of the late fiction and highlights the master's playfulness, humor, and extravagance of expression (rather than his artistic dedication and his alleged theoretical rigor).

19. Renato Poggioli, *The Theory of the Avant-Garde*, trans. Gerald Fitzgerald (Cambridge, Mass.: Harvard University Press, 1968), p. 8.

20. Poggioli makes this distinction on pp. 91-92.

21. Ironically, Henry's elder brother William is one of the few readers whom he seems to have entirely given up on. See the novelist's response to William's criticism of his "third" manner in general and *The Golden Bowl* in particular, both reprinted in Gard, pp. 392-394. Henry notes that William remains "constitutionally unable" to enjoy his late work.

22. Henry James, "Criticism," reprinted in *Literary Opinion in America*, ed. Morton Zabel (New York: Harper and Brothers, 1937), rev. ed., p. 50.

Chapter 1

1. "Letter to William James," 29 October 1888, *The Letters of Henry James*, ed. Percy Lubbock (New York: Charles Scribner's Sons, 1920) 1:141; hereafter cited as *LHJ*.

2. "Letter to William James," 29 October 1888, *LHJ* 1:141-142.

3. Henry James, *The Notebooks of Henry James*, ed. F.O. Matthiessen and Kenneth B. Murdock (New York: Oxford University Press, 1947), p. 99; hereafter cited as *Notebooks*.

4. "Letter to William Dean Howells," 2 January 1888, *LHJ* 1:135; and "Letter to Edmund Gosse," 3 January 1888, *Henry James Letters*, ed. Leon Edel (Cambridge: Harvard University Press, 1980), 3:210-211; hereafter cited as *HJL*.

5. Howells' editorial remarks are quoted in Leon Edel, *The Middle Years* (New York: J.B. Lippincott Company, 1962), pp. 243-244; hereafter cited as *MY*. The entire review has been reprinted in Albert Mordell, ed., *Discovery of a Genius* (New York: Twayne Publishers, Inc., 1961), pp. 126-128. Fulkerson's comment about supply and demand can be found in *A Hazard of New Fortunes* (New York: New American Library, 1965), p. 247.

6. James, *Notebooks*, pp. 82, 84, and 85. Matthiessen and Murdock have also noted James's shift in emphasis and tone. See their editorial comments on p. 85. Critics who insist upon

regarding James's middle period as a phase of his career wholly given over to thematic and technical experimentation are thus forced to either ignore *The Reverberator* or frankly acknowledge it as an exception. For an example of the latter tack, see Sergio Perosa, *Henry James and the Experimental Novel* (New York: New York University Press, 1983), pp. 34-38.

7. Of course as James's notebook entries reveal, he knew perfectly well that this was not the case. While *The Reverberator* was still appearing in serial form he was already at work on *The Tragic Muse*, a novel which would both portray and exploit the public's fascination with two of the most thoroughly newspaperized arenas of British life, parliamentary politics and the London stage. Although it was largely assumed at the time that the "New Journalism" was strictly an American import, contemporary historians now agree that the changes in English journalism were primarily due to internal economic and social developments. On this point, see Raymond L. Schulte, *Crusader in Babylon: W.T. Stead and the "Pall Mall Gazette"* (Lincoln: University of Nebraska Press, 1972) and Raymond Williams, *The Long Revolution* (New York: Columbia University Press, 1961), especially pp. 173-213. This quote from Howells' review of *The Reverberator* can be found in Mordell, p. 131. Along the same lines, see Howells' less enthusiastic review of "A London Life" (1889) in which he dutifully reminds James that "he must pay the penalty of being true" and broadly hints that James should "treat" or "vignette" his negatives in order to "flatter away those hard edges..." Mordell, p. 134.

8. Henry James, "The Art of Fiction," in his *Partial Portraits*, ed. Leon Edel (1888, rpt. Ann Arbor: University of Michigan Press, 1970), pp. 381-382.

9. These early reviews have been collected by Pierre de Chaignon la Rose in a volume entitled *Notes and Reviews By Henry James* (Cambridge, Mass.: Dunster House, 1921); hereafter cited as *N&R*.

10. One could even argue (and I, in effect, do so in chapter 6 below) that Milly Theale's mysterious fatal disease in *The Wings of the Dove* amounts to a severe case of female uselessness. For a detailed description and sensitive analysis of Alice's "career" as an invalid, see Jean Strouse's important new study, *Alice James: A Biography* (Boston: Houghton Mifflin Company, 1980).

11. James, *N&R*, p. 5.

12. See Leon Edel, *The Untried Years* (New York: J.B. Lippincott Company, 1953), pp. 291-294; hereafter cited as *UY* and Leon Edel, *The Conquest of London* (New York: J.B. Lippincott Company, 1962), pp. 130-132; hereafter cited as *CL*, regarding Henry's sources of income during this period and his elaborate justification of his European expenditures to his parents while they were still supporting him. Contrary to popular belief, the novelist did not inherit great wealth like his father. Henry always remained largely dependent upon income derived from his pen and suffered a lifelong anxiety, bordering on obsession, regarding money. In spite of this, he generously made over a large part of his relatively modest inheritance to his sister, Alice, when their parents died in 1882. Further information regarding Henry's relationship with his parents and siblings can be found in F.O. Matthiessen's *The James Family* (1947; rpt. New York: Vintage Books, 1980), Edel's five-volume biography of the novelist, especially *UY*, and Strouse's biography of Alice, especially pp. 3-82.

13. James, *N&R*, pp. 77-78. More detailed information on opposition to the novel because of its supposedly detrimental effect on women and the "lower orders" can be found in John Tinnon Taylor, *Early Opposition to the English Novel* (New York: Morningside Heights, King's Crown Press, 1943) and J.M.S. Tompkins, *The Popular Novel in England: 1770-1800* (London: Constable & Co. Ltd., 1932).

Notes for Chapter 1

14. Frank Luther Mott, *A History of American Magazines* (Cambridge, Mass.: Harvard University Press, 1957), III:90; hereafter cited as *History*. Twentieth-century students of American culture usually subscribe to Mott's point of view and accept this assumption as unproblematic. See, for example, Ann Douglas' controversial study of the rise of sentimental fiction, *The Feminization of American Culture* (New York: Alfred A. Knopf, 1977) and the first chapter of Nina Baym's more sympathetic analysis of novels written by popular women writers in America, *Woman's Fiction* (Ithaca: Cornell University Press, 1978), pp. 12-21. But while there is certainly evidence that women did form the majority of subscribers to the magazines, this does not mean that male family members were not reading them as well. In fact, women may simply have been functioning in their newly established role as purchasers for the entire family. This last point is developed in the first chapter of Nancy Cott's excellent study, *The Bonds of Womanhood* (New Haven: Yale University Press, 1977).

15. James, *N&R*, pp. 26, 28, and 33, emphasis mine. In a similar vein, James concluded his review of a recent Dumas novel by exclaiming: "Such writing is reading for men." On the novelist's admiration for Arnold, see John Henry Raleigh's *Matthew Arnold and American Culture* (Berkeley: University of California Press, 1961), pp. 17-46.

16. James, *N&R*, pp. 112 and 114.

17. James, *N&R*, pp. 202 and 207.

18. George Eliot, "Silly Novels By Lady Novelists," *Westminster Review*, LXVI (October 1856), pp. 460-461. Elaine Showalter devotes a chapter of her very useful study of British women novelists to the double critical standard. See *A Literature of Their Own* (Princeton: Princeton University Press, 1977), pp. 73-99.

19. For an account of this rise, see Ellen Moers' comparative study, *Literary Women* (New York: Anchor Books, 1977). Barbara Welter's "The Cult of True Womanhood: 1820-1860" (*American Quarterly,* no. 18 [1966], pp. 151-174) is the classic article by an American scholar on woman's "proper sphere" in the nineteenth century, while Cott's *The Bonds of Womanhood* is the best overall study of the origins, development, and consequences of this cult in America.

20. Hawthorne's remarks are quoted in Caroline Ticknor, *Hawthorne and His Publisher* (Boston: Houghton Mifflin Company, 1914), p. 141. Emphasis mine. (It is amusing to note that James would later refer to *The Lamplighter* as his first "grown-up" novel!) For more information on British male writers' similar fears of their female competitors, consult Showalter, pp. 37-72, 74, and 79.

21. Ticknor, p. 142.

22. These sales figures come from James D. Hart, *The Popular Book* (New York: Oxford University Press, 1950), pp. 93-94 and 112. James's reminiscences about *Uncle Tom's Cabin* can be found in his *Autobiography,* ed. Frederick W. Dupee (1917; rpt. New York: Criterion Books, 1956), p. 92.

23. This definition of a best seller is taken from Robert Escarpit, *The Book Revolution* (London: George G. Harrap & Co. Ltd., 1966), p. 116. It should be stressed that men as well as women were producing this new commodity. Timothy Shay Arthur, remembered today (if at all) as the author of *Ten Nights in a Bar Room,* was only one of several men who achieved popular success by catering to the demand for sentimental fiction. And, although he wrote no best sellers, Fanny Fern's brother N. P. Willis, made a highly successful career out of producing this type of fiction for the magazines. Ann Douglas Wood refers to Willis as "the high priest of the feminine subculture and mystique" in her valuable early article, "The 'Scribbling Women'

and Fanny Fern: Why Women Wrote," *American Quarterly,* vol. 23, no. 1 (Spring 1971), p. 16. Harriet Beecher Stowe's famous brother, the Reverend Henry Ward Beecher, would later achieve literary fame and immense profit with the publication of his sentimental novel, *Norwood.*

24. William Charvat, *The Profession of Authorship in America, 1800-1870,* ed. Matthew J. Bruccoli, foreword by Howard Mumford Jones (Columbus: Ohio State University Press, 1968), p. 262.

25. William Charvat, *Literary Publishing in America, 1790-1850* (Philadelphia: University of Pennsylvania, 1959), pp. 58-59. *Harper's, Putnam's,* and the *Atlantic* were founded in 1850, 1855, and 1857 respectively.

26. Henry James, *The Complete Tales of Henry James,* ed. Leon Edel (New York: J.B. Lippincott Company, 1962), III, p. 351; hereafter cited as *Tales.*

27. James, *Tales* 3:351, 352, and 353.

28. James, *Tales* 3:357.

29. Edel, Introduction to *Tales* 3:10 and James, *Tales* 3:358 and 365.

30. James, *Tales* 3:353. James would later use almost identical phrasing in describing the inner conflict which characterizes the two male protagonists of his theater novel, *The Tragic Muse.*

31. Henry James, *Watch and Ward* (1878; rpt. Boston: Houghton Mifflin and Co., 1886), p. 7. This serial (whose title is probably an ironic reference to Anthony Comstock and his "watch and ward" societies for the supervision of public morality) cannot be considered James's first novel because it was not published in book form until 1878 and only then at the suggestion of his publisher, James Osgood. There was no English edition of the novel, although by this time James was publishing his novels simultaneously on both sides of the Atlantic. It is obvious that he did not consider *Watch and Ward* to be of sufficient quality to satisfy the taste of the British public. Publishing details can be found in Leon Edel and Dan H. Lawrence, *A Bibliography of Henry James* (London: Rupert Hart-Davis, 1957), pp. 36-37.

32. James, *Watch and Ward,* pp. 41, 53, and 54. Just five months after this novel completed its serial run in the *Atlantic,* James left for Europe where he served as an escort for his sister and his aunt.

33. Foley, p. 9.

34. Foley, p. 9.

35. Several other commentators have noticed the melodramatic aspects of James's works. Peter Brooks's *The Melodramatic Imagination* (New Haven: Yale University Press, 1976) is the most recent attempt to focus upon and defend James's reliance upon melodrama. His analysis owes much to two earlier studies, Leo B. Levy's *Versions of Melodrama* (Berkeley: University of California Press, 1957) and Jacques Barzun's "Henry James, Melodramatist," a 1943 essay reprinted in *The Question of Henry James,* ed. F. W. Dupee (New York: Henry Holt and Co., 1945), pp. 254-266.

36. "Letter to Henry James Sr.," 1 February [1873], *HJL* 1:333-336. While Edel contradicts the popular assumption that it was Howells who gave James his start as a writer, an assumption Howells' late reminiscences did much to foster, he is quick to point out Howells' importance during the early years of James's career: "Howells was the first editor to take him seriously *as a writer of fiction* and to see that he had a future." Edel, *UY,* p. 269. Emphasis mine. By the time they met, Howells was the assistant editor to James T. Fields, owner-editor of the

Atlantic and former publisher of Hawthorne. By 1866 Howells had become its virtual editor, a title he was to claim officially in 1871. As such, Howells was instrumental in seeing to it that James's best work was placed in the *Atlantic*.

37. "Letter to William Dean Howells," 30 March [1877], *HJL* 2:104-106.
38. William Dean Howells, *Criticism and Fiction and Other Essays*, ed. Clara M. Kirk and Rudolph Kirk (1891; rpt. New York: New York University Press, 1965), p. 75. In 1890 Howells published *A Hazard of New Fortunes*, a semi-autobiographical novel which exposes the commercialization and "feminization" of American literature by exploring the personal dimensions of the professional dilemmas faced by Basil March, a magazine editor caught between the competing claims of his family and his conscience.
39. "Letter to Charles Eliot Norton," 10 August 1867, *Life in Letters of William Dean Howells*, ed. Mildred Howells (Garden City, N.Y.: Doubleday, Doran & Co., Inc., 1928), 1:117-118.
40. John Tebbel, *A History of Book Publishing in the United States* (New York: R. R. Bowker, 1972), 1:250; and Tebbel, 2:673.
41. Wilky's letter is quoted in Edel, *UY*, p. 200. All of the officers of the 54th regiment were white.
42. Foley reports that *Washington Square* was panned by some reviewers as "a clever bit of psychological anatomy" and "a difficult vivisection" while another critic insisted that James was capable of writing a great novel if only "he would stop experimenting and write one that would have life as well as art." Foley, pp. 24-26.
43. Justin Kaplan, *Mr. Clemens and Mark Twain* (New York: Simon and Schuster, 1966), p. 61. The famous episode in chapter 22 of *Huckleberry Finn* in which Colonel Sherburn faces down the lynch mob is generally taken to be Twain's ultimate assessment of (and heavy-handed attack upon) his own audience. The novel is virtually built upon similar (though much more subtle) excoriations of the taste and character of the American reading public.
44. The word "army" can be taken quite literally in some cases. Retired army officers and unemployed Civil War veterans formed a ready-made network, complete with hierarchy. For this reason they were frequently used as book agents by Bliss's firm and other subscription publishers and thereby became, in effect, one of the earliest postwar manifestations of that modern phenomenon, the travelling salesman or commercial traveller. James was to comment incisively on the relationship between the commercial traveller and American culture in his late work, *The American Scene* (1907). For a fascinating account of Twain's career as a subscription publisher of his own and others' works, see *Mark Twain, Business Man*, ed. Samuel Charles Webster (Boston: Little, Brown and Company, 1946).
45. This account of subscription publishing is drawn from Kaplan, pp. 61-62. The Grangerford-Shepherdson feud appears in chapters 17 and 18 of *Huckleberry Finn*. It is worth noting that Howells took a different point of view. As Kaplan reports, he would later state that "no book of literary quality was made to go by subscription except Mr. Clemens' books, and I think these went because the subscription public never knew what good literature they were" (Kaplan, p. 61). It should be pointed out that Twain's public also included "respectable" Easterners such as his social acquaintances and business friends in Hartford, Connecticut, a fact which suggests that at least in some cases, subscription books reached urban readers as well. Nevertheless, the attitude of Twain's Nook Farm neighbor (and future collaborator on *The Gilded Age*), Charles Dudley Warner, was probably quite typical of the Hartford community as well as most professional writers. In 1874 Warner counselled another friend, Helen Hunt Jackson, against publishing her works in subscription form: "I think if you were to see your dainty literature in such ill-conditioned volumes, you would just die. There is no

doubt, however, that 'by subscription' is the only way for the author to make any money." Quoted in Kenneth Andrews, *Nook Farm: Mark Twain's Hartford Circle* (Cambridge, Mass.: Harvard University Press, 1950), p. 122.

46. Kaplan, p. 61.

47. Quoted in Kaplan, p. 62. In 1875 Twain notified Howells that he could not afford to offer him *Tom Sawyer* for serialization in the *Atlantic*. As he candidly explained: "You see I take a vile, mercenary view of things—but then my household expenses are something almost ghastly." Quoted in Kaplan, p. 192. According to Hart, Twain usually received 50% of the profits from his books. (See Hart, pp. 148-152, regarding the distribution and sales of Twain's work.) In the very same year, Osgood offered James, through his father, a 15% royalty if he would agree to pay for his own stereotype plates or 10% on sales after the first 1000 if Osgood covered all costs. Edel and Lawrence, *Bibliography*, pp. 25-26.

48. "Letter to Thomas Sargeant Perry," 27 March 1868, *HJL* 1:84.

49. An account of these offers appears in *UY*, pp. 246-247.

Chapter 2

1. "Letter to John Hay," 21 July [1875], *HJL* 1:476-478.

2. "Letter to William James," 22 September [1872], *HJL* 1:300-301. One historian estimates that even under the earlier period of Greeley's editorship, the *Tribune* reached an audience of at least 200,000. James J. Barnes, *Authors, Publishers, and Politicians* (London: Routledge & Kegan Paul, 1974), p. 17.

3. "Letter to Whitelaw Reid," 22 November [1875], *HJL* 2:8 and "Letter to William James," 8 February [1876], *HJL* 2:27.

4. Lyall H. Powers, *Henry James and the Naturalist Movement* (Michigan State University Press, 1971), p. 34. A brief history of Flaubert's circle can be found on pp. 17-19. In regard to their narrowness of outlook, see "Letter to William Dean Howells," 28 May [1876], *HJL* 2:52, James's essay on Daudet in *Partial Portraits*, pp. 195-239, and his concluding remarks on Zola in "The Art of Fiction," *Partial Portraits*, p. 408.

5. "Letter to T.S. Perry," 3 February [1876], and [Postmarked 2 May 1876], *HJL* 2:24 and 44; and "Letter to William Dean Howells," 3 February [1876], *HJL* 2:23. This account of James's dealings with Reid is taken from Leon Edel and Ilse Dusoir Lind, Introduction to Henry James, *Parisian Sketches: Letters to the 'New York Tribune'* (New York: New York University Press, 1957), pp. xxiv and xxvi-xxvii.

6. "Letter to Whitelaw Reid," 30 August 1876, *HJL* 2:63-64.

7. "Letter to Henry James Sr.," 16 September [1876], *HJL* 2:66.

8. "Letter to William Dean Howells," 28 May [1876], *HJL* 2:53. In his 1903 essay on Zola's career, James would later recall "the chorus of contempt" which this incident elicited from Flaubert's cénacle. Their condemnation of the "superficiality, vulgarity, [and] intellectual platitude [,] was the striking note on this occasion..." This essay has been reprinted in George G. Becker, ed., *Documents of Modern Literary Realism* (Princeton: Princeton University Press, 1967), p. 517.

9. As his letters reveal, James was still struggling to achieve financial independence from his parents at this time. See, for example, the letter he wrote to his mother on 8 May [1876] in

which he insists that they keep the money from the sales of his first novel, *Roderick Hudson*, in order to cancel his debt to them. *HJL* 2:47.

10. "Letter to Mrs. Henry James Sr.," Christmas Eve [1876], *HJL,* 2:87. Henry went on to add: "I have been revelling in a subscription to Mudies..." Edel reports that the apprentice novelist borrowed "armfuls of books" from Mudie's circulating library during that winter. *CL,* p. 272. The parenthetical observation concerning American expatriates has been taken from Stanley Weintraub, *The London Yankees* (New York: Harcourt Brace Jovanovich, 1979), p. 4.

11. This description of Mudie's and the British book trade is drawn from Guinevere L. Griest, *Mudie's Circulating Library and the Victorian Novel* (Bloomington: Indiana University Press, 1970), pp. 18, 137, 140, and 40.

12. These estimates can be found in Griest, pp. 78-79. More information on the history of the circulating library can be found in Tompkins' *The Popular Novel in England* and Taylor's *Early Opposition to the English Novel*. On the relationship between this institution and the regular book trade, James J. Barnes's *Free Trade in Books* (Oxford: The Clarendon Press, 1964) has proved to be quite helpful, especially pp. 103-108.

13. The popular new weekly papers began to provide serial fiction for the multitude at still lower prices at about this time. My account of three-deckers is based upon Griest, pp. 101-119, while the description of "part issue" has been condensed from Kathleen Tillotsen's discussion of alternate modes of publication in *Novels of the Eighteen-Forties* (Oxford: The Clarendon Press, 1954), pp. 20-31.

14. "Letter to T.S. Perry," 5 August 1860, *HJL,* 1:27.

15. W. H. Smith operated the one railway library which gave Mudie serious competition in the field of "select" books. Rather than resort to literary piracy, Smith preferred to wait the required year or so before a triple-decker could be reprinted in single-volume format and supplemented his list with single-volume versions of high quality works on which the copyright had run out. These he sold through his chain of railway bookstalls, a method of distribution which enabled him to capitalize on the need of railway travellers for reading matter which was cheap and portable and yet "respectable." Griest, pp. 32-33. For more details on the unsuccessful attempts to pass an international copyright agreement prior to the last decade of the century and the effect which this situation had upon the Anglo-American literary scene, see Barnes's *Authors, Publishers, and Politicians* and Raymond Howard Shove, *Cheap Book Production in the United States, 1870 to 1891* (Urbana: University of Illinois Press, 1937).

16. Edel and Lawrence, *Bibliography,* pp. 25-30.

17. James's comments regarding the pirated edition as well as the details of its sales and publication are drawn from Edel and Lawrence, *Bibliography,* pp. 32-33. A photograph of the cover of the pirated version of *The American* appears in the *Bibliography* as well as in Edel, *CL,* p. 384.

18. Edel and Lawrence, *Bibliography,* p. 34. For more information on these arrangements, see "Letter to Henry James Sr.," 19 April [1878], *HJL* 2:166-167.

19. The use of advance sheets had been pioneered by two publishers, Carey of Philadelphia and Constable of London, in response to frantic competition among American publishers for the works of Scott and Byron early in the century. Tebbel, 1:115.

20. The *Home Journal* was an "urbane" New York magazine which Nathaniel Willis, brother of Fanny Fern, had once edited. Frank Luther Mott reports that "it devoted many of its columns to society chat." The *Living Age,* a weekly out of Boston, was considered an "eclectic" magazine. Although it took its material mainly from British periodicals, it rarely printed anything but second- and third-rate fiction because the better English novelists usually sold their advance sheets to other American magazines. Mott, *A History of American Magazines* 2:250, 3:101 and 256, and 1:748.

21. Edel and Lawrence, *Bibliography,* p. 39 and Edel, *CL,* p. 304.

22. Frank L. Schick, *The Paperbound Book in America* (New York: R. R. Bowker Company, 1958), p. 57 and Shove, pp. 1-5.

23. This line of thought was suggested to me by passages which develop the distinction between unpopularity by distribution and unpopularity by comprehension in Poggioli, pp. 43-45.

24. Howells' remarks are quoted in Edel, *CL,* p. 312. It is obviously too simple a view to see Daisy as an innocent young girl victimized by "corrupt" European society. In a sense she is just as much a victim of American society in the form of both her own inflexible notions of female freedom and independence and the equally rigid code of the expatriated Americans who cut her.

25. Edel and Lawrence, *Bibliography,* p. 49. For Henry's reaction, see "Letter to Henry James Sr.," 15 February 1880, *HJL* 2:270-272.

26. "Letter to William James," 23 July [1878], *HJL* 2:179.

27. "Letter to Elizabeth Boott," 30 October [1878], *HJL* 2:189 and Gard, p. 62. *The Europeans* began to appear in serial form just as *Daisy Miller* was concluding in the *Cornhill*. Due to the piracy discussed above, the book version of *The Europeans* actually appeared first. Within the next year Macmillan was to issue English editions of both *Roderick Hudson* and *The American* and publish a two-volume collection of James's earlier stories, entitled *The Madonna of the Future and Other Tales*. Because *The American* had already made an unauthorized appearance in the railway library, it was issued exclusively in one-volume form. But *Roderick Hudson* made his English debut as a three-decker, like any "new" English novel. James had to revise and divide the original thirteen chapters into twenty-six in order to stretch what had originally been one volume into three. Edel and Lawrence, *Bibliography,* pp. 30-33 and 42.

28. Richard Poirier, *The Comic Sense of Henry James* (New York: Oxford University Press, 1967), pp. 107-108.

29. Poirier, p. 108. "Us" refers primarily to a posthumous audience which can be roughly equated with Poirier himself and *his* imputed readers.

30. Henry's comments to his brother can be found in "Letter to William James," 14 November [1878], *HJL* 2:193. William Veeder observes that a tension between imitation and parody pervades James's apprentice novels. He also argues, less convincingly, that James's early style is virtually indistinguishable from that of the more popular Anglo-American novelists of his day. Although the sales figures and contemporaneous reviews of these novels do not support this line of argument, Veeder is quite effective in demonstrating James's reliance upon popular literary devices up to the time of *The Portrait*, which he treats as a break in this pattern. As I note in my Introduction, this interpretation of James's work will argue that James's flirtation with literary and theatrical conventions persisted throughout his entire career. Selected Anglo-American criticism of *The Europeans* can be found in Gard, pp. 49-73. This excerpt has been taken from p. 63.

31. James, *Notebooks*, p. 14 and "Letter to Mrs. F. H. Hill," 21 March [1879], *HJL* 2:221.

32. Henry James, *Hawthorne* (London, 1879; rpt. Ithaca: Cornell University Press, 1975), pp. 34-35 and 114.

33. "Letter to William Dean Howells," 31 January [1880], *HJL* 2:266-268.

34. "Letter to T.S. Perry," 22 February [1880], *HJL* 2:274-275. Interestingly enough, Foley maintains that "*Hawthorne* met with some of the most thoughtful and penetrating criticism that any work of James had received" (Foley, p. 20).

35. "Letter to William James," 14 November [1878], *HJL* 2:193. Emphasis mine. In contrast, James openly speaks of his next novel as a mere means of economic self-financing. In a letter to his mother, he expresses his hope that *Confidence* (probably James's worst novel) will provide him with the leisure he needs for what he refers to as his "big 'wine-and-water' novel." This big novel was to become *The Portrait of a Lady*. "Letter to Mrs. Henry James Sr.," 8 April [1879], *HJL* 2:229.

36. "Letter to William James," 14 November [1878], *HJL* 2:193-194. The other experiments James refers to here are probably *An International Episode* and *Four Meetings*, the two companion pieces to *Daisy Miller*.

37. Veeder, p. 89, and Henry James, *The Portrait of a Lady* (London, 1881; rpt. New York: The New American Library, 1963), pp. 80 and 256-257. On this point see Leo Levy's discussion of James's repeated use of the staple characters of melodrama (the orphan, the oppressor, the protector, the betrayed) in his *Versions of Melodrama*. Levy does, however, regard what he refers to as the "sensationalism" of James's fiction more as "an ingrained aspect of his [James's] way of looking at life" rather than as a "design of expediency" with respect to James's audience. (He cites *The Other House* as the one exception to this rule.) Levy, pp. 10 and 7. As I suggest in chapter 1, I think that both factors are at work. By arguing that James "was unable to escape the burden of his *self-imposed* conventions," Levy leaves little or no room for the role which the reading public (in the form of James's perception of popular taste) played in his career. Levy, p. 88. Emphasis mine. Veeder's *The Lessons of the Master* provides further evidence of James's reliance upon literary conventions established by popular Anglo-American novelists and French dramatists. Consult, for example, his documentation of James's reading of popular novels on pp. 16-17, on the basis of which he agrees with Oscar Cargill's assessment of James as "the *widest*, if not the *best*, read American of his day." Veeder, p. 18. In his notes Veeder also quotes a passage from Leon Edel's 1963 Introduction to *The Portrait* which deals with the melodramatic aspects of the plot. See Veeder, p. 253 n.1.

38. Henry James, "Nana," in his *The House of Fiction*, ed. Leon Edel (London: Rupert Hart-Davis, 1957), pp. 277-278. It is interesting to note that while visiting France during the preceding year, Mark Twain had listened "with delight" as the illustrator Edwin Abbey gave an unprintable speech to the all-male Stomach Club. According to his biographer, Twain "paid tribute to the high antiquity of masturbation" in his own talk, "Some Thoughts on the Science of Onanism," a speech which was obviously not intended to be heard by his wife Livy. Kaplan also recounts a subsequent visit by Twain to another all-male "club," West Point, during which the author supervised the private printing of his scandalous *1601* on the Academy's private press. As Kaplan documents here and elsewhere in this penetrating biography, Twain rigidly adhered to the Victorian distinction between "smoking-room sexuality and drawing-room purity" (to use Kaplan's apt phrase). Kaplan, pp. 221-222 and 229. It is much to James's credit that although he temporarily endorsed this particular version of the separation of "spheres" and the literary double standard, his middle and late works intentionally undermine this distinction.

39. James, *Partial Portraits*, p. 388. James's reference to the novel's "monstrous uncleanness" has often been quoted, perhaps with insufficient attention to the ironic tone with which he proceeds to remind his readers that this did not prevent *Nana* from reaching its thirty-ninth edition!

40. James, *The Portrait*, pp. 40 and 51.

41. James was to address this problem retrospectively in an explicit (if somewhat devious) manner in his preface to the New York Edition version of *The Portrait* where he asks: "... by what thinness, at the best, would such a subject not be vitiated? Millions of presumptuous girls, intelligent or not intelligent, daily affront their destiny, and what is it open to their destiny to *be*, at the most, that we should make an ado about it?" James, *The Art of the Novel*, ed. R. P. Blackmur (New York: Charles Scribner's Sons, 1934), p. 48. On this question, see also James's opening remarks in his preface to *Daisy Miller*, *The Art of the Novel*, pp. 267-270.

42. James, *The Portrait*, pp. 46-47, 13, and 42.

43. I owe my heightened awareness of both Henrietta's style and Isabel's occasional tendency to sound uncannily like her to Richard Poirier's perceptive treatment of Henrietta in *The Comic Sense of Henry James*, pp. 197-199. It is worth recalling that James also financed his travel abroad by writing letters for an American newspaper. Despite the obvious differences in the quality of mind and style as well as sex, it is certainly possible that James's caricature of the American journalist here and elsewhere in his work is tinged by an element of self-parody, perhaps even self-contempt.

44. James, *The Portrait*, pp. 175-178.

45. James, *The Portrait*, pp. 482-484, 23, 32-33, and 46-47.

46. James, *The Portrait*, p. 53.

47. James, *The Portrait*, pp. 279 and 325.

48. Laurence Holland, *The Expense of Vision* (Princeton: Princeton University Press, 1964), pp. 34-35. Holland correctly emphasizes and shrewdly analyzes James's enormous ambition and its consequences for his central characters throughout his fine study. James, *The Portrait*, pp. 138-139 and 531.

49. James, *The Portrait*, p. 396.

50. While William Veeder rightly insists that James succeeds in transforming conventional materials into personal style in *The Portrait*, he reads the ending of the novel, mistakenly in my opinion, as the novelist's ultimate reaffirmation of conventional notions of female character and the traditional values of courage, patience, and family affection. The deliberate ambiguity of the ending paradoxically accommodates yet *undermines* such a conventional reading, as contemporaneous readers uneasily sensed and as modern critics have amply documented in their various interpretations of the novel's conclusion. As previously noted, Veeder also argues that James's reliance upon literary conventions is permanently diminished by the achievement of *The Portrait*, an assertion which fails to take into account the psychological and financial contingencies which continued to impinge on James's career. See Veeder, *The Lessons of the Master*, pp. 183 and 66.

51. "Letter to T.S. Perry," 24 January 1881, *HJL* 2:335.

Chapter 3

1. The prefaces to *The Portrait, The Princess Casamassima*, and *The Tragic Muse* have been especially influential in this regard. See James, *The Art of the Novel*, pp. 40-97. Sergio Perosa, for example, embraces the conventional view that James's entire career "was marked and sustained by a *continuous and tireless* search for the new." He does, however, develop a valuable distinction between what he calls the "transitional" novels of the 1880s and the technically experimental novels of the post-theater period. On these points see Perosa, *The Experimental Novel*, pp. 3 and 5. Emphasis mine.

2. "Letter to T.S. Perry," 16 February 1881, *HJL* 2:341-342.

3. Young Henry's "Letter to Edgar Van Winkle," dated only [1856], can be found in *HJL* 1:5; and James's comments regarding the play version of *Daisy* have been taken from his *Notebooks*, pp. 44-45. Edel also considers this episode to be an early "harbinger" of James's subsequent siege of the theater. See *MY*, pp. 39-41. A letter addressed to the American actor Lawrence Barrett documents both James's continuing preoccupation with the theater during this period and the limits of his willingness to compromise his artistic values in order to achieve theatrical success. Barrett was interested in trying to mount a stage version of *The Portrait*, but James firmly refused to subject this work to the necessary rearrangements. Instead, he suggests an unfinished play version of his early novel, *The American*. "Letter to Lawrence Barrett," 18 July [1884], *HJL* 3:46-47.

4. "Letter to James R. Osgood," 19 April 1883, and "Letter to James R. Osgood," 5 May [1883], *HJL* 2:412-416.

5. My account of this shift has been taken from Mott, *History* 3:245 and Mott, *History*, 4:1-9. Charles Dudley Warner, owner/editor of the Hartford *Courant* and Mark Twain's friend and collaborator on *The Gilded Age*, represents the new breed of newspaper-trained magazine editors. In 1884 Warner became a contributing editor of *Harper's*, replacing Howells in "The Editor's Study" and "The Editor's Drawer."

6. Henry James, "Criticism," in Zabel, p. 47.

7. Edel and Lawrence, *Bibliography*, pp. 58-59; and "Letter to Frederick Macmillan," 29 January [1884], *HJL* 3:22-23.

8. James, *Partial Portraits*, pp. 382, 401-402, 405-406, 408, and 398. James's anticipation of criticism regarding the "lack of incident" in *The Portrait* can be found in his "Letter to T.S. Perry," 24 January 1881, *HJL* 2:335.

9. James, "A New England Winter," in *The American Novels and Short Stories of Henry James*, ed. F.O. Matthiessen (New York: Alfred A. Knopf, 1968), pp. 354, 363, and 374. Donald David Stone shares a similar view of these two stories. See his *Novelists in a Changing World* (Cambridge: Harvard University Press, 1972), p. 238.

10. James gently tried to dissuade this would-be disciple from dedicating her first novel, *Miss Brown*, to him in his "Letter to Violet Paget," 21 October [1884], *HJL,* 3:49-50. On the dissolution of Victorianism and the rise of modernism see Stone, p. 1 and George J. Becker's Introduction to his *Documents of Modern Literary Realism* (Princeton: Princeton University Press, 1967), pp. 15-16. Howells' *Century* review has been reprinted in Mordell, pp. 120-121.

11. "Letter to Grace Norton," 19 January [1884], *HJL,* 3:21, emphasis mine; "Letter to William Dean Howells," 21 February 1884, *HJL* 3:27-28; and "Letter to Thomas S. Perry," 12 December [1884], *HJL* 3:61.

Notes for Chapter 3   209

12. Quotations from this American review of *The Bostonians* are taken from Gard, pp. 164-165. Henry's letter to William, dated 14 February [1885], can be found in *LHJ* 1:115-117.

13. Both reviews are reprinted in Gard, pp. 166-168 and 173-174.

14. Hutton's assessment can be found in Gard, p. 175. William's letter, dated May 1886, is also quoted in Gard, pp. 159-160.

15. Howard Kerr, *Mediums, Spirit Rappers, and Roaring Radicals* (Chicago: University of Illinois Press, 1972), pp. 211-212 and 214-215. Appropriately enough, Kerr's title is taken from a phrase in *The Bostonians*. See his chapter on the novel in its entirety, pp. 190-222. Henry's fear of being "superficial and cheap" was probably rooted in his lack of firsthand knowledge of either spiritualism or the women's rights movement in America. On this last point see Marcia Jacobson's interpretation of *The Bostonians* as a reworking of two popular genres, the Civil War romance and the feminist novel of the eighties, in *Henry James and the Mass Market*, pp. 20-40. Henry's letter to William, dated June 1886, is quoted in Gard, p. 161.

16. For an extended discussion of Ransom's subversion of chivalry and a revealing analysis of what she calls "phallic" criticism of this novel, consult Judith Fetterly's fine chapter on *The Bostonians* in *The Resisting Reader: A Feminist Approach to American Fiction* (Bloomington: Indiana University Press, 1978), pp. 101-153, especially pp. 128-130.

17. Henry James, *The Bostonians* (London, 1886; rpt. New York: Random House, Inc., 1956), p. 343. Richard Foley states that the novel "brought down an avalanche of hostile criticism," noting that "it was the first book of James's to receive an almost unanimously poor press and it marked a turning point in the response of the public to his work" (Foley, p. 39).

18. This account is based upon Edel, *MY*, pp. 137-139 and 145 and Edel and Lawrence, *Bibliography*, pp. 73-76.

19. Mott, *History* 4:255. Although he concedes that James "perhaps exaggerated the scenic quality" of *The Tragic Muse* in his preface, Sergio Perosa not only regards this novel as "the swan song of the 'naturalistic' period" but also goes so far as to argue that in this work we can see "thematic experimentation" giving way to "technical experimentation." Perosa, *The Experimental Novel*, p. 43.

20. Henry James, *The Scenic Art*, ed. Allan Wade (New Brunswick: Rutgers University Press, 1948), p. 93. This valuable collection of James's theater essays remains one of the best introductions to his theater period. Several critics have cited *Miss Bretherton* as a literary source for *The Tragic Muse*. See D.J. Gordon and John Stokes, "The Reference of *The Tragic Muse*," in *The Air of Reality*, ed. John Goode (London: Methuen and Co. Ltd., 1972), p. 120; and Powers, p. 131. However, I do not subscribe to their view of the novel as an example of James's naturalist phase.

21. "Letter to Thomas Bailey Aldrich," 3 March 1888, *HJL* 3:223. This version of the Vizetelly incident comes from Becker, pp. 350, 372, 374, and 380-381. Graham Hough reveals Vizetelly's use of James's review in his "George Moore and the Nineties," in *Edwardians and Late Victorians*, ed. Richard Ellmann (New York: Columbia University Press, 1960), pp. 4-5. Hough contends that the publisher was deliberately seeking a "scandalous success" only to be mistakenly regarded as "a sort of martyr for culture." But he does acknowledge Vizetelly's contribution to the trend towards realism and the battle for freedom of subject matter.

22. These excerpts have been quoted from Becker's reprint of the Gosse article, pp. 385-386, 388, and 392; and Becker's reprint of the Manifesto, pp. 344 and 346-348. The information on Lee's defense of Zola can be found in Becker, p. 383. In an editorial note Becker also states

that the five signers of the Manifesto, far from being acknowledged disciples of Zola, were not even known to him and he even suggests that their attack may have been the result of a "cabal led by Daudet or Goncourt out of jealousy towards Zola." See Becker, p. 344.

23. Henry James, *The Tragic Muse* (1886; rpt. New York: Thomas Y. Crowell Company, 1975), pp. 72-73. Following James's lead, I have used the words "aesthete" and "raffiné" interchangeably. Gordon and Stokes have traced James's first use of the French term, which derives from Baudelaire, to his 1879 essay on the Goncourt brothers in which he notes: "...they are *raffinés* and they write for raffinés" (Goode, p. 148). Critics disagree sharply as to whom, if anyone, Nash was modelled upon. Oscar Wilde, Henry James Sr., Herbert Pratt (a friend of William James), and the novelist himself have each been put forward as likely candidates.

24. James, *Notebooks*, p. 90; and James, *The Tragic Muse*, pp. 284-285. The aspiring playwright can also be seen exploring (and vacillating between) his career options in two dialogues which he published in 1889. "After the Play," reprinted in *The Scenic Art* (pp. 226-242), is yet another description of contemporary theater conditions while "An Animated Conversation," later published in his *Essays in London* ([London: James R. Osgood, McIlvane & Co., 1893], pp. 267-305), deals with the question of international copyright and the possibility of consolidating the Anglo-American literary scenes. Although these two essays seem to point in different vocational directions, the fact that they are both cast in scenic form indicates that James's decision had, in effect, already been made. Gordon and Stokes rightly stress *The Tragic Muse's* personal *and* public topicality as well as the intersection between the conditions of the practice of art and the practice of politics. As they observe, both professions suffer corruption because both are primarily "affair[s] of words" which depend upon the manipulation of an audience. Goode, pp. 118 and 88.

25. James, *Notebooks*, p. 99; and Edel, *MY*, p. 265.

26. See, for example, "Letter to William James," 7 November 1890, *HJL* 3:306; "Letter to Urbain Mengin," 3 janvier [1891], *HJL* 3:319; and "Letter to Robert Louis Stevenson," 12 January 1891, *HJL* 3:326.

27. "Letter to Frederick Macmillan," 28 March 1890, *Selected Letters of William James*, ed. Leon Edel (London: Rupert Hart-Davis, 1956), pp. 123-124; hereafter cited as *SL*. By the time he resumed work on a full-length novel, the contours of the English literary scene had undergone significant alterations, not the least of which was the banning of the three-decker in 1895 and the subsequent decline of Mudie's power and prestige. See Griest, pp. 193-213, and chapter 4 below.

28. Leon Edel, Introduction to *The Complete Plays of Henry James* (New York: J. B. Lippincott Company, 1949), pp. 43-49; "Letter to William James," 12 February [1891], *HJL* 3:332-333; "Letter to William James," 1 September [1891], *HJL* 3:355; and "Letter to Isabella Stewart Gardner," 7 June [1891], *HJL* 3:342. Samuel Hynes groups Pinero with Henry Arthur Jones and Oscar Wilde as playwrights whose conservative attitudes towards women and marriage undercut and made safely respectable the potentially avant-garde subject matter of their plays. Hynes, *The Edwardian Turn of Mind* (Princeton: Princeton University Press, 1968), p. 181.

29. James's comment about critics can be found in his "Letter to William Dean Howells," 2 January 1888, *LHJ* 1:136. James, *The Bostonians*, p. 343.

30. Michael Egan, *Henry James: The Ibsen Years* (Plymouth, England: Vision Press, printed by Clarke, Doble & Brundon Ltd., 1972), p. 27. The notebook entry, dated 12 May 1889, can be found in James, *Notebooks*, p. 100.

31. Egan, pp. 28-29. James's continuing ambivalence towards Ibsen is discussed in Egan, pp. 37-56, especially on pp. 37-38, and throughout Elizabeth Robins' *Theatre and Friendship* (New York: G. P. Putnam's Sons, 1932).

32. Holbrook Jackson, *The Eighteen-Nineties* (New Jersey: Humanities Press, Inc., 1976), pp. 205, 207, and 209. In 1893 Robins (anonymously) co-authored, produced, and acted in *Alan's Wife*, a "shocking" Ibsenist play concerning euthanasia which epitomized the highly unconventional aspirations of the new movement. She would later write and star in *Votes for Women* (1907), a commercially successful play which propogandized in behalf of woman suffrage. According to Robins' biographer, Jane Marcus, James's close friend Florence Bell was the co-author of *Alan's Wife*. Marcus, "Elizabeth Robins: A Biographical and Critical Study," Diss. Northwestern University 1973, pp. 196 and 311. For more information on Robins' suffrage play, see Hynes, pp. 201-204.

33. "Letter to William James," 6 February [1891], *HJL* 3:329, second emphasis mine. James also refers to the drama as his "real form" in a subsequent letter to Robert Louis Stevenson dated 18 February 1891 where he describes the "Scène Anglaise" as "a kindom to conquer." *HJL* 3:336-337.

34. I am grateful to Charles Feidelson for suggesting this line of reasoning to me. Bernard Shaw, *The Quintessence of Ibsenism* (New York: Brentano's, 1922), p. 4.

35. Edel, *MY*, p. 287 (see also pp. 297-298); and "Letter to William James," 6 February 1891, *LHJ*, 1:179-180. For a description of Alice's response to her brother's theatrical venture, see *The Diary of Alice James*, ed. Leon Edel (New York: Dodd, Mead & Company, 1934) and Strouse, pp. 287-289.

36. Edel, *MY*, p. 293. My account of the production and reception of James's plays relies heavily upon Leon Edel's invaluable research upon and discussion of the theater years in *MY*, pp. 279-389, *TY*, pp. 1-151, and his biographical chapters in both *The Complete Plays* and James's *Guy Domville* (1894; rpt. London: Rupert Hart-Davis, 1961), pp. 13-121. Edel's dissertation, *Henry James: Les Années Dramatiques* (Paris: Jouve & Companie, Editeurs, 1931) stands out as the first study to treat these years as a crucial period in James's development rather than as an unfortunate accident. Although Edel's later interpretation is much more penetrating, the dissertation forms the basis of that work and merits appreciation as a timely biographical effort which succeeded in retrieving factual information which might otherwise have been permanently lost.

37. "Letter to William James," 15 November 1892, *HJL* 3:397; and "Letter to William James," 10 October [1891], *HJL* 3:358-359. This account is largely based on Edel, *MY*, pp. 297-299. James's plan can be found in his *Notebooks*, pp. 99 and 102.

38. "Letter to William James," 23 July 1890, *LHJ* 1:170.

39. This story, first published in 1893, has been reprinted in F. O. Matthiessen's collection of James's *Stories of Writers and Artists* (New York: New Directions Books, 1944), pp. 192-210; hereafter cited as *SWA*. As we shall see, James was to treat the theme of a second chance with bitter irony in "The Next Time," another tale of the literary life which he began working on shortly after the disastrous opening night of *Guy Domville*. For a brief biographical treatment of James's relationship with his young disciples during this period see Edel, *MY*, pp. 310-314.

40. Beach does not seem to have been aware of the existence of the theater period in 1918 when he wrote the original version of *The Method of Henry James* (Philadelphia: Albert Saifer,

Publisher, 1954), his otherwise quite penetrating and pioneering study of James's artistic development. Edel's claim regarding "The Coxon Fund" can be found in *MY*, p. 373.

41. See, for example, "Letter to Morton Fullerton," 4 February [1893] and 16 January [1893], *HJL* 3:405 and 399, for James's recognition of this phenomenon.

42. The preceding account of the *Yellow Book* is based upon the following sources: Stanley Weintraub, *The London Yankees* (New York: Harcourt Brace Jovanovich, 1979), p. 59; Katharine Lyon Mix, *A Study in Yellow* (Lawrence: The University of Kansas Press, 1960), pp. 171-173, 254-257, 83-84, 87 and 90; and Stanley Weintraub, *The Yellow Book* (Garden City, New York: Anchor Books, 1964), pp. vii-viii and x-xii. Reginald Turner's story, which appeared in the October 1896 issue, celebrates the unknown artist Alan Herbert for his total devotion to art for art's sake. After producing one "perfect" short story at the cost of his health, young Herbert dies upon receiving a rejection notice from a review. This story has been reprinted by Weintraub in *The Yellow Book*, pp. 310-319.

43. "Letter to Mr. & Mrs. William James," 28 May 1894, *LHJ* 1:217. Renato Poggioli has identified such "little magazines," periodicals characterized chiefly by their noncommercial nature, as one of the key external signs of a developing avant-garde movement. He observes that these journals define themselves as a reaction against the "spread of culture out to (or down to) the vulgar" (Poggioli, pp. 21-23). On the moral impropriety of the Anglo-American avant-garde, see for example Weintraub's biographical treatment of American expatriates such as Morton Fullerton, Harold Frederic, and Stephen and Cora Crane—each of whom was a friend or acquaintance of James—in his book, *The London Yankees*. The most infamous indigenous example of the "perversity" of the avant-garde in England is, of course, Oscar Wilde.

44. "Letter to William Heinemann," 30 November 1894, in Henry James, *A Most Unholy Trade* (Cambridge, Mass.: The Scarab Press, privately printed by Dunster House, 1923), pp. 14-15. The notebook entry can be found in James, *Notebooks*, p. 111. Leon Edel also suggests that James was happy to find an editor who would accept his short stories in spite of their length, which was inordinate by contemporaneous magazine standards. Given the nature of the changes in American magazine publishing discussed earlier in this chapter, Edel's suggestion is quite to the point.

45. "Letter to Elizabeth Robins," [6 December 1893], *HJL* 3:443-444; "Letter to Augustin Daly," 7 December 1893, *HJL* 3:444-445; and "Letter to Augustin Daly," 11 December 1893, *HJL* 3:446-449. Information on Daly's response comes from Edel's note 1, p. 445.

46. "Letter to Mr. and Mrs. William James," 29 December 1893, *HJL* 3:449-453, first emphasis mine.

47. "Letter to Robert Louis Stevenson," 5 December [1887], *LHJ* 1:132. Writing to William near the outset of his theater years, Henry had drawn an explicit if tongue-in-cheek analogy between the birth of his brother's third son and his own "dramatic first-born," *The American*. See "Letter to William James," 3 January [1891], *HJL* 3:317.

48. Henry James, *Theatricals/Two Comedies* (London: Osgood, McIlvane & Co., 1894), p. vi; and Henry James, *Theatricals: Second Series* (London: Osgood, McIlvane & Co., 1894), pp. v-vi.

49. This assessment of Alexander is based upon Edel, *MY*, pp. 338-339 and Edel, *TY*, p. 26. According to Edel, Oscar Wilde wrote *The Importance of Being Earnest* especially for Alexander. James's dismissal of Wilde's play as "infantine" can be found in *HJL* 3:372.

50. This description of Guy's destiny appears in a "Letter to Edward Compton," dated [2 May 1893], *HJL* 3:411. For the widely accepted interpretation of the play as a literary text, see Edel's remarks in his biographical chapters in James, *Guy Domville*, pp. 19-80.

51. James's comments about Robins' Ibsen audience come from Robins, p. 103. His distinction between these two publics can be found in a subsequent "Letter to William James," dated 19 January 1895, *HJL* 3:508; and his analysis of Wilde's appeal can be followed in his "Letter to Mrs. Hugh Bell," [23 February 1892], *HJL* 3:373.

52. "Letter to William James," 2 February 1895, *LHJ* 1:233.

53. Shaw's review has been reprinted by Edel following the script of *Guy Domville*, pp. 207-208. My account of the audience reaction to the opening night of the play and James's activities that evening is based largely on information provided by Edel in *TY*, pp. 64-80; Edel's biographical chapters in James's *Guy Domville*, pp. 83-108; and the theater reviews which he reprints at the end of *Guy Domville*, pp. 205-218. But it should become clear that I question some of Edel's assumptions about the nature and significance of that response and its effect upon James. For example, Edel assumes an a priori split in the taste of the theater audience along class lines, attributing the desire to be entertained only to the pits and the gallery. See "Henry James: The Dramatic Years" in James, *Guy Domville*, p. 85.

54. Edel, "The Dramatic Years," in James, *Guy Domville*, p. 93.

55. H.G. Wells, "A Pretty Question," in James, *Guy Domville*, pp. 212-213; Edel, "The Dramatic Years," in *Guy Domville*, p. 96; and "Letter to William James," 9 January 1895, *HJL* 3:507-508. According to Edel, Henry's suggestion of "malice prepense" probably refers to unsubstantiated rumors about an actress' attempt to seek revenge against Alexander. See Edel, "The Dramatic Years," in James, *Guy Domville*, pp. 101-103.

56. Edel, "The Dramatic Years," in James, *Guy Domville*, pp. 99-100 and 104.

57. Bernard Shaw, "The Drama's Law," in James, *Guy Domville*, pp. 206-207; and Wells, "A Pretty Question," in James, *Guy Domville*, p. 212. Edel's approving remarks and an excerpt from Walkley's review can be found in "The Dramatic Years," his Introduction to James, *Guy Domville*, pp. 106-107.

58. Edel, *TY*, pp. 109-110; and "Letter to William James," 9 January 1895, *HJL* 3:508-509.

59. "Letter to Mrs. Edward Compton," 15 March [1895], *HJL* 3:520-521. James took his time to respond to her letter and was obviously milking his part for all it was worth.

60. "Letter to William James," 2 February 1895, *HJL* 3:515-517, emphasis mine; and "Letter to William James," 4 February [1895], *HJL* 3:518-519. Ironically, *Guy Domville* was succeeded at the St. James's Theatre in February by Oscar Wilde's *The Importance of Being Earnest*.

Chapter 4

1. "Letter to William Dean Howells," 22 January 1895, *LHJ* 1:230-232.

2. "Letter to William Dean Howells," 22 January 1895, *LHJ* 1:232.

3. This summary is based upon Griest, pp. 193-208. For more information on George Moore's leading role in the attack on the triple-decker, see pp. 148-155. The observation concerning three-deckers as a form can be found in Jackson, p. 218.

4. "Letter to the American Copyright League," 15 November 1887, *SL*, pp. 115-120.

214 Notes for Chapter 4

5. Griest, p. 211 and Clarence Gohdes, "British Interest in American Literature During the Latter Part of the Nineteenth Century As Reflected by Mudie's Select Library," *American Literature*, vol. 13 (January 1942), p. 360.

6. James, *Notebooks*, p. 180. This entry is dated 26 January 1895.

7. Henry James, "The Next Time," *SWA*, p. 272. The phrase first appears in a letter to William James dated 9 January 1895. See *LHJ* 1:229.

8. James, *SWA*, p. 245. Emphasis mine.

9. James, *SWA*, pp. 246 and 260-261. Gilbert Osmond in *The Portrait*, at least as he first appears to Isabel, is in certain respects the prototype of this kind of reader in James's work. My reading of "The Next Time" is supported by Holbrook Jackson's shrewd observation that there were definite parallels (as well as obvious contrasts) between the two types of culture represented by the *Yellow Book* and the Yellow Press. As he remarks: "The characteristic excitability and hunger for sensation are exemplified in the one as much as the other, for what after all was the 'brilliance' of Vigo Street but the 'sensationalism' of Fleet Street seen from the cultured side?" Jackson, pp. 52-53.

10. James, *SWA*, p. 262 and 257-258. The *Yellow Book* prospectus is quoted in Weintraub, *The Yellow Book*, p. xi.

11. Matthiessen's remarks on this story appear in his Introduction to *SWA*, p. 6, while Edel's discussion of this tale can be found in *TY*, pp. 148-151. Two notable exceptions to this rule are Ronald Wallace's interpretation of this story in *Henry James and the Comic Form* (Ann Arbor: The University of Michigan Press, 1975), pp. 173-175; and Perry Westbrook's "The Supersubtle Fry," *Nineteenth-Century Fiction*, 8 (Sept. 1953), pp. 137-140. Both Wallace and Westbrook stress the narrator's and Vereker's unreliability, though neither identifies their relationship as avant-garde.

12. James, *Notebooks*, p. 220.

13. James, *SWA*, p. 282.

14. See James, *Notebooks*, pp. 225-229.

15. James, *SWA*, p. 287.

16. These reviews are quoted in Foley, pp. 54, 56, and 59-60. On Logan Pearsall Smith's conversion see Weintraub, *The London Yankees*, p. 103.

17. Edel, *TY*, pp. 156-157. This account is also based upon Matthiessen and Murdock's commentary in James, *Notebooks*, pp. 141-142.

18. Joseph Wiesenfarth in his study, *Henry James and the Dramatic Analogy* (New York: Fordham University Press, 1963), ignores *The Other House* entirely, while Joseph Warren Beach relegates the novel to a footnote because, as he candidly admits, it undercuts his assertion that "James never yielded an inch of the ground he had gained" during his middle years. Beach, p. 236.

19. Egan, p. 59 and Edel, *TY*, p. 167.

20. James, *Notebooks*, p. 179. This entry is dated 23 January 1895.

21. "Letter to William James," 2 February 1895, *LHJ* 1:234. James draws this distinction between the theater and the drama in several letters written during the theater years. See, for example, his comment in a letter to Henrietta Rubell written on 31 December 1894: "I may

have been meant for the Drama—God knows!—but I certainly wasn't meant for the Theatre." *LHJ* 1:226.

22. Henry James, *The Other House* (New York: The Macmillan Co., 1896), p. 362. Both Egan and Edel detect a relationship between James's theater experience and Effie's murder. While he does not push his perception to its ultimate conclusion, Egan does draw a highly suggestive parallel between the child murder in *The Other House* and Hedda's burning of Eilert's manuscript, which she refers to as his child, in Ibsen's *Hedda Gabler*. Egan, p. 63. Edel reads Effie's death as "the murder of innocence—as if some remote little being within James himself had been killed by the audience" during the opening night of *Guy Domville*. Edel, *TY*, p. 168. As I hope will become clear, this interpretation is quite misleading, for it presents James as a passive victim of the failure of *Guy Domville*, and makes no allowance for the very aggressive and highly manipulative stance which he is able to maintain in regard to both his fictional characters and his audience in this work and the other novels of the late nineties.

23. "Letter to William James," 9 January 1895, *LHJ* 1:229.

24. James, *Notebooks*, p. 188.

25. See, especially, Egan's interpretation of these novels, Wiesenfarth's analysis of their structure in terms of the "dramatic analogy," and Perosa's account of the experimental techniques tested by James during the second phase of his middle period.

26. See, for example, the comparison between the scenario for *The Spoils of Poynton* and the completed novel later in this chapter. Several critics, both contemporaneous and posthumous, have also asserted that James's habit of dictation, which (according to his biographer) was begun during the composition of *Maisie* in 1897, greatly altered the style and texture of his post-theater fiction (though James firmly denied this assumption when it came to his attention). On this point consult Edel, *TY*, pp. 175-177. If there is a connection, it may have begun to develop during the theater years when James helped Elizabeth Robins translate Echegary's *Mariana* from Spanish into English. *Theatre and Friendship* contains an interesting description of his method of dictation. See Robins, pp. 176-177. The most vivid firsthand account was left by one of James's typists, Theodora Bosanquet, in her recollections of *Henry James At Work* (London: The Hogarth Press, 1924), especially pp. 7-12.

27. Edel, *TY*, pp. 94, 168, 250, and 110. Marcia Jacobson has recently taken issue with Edel's application of the term "regressive" to these works. Stressing the literary context of the post-theater novels, she attributes James's preoccupation with children to his familiarity with the popularity of contemporaneous fiction focusing on "a helpless child-protagonist." While her account of this context serves as an extremely valuable corrective, it is important to note that Jacobson's interpretation fails to account for James's marked preference for *female* child-protagonists. See Jacobson, pp. 81-138, especially pp. 92-93 and 103.

28. Howells, *Criticism and Fiction*, pp. 70-71, 73, and 75.

29. James, *Notebooks*, p. 188. This entry is dated 14 February 1895.

30. Howells, *Criticism and Fiction*, p. 75.

31. The phrase "dramatic analogy" comes from Wiesenfarth. Ironically enough, after reading the first of these experimental novels, *The Spoils*, James's admirer and fellow professional, Joseph Conrad, is reported to have been concerned not with the fate of James's characters but with the suffering of "the man in the street" trying to read it! "One could amost see the globular lobes of his [the reader's] brain painfully revolving, and crushing and mangling the delicate thing. As to his exasperation, it is a thing impossible to imagine and too horrible to contemplate." Quoted in Gard, p. 268.

Notes for Chapter 4

32. James's notebook reference to the public, dated 23 January 1895, appears on p. 180.
33. Henry James, *The Aspern Papers/The Spoils of Poynton* (London, 1896; rpt. New York: Dell Publishing Co., Inc., 1975), p. 166.
34. James, *The Spoils*, p. 152.
35. James, *Notebooks*, pp. 211 and 214. These entries are dated 8 September 1895 and 15 October 1895. James's application of the scenic system to the germ of *The Spoils* can be followed in the notebooks on pp. 81, 136-138, 198-200, 207-212, 214-220, and 247-256. For an extended treatment of James's use of and deviation from this scenario, consult Oscar Cargill's chapter on *The Spoils* in *The Novels of Henry James* (New York: The Macmillan Company, 1961), pp. 218-243.
36. James, *Notebooks*, p. 215.
37. James, *The Spoils*, p. 172.
38. See, for example, James, *The Spoils*, pp. 165 and 260-268.
39. James, *The Spoils*, p. 253.
40. This review is reprinted in Gard, p. 267.
41. The *Academy* review is reprinted in Gard, p. 266. Emphasis mine.
42. Charles Feidelson, "James and the 'Man of Imagination,'" in *Literary Theory and Structure*, ed. Frank Brady, John Palmer and Martin Price (New Haven: Yale University Press, 1973), p. 351. My sense of James's curious relationship with his characters is somewhat different from but owes much to Feidelson's illuminating discussion of the unique "predicament" which James "visits upon" them in an effort to fulfill what he perceives as James's "obsessive quest for sense-in-general." Although my own interpretation of James's predicament finds expression in less philosophical terms, I have been greatly influenced by this essay.
43. James, *Partial Portraits*, pp. 405-406. Emphasis mine.
44. James, *Notebooks*, pp. 169-170. Much has been made of James's supposed prudery, his "failure" to marry, and his possible homosexuality. Although I am not unaware of the possibility that James was using Anglo-American literary conventions regarding sex to mask, evade, or even explore his personal difficulties in dealing with sexual intimacy, I think that more can be gained in a study such as this by following James's lead and treating the question primarily as a literary one. In either case, James's evident fascination with the other side of the literary coin, the Continental obsession with sexual relations and sensuality in general, greatly complicates the issue and has to be accounted for.
45. James, *Notebooks*, p. 170. On the following page, near the end of this entry, James notes that this "little story" reminds him of Edmond About's *Germaine*, "read long years ago and but dimly remembered." While the influence of conventional French theater is especially strong during this period in James's career, one must wonder why James continued to respond so powerfully to what was, after all, quite a shop-worn cliché.
46. James, *Notebooks*, pp. 187-188. The germ of *The Awkward Age* can be found on p. 192.
47. James, *Notebooks*, p. 236. The fact that *Maisie* was eventually serialized in the *Chap Book*, a Chicago little magazine, rather than the *Yellow Book*, does not fundamentally affect my argument here since both outlets were equally unconventional. James ended up sending Harland "She and He," a review of the George Sand/Alfred de Musset love letters, instead.

48. See the preface to the volume of tales containing "The Lesson of the Master" in James, *The Art of the Novel*, p. 219.

49. James, *SWA*, pp. 220-221 and 242. According to Mix, critics have identified Guy Walsingham with "George Egerton," the female author who appeared with James in the first and sixth volumes of the *Yellow Book*. For a brief sketch of Egerton's reputation for sexual frankness and her avant-garde career see Mix, pp. 171-174.

50. Matthiessen and Murdock in James, *Notebooks*, pp. 245-247. Second emphasis mine. This germ eventually became "John Delavoy," a story which James published in *Cosmopolis* in January and February of 1898.

51. Edel, *TY*, p. 156. Except for the information regarding the headlines, Edel's account of this incident is virtually identical to the earlier account provided by Matthiessen and Murdock.

52. W.C.D. Pacey, "Henry James and His French Contemporaries," *American Literature*, 23 (November 1941), p. 243.

53. Henry James, *What Maisie Knew* (London, 1897; rpt. New York: Anchor Books, 1954), pp. 27-28.

54. Walter Isle, *Experiments in Form* (Cambridge, Mass.: Harvard University Press, 1968), p. 130.

55. James, *Maisie*, p. 221. One wonders if James harbored a much more anxious awareness about his own role in their "development." For a somewhat different interpretation of *Maisie* which treats Mrs. Wix's relationship to her young charge in a decidedly negative light, see Tony Tanner's *The Reign of Wonder* (Cambridge: University of Cambridge Press, 1965), pp. 261-335, especially pp. 291-297.

56. Foley, pp. 68-69.

57. The reviews from the *Academy* and the *Spectator* are reprinted in Gard, pp. 270-271.

58. This review has been reprinted in Gard, pp. 272-273. It should be clear by now that I do not subscribe to the modern tendency to dismiss such criticism without considering its serious implications by relegating it to the category of mere "Victorian prudery." Critical reaction of this nature sheds an extremely interesting light on the career of the novel in Anglo-American culture, for it implies the role of the novel as a key medium for educating and entertaining the public and has the additional virtue of taking the social role of the novelist seriously. It is instructive to compare Anglo-American criticism of fiction in the nineteenth century with twentieth-century criticism of television, another "family" medium which has the potential to entertain and educate its audience, for better or for worse. Our comfortable sense of superiority to the Victorian code of literary propriety diminishes (and the self-reflexive irony of *Maisie's* contemporaneous reception increases) when we learn from Oscar Cargill that as recently as 1950, CBS found an adaptation of *Maisie* to be inappropriate for its television audience. See the notes to *What Maisie Knew* in Cargill, p. 259.

59. Edel's account of James's reaction to the Jubilee and his discussion of the Oxford incident can be found in *TY*, pp. 178-179 and 182-185, respectively. An interesting account of James's social interaction with his avant-garde Sussex neighbors, Stephen and Cora Crane, can be found in Weintraub's *The London Yankees*.

60. Edel, *TY*, p. 183. Emphasis mine.

61. See "Letter to H. G. Wells," 9 December 1898, *LHJ* 1:298-299, where James thanks Wells for his praise of "The Turn of the Screw" and discusses the difficulties involved in its composition, yet insists: "But the thing is essentially a pot-boiler and a *jeu d'espirit.*"

62. I am not even sure whether James himself could provide a definitive answer to this question, for if one accepts and extends the logic of my treatment of James's relationship with his characters and his readers, it becomes quite possible that he and they are the ultimate source of any "corruption" which the tale may evoke or represent. James all but acknowledged this in his preface to "The Turn of the Screw" when he explained why he refused to specify the exact nature of the corruption in this story. He insisted: "There is for such a case no eligible *absolute* of the wrong; it remains relative to fifty other elements, a matter of appreciation, speculation, imagination—these things moreover quite exactly in the light of the spectator's, the critic's, the reader's experience. Only make the reader's general vision of evil intense enough, I said to myself—and that already is a charming job—and his own experience, his own imagination, his own sympathy (with the children) and horror (of their false friends) will supply him quite sufficiently with all the particulars. Make him *think* the evil, make him think it for himself, and you are released from weak specifications." Preface to *The Aspern Papers* in James, *The Art of the Novel*, p. 176. Interestingly enough, Richard Ellmann links James with Oscar Wilde because of their refusal to specify the precise nature of the corruption they describe. Ellmann cites "The Turn of the Screw" and Wilde's *The Picture of Dorian Grey* as two of the most prominent examples of the non-pornographic treatment of homosexuality in nineteenth-century English literature. See his essay, "A Late Victorian Love Affair," in *Oscar Wilde: Two Approaches* (Los Angeles: University of California Press, 1977), pp. 6-7.

63. Henry James, *"The Turn of the Screw"* and *"Daisy Miller"* (London, 1898; rpt. New York: Dell Publishing Company, 1965), p. 11. James covertly participates in and completes the "seduction" of *his* audience by refusing to provide them with a closing and containing frame to match the opening one. He thus contributes *directly* to their mutual and vicarious "corruption," transforming the story itself into an ironic (and, in one sense, erotic) "go between" in respect to both himself and his own quite sexually mixed public.

64. Edel and Lawrence, *Bibliography*, p. 114.

65. James's discussion of Gyp and her school can be found in his preface to *The Awkward Age* in *The Art of the Novel*, pp. 106-108, while his comments on the public appear in the same preface, p. 106: "One had noted this reader [the Anglo-Saxon reader] as perverse and inconsequent in respect to the absorption of 'dialogue'—observed the 'public for fiction' consume it... on the scale and with the smack of lips that mark the consumption of bread-and-jam by a children's school-feast, consume it even at the theatre... and yet as flagrantly reject it when served, so to speak, *au naturel....* " James went on to add: "'Dialogue,' always 'dialogue!' I had seemed from far back to hear them [editors and publishers] mostly cry... " The term "roman dialogué" is taken from Oscar Cargill's description of the novels of Gyp and Lavedan in his chapter on *The Awkward Age*, p. 264.

66. Isle, p. 179.

67. James, *The Art of the Novel*, pp. 99-100.

68. Henry James, *The Awkward Age* (New York, 1908; rpt. Middlesex: Penguin Books Ltd., 1974), p. 356. Despite her age, "little Aggie" is initially described in terms strikingly similar to those used by the narrator of *The Portrait* to introduce her younger prototype, Pansy Osmond: "Little Aggie presented, up and down, an arrangement of dress exactly in the key of her age, her complexion, her emphasized virginity. She might have been prepared for her visit by a cluster of doting nuns... " James, *The Awkward Age*, p. 87.

69. James, *The Awkward Age*, p. 64.

70. George Gissing had challenged this crude and cruel literary and social stereotype in his admirable portrait of five unmarried women, aptly entitled *The Odd Women*. First published in 1893, the novel was reprinted by W. W. Norton and Co. in 1971, probably as the result of the 1960s revival of feminism and the renewed interest which this revivial sparked in women as characters in fiction.

71. James, *The Awkward Age*, p. 28. This is only one of several such speeches. See also pp. 30-31, where Longdon insists that he "belongs to a different period of history" and admits to feeling as if he had been "disinterred—literally dug up from a long sleep."

72. James, *The Awkward Age*, p. 143. James had previously used the same old-fashioned plot device in *The Tragic Muse*, where Nick Dormer's benefactor makes it clear to him that he will receive a substantial inheritance upon his death, but only if Nick marries Julia Dallow. In an earlier novel, *The Portrait of a Lady*, James employed an interesting variation on both the figure of the uncle-benefactor and the device of the inheritance.

73. James, *The Awkward Age*, pp. 302-303.

74. James, *The Awkward Age*, pp. 309-310.

75. James, *The Awkward Age*, p. 368.

Chapter 5

1. James, *Notebooks*, p. 269. This entry is dated 27 January 1899.

2. James, *Notebooks*, pp. 268-269. According to Matthiessen and Murdock, James reluctantly agreed to let Alexander produce the play, "only to have it rejected." They also point out, however, that Forbes-Robertson later convinced James to rewrite the play and that it was produced in Edinburgh on March 26, 1908, "with considerable success," after which it was given five matinee performances in London, where it was also "favorably received." See their commentary in James, *Notebooks*, pp. 186-187.

3. Both reviews are reprinted in Gard, pp. 282 and 285.

4. Foley, p. 73. Two exceptions can be found in the *Critic* for April and August of 1899. Foley cites the former, "The Evolution of Henry James," as one of the first studies which attempted to assess the cumulative effect of James's career as well as its experimental nature. (See Foley, p. 77.) The anonymous author of the second review acutely observed that "there always have been nice girls...although they may have to develop under circumstances which have hitherto been considered prohibitive. Nanda is prophecy... Mr. Longdon is history." While this reviewer clearly appreciated the character of Nanda and Mr. Longdon, he (or she) took "a certain satisfaction in observing that even Mr. James's art has a limitation. Although he writes, with equal sympathy, of the righteous and the unrighteous, he simply cannot achieve a fellow-feeling for the people who ought to have right feelings and do not." Mrs. Brook and Vanderbank were identified as supreme examples of "characters in the book which do not impress the reader as they seemed to impress their associates." Quoted in Gard, pp. 296-297.

5. Gard, pp. 298, 294, 282, and 283.

6. Gard, pp. 286-288. This reviewer also pointed out that James's drama focused on a "fast life" which produced "an atrophying cleverness that has learned to anticipate naif opinion of its depravity." He shrewdly noted the way in which James's "fast" characters "vie with one

another in their appreciation of the old-world chivalrous gentleman (Longdon) who sits like a bewildered stranger at their feasts."

7. "Letter to Howard Sturges," *LHJ* 1:317-318.

8. Henry James, "The Future of the Novel," in his *The House of Fiction*, ed. Leon Edel (London: Rupert Hart-Davis, 1957), pp. 48-51.

9. James, *The House of Fiction*, pp. 51-53.

10. James, *The House of Fiction*, pp. 53 and 57-58. Emphasis mine.

11. James, *The House of Fiction*, pp. 58-59. In his useful study, *The Social Context of Modern British Literature* (New York: Schocken Books, 1971), Malcolm Bradbury argues that between 1900 and 1915, London temporarily replaced Paris as the international capital of modernism. He also suggests that "the Tradition of the New" in England had its roots in the work of James's middle period. Bradbury, pp. 94-95.

12. James, *Notebooks*, pp. 299-301. Entry dated 9 August 1900. Regarding editors' emphasis on word counts, see "Letter to William Dean Howells," 10 August 1901, *LHJ* 1:375 and the unpublished letters which James wrote to James B. Pinker in 1889. For example, a letter from James to his literary agent, dated 17 September 1889, details his unsuccessful attempts to, as he put it, "work down" (Beinecke).

13. This account is taken directly from Matthiessen and Murdock's commentary in James, *Notebooks*, pp. 301-302, where they also state: "On the shelf it stayed until 1914, when he undertook to finish it." They have reprinted James's "'preliminary' sketch" for the novel (which remains unfinished) on pp. 361-369. The full text of James's long letter to Howells, dated 9 and 14 August 1900, can be found in *LHJ* 1:354-360.

14. "Letter to William Dean Howells," 9 August 1900, *LHJ* 1:356, second emphasis mine. *The Fount* was the first of James's works to be published by Scribner's (see Edel and Lawrence, *Bibliography*, p. 119 for publishing details). In 1903, Howells would refer to *The Fount* as "that troubled source" and urge puzzled readers not to expect too much of it. This comment appears in "Mr. Henry James's Later Work," an essay which has been reprinted in *The Question of Henry James*, ed. F. W. Dupee (New York: Henry Holt and Company), pp. 16-17.

15. For a sampling of some of the major critical responses to this novel, see: Lawrence B. Holland's fascinating but exhausting interpretation of *The Fount* as a controlled self-parody in *The Expense of Vision* (Princeton: Princeton University Press, 1964), pp. 183-226; Edmund Wilson's "The Ambiguity of Henry James," a penetrating and influential but heavy-handedly Freudian reading of *The Fount* in conjunction with "The Turn of the Screw" in *The Triple Thinkers* (New York: Farrar, Straus and Giroux, 1976), pp. 88-132; Leon Edel's uneven and somewhat belabored effort to pass the novel off as "a masterpiece of the story-teller's art" in his 1953 Introduction to the Grove Press edition; and, more recently, Sergio Perosa's highly intelligent but ultimately unpersuasive attempt to present *The Fount* as a "novel *on* the novel" which should be viewed as a "link" between James, the twentieth-century novel, and the anti-novel in *The Experimental Novel*, pp. 77-104.

16. Edel, Introduction to Henry James, *The Sacred Fount* (1901; rpt. New York: The Grove Press, 1953), pp. xxiii-xxiv and Wilson, *The Triple Thinkers*, p. 99.

17. Henry James to James B. Pinker, 19 June 1900, Beinecke; "Letter to William Dean Howells," 11 December 1902, *LHJ* 1:408-409; and James, *The Art of the Novel*, pp. 320-321.

Notes for Chapter 5   221

18. Norma Phillips, "*The Sacred Fount*: The Narrator and the Vampires," *PMLA* 76 (1961), pp. 409-411, emphasis mine.

19. James, *Notebooks*, pp. 150-151. This entry is dated 17 February 1894. As Ora Segal has observed, the professional men of letters who narrate the tales of the literary life "combine literary passion with critical discrimination: they are sensitive to and appreciative of the finer shades of the Master's works, which they hold in high esteem, but are at the same time its sharpest critics, quick to detect any false note which might be indicative of artistic decline." Ora Segal, *The Lucid Reflector* (New Haven: Yale University Press, 1969), p. 110.

20. James, *The Sacred Fount*, pp. 131-136 and 184.

21. James, *The Sacred Fount*, pp. 176 and 295. Third, fourth, and fifth emphasis mine. Philip Weinstein presents the narrator in a much more flattering light in his reading of *The Fount*, which he considers to be James's general critique of his calling as a novelist (rather than his peculiar and highly idiosyncratic artistic procedures). See Weinstein, *Henry James and the Requirements of the Imagination* (Cambridge: Harvard University Press, 1971), p. 115.

22. Peck is quoted in Gard, p. 308. The information about the effect which *The Fount* had on James's sales and his relationship with the public can be found in Foley, pp. 81-82.

23. Henry James, "The Question of the Opportunities," in *Literary Opinion in America*, ed. Morton Zabel (New York: Harper and Brothers, 1937), pp. 51 and 54-55.

24. In "Mr. Henry James's Later Work," first published in the January 1903 issue of the *North American Review*, Howells implies that women readers were especially hostile to this novel.

25. "Letter to William Dean Howells," 9 August 1900, *LHJ*, 1:357. *The Ambassadors* was actually written before *The Wings of the Dove* (1902), but the former novel did not appear in book form until 1903 because of a delay in serialization. After its serial publication in the *North American Review* from January through December of 1903, the novel was issued in England by Methuen and in America by Harper and Brothers. Edel and Lawrence, *Bibliography*, pp. 120 and 123-124. For a discussion of how this alteration effected James's presentation of his career in his Prefaces to the New York Edition of his work, see chapter 6 below.

26. Henry James Jr., "The Novels of George Eliot," *Atlantic Monthly*, vol. 28 (1866), p. 485.

27. The donnée can be found in James, *Notebooks*, pp. 225-228. Writing in October of 1895, the year of the *Guy Domville* incident, James meditated upon Jonathan Sturges' account of a recent Parisian encounter with Howells. It was the tone of the aging editor's remarks to James's young friend and disciple which immediately touched his imagination; and, interestingly enough, he soon began to embroider upon the bare facts by imagining that the speaker has "sacrificed some one, some friend, some son, some younger brother, to his failure to feel, to understand, . . . " James went on to project a "wave of reaction, of compunction," on the part of the elder man in response to his vision of "the sense, the nature, the temperament of this victim," who has "struggled and suffered" under the constraints of his elderly friend, father, brother or guardian. This vision, in turn, was to be triggered by the elderly friend's confrontation with the "case of some other person or persons . . . some other young life in regard to which it's a question of his interfering, rescuing, bringing home." The "terror" as well as the "pity" of James's post-theater career is clearly prefigured here, as if James "knew" on some subconscious level where he was heading. See also James's "project" for the novel, which he addressed to the Harpers and from which he deviated in several key instances, most notably by excluding most of the detail he provides on Strether's relationship with his wife and son, who have died before the novel begins. *Notebooks*, pp. 370-415.

222 Notes for Chapter 6

28. James, *Notebooks*, p. 375. Although Weinstein also stresses the many points of contact between *The Fount* and *The Ambassadors*, his interpretation turns out to be almost the exact reverse of the one offered here. Most importantly, he credits the narrator of *The Fount* with being protective (despite his evident cruelty) and he charges Strether with having exploited Maria Gostrey in a manner similar to Chad's exploitation of Madame de Vionnet. See Weinstein's chapters on these two novels, pp. 97-164.

29. John E. Telford, "James the Old Intruder," *Modern Fiction Studies*, IV (Summer, 1958), pp. 158 and 160-161. Telford records more than 65 instances of the use of "our friend," for example.

30. Like Maria Gostrey, Miss Barrace (a connoisseur of strange and amusing situations) and Little Bilham (an expatriated American artist) represent and form a composite portrait of James's avant-garde audience. While Miss Barrace's perpetual "oh oh oh" and Little Bilham's conspicuous lack of artistic productivity suggest that James may have found it difficult to take the younger generation seriously as an artistic force, this implication is more than counter-balanced by his striking portrait of the celebrated and prolific avant-garde sculptor, Gloriani, a man who combines considerable artistic force with the almost irresistible sexual attraction of a "glossy male tiger, magnificently marked."

31. Henry James, *The Ambassadors* (London, 1903; rpt. New York: W. W. Norton and Company, Inc., 1964), pp. 42-43, 175-176, and 190. Strether's reply to Maria's pronouncement is uncannily reminiscent of the repartee between Mrs. Briss and the narrator of *The Fount*: "It's quite true. I'm extremely wonderful just now. I dare say in fact I'm quite fantastic, and I shouldn't be at all surprised if I were mad."

32. James, *The Ambassadors*, pp. 226-227.

33. James, *The Ambassadors*, pp. 228 and 279-280.

34. James, *The Ambassadors*, pp. 265, 307, and 309-313. It is worth noting that the pavilion in which this scene occurs resembles a makeshift stage: "It consisted of little more than a platform, slightly raised, with a couple of benches and a table, a protecting rail and a protecting roof..."

35. James, *The Ambassadors*, pp. 313, 328, 330, and 332.

36. James, *The Ambassadors*, p. 344.

37. As in the case of *The Portrait*, James made the ending of *The Ambassadors* deliberately ambiguous. Strether's last words, "Then there we are!", implicitly force the reader to supply a meaning of his or her own, thus insuring (or at least making it possible) that the *reader's* education will continue on well beyond the confines of the novel, perhaps beginning anew where Strether's (seems to?) leaves off. For a valuable introduction to some of the main lines of critical responses to this novel, both contemporaneous and posthumous, see the Norton critical edition (cited above), pp. 413-484.

Chapter 6

1. Leon Edel, *The Master* (New York: J. B. Lippincott Co., 1972), p. 112; hereafter cited as *TM*. It should be noted that Edel stresses the biographical rather than the purely literary aspects of this past by treating *The Portrait* as the story of James's cousin, Minnie Temple, and linking Minnie's premature death with Milly Theale's in *The Wings of the Dove*.

2. Quoted by Edel in *TM*, p. 165.

Notes for Chapter 6

3. Henry James, "Matilde Serao," in *Notes on Novelists* (London, 1914; rpt. New York: Biblo and Tannen, 1969), pp. 309 and 312-313. This article originally appeared in the March 1901 issue of the *North American Review*. James had met "the 'she-Zola' of Italy" in Rome in 1894 and described her as "a wonderful little burly Balzac in petticoats..." See Edel, *MY*, p. 376.

4. James, *Notes on Novelists*, p. 299. As we have seen, James had appeared side by side with some of the most notorious Anglo-American producers of "sexual fiction," many of them female, in the pages of the *Yellow Book*.

5. James, *The Ambassadors*, pp. 322-323.

6. James, *Notebooks*, pp. 174 and 169.

7. "Letter to H.G. Wells," 15 November 1902, *LHJ* 1:404-406.

8. On James's attempts to serialize *The Golden Bowl*, see, for example, Henry James to James B. Pinker, 30 June 1904, Beinecke. *The Ambassadors* thus became the last of James's novels and the only novel of his major phase to appear as a serial prior to publication in book form. James's failure to achieve serialization had several consequences, not the least of which was a loss of an additional source of income. Furthermore, in the absence of external restraints regarding length imposed by the magazines, *The Wings* and *The Golden Bowl* both became extremely long novels (each appeared as a double-decker in America) precisely at a time when the English book trade was actively discouraging the production of expensive multi-volume fiction.

9. James, *The Art of the Novel*, p. 302.

10. James, *The Art of the Novel*, pp. 285-286. These observations appear in the preface to *Daisy Miller*, but they refer specifically to "The Story In It," a tale which James published in 1902. This tale, which contrasts Anglo-American and Continental literary conventions regarding adultery, turns on the question of whether a "decent" (i.e., sexually innocent) woman can have the kind of fictional "adventure" which would qualify as the subject of a story. Appropriately enough, James's discussion of this issue immediately precedes the preface to *The Wings*.

11. James, *The Wings of the Dove* (1902; rpt. Baltimore: Penguin Books, 1976), p. 144. In his preface to the novel, James simultaneously points to and throws the reader off the track of the true nature of his "failure" by stating that the problem is "lodged in Book Fifth" but referring to it as a case of a "misplaced pivot." See *The Art of the Novel*, p. 306.

12. James, *The Wings*, pp. 150-151 and 161-162.

13. In his preface to the novel, James acknowledges the extraordinary indirectness of his treatment of Milly but passes it off exclusively in terms of his desire to be "merciful" to her. His effort to keep the pressure all around her "easy" thus becomes evidence of his "tenderness of imagination about her." *The Art of the Novel*, p. 306. Sallie Sears also finds the ending of the novel to be "unpersuasive, even unreal," though she places the blame on James's preoccupation with what she calls "the mathematics of the situation." See her chapter on *The Wings* in *The Negative Imagination* (Ithaca: Cornell University Press, 1968), especially pp. 94-98.

14. The word "failure" recurs in several different contexts in this preface, as when James presents the novel as "the most striking example" of "my regular failure to keep the appointed halves of my whole equal." *The Art of the Novel*, p. 302. (He had previously used similar terms in a letter to Mrs. Caldwalader Jones dated 23 October 1902. See *LHJ* 1:403.) Due to the forementioned publishing delays, *The Ambassadors* had not yet appeared in serial or book

form. But when it was published in 1903, after *The Better Sort* and just before *The Golden Bowl*, it too was hailed as a great improvement. According to Richard Foley, Strether and Maria Gostrey were praised as two of James's "most delightfully human" characters. Foley, pp. 93-94.

15. These reviews are reprinted in Gard, pp. 339-340 and 319; while the excerpts from Howells' essay on James can be found in Dupee, pp. 8-9. Foley offers indirect confirmation of Howells' point of view when he notes that 1903 and 1904 were especially good years for James's literary reputation. Interest revived in earlier novels such as *The American* "and James as a 'literary topic' was more in evidence than he had been since the time of *Daisy Miller*." Foley, p. 97.

16. The donnée for *The Golden Bowl* can be found in James, *Notebooks*, pp. 187-188. This entry is dated 14 February 1895.

17. From a review reprinted in Gard, p. 350.

18. Henry James, *The Golden Bowl* (1904; rpt. Baltimore: Penguin Books, 1973), p. 33.

19. The Prince thinks of these traits as constituting Charlotte's "world quality," a quality "of which, in Rome, he had had his due sense, but which clearly would show larger on the big London stage." James, *The Golden Bowl*, p. 95.

20. James, *The Golden Bowl*, pp. 301, 287, and 286.

21. James, *The Golden Bowl*, p. 51. Colonel Bob Assingham is the only non-super-subtle major character who is given lines to speak in this novel. To the extent that he is viewed as a stand-in for resisting, baffled, and/or unsympathetic readers, his early dialogues with his wife can be seen as attempts on James's part to gradually initiate such readers into the complexities of the novel. A contrasting (though complimentary) account of the Assinghams' complex function in the novel can be found in R.B.J. Wilson's subtle and highly original study, *Henry James's Ultimate Narrative: "The Golden Bowl"* (London: University of Queensland Press, 1981), pp. 169-182. In his extended discussion of Fanny and Bob's respective roles as *ficelles*, Wilson persuasively argues that "she endlessly embroiders" while he "peremptorily edits" life. According to Wilson, the Assinghams' education forms a large part of the reader's education; yet their role gradually diminishes and their education reaches its limits long before the reader's does. As Wilson shrewdly observes, "she is clearly too close to the imbroglio and he is clearly too far from it, neither—James implies—attains the distance he recommends to us" (Wilson, pp. 170-172 and 181).

22. James, *The Golden Bowl*, p. 385. This language is clearly reminiscent of the terms in which Isabel Archer perceives her unconventional decision to refuse Lord Warburton's proposal in *The Portrait*. R.B.J. Wilson has recently taken issue with those critical responses to this novel which—like my own—tend to focus on one or two of the four principals at the expense of the others. Quite accurately observing that "an actual authorial mobility" lies behind "the apparent consistency of a fixed 'centre,'" Wilson goes on to insist that Maggie, Adam, Charlotte, and the Prince each deserve *equal* emphasis and attention. This point is developed in his useful but rather acerbic second chapter, in which he summarizes the history of the critical debate over *The Golden Bowl*. See Wilson, pp. 13-39, especially pp. 27 and 35-36.

23. James, *The Golden Bowl*, p. 439.

24. James, *The Golden Bowl*, pp. 455, 456, and 459.

25. James, *The Golden Bowl*, pp. 468-469.

26. James, *The Golden Bowl*, pp. 507-508 and 509. These two scenes bear an uncanny resemblance to (and should be considered as revisions of) similar incidents in James's post-theater fiction. Both are reminiscent of the moment in *The Awkward Age* when Mrs. Brook publicly confronts Nanda regarding the French novel and the narrator's callous pursuit of Mrs. Server in *The Sacred Fount*.

27. James, *The Golden Bowl*, p. 546.

28. Henry James, *The Question of Our Speech/The Lesson of Balzac* (1905; rpt. New York: Norwood Editions, 1976), pp. 96-97. On the supposed cruelty of James's treatment of Charlotte see, for example, Edel, *TM*, p. 232. Sallie Sears has gone so far as to pronounce this novel "morally absurd," a judgment with which Philip Weinstein agrees, though he is willing to concede that this was *not* James's intention. See Sears, p. 222, and Weinstein, pp. 174 and 189. Walter Wright offers an even-handed analysis of the Ververs' alleged immorality in "Maggie Verver: Neither Saint Nor Witch," in *Henry James: Modern Judgments*, ed. Tony Tanner (London: The Macmillan Co., 1968), pp. 316-326.

29. James, *The Golden Bowl*, p. 124. Daniel Mark Fogel also detects a crucial parallel between the shape of the careers of Adam Verver and Henry James in his penetrating study, *Henry James and the Structure of the Romantic Imagination* (Baton Rouge: Louisiana State University Press, 1981). Discussing *The Golden Bowl*, Fogel shrewdly demonstrates how Adam himself presents his own career "specifically as a spiral ascent." He then goes on, in his persuasive concluding chapter, to reveal the extent to which James's entire career can be viewed in terms of the Romantic dialectic of spiral ascent and return. This formulation, in turn, leads to Fogel's ultimate observation regarding the master's career. Citing James's amazing "recovery of his powers of affirmation following the dark middle period," Fogel justifiably insists that we should regard this phenomenon as one of the "greatest sustained acts of literary heroism." See Fogel, pp. 85-175, especially pp. 99-101 and 172-175.

30. James would deprecatingly refer to the latter edition as "the British brick." See "Letter to H.G. Wells," 19 November 1905, *LHJ* 2:41. He was probably in no position to argue with Methuen at this time. Archibald Constable & Co., another of his British publishers, had recently explained to him through Pinker that they were reluctant to take on *The Golden Bowl* due to the disappointing sales of *The Wings*, especially in view of the fact that the circulating libraries now refused to pay the high price of multi-deckers. See Archibald Constable & Co., Ltd. to James B. Pinker, 13 March 1903, Beinecke.

31. Scribner's Sons to James B. Pinker, 16 March 1903 and 20 September 1904, Beinecke. As they confided to Pinker, the American firm was "very anxious to bring the novel out while Mr. James is here, so as to secure for it and for him the benefit... of his presence in this country and the interest that naturally attaches thereto." Edel's account of this ten-month tour of the American scene can be found in *TM*, pp. 234-235. James's "oral essays" were addressed primarily to literary clubs and women's colleges, including Smith and Bryn Mawr (where he also served as commencement speaker in the spring of 1905).

32. He went on to praise the "very pretty form" of the Scribner edition of the novel. Henry James to James B. Pinker, 2 March 1905, Beinecke. It is also worth noting that Henry frequently adopts this identity (or at least tries to) in his letters to his older brother. See, for example, his letter to William of 24 May 1903, where he implies that the primary motive for his forthcoming trip is "absolutely economic." *LHJ* 1:419.

33. Henry James to James B. Pinker, 6 March 1905, Beinecke. James takes similar pride in his public exploits in a letter he wrote to Edmund Gosse on 16 and 18 February 1905. See *LHJ* 2:27-28.

34. Foley, pp. 105-106. Edel similarly describes James's manner of delivery as "an admirable piece of conversational reading" in *TM*, p. 280. His description of James's appearance can be found on pp. 169-170, and he treats the subject of the mixed reaction which James's lectures evoked on pp. 301-303.

35. Percy Lubbock, H. G. Wells, and Ford Madox Ford followed by Ezra Pound, T. S. Eliot, and Leon Edel are among the key figures in the formation and perpetuation of the legend of the master. It should be stressed, however, that Edel's work on James's theater years has helped to undercut this stereotypical view of James's career. Despite the fact that James eventually broke with Wells after a long dispute over the relationship between art and life, both Wells and James's highly influential disciple, Lubbock, promoted the view of the master as a writer preoccupied almost exclusively with questions of form and technique. See, for example, Wells's much-quoted parody of James in his novel, *Boon*, reprinted in the Norton critical edition of *The Ambassadors*, p. 426. (James's dispute with Wells can be followed in *Henry James and H. G. Wells: A Record of Their Friendship, Their Debate on the Art of Fiction, and Their Quarrel*, ed. Leon Edel and Gordon N. Ray [Urbana: University of Illinois Press, 1958].) Lubbock's pioneering study of James's technical experiments with point of view, *The Craft of Fiction* (London: J. Cape, 1921), did much to inaugurate "the modern era of James appreciation," converging as it did all too neatly with many of the central concerns of the New Critics (who often reinforced and expanded upon this one-sided appraisal). This estimate of Lubbock's influence can be found in Tony Tanner's Introduction to *Henry James: Modern Judgements* (London: the Macmillan Company, 1968), a collection of some of the most important post-1943 criticism of the master. See Tanner, pp. 25-26.

36. James, *SWA*, pp. 287-288 and the preface to "The Lesson of the Master" in James, *The Art of the Novel*, p. 221.

37. Percy Lubbock, "The New York Edition of the Novels and Tales of Henry James," *Times Literary Supplement*, 8 July 1909; and "Letter to William Dean Howells," 17 August 1908, excerpted in R. P. Blackmur's Introduction to *The Art of the Novel*, p. vii (the complete text of this letter can be found in *LHJ* 2:98-104.) According to Elsa Nettels, Joseph Conrad and Ford Madox Ford also participated in this process by devoting editorials to the New York Edition in the first issue of the *English Review*, which Ford began to edit in 1909. My account of James's response to Lubbock's review is also taken from Nettels, pp. 8-10.

38. James, *The Golden Bowl*, pp. 124-125.

39. Leon Edel, "The Architecture of Henry James's New York Edition," *New England Quarterly*, 24 (1951), pp. 169-170 and 176. Interestingly enough, he omits any reference to James's exclusion of *The Sacred Fount*.

40. "Letter to Robert Herrick," 7 August 1907, *SL*, pp. 190-191. Edel also quotes from this passage in his article on the architecture of the edition, but he omits the last two lines and thus interprets the letter quite differently, concluding that "James seems to have been caught between the Scylla of amplitude and the Charybdis of amputation." Edel, "The Architecture," p. 172.

41. Edel, "The Architecture," p. 177. James actually uses the term "disown" in a letter to Pinker in which he reveals his decision "not to let it (the edition) include absolutely everything. It is best, I think, that it should be selective as well as collective; I want to *quietly disown* a few things by not thus *supremely adopting* them." Henry James to James B. Pinker, 6 June 1905, Beinecke. Emphasis mine. For an alternative explanation which seeks to explain James's exclusion of *The Fount* on strictly technical grounds see Claire Raeth, "Henry James's Rejection of *The Sacred Fount*," *Journal of English Literary History* 26 (Dec. 1949), pp. 308-324.

42. "Letter to William Dean Howells," 17 August 1908, *LHJ* 2:100. James then went on to add: "I feel at the same time how the series suffers commercially from its [*The Bostonians*] having been dropped so completely out." This remark is disingenuous, to say the least, considering the extremely poor reception and sales of this novel; but James knew that Howells admired *The Bostonians* and was probably trying to justify its exclusion as gracefully as possible without insulting his old friend's taste and judgment.

43. This last phrase appears in the preface to *The Tragic Muse* and can be found in James, *The Art of the Novel*, p. 84. I am grateful to Charles Feidelson for reminding me that while not every aspect of James's development as an artist was premeditated, the overall process does take on a rather uncanny air of predestination, at least in retrospect—even without the Prefaces. It is also important to note that James slyly punctuates almost every preface with disarmingly candid references to the many accidents and setbacks that befell him, disclosures which are meant to add to the "suspense" by deliberately undercutting his ostensible aura of absolute authorial control. (However, these references have predictably been ignored by most scholars or dismissed as proof of the Anglo-American public's supposedly total lack of appreciation.)

44. The sequence runs as follows: volume 1—*Roderick Hudson*, volume 2—*The American*, volumes 3 and 4—*The Portrait*, volumes 5 and 6—*The Princess Casamassima*, volumes 7 and 8—*The Tragic Muse*, volume 9—*The Awkward Age*, volume 10—*The Spoils* (etc.), volume 11—*Maisie* (etc.), volume 12—*The Aspern Papers* (etc.), volume 13—*The Reverberator* (etc.), volume 14—*Lady Barberina* (etc.), volume 15—*The Lesson of the Master* (etc.), volume 16—*The Author of Beltraffio* (etc.), volume 17—*The Altar of the Dead* (etc.), volume 18—*Daisy Miller* (etc.), volumes 19 and 20—*The Wings*, volumes 21 and 22—*The Ambassadors*, volumes 23 and 24—*The Golden Bowl*. The most conspicuous departures from chronology are the placement of *The Awkward Age* (which appears before its predecessors, *The Spoils* and *Maisie*), *Daisy Miller* (which James moved to the end rather than the beginning of the volumes containing short stories), and *The Wings* (which precedes *The Ambassadors*, though it followed it in order of composition). In the case of the short stories, word counts as well as thematic considerations influenced James's groupings. Yet despite all his careful preparation, he was forced to spill over into a twenty-fourth volume. On this last point, see Edel, *TM*, pp. 323-324.

45. James, *The Art of the Novel*, p. 4. The wording of the Scribner prospectus confirms this view, for it emphasizes the "patriotic" aspects of James's career. See Edel, *TM*, p. 324.

46. See James, *The Art of the Novel*, pp. 15, 37, 85-86, 123, 146, 296, 317, and 329-330, respectively. There are many other subplots running throughout the Prefaces, although the two above-mentioned are the most consistent and conspicuous. For example, James's attempt to perfect the dramatic analogy is followed in the prefaces to *The Tragic Muse, The Awkward Age*, and the major novels, while his running battle with editors, journalism, and the debased taste of the common reader is chronicled in almost every preface, especially the ones which introduce *The Reverberator* and the volumes containing the stories of writers and artists.

47. James's hopes and expectations proved to be correct. In August of 1918, a little more than two years after his death, the *Little Review* published two appreciations of the master's greatness, one by Ezra Pound and the other by T.S. Eliot. These influential essays have been reprinted in Pound, *Essays*, pp. 295-338, and *The Shock of Recognition*, ed. Edmund Wilson (New York: Farrar, Straus, and Cudahy, 1955), pp. 854-865, respectively. Both writers obviously felt a special kinship with and admiration for James as a fellow expatriate, a key factor which has affected his reputation (for better *and* for worse).

48. James, *The Art of the Novel*, pp. 96-97.

49. James, *The Art of the Novel*, p. 309. However, James candidly if parenthetically exposes this sleight of hand in the following paragraph, where he calls the careful reader's attention to this reversal of the two novels. This tactic recalls Neil Harris' shrewd assessment of P. T. Barnum's "operational aesthetic": Barnum knew that his audiences would accept guile "because it was more complicated than candor." Perhaps James did too! See Harris' *Humbug: The Art of P. T. Barnum* (Boston: Little, Brown and Co., 1973), p. 57. In this context, the Prefaces taken as a group can be seen as an elegant (if devious) variation on that all-American institution, the "how to" manual.

50. James, *The Art of the Novel*, p. 335. Emphasis mine. As this passage continues, James virtually becomes his own "ideal" reader, for he states: "As the historian of the matter sees and speaks, so my intelligence of it, as a reader, meets him halfway, passive, receptive, appreciative, often even grateful; unconscious, quite blissfully, of any bar to intercourse, any disparity of sense between us." *The Art of the Novel*, pp. 335-336. On the success of *The Golden Bowl*, see James's reference to "the altogether better literary manners" of that novel and *The Ambassadors*, in *The Art of the Novel*, p. 344.

51. James, *The Art of the Novel*, pp. 346-347. Citing this passage, R. B. J. Wilson also places a significant emphasis upon the role played in James's mature authorial discourse by his desire to appeal to "the mental voice" through "the play of tone." Arguing that the master came to draw upon the rhetorical principle of the *histrionique* of the French classical theater, Wilson offers a brilliant interpretation of the effect of James's revisions upon the rhythm of the rhetoric of his major phase. I heartily concur with Wilson's observations that "[t]he resulting prose has more affinities with the *tirades* of the *Theatre Française* than has been realized" and that "James's own speech in other quarters was certainly as rhythmic." See Wilson, pp. 261-292, especially pp. 262-264, 275, and 282-283.

52. H.G. Dwight, "Henry James—In His Own Country," reprinted in Gard, pp. 442-444. This article originally appeared in the May and July 1907 issues of *Putnam's Monthly*.

53. As we have seen in chapter 3, the theme of a substitute performance first emerged in the prefaces James wrote to accompany and introduce his unacted plays, the two volumes of *Theatricals*.

54. James, *The Art of the Novel*, pp. 337, 344, 348 and 341. James employs this imagery throughout the Prefaces, especially when dealing with works which were ignored or abused by the reading public. See, for example, his reference to "unacknowledged births" and "pregnant themes" in the preface to *The Tragic Muse* (*The Art of the Novel*, pp. 79-80), to the "unforseen principle of growth" by which small things turn into "monsters" in the preface to *The Awkward Age* (p. 98), to shirked parental burdens in the preface to *Maisie* (pp. 142-143), to his "family" of small productions in the preface to *The Aspern Papers* (p. 177), and to "the ultimately most prosperous child" of his invention in the preface to *Daisy Miller* (p. 277). However, its most sustained use occurs, quite appropriately, in the preface to *The Golden Bowl*.

55. Even the most avant-garde modern critics of James's work tend not to question the reliability of the narrator of the Prefaces. A good example of this tendency is Susanne Kappeler's recent study of *Writing and Reading in Henry James* (New York: Columbia University Press, 1980). Despite the fact that she regards literature as a game of skill and recognizes the effect upon James's short stories of "the pressure of originality and novelty that the dialectic race between connoisseur readers and writers" exerts, she persists in regarding James's role in the Prefaces as that of an impersonal guide and trustworthy teacher instead of a devious game-player.

Kappeler, pp. 12, 175, and 179-180. A notable exception to this rule is Wayne Booth's penetrating treatment of James in *The Rhetoric of Fiction* (Chicago: University of Chicago Press, 1961). Booth's approach to James's work in particular and the dilemma of the modern writer in regard to the problem of audience, while somewhat different from the one offered here, largely coincides with and frequently supports my reading of James's career. See especially pp. 348-350, 373-374, and 392-396.

56. "Letter to James B. Pinker," 23 October 1908, *LHJ* 2:106-107. For a detailed account of this breakdown, see Edel, *TM,* pp. 433-447. Precise information concerning the sales of the New York Edition can be found in Gard, p. 556.

57. Henry James to James B. Pinker, 20 December 1911, Beinecke. Edel and Lawrence report that although 100 sets of sheets were imported to England for the Macmillan version of the New York Edition, only a fraction of these were bound. The rest were used as package wrapping during the Second World War! See *Bibliography,* pp. 138-139. However, Gard states that Macmillan informally denied this when he requested confirmation. See Gard, p. 556. James's letter to Gosse is quoted in Gard, p. 531.

58. Edel, *TM,* pp. 562-563. Interestingly enough, one of James's contemporaries virtually predicted the effect which the rapid expansion of college and graduate level education would have on both the contour and the taste of the American reading public. Writing in the *Atlantic Monthly* in 1896, Paul Shorey lamented the omnipresence of ephemeral (i.e., "cheap and easy") literature; but he took refuge in the hope that the past two decades of growth in graduate instruction in the United States would help to remedy the situation. Noting that there were already more than one thousand professors wholly or partly engaged in what he revealingly referred to as "*non-professional* graduate instruction to more than three thousand students," he insisted that this phenomenon would have a decisive effect on future producers, critics, and readers of literature, especially in terms of the establishment of "a non-local, non-provincial" standard of literary quality. Shorey concluded his perceptive survey of the American literary and academic scenes by speculating upon the effect which Ph.D. dissertations would have in the future: "Collectively, they will combine with other forces to form a small but influential reading public, that will not only tolerate but demand stronger food than American literature has usually supplied in the past." Paul Shorey, "Present Conditions of Literary Production," *Atlantic Monthly* 78 (August 1896), pp. 158 and 165-168. Emphasis mine. Shorey might have been less sanguine about this new development had he lived to see the elaborate posturing indulged in by some modern professors of literature or the extent to which the typical doctoral dissertation would fail to achieve (or deliberately reject) the "vigorous and readable" style which he so confidently envisioned in his concluding remarks.

Bibliography

Manuscript Collections

James-Pinker Correspondence. Collection of American Literature, Beinecke Rare Book and Manuscript Library, Yale University, New Haven, Connecticut. This correspondence consists of three bound volumes of letters from Henry James to James B. Pinker covering the period from 7 May 1898 through 30 October 1915. The collection also contains several folders of letters to Pinker written by the novelist and his nephew, Henry James Jr., and correspondence written by various publishers and editors to James (though it is frequently addressed to Pinker).

Published Primary Sources

N.B. Due to the nature of this study, in most cases I have avoided using the revised texts of the New York Edition of James's novels and tales. An exception to this is the late novels, where any variation between the original and revised versions of the text would not fundamentally effect my argument.

Edel, Leon and Gordon N. Ray, eds. *Henry James and H.G. Wells: A Record of Their Friendship, Their Debate on the Art of Fiction, and Their Quarrel.* Urbana: University of Illinois Press, 1958.
Edel, Leon, ed. *Henry James Letters.* 3 vols. Cambridge, Mass.: The Belknap Press of Harvard University Press, 1974-1980.
_____. ed. *Selected Letters of Henry James.* London: Rupert Hart-Davis, 1956.
Eliot, George. "Silly Novels By Lady Novelists." *Westminster Review* 66 (October 1856), pp. 442-461.
Howells, Mildred, ed. *Life In Letters of William Dean Howells.* 2 vols. Garden City, New York: Doubleday, Doran & Co., Inc., 1928.
Howells, William Dean. *Criticism and Fiction and Other Essays.* Ed. Clara Marburg Kirk and Rudolph Kirk. 1891; rpt. New York: New York University Press, 1959.
James, Alice. *The Diary of Alice James.* Ed. Leon Edel. New York: Dodd, Mead & Co., 1934.
James, Henry. *The Ambassadors.* Ed. S.P. Rosenbaum. 1909; rpt. New York: W.W. Norton and Company, Inc., 1964.
_____. *The American.* Intro. Joseph Warren Beach. 1877; rpt. New York: Holt, Rinehart and Winston, Inc., 1949.
_____. *The American Novels and Stories of Henry James.* Ed. F.O. Matthiessen. New York: Alfred A. Knopf, 1968.
_____. *The American Scene.* London: Chapman and Hall, 1907.

Bibliography

———. *The Art of the Novel*. Intro. R.P. Blackmur. 1907-1909; rpt. New York: Charles Scribner's Sons, 1934.
———. *The Aspern Papers/The Spoils of Poynton*. Intro. R.P. Blackmur. London, 1888 and 1897, respectively; rpt. New York: Dell Publishing Co., Inc., 1975.
———. *Autobiography: A Small Boy and Others/Notes of a Son and Brother/The Middle Years*. Ed. and intro. F.W. Dupee. 1913, 1914, and 1917, respectively; rpt. New York: Criterion Books, 1956.
———. *The Awkward Age*. New York, 1908; rpt. Middlesex, England: Penguin Books, 1974.
———. "Benvolio." In *The Complete Tales of Henry James*. Ed. and intro. Leon Edel. Vol. 3. 1875; rpt. New York: J.B. Lippincott Company, 1962, pp. 351-401.
———. *The Better Sort*. London: Methuen and Company, 1903.
———. *The Bostonians*. Introd. Irving Howe. London, 1886; rpt. New York: Random House, Inc., 1956.
———. "A Bundle of Letters." In *The Complete Tales of Henry James*. Ed. and intro. Leon Edel. Vol. 4. 1879; rpt. New York: J.B. Lippincott Company, 1962.
———. *The Collective Edition of Mr. Henry James's Novels and Tales*. 14 vols. London: Macmillan and Company, 1883.
———. *The Complete Plays of Henry James*. Ed. and intro. Leon Edel. New York: J.B. Lippincott Company, 1949.
———. *Confidence*. Ed. and intro. Herbert Ruhm. 1880; rpt. New York: Grosset & Dunlap, 1962.
———. *Daisy Miller: A Comedy In Three Acts*. Boston: James R. Osgood and Company, 1883.
———. *Embarrassments*. London: William Heinemann, 1896.
———. *Essays in London and Elsewhere*. London: James R. Osgood, McIlvaine & Co., 1893.
———. *French Poets and Novelists*. London: Macmillan and Company, 1878.
———. *The Golden Bowl*. 1904; rpt. Baltimore: Penguin Books, 1966.
———. *Guy Domville/A Play in Three Acts with Comments by Bernard Shaw, H.G. Wells, Arnold Bennett/Preceded by Biographical Chapters "Henry James: The Dramatic Years," by Leon Edel*. London: Rupert Hart-Davis, 1961.
———. *Hawthorne*. London, 1879; rpt. Ithaca, New York: Cornell University Press, 1975.
———. *The House of Fiction: Essays on the Novel by Henry James*. Ed. and intro. Leon Edel. London: Rupert Hart-Davis, 1957.
———. Introduction to *The Tempest*. In *The Appreciation of Shakespeare*. Ed. Bernard M. Wagner. London, 1907; rpt. Washington, D.C.: Georgetown University Press, 1949, pp. 475-481.
———. "The Madonna of the Future." In *The Complete Tales of Henry James*. Ed. and intro. Leon Edel. Vol. 3. 1873; rpt. New York: J.B. Lippincott Company, 1962, pp. 11-52.
———. "Matilde Serao." In *Notes on Novelists with Some Other Notes*. 1914; rpt. New York: Biblo and Tannen, 1969, pp. 294-313.
———. *"A Most Unholy Trade": Being Letters on the Drama By Henry James*. Cambridge, Mass.: The Scarab Press, privately printed by Dunster House, 1923.
———. *The New York Edition of the Novels and Tales of Henry James*. 24 vols. New York: Charles Scribner's Sons, 1907-1909.
———. *The Notebooks of Henry James*. Ed. F.O. Matthiessen and Kenneth B. Murdock. New York: Oxford University Press, 1947.
———. *Notes and Reviews By Henry James*. Preface Pierre de Chaignon la Rose. Cambridge, Mass.: Dunster House, 1921.
———. "The Novels of George Eliot." *Atlantic Monthly* 28 (1866), pp. 479-492.
———. *The Other House*. New York: The Macmillan Company, 1896.
———. *Parisian Sketches: Letters to the 'New York Tribune,' 1875-1876*. Ed. and intro. Leon Edel and Ilse Dusoir Lind. London: Rupert Hart-Davis, 1958.

_____. *Partial Portraits*. Intro. Leon Edel. London, 1888; rpt. Ann Arbor: The University of Michigan Press, 1970.
_____. *A Passionate Pilgrim and Other Tales*. Boston: James R. Osgood and Company, 1875.
_____. *The Portrait of a Lady*. Afterword Oscar Cargill. London, 1881; rpt. New York: New American Library, 1963.
_____. *The Princess Casamassima*. London, 1886; rpt. New York: Harper and Row, Publishers, 1968.
_____. *The Question of Our Speech/The Lesson of Balzac: Two Lectures*. 1905; rpt. n.p.: Norwood Editions, 1976.
_____. *The Reverberator*. Intro. Simon Nowell-Smith. London, 1888; rpt. New York: Grove Press, Inc., n.d.
_____. *Roderick Hudson*. Boston: James R. Osgood and Company, 1876 [1875].
_____. *The Sacred Fount*. Intro. Leon Edel. 1901; rpt. New York: The Grove Press, 1953.
_____. *The Scenic Art/Notes on Acting and the Drama: 1872-1901*. Ed. and intro. Allan Wade. New Brunswick: Rutgers University Press, 1948.
_____. "The Siege of London." In *The Complete Tales of Henry James*. Ed. and intro. Leon Edel. Vol. 5. 1883; rpt. New York: J.B. Lippincott Company, 1963.
_____. *Stories of Writers and Artists*. Ed. and intro. F.O. Matthiessen. New York: New Directions Books, 1944.
_____. *Terminations*. London: William Heinemann, 1895.
_____. *Theatricals: Second Series*. London: Osgood, McIlvaine and Company, 1894.
_____. *Theatricals/Two Comedies/Tenants/Disengaged*. London: Osgood, McIlvaine and Company, 1894.
_____. *The Tragic Muse*. Intro. Fred W. Bornhauser. 1890; rpt. New York: Thomas Y. Crowell Company, 1975.
_____. *Transatlantic Sketches*. Boston: James R. Osgood and Company, 1875.
_____. *"The Turn of the Screw" and "Daisy Miller."* London, 1898 and New York, 1878, respectively; rpt. New York: Dell Publishing Company, 1965.
_____. *The Two Magics*. London: William Heinemann, 1898.
_____. *Washington Square/The Europeans*. Intro. R.P. Blackmur. 1880 and 1878, respectively; rpt. New York: The Dell Publishing Company, 1967.
_____. *Watch and Ward*. 1878; rpt. Boston: Houghton, Mifflin, and Co., 1886.
_____. *What Maisie Knew*. 1908; rpt. Garden City, New York: Doubleday and Company, Inc., 1954.
_____. *The Wings of the Dove*. 1902; rpt. Baltimore: Penguin Books Inc., 1976.
Lubbock, Percy, ed. *The Letters of Henry James*. 2 vols. New York: Charles Scribner's Sons, 1920.
Paige, D.D., ed. *The Letters of Ezra Pound: 1907-1941*. New York: Harcourt, Brace and World, Inc., 1950.
Robins, Elizabeth, comp. *Theatre and Friendship: Letters from Henry James to Elizabeth Robins With a Commentary by Elizabeth Robins*. New York: G.P. Putnam's Sons, 1932.

Secondary Sources

Andrews, Kenneth. *Nook Farm: Mark Twain's Hartford Circle*. Cambridge, Mass.: Harvard University Press, 1950.
Barnes, James J. *Authors, Publishers, and Politicians: The Quest for an Anglo-American Copyright Agreement 1815-1854*. London: Routledge & Kegan Paul, 1974.
_____. *Free Trade in Books: A Study of the London Book Trade Since 1800*. Oxford: The Clarendon Press, 1964.

Bibliography

Baym, Nina. *Woman's Fiction: A Guide to Novels by and about Women in America, 1820-1870.* Ithaca: Cornell University Press, 1978.
Beach, Joseph Warren. *The Method of Henry James.* Philadelphia: Albert Saifer, Publisher, 1954.
Becker, George J., ed. *Documents of Modern Literary Realism.* Princeton: Princeton University Press, 1967.
Booth, Wayne C. *The Rhetoric of Fiction.* Chicago: University of Chicago Press, 1961.
Bosanquet, Theodora. *Henry James At Work.* London: The Hogarth Press, 1924.
Bradbury, Malcolm. *The Social Context of Modern English Literature.* New York: Schocken Books, 1971.
Brooks, Peter. *The Melodramatic Imagination: Balzac, Henry James, Melodrama, and the Mode of Excess.* New Haven: Yale University Press, 1976.
Brooks, Van Wyck. *The Pilgrimage of Henry James.* 1925; rpt. New York: Octagon Books, 1972.
Cargill, Oscar. *The Novels of Henry James.* New York: The Macmillan Company, 1961.
Charvat, William. *Literary Publishing In America, 1790-1850.* Philadelphia: University of Pennsylvania Press, 1959.
_____. *The Profession of Authorship in America, 1800-1870, The Papers of William Charvat.* Ed. Matthew J. Bruccoli. Columbus: Ohio State University Press, 1968.
Cott, Nancy. *The Bonds of Womanhood: "Women's Sphere" in New England, 1780-1835.* New Haven: Yale University Press, 1977.
Donovan, Alan. "My Dear Pinker: The Correspondence of Henry James With His Literary Agent." *Yale University Library Gazette* 36, no. 2 (October 1961), pp. 78-88.
Douglas, Ann. *The Feminization of American Culture.* New York: Alfred A. Knopf, 1977.
Dupee, Frederick W., ed. *The Question of Henry James.* New York: Henry Holt and Company, 1945.
Edel, Leon, and Dan Lawrence. *A Bibliography of Henry James.* London: Rupert Hart-Davis, 1957.
Edel, Leon. "The Architecture of Henry James's New York Edition." *New England Quarterly* 24 (1951), pp. 169-178.
_____. *The Conquest of London.* Vol. 2 of *The Life of Henry James.* New York: J.B. Lippincott Company, 1962.
_____. *Henry James: Les Années Dramatiques.* Diss. Paris: Jouve & Companie, Editeurs, 1931.
_____. *The Master.* Vol. 5 of *The Life of Henry James.* New York: J.B. Lippincott Company, 1972.
_____. *The Middle Years.* Vol. 3 of *The Life of Henry James.* New York: J.B. Lippincott Company, 1962.
_____. *The Treacherous Years.* Vol. 4 of *The Life of Henry James.* New York: J.B. Lippincott Company, 1969.
_____. *The Untried Years.* Vol. 1 of *The Life of Henry James.* New York: J.B. Lippincott Company, 1953.
Egan, Michael. *Henry James: The Ibsen Years.* Plymouth, England: Vision Press, printed by Clark, Doble & Brendon Ltd., 1972.
Eliot, T.S. "Henry James." In *The Shock of Recognition; The Development of Literature in the United States Recorded by the Men Who Made It.* Ed. Edmund Wilson. New York: Farrar, Straus & Cudahy, 1955, pp. 854-865.
Ellmann, Richard, ed. *Edwardians and Late Victorians: English Institute Essays, 1959.* New York: Columbia University Press, 1960.
_____. "A Late Victorian Love Affair." In *Oscar Wilde: Two Approaches.* Los Angeles: University of California Press, 1977.
Escarpit, Robert. *The Book Revolution.* London: George G. Harrap & Co., Ltd., 1966.

Feidelson, Charles. "James and the 'Man of Imagination.'" In *Literary Theory and Structure*. Ed. Frank Brady, John Palmer, and Martin Price. New Haven: Yale University Press, 1973, pp. 331-352.
Fetterly, Judith. *The Resisting Reader: A Feminist Approach to American Fiction*. Bloomington: Indiana University Press, 1978.
Firebaugh, Joseph J. "The Ververs." *Essays In Criticism* 4 (1954), pp. 400-410.
Fogel, Daniel Mark. *Henry James and the Structure of the Romantic Imagination*. Baton Rouge: Louisiana State University Press, 1981.
Foley, Richard N. *Criticism in American Periodicals of the Works of Henry James from 1866 to 1916*. Washington, D.C.: The Catholic University Press, 1944.
Gard, Roger, ed. *Henry James: The Critical Heritage*. New York: Barnes & Noble Inc., 1968.
Gohdes, Clarence. "British Interest in American Literature During the Latter Part of the Nineteenth Century As Reflected By Mudie's Select Library." *American Literature* 13 (January 1942), pp. 356-362.
Gordon, D.J. and Stokes, John. "The Reference of *The Tragic Muse*." In *The Air of Reality: New Essays on Henry James*. Ed. John Goode. London: Methuen and Co., Ltd., 1972.
Griest, Guinevere L. *Mudie's Circulating Library and the Victorian Novel*. Bloomington: Indiana University Press, 1970.
Harris, Neil. *Humbug: The Art of P.T. Barnum*. Boston: Little, Brown and Co., 1973.
Hart, James D. *The Popular Book: A History of America's Literary Taste*. New York: Oxford University Press, 1950.
Holder, Alan. *Three Voyagers in Search of Europe: A Study of Henry James, Ezra Pound, and T.S. Eliot*. Philadelphia: University of Pennsylvania, 1966.
Holland, Lawrence B. *The Expense of Vision: Essays on the Craft of Henry James*. Princeton: Princeton University Press, 1964.
Hynes, Samuel. *The Edwardian Turn of Mind*. Princeton: Princeton University Press, 1968.
Isle, Walter. *Experiments in Form: Henry James's Novels, 1896-1901*. Cambridge, Mass.: Harvard University Press, 1968.
Jackson, Holbrook. *The Eighteen-Nineties: A Review of Art and Ideas at the Close of the Nineteenth Century*. New Jersey: Humanities Press, Inc., 1976.
Jacobson, Marcia. *Henry James and the Mass Market*. University, Alabama: University of Alabama Press, 1983.
Jefferson, D.W. *Henry James and the Modern Reader*. New York: St. Martin's Press, 1964.
Kaplan, Justin. *Mr. Clemens and Mark Twain: A Biography*. New York: Simon and Schuster, 1966.
Kappeler, Susanne. *Writing and Reading in Henry James*. New York: Columbia University Press, 1980.
Kerr, Howard. *Mediums, and Spirit-Rappers, and Roaring Radicals: Spiritualism in American Literature, 1850-1900*. Chicago: University of Illinois Press, 1972.
Levy, Leo B. *Versions of Melodrama: A Study of the Fiction and Drama of Henry James, 1865-1897*. Los Angeles: University of California Press, 1957.
Lubbock, Percy. *The Craft of Fiction*. London: J. Cape, 1921.
_____. "The New York Edition of the Novels and Tales of Henry James." *The Times Literary Supplement*, 8 July 1909, p. 249.
Marcus, Jane Connor. "Elizabeth Robins: A Biographical and Critical Study." Diss. Northwestern University, 1973.
Margolis, Anne T. "The James Family." *American Quarterly* 34 (Winter 1982), pp. 562-570.
Matthiessen, F.O. *The James Family*. New York: Alfred A. Knopf, 1947.

Mix, Katharine Lyon. *A Study in Yellow: The "Yellow Book" and Its Contributors.* Lawrence: The University of Kansas Press, 1960.

Moers, Ellen. *Literary Women: The Great Writers.* Garden City, New York: Doubleday & Co., Inc., 1977.

Mordell, Albert, ed. *Discovery of A Genius: William Dean Howells and Henry James.* New York: Twayne Publishers, Inc., 1961.

Mott, Frank Luther. *A History of American Magazines.* Vols. 1-3. New York: D. Appleton & Co., 1930.

_____. *A History of American Magazines.* Vol. 4. Cambridge, Mass.: Harvard University Press, 1957.

Nettels, Elsa. *James and Conrad.* Athens: The University of Georgia Press, 1977.

Pacey, W.C.D. "Henry James and His French Contemporaries." *American Literature* 13 (November 1941), pp. 240-256.

Perosa, Sergio. *Henry James and the Experimental Novel.* New York: New York University Press, 1983.

Phillips, Norma. "*The Sacred Fount:* The Narrator and the Vampires." *PMLA* 76 (1961), pp. 407-412.

Poggioli, Renato. *The Theory of the Avant-Garde.* Trans. Gerald Fitzgerald. Cambridge, Mass.: The Belknap Press of Harvard University Press, 1968.

Poirier, Richard. *The Comic Sense of Henry James: A Study of the Early Novels.* New York: Oxford University Press, 1967.

Pound, Ezra. "Henry James." In *The Essays of Ezra Pound.* Ed. T.S. Eliot. London: Faber and Faber Limited, 1954.

Powers, Lyall H. *Henry James and the Naturalist Movement.* n.p.: Michigan State University Press, 1971.

Raeth, Claire. "Henry James's Rejection of *The Sacred Fount.*" *Journal of English Literary History* 16 (Dec. 1949), pp. 308-324.

Raleigh, John Henry. *Matthew Arnold and American Culture.* Berkeley: University of California Press, 1961.

Schick, Frank L. *The Paperbound Book In America.* New York: R.R. Bowker Company, 1958.

Schulte, Raymond L. *Crusader In Babylon—W.T. Stead and the "Pall Mall Gazette".* Lincoln: University of Nebraska Press, 1972.

Sears, Sallie. *The Negative Imagination: Form and Perspective in the Novels of Henry James.* Ithaca: Cornell University Press, 1968.

Segal, Ora. *The Lucid Reflector: The Observer in Henry James's Fiction.* New Haven: Yale University Press, 1969.

Shaw, Bernard. *The Quintessence of Ibsenism.* New York: Brentano's, 1922.

Shorey, Paul. "Present Conditions of Literary Production." *Atlantic Monthly* 78 (August 1896), pp. 156-168.

Shove, Raymond Howard. *Cheap Book Production in the United States, 1870 to 1891.* Urbana: The University of Illinois Library, 1937.

Showalter, Elaine. *A Literature of Their Own: British Women Novelists From Brontë to Lessing.* Princeton: Princeton University Press, 1977.

Smith, Henry Nash. *Democracy and the Novel: Popular Resistance to Classic American Writers.* New York: Oxford University Press, 1978.

Stone, Donald David. *Novelists In A Changing World; Meredith, James, and the Transformation of English Fiction in the 1880's.* Cambridge: Harvard University Press, 1972.

Strouse, Jean. *Alice James: A Biography.* Boston: Houghton Mifflin Company, 1980.

Strout, Cushing. "Henry James's Dream of the Louvre, 'The Jolly Corner,' and Psychological Interpretation." *Psychohistory Review,* 8, nos. 1-2 (Summer-Fall 1979), pp. 47-52.

Tanner, Tony, ed. *Henry James: Modern Judgements.* London: The Macmillan Co., 1968.
_____. *The Reign of Wonder.* Cambridge: University of Cambridge Press, 1965.
Taylor, John Tinnon. *Early Opposition to the English Novel: The Popular Reaction from 1760-1830.* New York: Morningside Heights, King's Crown Press, 1943.
Tebbel, John. *The Creation of an Industry, 1630-1865.* Vol. 1 of *A History of Book Publishing in the United States.* New York: R.R. Bowker, 1972.
_____. *The Expansion of an Industry, 1865-1919.* Vol. 2 of *A History of Book Publishing in the United States.* New York: R.R. Bowker, 1975.
Telford, John E. "James the Old Intruder." *Modern Fiction Studies* 4 (Summer, 1958), pp. 157-164.
Ticknor, Caroline. *Hawthorne and His Publisher.* Boston: Houghton Mifflin Co., 1913.
Tillotsen, Kathleen. *Novels of the Eighteen-Forties.* Oxford: The Clarendon Press, 1954.
Tompkins, J.M.S. *The Popular Novel in England, 1770-1880.* London: Constable & Co., Ltd., 1932.
Veeder, William. *Henry James—The Lessons of the Master: Popular Fiction and Personal Style in the Nineteenth Century.* Chicago: University of Chicago Press, 1975.
Wallace, Ronald. *Henry James and the Comic Form.* Ann Arbor: The University of Michigan Press, 1975.
Webster, Charles, ed. *Mark Twain, Business Man.* Boston: Little, Brown and Company, 1946.
Weinstein, Philip M. *Henry James and the Requirements of the Imagination.* Cambridge: Harvard University Press, 1971.
Weintraub, Stanley. *The London Yankees: Portraits of American Writers and Artists in England, 1894-1914.* New York: Harcourt Brace Jovanovich, 1979.
_____, ed. *The Yellow Book: Quintessence of the Nineties.* Garden City, New York: Anchor Books, 1964.
Welter, Barbara. "The Cult of True Womanhood: 1820-1860." *American Quarterly* 18 (1966), pp. 151-174.
Westbrook, Perry D. "The Supersubtle Fry." *Nineteenth-Century Fiction* 8 (Sept. 1953), pp. 134-140.
Wiesenfarth, Joseph. *Henry James and the Dramatic Analogy: A Study of the Major Novels of the Middle Period.* New York: Fordham University Press, 1963.
Williams, Raymond. *The Long Revolution.* New York: Columbia University Press, 1961.
Wilson, Edmund. "The Ambiguity of Henry James." In *The Triple Thinkers: Twelve Essays on Literary Subjects.* New York: Farrar, Straus and Giroux, 1976, pp. 88-132.
Wilson, R.B.J. *Henry James's Ultimate Narrative: "The Golden Bowl."* New York: University of Queensland Press, 1981.
Wood, Ann Douglas. "The 'Scribbling Women' and Fanny Fern: Why Women Wrote." *American Quarterly* 23 (Spring 1971), pp. 3-24.
Zabel, Morton D., ed. *Literary Opinion In America.* New York: Harper and Brothers, 1937.

Index

Academy, reviews cited: of *Awkward,* 140; of *Maisie,* 26; of *Spoils,* 117
Actor-manager system, 79; James's bitterness toward, 87
"Adulterine element," James's treatment of, 110–12, 118–20, 129–30, 147; and "divine principle of the scenario," 111, 120–21, 134; criticism of, 126–27; in post-theater fiction, 110, 119, 155; treatment of in literature, 118–19, 123, 129–30, 139–40, 166–67, 169
Aesthetes. *See* Avant-garde, Anglo-American
Alcott, Louisa May, 12
Aldrich, Thomas Bailey, 69
Alexander, George, 89–90, 138; on reception of *Guy Domville,* 92–93
American Copyright League, James's letter to, cited, 99
American culture, James's criticism of, 40–41
American Publishing Company, 21
Appleton's Journal, 8; review of *Europeans,* 39
Archer, William, 77, 94; on *Guy Domville,* 94
Arnold, Matthew, 9
Atlantic Monthly, 1, 3, 18–19, 34, 114–16; criticism of *Terminations,* 107; female audience of, criticised, 8; James published in, 12, 16, 37, 43; James reviewed in, 65
Audience, 38
  American, expectations of, 7, 37, 123; James's criticism of, 38–40
  Anglo-American: expectations of, xv, 4–5, 17, 36, 45, 54, 153; James's dependence on, 2, 7; his criticism of, 7–9
  avant-garde, James and, 90, 93–94, 98, 183–84, 191–93; alienated by *The Americans,* 81; his ambivalence toward, 74–76, 104, 106–7; his attempt to compel, 91; his contempt of, 96; Prefaces and, 186–88; of short stories, 83; of theater, 69, 72–73, 80; women, 143
  avant-garde, Anglo-American, James's success with, 154–55
  Civil War enlarges, 20
  conventional, James and, xv
  expanded by paperbacks, 20, 33–35
  expensive book format, effect on, xiv, 30–31
  female, James's criticism of, 6–8, 153
  Hawthorne's criticism of, 10–11
  H.G. Dwight cited on, 190
  influence of: on James's desire for commercial success, xii–xiv; in major phase, xvi; on themes and structures, xii
  James and: his attitudes toward, discussed, xiii–xiv; his criticism of, xiii–xiv, 7–8, 12–13, 22, 26, 29, 40, 55–56, 96, 101, 108, 141–43, 153; his dependence on, 2, 7, 18; his "education" of, xiv, xvii, 12–13, 152, 155; his ideal of, 6, 14, 22–23; his interaction with, xii, xv–xvii; his perceptions of, xii, xv–xvii; his reputation as difficult, xiv; on size and quality of, 152–53; on reading aloud and, 189–91
  mass culture, effect on, and James's criticism of, xii–xiv
  of magazines: change, and newspaper competition, 58; expansion of, 58–59
  of short stories, 82; avant-garde, James and, 83
  of theater: avant-garde drama unpopular with, 90; interest in, 69; James's criticism of, in *Muse,* 72–73; strictures on, 72
  of yellowbacks, 32–33
  quality and size of, Howells on, 19–20
  Twain's attitude toward, 21

Authors: effect of subscription publishing on, 21-22
　female, xi; G. Eliot's criticism of, 10-11; Hawthorne's criticism of, 10-12; James and, Veeder on, xi-xiii; James on competition with, 9-10, 12-14; success of, 11-12, 22
　male: James's criticism of, 9-10; James on, 6-8
Avant-garde, Anglo-American, 62; emergence of, James and, xii, xvi-xviii, 62-63; James's ambivalence toward, xiv-xvi; his relationship with, xv; literary compared to theatrical, 79; Poggioli on, xvi; use of, defined, xvi-xvii
Avant-garde, French. *See* French realists

Balestier, Wolcott, 2-3
Balzac, Honoré, 181-87; James on, 9; *Comédie Humaine,* 187
Beach, Joseph Warren, on James's short stories, 82
Beadle, dime novels and ads of, 20
Beardsley, Aubrey, 83-84, 121
Becker, George, 70
Bennett, on *Guy Domville,* 93
Bernhardt, Sarah, 56-57
Besant, Walter, 60; *Sweet Nelly,* 36
Blackmur, R.P., *The Art of the Novel,* 185
Bliss, Elisha, 21
Book trade, xv, 22, 29-30 (*See also* Subscription publishing); effect of Copyright Law (1891) on, 99; effect of subscription publishing on, 30-31
Bookman, reviews cited: of *Spoils,* 116-17; of *Wings,* 175
Boott, Lizzie, 42; James's letter to, 37
Boston Herald, James published in, 123
Bourget, Paul, 62, 127; Edel on, 127-28; lecture on Flaubert, 127-28; *Le Disciple,* 62
Braddon, Miss, 12; *Aurora Floyd,* James on, 9
Browning, Elizabeth Barrett, 9
Business and businessmen, James on, 152-53

Censorship: James's criticism of, 122; of French realists, reasons for, 70-71
Century Magazine, 3, 63, 122-23; Civil War, publications on, 64; James's criticism of, 122-23; James published in, 64
Characterization, from national traits, James's criticism of, 1-2
Charles, Mrs. E.R., 12
Charles Scribner's Sons, 192; publication of *Golden Bowl,* 182; publication and poor sales of New York Edition, 187, 192

Charrington, Charles, production of *A Doll's House,* 77
Charvat, William, 11-12
Circulating libraries, 32, 100, 102; and censorship, 70; audience of, 31; criticism of, 62; effect on book trade, 30-31, 70; effect of Copyright Law (1891) on, 99; Moore's criticism of, 70
Civil War, expands paperback audience, 20
Clifford, Mrs. W.K., 107
Coburn, Alvin Langdon, 189
Colby, F.M., on *Wings,* 175
Collier's Weekly, James published in, 129
Collins, Wilkie, James on, 9
Compton, Edward, 2-3, 73-74, 81
Compton, Mrs. Edward, 95
Conrad, Joseph, 62
Contemporary Club of St. Louis, James's lecture to, 183
Copyright Law (1891), 32, 99; effect on book trade and circulating libraries, 99
Cornhill Magazine, 31, 33; James published in, 33; Thackeray in, 30
Crackanthorpe, Herbert, 84
Craigie, Mrs. Pearl Richards. "John Oliver Hobbes," 84
Craik, Mrs. D.M.M., 12
Crane, Stephen, 127
Crawford, Frances Marion, James's criticism of, 63
Critics: and James's final success, 193; James's criticism of, 76; New, 184
Cummins, Maria S., 10; *The Lamplighter,* success of, 10-11

Daily Telegraph, The, review of *Ghosts,* 80
Daly, Augustin, 85; James's quarrels with, 86-87
Daudet, Alphonse, 27, 63; *L'Evangeliste,* plot of, 66
de Goncourt brothers, 27
de Goncourt, Edmonde, 28, 63
Dent, publication of James, xiv
Dickens, Charles, 63
Dime novels (*See also* Paperbacks; Yellowbacks): ads, 20, 25; success of, 20
Drama vs. theater. *See* James, Henry: theater vs. drama
Dramatists, avant-garde: goals of, 79; public unpopularity of, 80
Dumas *fils,* James on, 122-23
Dwight, H.G., on James and reading aloud, 190

Edel, Leon, xvi, 3, 18, 28, 34; on "Benvolio," 14; on Bourget's lecture on

Index   241

Flaubert, 127-28; on dramatization of *The American*, 80; on "The Figure in the Carpet," 1-4; on *Fount*, 146; on *The Golden Bowl*, 165; on *Guy Domville*, 93-94; on Ibsen's influence on James, 108; on James and theater, 73; on James's post-theater fiction, 110; on James's final success, 192; on selections for New York Edition, 186-87; on short stories, 82; on *Wings*, 165; *The Complete Plays*, 74

Egan, Michael, 77; on *Henry James: The Ibsen Years*, 77; on Ibsen's influence on James, 108
"Egerton, George." Mary Chavelita Dunne, 84; *Discords*, 84; *Keynotes*, 84
Eliot, George, 9-10, 27; criticism of female authors, cited, 10; James's criticism and reviews of, 10, 154
Eliot, T.S., xiv
England, French realists, censorship of, reasons for, 69-71

Feidelson, Charles, on James's characters, 118
Fern, Fanny: Hawthorne on, 11; *Fern Leaves*, success of, 11; *Ruth Hall*, 11
Fiction (*See also* Paperbacks)
  American: increased demand for, 152; James on size and quality of audience, 152-53; James on women as audience, 152-53
  Anglo-American, James's challenge of conventions in, xiii, 17-19, 60-61, 112-14; and adulterine element, treatment of, 110-12, 118; and vulgarity, 166-68
  James on, 60-61
Fireside Library, 34
Flaubert, Gustave, xv, 27-28, 106; attitudes toward audience, 29; Bourget lecture on, 127-28; *Madame Bovary*, 127
Foley, Richard, xvi; on James's characterization, 17; on *Maisie*, 126; on success of James's lectures, 183
Ford, Ford Madox, 62, 127
Forum, E. Gosse in, on French realists, 71
French realism, 115-16
French realists, 60; and English avant-garde, 63; censorship of, reasons for, 69-71; Gosse on, 71; Howells's praise of, 63; influence of, 62, 64; James and, 27; James's avoidance of, 120; James differs from, 123-24; James on, 7-9; his criticism of "latitude," 122
Fuller, Margaret, 25
Fullerton, Morton, 62, 84

Galaxy, 34; female audience criticised, 8; James published in, 12-13
Gard, Roger, xvi
Gardner, Isabella Stewart, 75
Gaskell, Mrs., 12
Gohdes, Clarence, 100
Gosse, Edmund, 3, 78, 84; James's letter to, 2; his letter to on failure of New York Edition, 192; on French realists, 71; "The Limits of Realism," 71
Greeley, Horace, 25
Grein, J.T., 77
Griest, Guinevere, 31; cited, 99

Hamilton, Gail, 9
Hardy, Thomas, 62
Harland, Henry, 62, 83, 103, 121
Harper's Half-Hour Series, publication of *Daisy Miller* in, 34
Harper's Magazine, 3; female audience criticised, 9; Howells on James's popularity, 3
Harper's New Monthly Magazine, 5
Harper's Weekly, 120; James's letters for, 128; publication of *Awkward* in, 129
Hawthorne, Nathaniel, xv, 6-7, 64, 68; criticism of audience, 10-11; criticism of female authors cited, 10-12; James's biography of, 39; letter to G. Ticknor, 10-11; on *Ruth Hall*, 11; popularity of, compared to female authors, 11-12; work unsuited for serialization, 12; *The Blithedale Romance*, 66; *The Scarlet Letter*, 11
Hay, John, 25
Heinemann, William, 78; James's letter to criticising theater audience, 85; publication of James's works, 108; publication of *Maisie*, 126; publication of *Spoils*, 116
Henry James—The Lessons of the Master, cited, xi
Herrick, Robert, James's letter to, 187
"Hobbes, John Oliver." Mrs. Pearl Richards Craigie, 84
Holland, Laurence, on characterization in *Portrait*, 51
Home Journal, 34
Home Library, 34
Houssaye, Arsene, 25
Howells, William Dean, xiv, xv, 3, 22, 64, 98-99, 103, 144, 154-55; and publication of *Ambassadors*, 156; criticism of "The Madonna of the Future," 18; on *The American*, 18-19; on avant-garde, 63; on *Daisy Miller*, 35; on "delicate subjects," 112; on literary marketplace, 3; on Henry James Jr., 63; on James's popularity, 3;

on mass culture, 3; on *Wings*, 175; praises French realists, 63; review of *The Reverberator*, 5; Twain's letter to, 22 James's letters to, 2, 19, 63, 97-99, 104; on critics, 76; on *Fount*, 146, 151; on Prefaces, 185; on *Sense*, 144-45
letters of: to C.E. Lowell on audience, 19-20; to J.R. Lowell, 35
works: *A Hazard of New Fortunes* (1890), 3; "Criticism and Fiction," 111; *Dr. Breen's Practice* (1881), 66; *The Undiscovered Country* (1880), 66
Hutton, R.H., review of *Princess*, 65-66

Ibsen, Henrik, 71, 90, 134; and avant-garde theater, 77; influence of on James, 108; James and, 77-79; newspapers cited on, 80; Shaw on, 80; unpopularity of with public, 79-80; work of, compared to *Muse*, 77
works: *A Doll's House*, production of, 77; *Ghosts*, review of, 80; *Hedda Gabler*, 77, 90; *The Master Builder*, 90
Illustrated London News, 107; publication of *The Other House*, 107-8
Inner Shrine, The, xiii
Isle, Walter: on *Awkward*, 129; on *Maisie*, 124-25

Jackson, Holbrook: cited, 99; on British avant-garde theater, 77-78
James, Alice, 6-7, 19; death of, 74
James, Henry (*See also* individual works)
American culture, his criticism of, 40-41
and "adulterine element," treatment of, 111-12, 118-21, 129, 134, 153, 155, 166, 169
and audience, xv, xvi-xvii, 26, 38; ambivalence toward, 74-76, 90, 104, 106-7; criticism of, xii, xiv, 7-9, 13-14, 19, 22, 26, 38-39, 55-56, 76-77, 85, 101, 104, 108, 154; dependence on, 2-3, 6-7, 18; effect of expensive format on, xiv; his education of, xiv, xvii, 13, 152, 154-55; his ideal of, 6-7, 14, 22-23; in major phase, xvi; his perceptions of, xii, xv-xvii, 2-3, 5-9; his reputation as difficult, xiv, 190; its expectations, xv, 169-71; mass culture, effect on, xiii-xiv, 4-5; on size and quality of, 19-20, 152-53
and audience, American: his criticism of, 38-40; his dependence on, 7; its expectations, 7, 37, 123
and audience, Anglo-American: his criticism of, 7-9; his dependence on, 2-3, 6-7; his ideal of, 6-7; his perceptions of, 3; its expectations, xv, 4-5, 17, 36, 45, 54, 153; on taste of, 43
and audience, British, 36-37
and audience, female, 16-17; his attitude towards, 6; his criticism of, 13-14, 16-17, 43-44, 153
and authors, male and female, criticism of, 6-10, 12-14
and avant-garde, xv-xviii, 19, 83, 90, 94, 98, 102, 183-84, 191-93; Anglo-American, his success with, 154-55; his ambivalence toward, xiv, 74-76, 104, 106-7; his attitude towards, xiv, xvi; his criticism of, xii-xiv, 96, 101, 104, 108, 183-84; British, 36-37; James on, 143
and censorhip, 69-71
and challenge of literary conventions, xi-xiii, 17-19, 60-61, 112-14; and vulgarity, 166-68
and critics, 184
and fear of failure, 2, 57-58, 97-98, 154
and fiction, cited on, 60-61, 152-53
and French realists, 27; his ambivalence toward, 122; influence of, 17, 44, 60-61; "larger latitude," 168
and Ibsen, 78-79, 90; ambivalence toward, 77; review of *Hedda Gabler*, 90
and "larger latitude," 168; and attempts to educate audience, 152; and French realists, ambivalence toward, 122; and "new woman," 143; and writing for *Yellow Book*, 121-22
and literary agents, 2; letters to, xii, xvi, 2, 69; relationship with, 2-3
and literary marketplace, perceptions of, xv
and magazines: difficulty of publication in, 58, 98; effect on his career, 18-19; his criticism of, 59; serialization in, 33-34, 37
and modernism, resistance to, xii-xiv
and Mudie's, 30, 100
and naturalism, 63-64
and "newspaperization," xii-xiv, 4-5
and novels, experimental: criticism of, as avant-garde, 106-7; influence of theater on, 109-12; techniques in, 109-11; triple-deckers, 31, 99-100
and popular novelists. *See* James, Henry: and authors
and popular vs. artistic success, xii-xiv, 15, 17, 25-26, 29, 137-38, 140-42 (*See also* James, Henry: desire for

Index   243

commercial success); ambivalence to avant-garde, xiv, 75–76, 104, 137–38; during major phase, 55; during theater phase, 56–57, 72–76, 79–80, 90–91
and public opinion, restricting effect of, 69–71
and realism, abandonment of, 69–71
and relationship with characters, 42, 137, 151–54
and theaters: ambivalence toward, 72–74, 76–77, 81–82, 85–88, 90; audience, his criticism of, 72–73, 85, 154; avant-garde, 90; bitterness toward actor-manager system, 85–88; British, avant-garde, 77–78; criticism of, 85, 96; desire for success, 56–58, 72–76, 79–84, 87–91; failure in, effect on his development, 96, 154; fear of failure, 57–58, 76–77, 97–98; intellectual attractions of, 78–79, 81; L. Edel on, 73; letter to Wm. James on, 75, 78–80; M. Egan on, 77; on publication of plays, 88–89; theater vs. drama, 72, 77–79, 81, 87, 110
career of, compared to Twain, 21
characterization of, 18; break from, 64; development of, 17; Foley on, 17; international American girl, 56, 61
children, use of, 110–12, 118–19; criticism of, 127
criticism of F.M. Crawford, 63
desire for commercial success, 2–3, 14–15, 56–57, 106; factors in failure of, xiv
Edel on success of, 192
emigration of, 6, 9; James on, 29–30; Pound on, xv
Howells on, 63
inheritance from Alice James, 74
internationalism of, 35–36, 38, 43; and audience, 2–3, 6, 23; departure from, unpopular, 3–4; his criticism of, 1–2; in major phase, 165, 182
leases Lamb House, 106, 127
lectures of, 182–83; Foley on success of, 183
letters of: on literary scene, changes in, 100–101; on magazines, difficulty of publication in, 98; on writing for *Yellow Book*, 121; to American Copyright League, 99; to G. Norton, 63; to H.G. Wells, 168–69; to H. James, Sr., 28; to J.B. Pinker, xiii–xv, 146, 182–83, 186, 192; to literary agents, 2–3, 146, 169, 182–83, 192; to Lizzie Boott, 37; to Mrs. H. James, Sr., 29; to Osgood, 58; to R.L. Stevenson on work, 88; to T.S. Perry, 22, 27, 31, 41, 53, 64; to W.D. Howells, 2, 19, 29, 63, 76, 97–99; to Whitelaw Reid, 28; to Wm. James, 1–2, 26, 42, 85, 91
major phase of, xii; audience in, xvi; artistic dilemma of, 55; compared to earlier works, 165, 181–82; internationalism in, 165, 182; James on, 119, 166, 168; literary conventions and "adulterine element," 166–69
melodrama, taste for, 14–17
Methodist Times, criticism of James, 70
newspaper journalism, 25–29; letters on, 27–28
notebooks of, cited, 2–3, 40, 109–10; on big effect, 138–39; on "Figure," 104; on *Golden Bowl*, 175; on major phase, 119; on "Next Time," 100; on *Spoils*, 115; on terror, 144; on theater, 73, 85; on the Divine principle of the Scenario, 109–10; on treatment of adulterine element, 111, 120–21, 134
on Balzac, 9
on business and businessmen, 152–53
on Dumas *fils*, 122–23
on G. Eliot, 10, 154
on *Lindisfarn Chase*, 9
on literary double standard, 9–10
on *Nana*, 67; cited by Vizetelly, 70
on novels of M. Serao, 167–68
on Prescott's *Azarian*, 9
on reading aloud, 189–91; H.G. Dwight on, 190
on the Divine principle of the Scenario, 109–10; and treatment of adulterine element, 111, 120–21, 134
on *Theatricals*, 88
on triple-decker format, 31
on *Uncle Tom's Cabin*, 11
parents, death of, 59
plays of, xii, 2, 70–71; contrasted with short stories, 82–83
post-theater phase, 110; author-character relationship of, 151–54; fiction of, xii; his understanding of, 151; L. Edel on, 110; Peck on, 151–52; restrictions in, and artistic development, 119; treatment of adulterine element in, 111–12, 118–20, 153; use of conventional themes, 155; use of houses and children, 110–12, 118–19
refusal of editorial offers, 22
return to America, 182–83
serialization of works: in America, 37; in

England, 33-34
short stories of, 106; audience, avant-garde, 83, 106; compared with theatrical writing, 81-83; criticism of, 107; difficulty in publication, 58; effect on development of style, 82; innovative characters in, 61-62; J.B. Beach on, 82; L. Edel on, 82; published in *Yellow Book*, 83-85; themes, subtlety of, 62
Smith, Henry Nash on, xii-xiii
style, development of, confusion in, 97-99, 101, 109-10
themes of: children and houses, 121; conflict in, 15-16; experimental treatment of "larger latitude," 121-22; invasion of privacy, 4; subtlety of, in short stories, 62; transition in, 114
Works
A Bundle of Letters, pirated, 36
The Album, 85
"The Altar of the Dead," criticised as avant-garde, 107
The Ambassadors (1903), 105, 165-66, 187, 189, 192; and audience, 161-62, 164, 170; and avant-garde audience, 158-59, 163-64; and James's audience "education," 154, 156-58; compared to *Fount*, 156-57, 165; compared to later works, 160, 166; Howells and publication of, 156; international girl in, 166; internationalism and, 155-57, 159; Preface to, 146-47; serialization of, 156; treatment of adulterine element in, 155, 159-60, 166-68; use of *ficelle* in, 160-61, 163-64; use of narrator in, 157-59; Telford on, 157
The American (1877), 42, 47, 59, 168, 187; alienation of avant-garde, 81; characterization, 18; criticism of, 80; dramatization of, 2, 73-76; ending, 37; E. Robins on, 78; Howells on, 18-19; James on, 19; L. Edel on, 80-81; letter to Wm. James on, 81; melodrama in, 18; pirated, 32-33; Preface to, 188; success of, 80
"The Art of Fiction" (1884), 43-44, 60-63, 118-19, 141, 143; challenge of convention in, 69, 111; James on, 5; James on reviewers in, 140
"The Author of Beltraffio," 61-62, 85; innovative characters in, 61-62; theme, subtlety of, 62
The Awkward Age (1899), 70, 110, 121, 128, 137, 147, 155, 166; characters, and audience, 135-36; compared with *Fount*, 148-49; compared with *Wings*, 175; criticism of, 138-40; distancing of author in, 129-30, 132, 147, 155; experimental aspects of, 118-19, 129-30, 135-36; James's letter to H. Sturges on, 140; R. Foley on, 139; serialized, 137; treatment of adulterine element in, 129, 131; use of young girl in, 129-36, 155; use of *"roman dialogué"* in, 129; W. Isle on, 129
"Benvolio," 79; audience of, criticised, 13; conflict in, 15-17; L. Edel on, 14; plot of, 13-15; style of, 13-14
The Better Sort, 182
The Bostonians (1886), 59, 64, 76, 96-97; characterization in, 64-65; criticism of women in, 67-68; ending, compared to *Reverberator*, 5; excluded from New York Edition, 186-87; French realism, influence of, 64; Gosse on, 71; H.E. Scudder review, 65, 67; H. Kerr on, 66; innovations of, 64; James on, 67; naturalism in, 65-67; plot of, 66; publication, difficulties of, 68, 74; serialization of, 64; unpopularity of, 2-4; Wm. James on, 66
Confidence, 59; excluded from New York Edition, 186-87
Covering End, production, James's ambivalence toward, 138
"The Coxon Fund," 82, 85; criticism of as avant-garde, 107
"Criticism," xvii, 59; James on reviewers in, 140
Daisy Miller (1878), 1, 33, 37, 42, 47, 59, 76; discussed, 35; dramatization of, 56; editions of, 34, 36; Howells on, 35; in New York Edition, 188; international American girl in, 44, 153, 155; James on, 36; pirated, 34; sales of, 34-36; serialization of, 34-35; success of, 56
Daisy Miller: A Comedy, 56-57; failure of, 57; James on, 57; melodrama in, 56; publication of, 58
"The Death of the Lion," 83-84, 100-102, 104, 148; criticism of, as avant-garde, 107; parody on pseudonyms in, 121-22
"Dr. Fargo," 66
Embarrassments, 116; criticism of, 107; publication of, 108
Essays in London, criticism of as avant-garde, 107
The Europeans, 59, 91; excluded from New York Edition, 186-87; James

reaction to criticism of, 41-42; Poirier on style of, 37-39; reviews of, 39; serialization of, 37
"The Figure in the Carpet," 145, 148, 184-85; author and audience in, ambivalence, 104-6; criticism of, 107; F.O. Matthiessen on, 104; L. Edel on, 104; notebook entry on, 104
Four Meetings, 36
French Poets and Novelists, 33
"The Future of the Novel," 167; James criticism of audience in, 141-43; his personal interest in, 141-43
"Glasses," criticism of, 107
The Golden Bowl (1904), 120, 165-66, 189; ending of, 180-81; internationalism in, 182; James attempts to serialize, 169; L. Edel on, 165; letter to J.B. Pinker on, 182-83; notebook on, 175; Preface to, 188; treatment of adulterine element in, 175-78, 181
Guy Domville, 89, 91, 97, 100, 103, 108, 175; A.B. Walkley on, 93; Alexander's reception of, 92-93; and avant-garde audience, 93-95; attempt to compel audience, 91, 95; Bennett on, 93; defense of, 93-95; effect on James's career, 95-97; G.B. Shaw on, 91, 93-94; H.G. Wells on, 92-94; James on, 92-95, 109; James's ambivalence toward theater in, 89-90; L. Edel on, 93-94; reviewed, 94; themes, conflict in, 15; unpopularity of, 92-93, 95-96, 106
Hawthorne, 39-40; criticism of, 40-41
An International Episode, 36
"The Lessons of the Master," xiv, 148
"The Madonna of the Future" (1873), Howells criticism of, 18
"The Middle Years," 82, 84, 96, 104, 113, 148, 165; criticism of as avant-garde, 107
Mrs. Jasper, 85-86; James quarrel with Daly, 86
"A New England Winter," innovative characters in, 61
New York Edition: and audience, 188, 191; failure of, 191-92; high price of, xiv-xv; James and internationalism of, 187-89; James's arrangement of, and critics' view of artistic unity, 184-89, 191; James's desire for commercial success and, 185-86, 188; letter to Gosse on, 192; letter to Pinker on, 192; letter to R. Herrick on, 187; P. Lubbock on, 185; selections for, 186-89

"The Next Time," xiii, 100-101, 104, 148, 155, 192; audience of, 102-4; criticism of, 107; notebook entry, 100; publication in *Yellow Book,* 104
The Other House: excluded from New York Edition, 186-87; influence of Ibsen on, 108; James's ambivalence toward, 108-9; L. Edel on, 108; M. Egan on, 108; serialization of, 107-8; violence in, 107-8
"Pandora," 61
"The Parisian Stage," 90
A Passionate Pilgrim and Other Tales (1875), 22, 32; price of, 22
The Portrait of a Lady (1881), xii, xv, 37, 42-43, 56, 58-59, 120, 165-66, 172, 187, 189; Anglo-American conventions of, 43-44, 51-52; characterization, L. Holland on, 48-51; characters, James's identification with, 49-51; conflict in, 49-50, 52; conventions challenged in, 60; criticism of, 60; ending of, controversial, 52; French influence on, 51-52; in New York Edition, 188; international American girl in, 43-44, 45-49, 52-53, 153; irony in, 46-48; James on, 53; publication of, 52; serialization of, 43; success of, 55; Veeder on, xi
Prefaces to the New York Edition, 41, 55, 88, 105, 110, 121, 189; and arrangement, effect on critics' view of artistic unity, xvi, 41, 56, 104, 173, 175, 184-91; James and audience, 191; letter to Howells, 185
The Princess Casamassima (1886), 64, 74, 97; characterization in, 64-65; French realism, influence of, 64; innovations of, 64; James's attitude toward characters, 67; J. Wedgwood review of, 65; naturalism in, 65; poor sales of, 2-4; publication difficulties of, 68, 74; R.H. Hutton review of, 65-66; themes, conflict in, 15
The Question of Our Speech/The Lesson of Balzac, 182, 190
"The Question of the Opportunities," James on audience in, 152-54, 156
"The Real Thing," criticism of as avant-garde, 107
The Reprobate, 85
The Reverberator (1888), 47, 68-69; ending, compared to *Bostonians,* 5; Howells's review of, 5; internationalism of, 4; irony in, 5; plot of, 4; themes of, 4
Roderick Hudson (1875), 32, 42, 47, 59;

in New York Edition, 187–88; poor reception of, 17
The Sacred Fount, 118, 156–57, 165; compared with *Ambassadors*, 165–66; compared with *Awkward*, 148–49; compared with *Wings*, 175; decreases sales, 152; E. Wilson on, 146; excluded from New York Edition, 186–87; H.T. Peck on, 151–52; James on, and *Sense*, 145; James's reaction to, 146–47, 153–55; L. Edel on, 146; letter to Howells on, 146, 151; letter to J.B. Pinker on, 146; "master-pupil" and "character-reader" in, 148–49; N. Phillips on, 148; publication of, 182; treatment of adulterine element in, 147, 155; use of narrator in, 145–47, 149–51, 153, 159
The Sense of the Past: James on, and *Fount*, 145; letter to Howells on, 144–45, 151, 153
"The Siege of London," 59
The Spoils of Poynton (1897), 110, 121, 146–47; experimental aspects of, James on, 115–16; notebook entry, 115; Preface to, 188; published by Heinemann, 116; reviews of, 116–17; transitional aspects of, 112–14, 117–18
Tenants, 85
Terminations, 116; criticism of as avant-garde, 107; publication, 108
The Tragic Muse, 68, 77, 89, 186; and audience interest in theater, 69; compared to Ibsen's work, 77; criticism of British stage in, 72–73; James on, 1–2; letter on poor sales of, 81; Preface, 188; publication difficulties of, 74; themes, conflict in, 5
Transatlantic Sketches, 32
"The Turn of the Screw" (1898), 128; James's distancing in, 128; publication, 129; use of children in, 128
The Two Magics, 138
"The Universal Anthology," James on novel in, 140
Washington Square (1880), 59; excluded from New York Edition, 186–87
Watch and Ward (1871), 42, 109; and audience, female, 16–17; conflict in, 16; excluded from New York Edition, 186–87; melodrama in, 16; plot of, 16; publication of, 33; Veeder on, xi
"The Way It Came," criticism of, 107
What Maisie Knew (1897), 110, 122, 129, 133, 146–47; character in and audience of, 123–26; compared to *Ambassadors*, 156; distancing in, 147; experimental aspects of, 118–19; Preface, 188; public reception, unfavorable, 126–27; reviews of, 126–27; treatment of adulterine element in, 123–26; use of young girl in, 155; W. Isle on, 124–25; W.C.D. Pacey on, 124
The Wings of the Dove (1902), 119, 165–66, 189; and James's desire for commercial success, 168; characters, and audience's expectations, 169–75; compared to *Awkward* and *Fount*, 175; F.M. Colby on, 175; Howells on, 175; James on, 120, 169; L. Edel on, 165; Preface, 188; publication of, 182; review, 175; treatment of adulterine element in, 119–20, 174; use of young girl in, inadequacy of, 166, 170–175

James, Henry Jr., on H. James lack of commercial success, xiv–xv
James, Henry Sr., 7, 25; H. James's letters to, 28
James, Mrs. Henry Sr., H. James's letters to, 29
James R. Osgood and Company, 22, 32; prices, 32; publication of *Watch and Ward*, 33; H. James's letters to, 58; James loses money on failure of, 68; publication of plays, 88–89
James, Wilky, cited, 20
James, William, xiv, 7, 19; H. James letters to, 1–2, 26, 42, 85, 91; on *The American*, 81; on *The Bostonians*, 66–67; on *Guy Domville*, 92–95; on quarrel with Daly, 86; on short stories, 85; on theater and desire for success, 75, 78–80; on *Tragic Muse*, 81
Johnson, Robert Underwood, 122–23
Jones, Henry Arthur, *The Dancing Girl*, success of, 75

Kaplan, Justin: on subscription publishing, 22; on Twain's audience, 21
Kerr, Howard, on *The Bostonians*, 66

Lakeside Library, 34
Lane, John, 83
Lea, Marion, 77
Le Gallienne, Richard, "Tree-Worship," 84
"Lee, Vernon." Violet Paget, 84
Libraries, circulating. *See* Circulating libraries; Mudie's
Lippincott's, female audience of criticised, 8
Literary agents, 2–3; James's letters to, 2–3, 146, 169, 182–83
Literary double standard, James on, 9–10, 12–13
Literary marketplace, Anglo-American, 29–30

(*See also* Book trade)
Literary piracy, 32–34 (*See also* Yellowbacks)
Literary World: Awkward criticised in, 139; *Maisie* reviewed, 126–27
Literature, *Awkward* criticised in, 139
Littell's Living Age, 34
Little Review, xv
London Times, 62
Loring, pirates *A Bundle of Letters*, 36
Lowell, James Russell, Howells's letter to, 35
Lubbock, Percy, on unity in New York Edition, 185

Macmillan, Frederick, 74
Macmillan and Company, 31; publication of James's works, 33, 59, 68, 74
Macmillan's Magazine, James published in, 43
Magazines: advertising, and price decrease of, 58–59; audience, James's criticism of, 6–8; audience, American, James's dependence on, 29; audience, Anglo-American, and censorship, James's criticism of, 122; audience, female, James's criticism of, 7–10; James's dependence on, 18; James on difficulties of publication in, 98; serialization in, 31
"Manifesto of Five Against *La Terre*," 71
Margot la Balafrée, James on, 60
Mass culture (*See also* Newspaperization): effect on James's audience, xiii–xiv; Howells on, 3
Matthiessen, F.O., 104; on "Figure," 104; on James's article on Dumas *fils*, 122; on *The Other House*, 108
Melville, Herman: *Moby Dick*, 11; *Typee*, 11
Mencken, H.L., xiv; *Book of Prefaces*, xiv
Methodist Times, criticism of James, 70
Methuen and Company, publication of *Golden Bowl*, 182
Mix, Katharine Lyon, 84
Modernism, James's resistance to, xii–xiv
Moore, George, 62, 99; "Literature at Nurse, or Circulating Morals," 62; on circulating libraries, 70
Morley, John, commissions James, 39
Mott, Frank Luther, 58–59; on criticism of female audience, 8
Mudie, Charles Edward, 30
Mudie's Library, 32, 100; criticism of, 84; effect of Copyright Law (1891) on, 99; effect on British book trade, 30–31; James and, 30, 100
Murdock: on James article on Dumas *fils*, 122; on *The Other House*, 108

Nation, 22; *Awkward* criticised in, 139; James published in, 12; James's work for, criticised, 26
National Vigilance Association, 70
Nelson, publication of James, xiv
New Review, James published in, 123
New York Herald, James published in, 123
Newspaperization: as American problem, 5; James on, 4; of theater, 72
North American Review, 18, 22; *Ambassadors* serialized in, 156; Howells in, on *Wings*, 175; James published in, 12, 166
Norton, Charles Eliot, 18; Howells's letter to, 19–20
Norton, Grace, 19; James's letters to, 63, 166

Obscenity, 69–71
Osgood and Company. *See* James R. Osgood and Company

Pacey, W.C.D., "Henry James and His French Contemporaries," 124
Paget, Violet. "Vernon Lee," 62
Pall Mall Gazette, review of *Guy Domville*, 94
Paperbacks (*See also* Dime novels; yellowbacks), 34–35; audience, expansion of, 33–35; format of, 34–35; popularity of, 33–35; Schick on, 34
Pattee, Fred, cited, 11
Peabody, Elizabeth, 64
Peck, Harry Thurston, on James's post-theater career, 151–52
Perry, Thomas Sergeant, 55; James's letters to, 22, 27, 31, 41, 53, 64
Phillips, N., on *Fount*, 146
Pinker, James B., 2, 182; James's letters to, xiii–xv, 146, 182–83, 186, 192; H. James Jr.'s letters to, xiv, xv
Poggioli, Renato, on avant-garde, xvi
Poirier, Richard, on *The Europeans*, 37–39
Pound, Ezra, xiv; on James, xv
Prescott, Miss, 12; *Azarian*, James's review of, 9
Public. *See* Audience
Putnam's Magazine, xiii

Raffinés. *See* Avant-garde, Anglo-American
Reading aloud: H.G. Dwight on James on, 190; James on, 190–91
Rehan, Ada, 85–86
Reid, Whitelaw, 25, 28, 76, 100; James's letters to, 28
Rice, J., *My Heart's Delight*, 36
Riverside Library, 34

Index

Robins, Elizabeth, 77, 86, 90; acting/production of Ibsen, 90; *Theatre and Friendship,* 78

St. James Theatre, 89, 91, 94–97
Sand, George, 9
Saturday, Awkward criticised in, 138–39
Savoy, 83
Schick, Frank L., on paperbacks, 34
Schoenberg-Cotta Family, The, James's review of, 7
Scott, Clement, on *Guy Domville,* 94
Scribbling women. *See* Authors, female
Scribner's, 3; female audience of, criticised, 8
Scudder, H.E., 115; review of *Bostonians,* 65
Seaside Library, 34; piracy of James's works, 36

Seemuller, Mrs. A.M.C., 12
Senior, Nassau, *Essays on Fiction,* 44; James criticism of, 6
Serao, Matilde, 167; James on novels of, 167–68
Serialization. *See* Magazines: serialization; and specific works
Shaw, George Bernard, 78; on *Guy Domville,* 91, 93–94; on Ibsen, 80
Shorter, Clement, 107–8
Smith, Henry Nash, *Democracy and the Novel,* xii–xiii
Smith, Logan Pearsall, 62, 107
Southworth, Mrs. E.D.E.N., Veeder on characters of, 42–43; *Ishmael,* 43
Spectator, Awkward criticised in, 138; review of *Princess,* 65–66; review of *Maisie,* 126
Stephen, Leslie, 33
Stevenson, Robert Louis, 79, 88, 142; James's letter to on work, 88
Stone, Donald David, 62
Stone, Herbert S., publication of *Maisie,* 126
Stowe, Harriet Beecher: success of, 11; *Uncle Tom's Cabin,* James on, 11
Sturges, Howard, James's letter to on *Awkward,* 140
Sturges, Jonathan, 105
Subscription publishing (*See also* Book trade; Mudie's), 21; effect on authors, 21–22; success of, 21

Tebell, John, and audience, creation of, 20
Telford, John E., on narrator in *Ambassadors,* 157
Terry, Ellen, 94
Terry, Marion, 89
Thackeray, W., 63; cited, 30

Theater, and James's theater phase (*See also* Actor-manager system): audience strictures on, 72–73; British, avant-garde, emergence of, 77; criticism of British theater in *Muse,* 58
Ticknor, George, Hawthorne's letters to, 10–11
Ticknor and Fields, prestige of, 22
Times, review of *Maisie,* 126
Times Literary Supplement, reviews: of New York Edition, 185; of *Wings,* 175
Triple-decker, 100, 102; demise of, 99–100; effect of Copyright Law (1891) on, 99; James and, 99–100; effect on book trade, 31
Tribune: dime novel ads, 25; James's work for, 25
Trollope, Anthony: *Lindisfarn Chase,* James on, 9
Trübner and Company, 32
Turgenev, Ivan, 27–28
Turner, Reginald, "A Chef d'Oeuvre," 84
Twain, Mark, xv; career of, compared to James, 21; on subscription publishing, letter to Howells, 22; *Huckleberry Finn,* 21; *The Innocents Abroad,* 21

Veeder, William, xii; on James and popular novelists, xi; on characters of Southworth, 42–43
"Vernon Lee." Violet Paget, "The Moral Teachings of Zola," 71
Victoria, Queen, Diamond Jubilee, 127
Vizetelly, Henry, 69; obscenity trial of, 70–71

Walkley, A.B., 78; on *Guy Domville,* 93–94
Ward, Mrs. Humphrey, *Miss Retherton,* 69
Ward, Lock, and Company, pirates *The American,* 32–33
Watt, A.P., 2
Wedgwood, Julia, review of *Princess,* 65
Weintraub, Stanley, 107; on *Yellow Book,* 83–84
Wells, H.G., 62, 84, 183; on *Guy Domville,* 92–94; James's letter to, 168–69; "A Pretty Question," 94
Wilde, Oscar, 83, 90; James on *An Ideal Husband,* 91; *Lady Windermere's Fan,* 89
Westminster Review, 10
Wilson, Edmund, on *Fount,* 146
Women (*See also* Authors, female): as audience, James's criticism of, 8, 43–44; French view of, 44; James's criticism of, 6–10

Yellowbacks (*See also* Dime novels; Paperbacks), 32–33

Yellow Book, 62, 83–84, 103–4, 121–22; audience of, 121; James's ambivalence toward, 83–85; James on writing for, 121–22; success of, 84; S. Weintraub on, 83–84

Zola, Emile, 27, 43, 63, 148; censorship of, 70; Gosse, criticism of, 71; James's criticism of, 27–29; James's review of, 45; V. Lee on, 71; Vizetelly translation, success of, 69–70; *Works: La Joie de Vivre,* Gosse on, 71; *Le Roman Expérimental,* 63; *Nana,* James's review of, 9, 60, 67; review of cited by Vizetelly, 70

DATE DUE

DEMCO 38-297